THE BLACK DEATH

The Black Death

⇥ A PERSONAL HISTORY ⇤

John Hatcher

DA CAPO PRESS
A Member of the Perseus Books Group

Library of Congress Cataloging-in-Publication Data

Hatcher, John.
    The Black Death : a personal history / John Hatcher. — 1st ed.
        p.   cm.
    Includes bibliographical references and index.
    ISBN-13: 978-0-306-81571-3 (hardcover : alk. paper)
    ISBN-10: 0-306-81571-0 (alk. paper)
    1. Black Death—England—Fiction.   2. Walsham le Willows
(England)—Social conditions—Fiction.   3. Great Britain—
History—14th century—Fiction.   I. Title.
    PR6108.A87B57 2007
    823'.92—dc22

                                                    2007044922

First edition 2008

Published by Da Capo Press
A Member of the Perseus Books Group
www.dacapopress.com

Da Capo Press books are available at special discounts for bulk
purchase in the U.S. by corporations, institutions, and other
organizations. For more information, please contact the Special
Markets Department at the Perseus Books Group, 2300 Chestnut
Street, Suite 200, Philadelphia PA 19103, or call (800) 810-4145,
extension 5000, or e-mail special.markets@perseusbooks.com.

1 2 3 4 5 6 7 8 9 10

To Melissa and Zara,
who have suffered from the Black Death since birth.

⇥ CONTENTS ⇤

MAPS

⊰ PREFACE ⊱

The Nature of This Book

This book is an experiment in combining history and fiction. It evolved from a search to find a new way of adding to our knowledge and understanding of a distant but massively important and very well-worn historical topic. Although it contains an abundance of historical facts and context and its content is based as far as possible on what is known about the mid-fourteenth century and the Black Death, it also contains fiction. The fiction is there with the intention of supplying a framework for the presentation of the facts, as well as to add a further and more vivid dimension to the manner in which they can be observed. Great care has been taken to ensure that the fiction does not conflict with the facts, but the result is literary docudrama rather than conventional history.

Having researched and published on the history of the fourteenth century for the past forty years, I wanted to write a book about the Black Death, the greatest natural disaster the world has ever seen. Within the space of a few years in the mid-fourteenth century this horrific pestilence swept across the whole of the known world killing at least 35 percent and probably more than 40 percent of the population. Even to our own age, which is highly skeptical of historical turning points and generally favors evolution over revolution, the Black Death is commonly recognized as an event of immense significance.

Yet I was undecided what sort of book to write. The Black Death has exerted a perennial fascination for scholars, students, and readers of history. But if the appetite for learning about it is enormous, so is the number of books and articles that have been written to feed that hunger. One obvious choice for me was to write a survey tracing the doleful progress of the plague across Europe, from its origins in the Asiatic steppes in the early 1340s to its demise in Russia and Scandinavia in 1350. As is customary in such books, the narrative could dwell in each of the cities and countries ravaged by the disease, and a series of pictures painted of the devastation it caused using contemporary accounts, ranging from Boccaccio's elegant report of the ruin of Florence to al-Maqrizi's reflective description of the plague's journey through the Middle East, and Emperor Ioannes Cantacuzenos's eyewitness testimony of the ravaging of Constantinople. It would then be conventional to add a multitude of descriptions of the nature of the disease and the symptoms it caused, drawn from the observations of those who witnessed it as well as from modern medical science. Then an attempt could be made to calculate the spectacular death rate. Finally, a conclusion could be added consisting of a general assessment of the impact that this and later outbreaks of pestilence had on succeeding generations.

But such books have been written many times before, and all the best narrative sources on which they must be based are very well-known. So instead of embarking on yet another general survey of the Black Death's rampage across the known world or even through a single country, I started planning a very different sort of book. I wanted to probe deeper, to focus on the particular rather than the general, and to uncover as much as I could about what it was like for ordinary people to live and die in these momentous years. Therefore, I decided to try to tell the story of the great pestilence from the perspective of the inhabitants of a single village. The place I chose was Walsham le Willows, a large rural parish in northwest Suffolk that possesses exceptionally good local records which run continuously through the crucial years, from the mid-1340s to 1350. But as I began to work on the book, it soon became clear why nothing like this had ever been done before. Even in the best documented of places, the sources surviving from the fourteenth century are silent, or severely deficient, on most of the issues that were central to the lives of the villagers. There are no diaries, reminiscences, or correspondence, and no accounts of what people believed or how they spent their days. In fact, there is scarcely any truly personal information on the vast majority of men and women who lived at the time, for they were illiterate and their rulers and betters were not concerned to write much about them. Thus, despite being of exceptional quality for the period, Walsham's sources fall far short of enabling the historian adequately to explore the experiences of its inhabitants during the Black Death. As a result, any conventional historical account which is written about this village, or any other village for that matter, rather than being comprehensive and intimate will inevitably be selective and impersonal.

Historians seeking to write an intimate social history of the great pestilence will find themselves constantly thwarted by the lack of evidence. Instead of writing the story they might seek to tell, they will have their focus set by the very different priorities and motives of the fourteenth-century clerks and administrators who compiled the records. While we would wish to discover what the people who lived and died in these tumultuous years experienced, heard, thought, did, and believed, even the very best sources—the local court records—tell us primarily about such matters as the straying of sheep and cows, the failure to repay debts, the obstructions which careless or selfish villagers left in the way of paths and watercourses, the poaching of rabbits, the election of villagers to manorial offices, or the buying, selling, and inheritance of plots of land. And what is more, they rarely do so in other than brief and formulaic language. Pieces of information like this, of course, capture an essential part of the routine of rural society and they can occasionally be supplemented by notices of deaths, marriages, and illegitimate births, but much of the world in which Walsham villagers lived is left in deep, impenetrable shadow. Local records tell us frustratingly little in a direct manner about the impact of the Black Death. The intimate history of the Black Death, as it was witnessed by those who experienced it, was never recorded.

Yet it would be wrong to suggest that the fourteenth century is poorly documented; rather, its relatively abundant archives cast their light in other places. There are multitudes of records which illuminate significant areas of the religious, political, legal, and economic affairs of the time, although the vast majority of them relate to the affairs of nations and to major occurrences in the world at large, or were created by the bureaucracies of institutions and deal with administrative processes. Such archives support the writing of macrohistories or provide wondrous detail on such matters as the income and expenditure of great households or the performance of the great farms of the rich, but they are largely silent on the microhistories of ordinary people. Such a state of affairs is not uncommon, for throughout history institutions have generated the bulk of vellum and paper, while daily living and individual lives have left little or no trace. The absence of personal information is particularly acute in the Middle Ages, where the sources simply do not survive which would enable even partial biographies of the great mass of ordinary folk who dwelled in villages and towns to be reconstructed. The same is true of religion, which was of immense importance to fourteenth-century society. A considerable amount is known about the English Church and the organization and operation of dioceses and parishes. In addition, many sermons, manuals for priests, confessionals, liturgies, pious handbooks, and suchlike survive. But little of this information directly relates to the beliefs of the common people, and little can be discovered about the church and its officers in Walsham. In fact, we do not even know the name of Walsham's parish priest, and nothing whatsoever can be discovered about the sort of man he was or how he shepherded his flock.

It will never be possible to know for certain more than a small part of what it was like to live and die in the Black Death. If a more rounded history of society during the great pestilence is to be written, it cannot be achieved using conventional academic methods. But this does not mean that historians should give up and leave the telling of it to novelists, dramatists, and filmmakers. There are huge holes in the local records, and the least unacceptable way for the historian to fill them is to draw heavily on what is known. The best way of writing history is to proceed from the known to the unknown, and the deep knowledge that historians have of many areas of mid-fourteenth-century England and the wider world can be applied to create a fuller picture of life in our chosen village. In order to move from the general to the particular and construct the lives of some of the individuals who lived in Walsham, our narrative will have to be extended beyond the fragmentary and often prosaic facts contained in surviving documents. In other words, this book will have to contain speculation as well as specifics, fiction as well as fact. The documents that survive, with all their limitations, will have to form the basis of a docudrama rather than a conventional history. As such it will be a hazardous project for a professional historian to undertake.

From the moment I proposed a book of this type I received a stream of advice on how it should be written. Unfortunately, much of it has been contradictory. Some historian colleagues counseled me to stay true to my vocation, stick very closely to the sources and keep speculation and invention to a minimum, while meticulously pointing out the limitations of the evidence and explaining the methodology I have adopted. By contrast, the advice I received from the literary end of the spectrum sought to push the book in precisely the opposite direction. I was urged to cast stuffy scholarly caution aside, concoct stronger storylines and fill them out with more invented and imaginative dialogue between more strongly drawn fictional characters. In other words, their advice is that I should write a novel rather than a history.

The former advice was closer to my natural instinct. I did not want to write a work of pure fiction or even a historical novel based firmly in the period. But I soon found that much of the cautious advice from historians would not work. For if, when trying to write the stories of individuals, I stuck too closely to the scraps of largely impersonal information that the sources could be made to yield up, and also explained what I was doing by drafting extensive conceptual and philosophical passages on the nature of history and historical writing, the resulting book would be very different from the one I wished to write.

Of course, there is no ideal compromise between keeping true to the sources and writing something akin to a historical novel. At least I have not been able to find one. Nor am I convinced that I have even found an acceptable balance somewhere between the two. Being a historian and desiring to convey what happened, or when the sources are silent, what was most likely to have happened, I decided that the balance of the book must be tilted decisively toward history rather than fiction. But in order to bring the lost history of the Black Death to life and to place the evidence that survives within a rich living context, I have had to invent situations and dialogue and employ techniques reminiscent of docudrama. The characters in the book are almost all based firmly on actual people who lived in Walsham and its region at the time, and the surviving evidence of who they were and what they did has been used to the fullest extent possible. But in order to provide a satisfactory narrative, it has often been necessary to flesh out these characters beyond the narrow limits set by the sparse and frequently oblique nature of the surviving records. In doing this, I have tried to be guided as far as possible by what I have been able to find out about the people themselves or of what the people of the mid-fourteenth century were like. When characters as well as situations have been created, it has been done with the overriding purpose of recapturing the real history of the period rather than telling a good story.

Given the nature of mid-fourteenth-century society, the parish priest of Walsham had to be a central character in the book. But because it is impossible to find out anything of significance about who he was or what he did, it was necessary to invent him. My decision to make Master John a good priest was arbitrary. Having made it, however, I based his character closely on the detailed portraits of good priests contained in near contemporary literary sources such as Geoffrey Chaucer and William Langland, and added depth and color by drawing on the rich information available in the sermons and moral literature of the mid-fourteenth century. Further guidance on the way in which my fictional priest carried out his duties has been provided by the best practice specified in the manuals, liturgies, and handbooks of the period. But Master John remains an invention nonetheless.

A priority of this book is to bring to life the key documents, events, and sequences of the period by integrating them into the history of the local community and the people who lived there. Eyewitness tales of the horrors of the pestilence are among the most colorful sources we have. The residents of Walsham, like those of other towns and villages, must have heard stories of the devastation wrought in distant lands, and there is no doubt that they became increasingly concerned as the death moved ever closer to England. But there is scarcely any record that this was the case. So when, in the ensuing chapters, tales of the devastation wrought by the pestilence are told to Walsham residents, they follow closely the substance and chronology of the reports that eyewitnesses and annalists have left to posterity. Again, from midsummer 1348 the English bishops were sending letters to be read out in plain English in all churches, warning parishioners of the advancing plague and advising them how they should respond. These fascinating documents have been studied by academics for what they reveal about late medieval theology and the responses of the ecclesiastical elites to plague, but in order to place them into the setting for which they were intended, a scene has been created in which just such a letter is read out by Master John to a shocked congregation in St. Mary's, Walsham. The letter is then interpreted by the priest in terms drawn faithfully from contemporary theology. The questions asked by parishioners, and the answers given to them, are based closely on the debates which raged at the time.

The structure of this book largely takes the form of a chronological narrative with much of the story and events imparted by the actions and words of the characters. A series of sequential set pieces have been created, including the deathbed of William Wodebite, the Lenten sermon in St. Mary's parish church, the assessment of the nature and progress of the pestilence by the librarian and chronicler of Bury St. Edmunds abbey, a pilgrimage undertaken by the villagers in the summer of 1348 to the shrine of Our Lady at Walsingham, the study of medical texts in the library of Bury abbey, the story of Agnes Chapman during the plague epidemic, the reconstruction of the epic court session of June 1349, when the deaths of around half of the tenants of Walsham were recorded, and so on. These tableaux are intended as windows through which the mentalities, sentiments, and experiences of mid-fourteenth-century people can be observed in a more vivid and intimate manner than would otherwise be possible from a conventional account using only what the surviving sources contain. We know exactly what constituted a "good death" in the mid-fourteenth century, we know how parish churches and parishioners celebrated Lent, we know that Bury St. Edmunds abbey had a chronicler and an extensive library and that a constant stream of visitors meant that monasteries were ideally placed to gather news. And we know that the numbers of people going on pilgrimages surged in 1348. But what we do not know is that the events in this book took place in Walsham and Bury and Walsingham in the way they are described here. We know only that they are likely to have done so in a broadly similar fashion in many places throughout England at this time.

Finally, and most importantly, this is an attempt to write history from the inside, and the profusion of illustrations are there to assist the reader in entering the world of the mid-fourteenth century. With the exception of the short historical introductions, printed in italic font, which preface each of the chapters, the reader is given a view of the Black Death entirely from within the period. The language spoken by the characters, though modernized, has as far as possible been adapted from that contained in contemporary sources, and the voice of the narrator, who from time to time links the action and offers introductions, summaries, amplifications, and judgments, is that of a male contemporary writing about the events soon after they had occurred. It could have been one of Master John's successors as Walsham's parish priest. The intention throughout has been to banish the hindsight, overviews, judgments, and perspectives of the twenty-first-century historian from the text.

My commitment to finishing this book received an enormous boost from the advice and encouragement of two leading historians of the period, Mark Bailey and Maryanne Kowaleski. Mark read a draft of the whole text, and Maryanne read large chunks of it; both provided a wealth of invaluable comments, added new dimensions, and saved me from many errors of fact and emphasis. But, most importantly, both urged me to continue broadly along the lines I had embarked on, namely, the writing of a docudrama. I hope its unusual perspectives help readers acquire a better understanding of the Black Death and the mid-fourteenth century. But it will also have served its purpose if it simply encourages some to dig deeper into real history books.

NOTE: Throughout the work, monetary denominations are referred to using their abbreviated forms; for instance, 5 shillings reads as 5s, 5 pence as 5d, etc.

Walsham in the Middle Ages

This intimate history of the Black Death is focused on the village of Walsham le Willows in west Suffolk. Walsham—it acquired the suffix "le Willows" only in the sixteenth century—lies some twelve miles northeast of what was the important monastic town of Bury St. Edmunds, and about the same distance from the market towns of Diss and Stowmarket. Walsham was chosen for a number of reasons for this experiment in combining history and fiction, the most important being the exceptional richness of the records that have survived from the fourteenth century, for both the village and its region. Moreover, Walsham's prime records, the manor court rolls, run continuously through the Black Death, and they are available in print for all to consult in translation. The region around Walsham is also extraordinarily well documented. A number of the neighboring villages, most notably Rickinghall, Hinderclay, and Redgrave, have particularly fine records, and the archives of both the borough and the monastery of Bury St. Edmunds are relatively rich. Thus the potential for recreating the life and experiences of the people of Walsham and its region in the mid-fourteenth century is as great as for almost anywhere in England, or Europe for that matter.

Walsham lay, as it still does today, tucked between the main roads leading from Bury St. Edmunds northeastward to Diss and southeastward

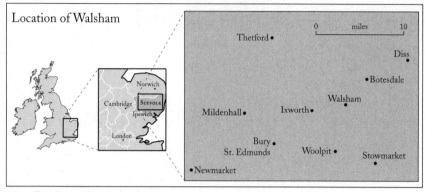

Source: Patti Isaacs of Parrot Graphics.

to Stowmarket. In the mid-fourteenth century it was a populous village with well over a thousand residents, possibly even fifteen hundred, as many as it was to have again before the nineteenth century. The village was coterminous with the parish of Walsham but was divided into two separate manors owned by different lords, who farmed part of the land directly and rented the rest out to free and unfree tenants. Walsham manor, by far the larger and more valuable of the two, was the property of Lady Rose de Valognes, who was born just before her father's death in 1282 and lived until 1353. Rose had been the lady of the manor since at least 1307, and in the 1340s she held Walsham jointly with her second husband, Sir Hugh de Saxham, until he died in the Black Death. The couple, who held other manors and properties, did not live in Walsham, but the owners of the small manor of High Hall did. Sir Nicholas Walsham, the lord of High Hall until he died in 1347, resided in a moated manor house in the center of his demesne farm of around 150 acres. He was succeeded as lord of the manor by Edmund de Welles, who lived in the manor house with his sister Margery, who was almost certainly Sir Nicholas's widow.

This part of England was among the richest and most populous in the country, and it had been growing and developing since late Saxon times. Walsham parish shared fully in this expansion. Over the centuries, as the old village center around the church filled up and then become crowded, new satellite settlements were planted around the edges.

Village of Walsham at the time of the Black Death

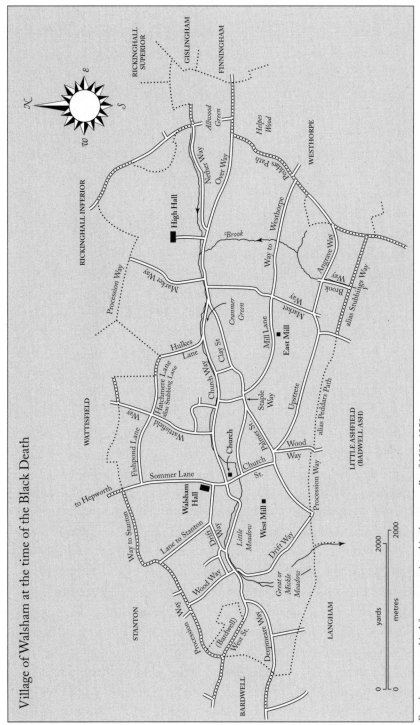

Based on topographical features mentioned in the court rolls of 1303–1350.

Source: Ray Lock (ed.), *The Court Rolls of Walsham le Willows, 1303–1350* (Suffolk Records Society, 1998), p. 16.

These new settlements, which consisted initially of scattered farm-houses, subsequently evolved into small clusters of dwellings and then into hamlets. As yet more land was brought into cultivation and exist-ing farmland was used more intensively, these hamlets expanded further in size, and then in turn threw out their own new shoots consisting of cottages, fields, and closes.

By the 1340s Walsham contained well over two thousand acres of farmland, but with well over a thousand inhabitants to support, land was scarce. Naturally, the great bulk of residents relied on cultivating crops and raising animals to provide their essential subsistence and employ-ment. As their numbers rose, the average amount of land per head fell. It was the custom of the manor to split inheritances equally among sur-viving male heirs, and as generations came and went, the strips on the great open fields were divided among ever more people, and the innu-merable odd parcels of land which lay hither and thither around the parish were shared among groups of brothers who farmed them cooper-atively or sliced them into ever tinier parcels. By the mid-fourteenth century few villagers held sufficient acres to provide a complete subsis-tence for their families.

The dwellings which peppered the landscape were of varying size and condition, and the majority sat in garden plots along the roads and tracks which crisscrossed the village. On the land around these houses, cottages, and hovels, vegetables and sometimes fruit were grown, and ubiquitous chickens, ducks, goats, and the odd pig or two scraped a subsistence. While the homes of the richer tenants were substantially built and generally well maintained, those of the poorer villagers were cramped and dilapidated, at worst little more than temporary struc-tures erected from whatever materials came to hand (see figure 1). As smallholdings descending by inheritance often had to be shared be-tween brothers or sisters, and their wives and husbands too, it was not uncommon for two or more families to live in a single dwelling, al-though an additional cottage might be erected in the gardens. House-hold furnishings and utensils tended to be few and rudimentary. Bronze cooking pots, iron hearth equipment, earthenware or wooden tableware, a minimum of clothing and bed linen, and a few pieces of rough furniture—a bed, a chair or two, a cupboard, and a trestle table—were all that were found in most households, while the more affluent villagers would possess a wider range of such items and notably more metal ware and textiles, and perhaps a bronze jug and basin, and a silver spoon or two.

In a region where large farms were rare, a relatively small number of families, like the Cranmers, Wodebites, and Syres, sat at the top of Walsham's peasant hierarchy because they possessed twenty or more acres of good farmland. These elite villagers primarily owed their wealth to being fortunate enough to enjoy secure hereditary possession of their sizable landholdings, which they held from their lords in return for low or even negligible rents. Though some of these privileged villagers were freeholders, others were unfree. One of the paradoxes of the Middle Ages was that men and women of the lowest legal status, the villeins and serfs, could enjoy the benefits of secure tenure for themselves and their heirs in return for relatively cheap money rents and an obligation to provide labor on the lord's demesne farm. These larger landholders had the choice of either farming their land or leasing it out in small plots at high rents to less fortunate villagers. If they decided to farm it, like their lords, they would grow wheat, barley, oats, peas and beans, and a little rye, and raise flocks of sheep and herds of cattle.

With an excess of people seeking food, land, and employment, life was very harsh for the majority of villagers in the 1340s. At the other end of the spectrum from the village elite lay a major part of the three hundred or so Walsham families who either had no land at all or possessed only garden-size plots or closes which they held on short leases at high rents from other villagers. If such poorly endowed folk did not possess any exceptional handicraft or commercial skills, they had to get by as best they could, buying most of their food at high prices and hiring themselves out for manual work in a labor market where they competed with each other for intermittent low-paid employment in the fields or the homes of their richer neighbors. The village common lands provided a little welcome assistance by offering pasture for a horse, a cow or two, or a few sheep for those fortunate enough to own them; the village woodlands, as well as backyards, allowed pigs and poultry to be reared.

But the pressure on such valuable resources was so great that access had to be strictly regulated by the village community. Times had been worse, especially from 1315 to 1322, when incessant torrential rains had brought appalling famines and livestock epidemics, but the 1340s were also punctuated by poor harvests that could cause perennial hardship to turn rapidly into acute distress.

A few villagers found more constant employment working for the lords of the manor. Robert Lene served Lady Rose and Sir Hugh de Saxham as shepherd, though we learn from the court rolls that they accused him of failing to apply sufficient ointment to the sheep in 1346, when many of the flock he was tending died. John the dairyman ran their dairy, and he was heavily fined in the same year for wasting firewood "beyond measure," an act of profligacy for which Matthew Tailor, who was employed as "custodian of the lord's firewood," was also held responsible. Some young, unmarried villagers secured annual contracts as live-in servants for their lords or more affluent peasant neighbors, with the men working largely on agricultural tasks and the women as housemaids and dairymaids. Somewhat more lucrative employment could be gained by those who had acquired special skills enabling them to undertake work for local customers as blacksmiths, carpenters, thatchers, tilers, weavers, tailors, cobblers and leatherworkers, and such like.

Opportunities for subsidiary incomes also came from providing services. Walsham, like most villages and towns, had a large number of alehouses and hostelries which operated on a temporary or permanent basis. A considerable number of Walsham women brewed ale, baked bread, and made pies for sale, and some hawked a range of cheap useful and decorative items around the roads and markets. More specialized, and much better rewarded, were the few literate persons who could charge for writing documents, or the cunning folk with high reputations who successfully dispensed medicines and prophecies.

It was a makeshift economy for many in late medieval England, but it was far from primitive. Life was unpredictable because income, employment, and expenses were critically dependent on the vagaries of the weather. Harvests fluctuated widely in quality, and along with them the yields of fields and the price of food; in addition, the health of livestock was often very uncertain as diseases came and went. Yet people generally made rational decisions about their lives and farmed efficiently within the constraints of custom, market conditions, and resources. The mix of arable and pastoral husbandry practiced in Walsham was closely geared to local soil and climate as well as to the needs and opportunities of the community. It was an overstretched society in which the majority often led a hand-to-mouth existence and frequently went hungry, but it was far from being a truly subsistence economy. Money and markets were essential and everywhere in evidence, and the folk of Walsham habitually lent and borrowed money and bought and sold a wide range of goods on credit.

Though most villagers grew at least part of the food they ate, all depended to some extent on sales and purchases. Those with larger farms produced surpluses and sold them for cash, which they used to buy a wide range of necessary and desirable goods that they could not produce for themselves, while those who needed to buy their subsistence sold their labor to get the money to do so. Although tucked away off the main roads of the region, Walsham received visitors and goods from far and wide. Exotic produce—wine, fruits, spices, foreign cloth—was brought from Bury St. Edmunds, and sometimes directly from London or Ipswich or another large port or market town, for the lords of the manor and the village elite. Walsham was well served with markets. The weekly market in the village supplied a range of mundane goods, and a somewhat greater variety was available just down the road at Ixworth, a settlement with some of the characteristics of a small market town. For those who chose to travel six or so miles to trade, there was a wider selection and keener prices at the thriving market of Botesdale. Such commerce also provided a number of residents with welcome subsidiary incomes from carting goods or driving animals to market.

Commercial and cultural links with nearby Bury St. Edmunds were constant and strong. Bury was a sizable town with a population of around seven thousand, and an abundance of large stone buildings. Country folk were impressed by the host of commercial and industrial occupations practiced by its citizens, and the bewildering miscellany of goods and services for sale in its streets and markets. In addition it housed one of the richest and greatest Benedictine monasteries in England. Among its eighty or so monks were scholars renowned for theology, astronomy, medicine, and a host of other disciplines, as well as chroniclers of historical and current events. Bury abbey generated a substantial demand for goods and services, and even closer to Walsham lay the small Augustinian priory of Ixworth, with its handful of resident monks.

Medieval communities were much less introspective and sedentary than they have often been portrayed. In addition to the multiple and frequent contacts that Walsham had with the wider world, many of its residents traveled far afield, either on a regular or occasional basis, and the village received a flow of visitors, temporary migrants, and settlers. While some of its long-term residents eventually left to seek their fortune elsewhere, those who stayed saw themselves as members of a wider community with rights as well as obligations. Above all, despite their parochial pressures, the ordinary folk of the village thirsted for news of the king and his nobility, of the local gentry, of goings-on in Parliament, of the levying of taxation, and, of course, of the progress of the war against the French, which had begun in 1337 when Philip VI confiscated Gascony and Edward III laid claim to the French throne.

Though life in Walsham was far less sophisticated and varied than it was in the city of Bury St. Edmunds, it was a civilized, complex, and generally well-ordered community, girded about with numerous laws, rules, codes, customs, and practices. Across England the universality of Christian teaching promoted a strict code of moral behavior and religious belief, the king and Parliament governed the realm, royal justice intervened in local affairs when it was deemed necessary and expedient, lords managed their estates and their tenants, and villages and manors were regulated by their local courts and the bylaws of the communities themselves. All in all, a good measure of order and justice was successfully imposed, and this applied to the regulation of business and commerce as well as to misdemeanors and crimes. Trade and contracts were regulated and enforced by numerous local and national tribunals, and in Walsham the manor court rolls reveal that the quality of ale and bread, as well as the measures by which they were sold, were closely specified, the numbers of animals that villagers might pasture on the commons or forage in woods were strictly regulated, the ownership and possession of land meticulously recorded, the boundaries of holdings precisely defined, and trespass by people or livestock on the lands and crops of others was prohibited and punished. People who broke contracts or failed to pay their debts were fined or suffered the loss of goods when they were distrained by bailiffs. Serious crime was subject to justice imposed by the leet and hundred courts that rested in the hands of the abbot of St. Edmunds and, at a higher level still, by the king's justices.

On the other hand, as always, order came at a price. The freedom of the common villagers was constrained in many ways by the judgment of their peers and the layers of social hierarchy above them. Costs as well as benefits flowed from the need to adhere to communal agreements and abide by collective decisions. This was evidenced in the farming of the irregular open fields of Walsham. Although individuals had more independence in how they cultivated their strips of land than in many other parts of the country, they were subjected to oversight of the standards of husbandry they practiced, the folding of sheep on the fallows, the protection of property against trespass, and so on. Custom and precedent rather than the letter of the law generally governed relations between lords and their men, and strictly limited the scale of the rent that was paid in money and labor each year for their landholdings. The unfree, of whom there were many in Walsham, were legally the chattels of their lords, who had the right in law to control many aspects of their lives, although most of these rights were rarely if ever exercised to the full. But the unfree in particular were subjected to a range of extra charges on a variety of occasions, some of which could be irksome and others expensive, including fines when they married or when they were discovered giving birth out of wedlock. The latter was frowned on, not merely because it was believed that marriage was a desirable state and fornication was sinful, but because it was thought there were enough poor to support in the parish of Walsham without single mothers and their children adding to the burdens.

Walsham was an ecclesiastical as well as a secular community, a parish as well as a manor, and the church and religion held a central place in the life of the residents. The lay community assumed obligations to help keep

St. Mary's church in good repair, and to provide a long list of objects to enable the church and its priests to carry out the conduct of worship and the cure of souls. In the fourteenth century the list of necessary objects for churches in the diocese of Norwich, within which lay the parish of Walsham, could include bells for the steeple and ropes for the bells, various books for the conduct of services, including a psalter, an ordinal, a manual, a lesson book, and books of music, elaborate vestments for the priest, cloths and surplices of various sorts, a set of banners for processions, a censer, a vat and a sprinkler for holy water, a lantern and a handbell, candlesticks, a font with a lockable cover, and, of course, a chalice for Communion wine and a pyx of silver or ivory to hold the Sacrament. In addition to gifts of money and objects, parishioners were expected to pay tithes to the church comprising a tenth of their corn and other crops, and on the increase of their livestock. On death they paid a mortuary fee, their second best beast.

Moral discipline was enforced primarily by the parish priest and his assistant clergy, but some miscreants found themselves appearing before church courts presided over by archdeacons and rural deans. The relationship of parishioners to their church and its priests, however, was more often one of piety and devotion than of payments and discipline. Though services were in Latin and almost all peasants were illiterate, lessons were learned by ear and by eye, from sermons, conversations and instructions with priests, from wall paintings, stained glass windows and images, from music, performance, and ceremony, and through the great mime that was the celebration of the Mass. A cycle of ecclesiastical feasts fitted well with the cycle of traditional popular celebrations, which in turn fitted well with the seasons and the turning points of the farming year. Michaelmas (September 29) marked the end of one farming year and the beginning of a new, when the harvest was complete and the autumn work in the fields began, especially the plowing and sowing of the winter corn. All Saints (November 1) was the start of the winter, when cattle were brought into the byre, as well as the time when the evil spirits abroad on Halloween had to be propitiated. The twelve days of Christmas were a welcome holiday after the autumn exertions, and they ended with Plow Monday (the Monday after January 6), when, if the land was not frozen or too sodden, the spring plowing was begun. With luck and good weather the spring plowing would be over by Easter, when another holiday led into the time for fallow plowing, weeding, lambing, and sheep shearing. Midsummer (June 24), the feast of the Nativity of St. John the Baptist saw haymaking begin, and the feast of St. Peter in Chains (Lammas Day, August 1) marked the time when, in good years, harvesting might commence. The twin perpetual cycles of agricultural tasks and religious festivals framed each year at Walsham and gave the momentum that helped provide the community's material and spiritual sustenance.

Master John

The thousands of ordinary parish priests who ministered to their flocks in four-teenth-century England have left scarcely a trace of their lives in surviving records. Their names, dates of appointment, and deaths or resignations can usu-ally be found noted in diocesan registers by the officials of the presiding bishops, but little else can be discovered about them. However, Master John, who is the central character in this book, has had to be entirely invented because the priests of Walsham were appointed by Ixworth priory rather than the bishop of Nor-wich, and not even their names have survived.

Yet if direct evidence of individual parish priests is lacking, except for a few odd notices of their agricultural and economic activities in manor court rolls, there is an abundance of rich material that throws welcome light on their duties in the fourteenth century and the manner in which they were, or should have been, performed. Manuals for the guidance of priests and rules for their moral, spiritual, and liturgical conduct are perhaps the most infor-mative, but together with sermons and commentaries, as well as a host of lit-erary works and administrative proceedings, they comprise just a part of the rich material from which the vocation of a priest at the time of the Black Death can be reconstructed. It is from these sources that I have created the life and work of Master John. Having chosen to make him especially devout, dili-gent, and learned, I have drawn further details of his character from Geoffrey Chaucer's portrait of a poor parson, a man who was "rich of holy thought and work" (see figure 2). The narrator throughout this book has a similar voice and character to Master John, and is conceived as writing his history within a decade or two of the Black Death. He may well have been one of Master John's successors as parish vicar.

⊰ ⊱

Master John, who had the cure of souls in Walsham, was a blessing to his parishioners. For many years before his arrival they had suffered sorely from the neglect of their parish priest, Robert Shepherd, a man who was more interested in accumulating earthly riches for himself than helping his flock to gain the spiritual rewards that await the righteous in Heaven.

Although Robert Shepherd drew only a modest stipend from the priory of Ixworth, which had long since appropriated the tithes and revenues of the parish for its own purposes, he was never troubled by a lack of income. This was not because he shunned worldly goods but because he was so skilled at making money. His surname was most inappropriate, for Shepherd's gifts lay more in the acquisition of wealth than in the curing of souls. In his many years at Walsham, he had grown steadily more wise in worldly things while neglecting the spiritual. He speculated in land and used his wealth prudently. Shepherd made many loans to villagers who were short of ready money but not out of charity, for he did not lend to the indigent. In fact he deemed it unwise to advance money unless it could be well secured against assets, and, in shameful disregard of his church's prohibition of usury, he always managed to take much more in repayment at the end of the term than he had lent at the beginning. If borrowers failed to repay the sum agreed in full at the specified date, he was not slow to sue them for debt in the manor court, claiming onerous damages on top. And if the bailiffs of the court could not seize enough cash or movable property to cover the poor debtor's obligations, Shepherd invariably found it necessary to speedily foreclose on the land put up as security.

By conducting his affairs in this manner, Shepherd had built up substantial landholdings, which, being at heart a lazy man, he chose to lease out at high rents rather than cultivate. His annual rent roll alone amounted to more than 40s. He allowed few opportunities for gain to pass him by, even if this sometimes meant bending the rules, and on more than one occasion he found himself in difficulties with the lord of Walsham. In 1336, for example, he was called to account by the manor court for illegally cutting down and selling trees growing on land that he was renting from the lord. His action was clearly wrong, since the law in Walsham decreed that trees belonged to the landlord and not to the tenant. Yet so great was Shepherd's reluctance to be parted from his money that he tried to avoid paying the 5s fine levied on him by claiming he had been forced out of great necessity to cut down the trees. However, since everyone knew the priest was a rich man, Shepherd's enemies heaped scorn on his head and disclosed to the lord that he had used the cash from the sale of the timber to buy a piece of freehold land in nearby Debenham.

Robert Shepherd might not have been blessed with a pure heart, but he was blessed with cunning. And it was soon after this humiliation, when the income he was receiving from his various speculations was at its highest, and the respect in which he was held in the parish at its lowest, that he began to consider appointing a deputy to perform the spiritual duties he had so lamentably neglected. Eventually, so loud and so persistent did the complaints from the parishioners become, that the prior of Ixworth was moved to express his concern and Shepherd made up his mind. Despite the miserable stipend that he offered, the throng of surplus clerics seeking employment in the region was so great that a host of well-qualified applicants pressed for the post. From among them Shepherd preferred John Bradfield, a mature and experienced man. He chose wisely, and after many years of neglect Walsham at last had a good man of religion who led his flock by noble example. With the willing complicity of Robert Shepherd and to the great benefit of the parishioners, John Bradfield soon assumed all the duties, responsibilities, and authority that should have been exercised by the parish priest.

Although John Bradfield had not been to university and had never run his own parish, he soon became known to his parishioners as Master John. This title was bestowed on him because he was such a learned and respected priest, as well as an excellent preacher. The lack of preferment that John had hitherto suffered in the Church had been due to an excess of holiness rather than a lack, and also to his plain speaking and daunting austerity. Time and again John had disappointed his friends and sponsors by refusing to offer flattering words or a bribe to gain promotion, or by turning down some toilsome office that did not directly serve God. His principles had brought him a harsh life with few comforts, but as he often said, using the words of the gospel, "If gold rust, what shall iron do?" This, he patiently explained, meant that the clergy had to be above reproach in order to provide a shining example to others: "If the priest, on whom we trust and who ought to be like gold, should instead be foul and corrupt, it is no wonder that ordinary men would rust." And he was very fond of telling his chaplains the cautionary parable of the "shiten shepherd and the clean sheep," in order to instruct them on the purity of the lives they must lead.

Master John dispensed an abundance of piety and wisdom to his parishioners and assiduously ministered to their spiritual needs. He would visit them regardless of the weather and often on foot, even in the most far-flung parts of the parish, with a staff in his hand and a bag containing essential ecclesiastical equipment across his shoulder. Despite imposing the harshest standards on himself and his colleagues, Master John did not lack mercy toward sinners. He was mindful of their constant temptations as well as their failings, and through considerate and kindly words he sought to draw them to Heaven. In his sermons, which he gave more frequently than was common among priests in neighboring parishes, he was fond of recounting how when a man went to a cobbler to buy a pair of shoes neither the cobbler nor the customer was able to open his mouth without uttering some falsehood, while at the same time swearing by all Christ's limbs that he was telling the truth. Yet, for all his understanding, Master John could be severe with transgressors who obstinately failed to reform. It made no difference to him whether his parishioners were of high or low estate, for he treated all sinners the same. In his behavior he set a splendid and often unmatchable example, not only to his parishioners but also to his junior clergy who assisted him in the large parish.

There were many more than a thousand souls to cure in Walsham, but there was no shortage of clerics seeking to labor with Master John and live off the fees they could earn by conducting services, administering rites, and saying Masses (see figure 3). Most of these clerics, in Walsham and elsewhere, had grown up in modest circumstances. Many were the presentable sons of peasant farmers, who in youth had shown a particular promise in learning and had caught the eye of their local priest, who enrolled them into his band of helpers as choristers. As they continued to develop academically and display appropriate qualities of character, these boys were selected for reading and writing lessons in small village schools, where they also acquired some Latin. Then, if they were deemed potentially worthy of eventual ordination into holy orders, they were moved on to more structured instruction in schools run by monks. One of Master John's assistants had even studied at the University of Cambridge. Having qualified as priests but lacking a benefice to support them, these junior clergy struggled to earn a modest living as chaplains. Master John was particularly pleased when John Beck and John Kebbil, two of his favorite protégés born in Walsham to well-established local families, returned to serve their native village.

Master John himself had been born of humble peasant stock in the nearby village of Bradfield. From an early age he had shown himself to be exceptionally bright, and when he was only seven he became renowned in his village for his ability to recite long prayers and passages from the Bible in Latin as well as English. A few years later, when his parish priest brought him to the attention of the monks of Bury, John made a great impression with his wide vocabulary and ability to grasp the subtleties of scholarly discourse, and he was sent to be educated in the almonry school at the abbey. There he spent many happy years studying and training for the monastic life, showing himself to be both an excellent scholar and an exemplary Christian. But when he reached eighteen years of age and was set to be professed into the community as a novice, doubts began to gather. It seemed to his favorite tutor, and then to John himself, that he was not best suited to the solitary life of a monk. For John thrived in company and was never happier than when he mixed with the common folk, advising them and persuading them to be better Christians. After much agonizing and many long discussions between his tutor and the abbot, it was decided that John should become a member of the secular clergy, devoted to the pastoral care of parishioners and the cure of their souls, rather than a monk sequestered in a cloister.

As a parting gift from his tutor, John had been given a precious book that thenceforth scarcely ever left his side. It was a leather-bound volume entitled *Oculus Sacerdotis*, a manual written in Latin for the guidance of parish clergy by William of Pagula, a most learned doctor of canon law. His tutor had painstakingly made this book for him in the abbey scriptorium by copying, in an elegant and clear hand onto new folios of vellum, the words contained in a manuscript that had recently been brought to Bury by a monk from a northern monastery. That was more than twenty-five years ago, but ever since the stoutly bound book had been John's most treasured possession, not merely because of its sentimental value or even for the profusion of detailed instructions it contained on how a good priest should carry out his varied duties, but because it spoke to him in a familiar and welcome voice and put his own deeply held beliefs into fine words.

Master John, like William Pagula, saw that administering confession was one of his most important tasks. Not for him was the annual hearing of confession of each of his flock a hurried matter of granting easy absolution. Following his precious manual, he learned how to use the confessional as an essential means of teaching and correcting. He did not merely encourage confession but always made time to inquire of penitents what lay behind their sins, so that they might not be repeated. If the sin was drunkenness, John asked the inebriate how he got drunk; if the sin was anger or caused by anger, he asked whether he was accustomed to curse men or innocent animals, and whether he believed that cursing was a sin. John had his own special questions designed to expose the potential weaknesses of all who came to him: the rich, the hirer of workmen, the manorial official, the brewer of ale, the baker of bread. And he required all men and women who labored with their hands to do an honest day's toil for an honest day's pay, and never to work on Sundays or holy days.

When deciding appropriate penances for the sins of his flock, Master John found it helpful to refer to the long lists contained in his manual, which told him the penances prescribed by canon law and the sins which were so serious that absolution was reserved to a bishop or even the pope. But as time passed and he gained more experience, Master John increasingly chose to follow his own instincts, and to do so with flexibility and humanity. He hesitated to use excommunication, which cast offenders beyond the cloak of protection offered by the Church, but was reluctant to grant absolution in return simply for the payment of money. He preferred always to make the penance fit the sinner as much as the sin.

Master John had faithfully learned how best to interrogate penitents on their religious knowledge, and he used this private meeting, as well as others during the course of each year, to test and teach his parishioners. He expected his flock to know by heart at least two prayers, including the Our Father and the Hail Mary, as well as the rudiments of the fourteen articles of faith, the seven sacraments, the seven works of mercy, the seven virtues, the ten commandments of the law and the two of the gospel, and the seven sins. And finally, he made sure they were aware of the chief joys of Heaven and the chief pains of Hell.

Master John also strove to give good practical advice to his flock. He told expectant mothers to avoid heavy work and new mothers to suckle their newborn children, and he instructed parents to be careful when taking infants into their beds, so that they might not be suffocated. He warned how easily an infant might be killed when left on its own, and how it could be smothered if its mouth were covered by a cloth for even a brief time. Nor did Master John lack the courage to remind those he felt were in temptation, either through poverty or cruelty, that infanticide was a dreadful sin, even if it should occur through neglect rather than a deliberate act.

Master John was quick to reprove his flock for sexual laxity. Although he hesitated to send adulterers and fornicators to be judged in the archdeacon's church court, he did so not out of leniency but because he believed he could deal with them better himself. He held tightly the secrets he learned in the confessional, but if the misdeeds were repeated and became public knowledge, Master John approved of public shaming, which most often took the form of a ritualized whipping of the offenders, barefooted, bareheaded, and stripped to their undergarments, through St. Mary's churchyard and the surrounding roads. He held strongly to Church teachings on the desirability of marriage and was never happier than when his parishioners married. In the autumn of 1345 in St. Mary's he took particular pleasure in blessing the marriages of members of a number of Walsham's leading families, including those of Hilary, the daughter of Robert Tailor, to John Patel, and Agnes, the daughter of Alice Helewys, to Nicholas Goche. Although Master John

was generous in dispensing charity to unmarried mothers and their children, he did all he could to discourage such pregnancies, on moral
grounds and because he agreed with village notables that there were already more than enough poor people in the parish. Yet, as in so many
areas of his life, Master John frequently allowed kindness to overcome
severity, and often it became known that he had begged the lords of the
manors of Walsham and High Hall to moderate the fines for "childwyte"
that they imposed on unwed mothers. In the face of considerable criticism he provided a full Christian burial in consecrated ground for
Catherine Cook when she died soon after giving birth to a bastard.

Master John did not confine his instruction to strictly religious matters, but saw it as an important part of his ministry to try to settle the differences that arose between the residents of Walsham. In addition to
exhorting his parishioners to live their lives in a manner that would give
rise to fewer quarrels, and to be conciliatory when disputes did flare up,
he was often called on to act as a mediator. By judging with great wisdom
and fairness, he brought many disagreements to an end before they esca-
lated into conflicts that had to be taken to the manorial court. On many
occasions he assessed the compensation that might be due to purchasers
who were unhappy with what they had bought, or to farmers when their
crops were damaged by straying animals, or to the victims of violence
when they had been attacked. And he was often successful in persuading
the lenders of money to grant some extra time for their debtors to repay
what they owed, though Robert Shepherd had rarely relented. Yet Master John was forever being disappointed that, in spite of his best efforts at
mediation, arguments continued to bubble up everywhere in very much
the same fashion as they had for decades before his arrival and would
continue to do for decades after his departure. It brought him particular
sadness that he was sorely rebuffed in his attempts to calm the bitter feud
which flared up between the children of William Wodebite soon after
their father's death in the late summer of 1345 (see figure 20).

2

Late Summer, 1345

Average life expectancy at birth was very low in the mid-fourteenth century, but significant numbers of people lived into middle and old age, even in peasant communities. Death in Walsham was less predictable and avoidable than today because of the harshness of most villagers' lives. They worked hard in the fields in all weather and suffered from frequent shortages of food, as well as a lack of effective treatments for many common ailments. However, despite being a period of hardship, the decades before the Black Death were largely free of epidemic diseases that infected and killed substantial numbers of people.

It is difficult to overstress the importance of a "good death," which was essential to ensure the safe journey of the soul from this world to the next, shortening the time spent in Purgatory and easing the pain of being there. In the later Middle Ages the deathbed was commonly portrayed as a battlefield where the forces of good and evil, mercy and condemnation fought over the soul of the dying person. While devils whirled around, tempting and terrifying the dying and seeking to snatch their souls and carry them to Hell, the priest, aided by the powers and accoutrements of his office, the Virgin Mary, and the intercession of the saints, strove to extract the contrition and confession that would deliver God's mercy and eventual salvation. Repentance and deathbed ministrations by the clergy could save even the gravest of sinners from damnation, but this alone did not purge all the sins that had been committed. Purging was achieved through the pains of Purgatory, though the prayers of the living could assist in speeding the souls of the dead toward Heaven.

According to the laws and customs of the time, the living could generally de-
volve their property as they wished, but strict inheritance customs, enforced in
Walsham's manor courts, determined how the bulk of estates would pass after
death. Landholdings were shared equally between surviving sons, with daugh-
ters inheriting only if they had no brothers. When multiple sons inherited land,
it was often more efficient if they farmed it cooperatively rather than splitting
it into small, uneconomic parcels. But sometimes brothers found it impossible to
work with each other.

⊰ ⊱

In the late summer of 1345, in the village of Walsham in west Suffolk, William Wodebite was close to death. Although he was an old man, thought to be at least sixty, William was accustomed to good health. But in the last two weeks he had become ever more frail, brought down by a fever, diarrhea, and constant vomiting. It had been more than four days since William had been able to digest any food, and he was now slipping in and out of consciousness. When awake he often lapsed into a gentle vagueness, muttering quietly to himself, and it seemed to those gathered around his bedside that at times he was barely breathing and his heart was scarcely beating. Family, friends, and neighbors clustered in his house and around his bed, offering spiritual and bodily support and comfort (see figure 5). They bathed him, encouraged him to eat and drink, prayed for his recovery, and, if that were not to happen, for the forgiveness of his sins and the salvation of his soul. As William continued to weaken, a discussion began about whether his end was near. When he lapsed into a long and unnaturally deep sleep, it was agreed that the time had come to summon the parish priest to his bedside to guide him through his final hours of death. Two of William's nephews hurried off to St. Mary's church, which stood just over a mile away, to summon Master John.

The priest was expecting the summons and immediately started to prepare himself to lead William safely through the crucial and dangerous stages of his last hours on earth. Master John called to his chaplain and to a group of young boys who acted as choristers and general helpers, and asked the sexton to begin his solemn pealing of the church bell in the tower. As John had often told his assistants, the administration of the last sacraments of shrift, housel, and annealing—confession, Communion, and anointing—required a specific range of texts, substances, and equipment to administer, and they now set about assembling them. John washed and dried his hands, and after crossing himself he carefully removed the ivory box, called a pyx, from the altar. Suspecting the imminence of William's death, he had saved a piece of the consecrated Host from the morning Mass in the box. He poured a little holy oil into a small brass pot and dipped another vessel, perforated with small holes in its lid, into the water in the font, and then hung them both on the belt he wore around his waist.

All the time, Master John offered the young boys a commentary on the function that each substance and vessel would serve, and impressed on them how these and other powerful weapons of the Church were essential to ward off the forces of evil striving to drag the dying man's soul into damnation. Then, one by one, he put on his vestments, with as much attention to detail as a knight would dress and arm for battle. First, the white alb, which reached to his ankles and covered his arms with long full sleeves, and then the red girdle that he tied around his waist. Next he slipped the blue sleeveless chasuble over his head, which covered his front and back and hung down to his calves. And then, with great awe, he took up a long red cope, embroidered with gold and blue silk, and draped it over his shoulders. The subdeacon had by now arrived, and he fetched a large brass cross from behind the altar and tied to it, with red ribbons, a finely carved and richly painted wooden figure of the crucified Christ. When he had done this, the subdeacon collected a small pewter chalice, engraved on its foot with a cross, together with a Bible and a leather-bound service book containing prayers and responses and a number of psalms, and then picked up a bundle of clean white cloths. The boys, who had put on their white surplices, fetched two handbells and two great candles, which they set in large, brightly polished pewter pricket candlesticks, before carrying into the church an iron lantern on a painted wooden pole. Master John once again reminded his young assistants of the significance of what they were doing: "The lights, cross, and handbells are to announce the coming of Christ's blessed body borne in the priest's hands." Nodding to the ivory pyx containing the Host, he added, "So that all who see it shall devoutly kneel down and worship his God by his paternoster, or whatever prayer that he can recite, and be summoned to follow the procession."

The priest then draped a narrow piece of embroidered blue cloth over his left arm and took the brightly painted wooden statue of Mary from the screen, which he passed to his deacon. Finally, with great reverence, he lifted the pyx up in his hands and then surveyed with satisfaction his assembled assistants, who had already been joined by a number of parishioners. In the fading summer sunlight a solemn chanting procession, armed with the weapons of Christ and the Virgin Mary, left the church door and made its way through the churchyard into Church Way. With a lighted lantern and candles at the head, servers carrying the cross and ringing the handbells just behind, the deacon carrying aloft the statue of the Blessed Virgin, the chaplain clutching the holy books, and in the center Master John, bearing in both hands before his breast the Body of Christ wrapped in a napkin, set in an ivory box, draped with a freshly laundered linen veil, the procession resolutely advanced toward William's cottage.

"Hail! Light of the world, Word of the Father, true Victim, Living Flesh, true God and true Man. Hail! Flesh of Christ, which has suffered for me! O flesh of Christ, let Thy blood wash my soul!"

The villagers who had gathered at the roadside knelt before the procession and prayed, and in the fading light of evening many followed behind, as Master John had foretold, "with bowed heads, devotion of heart, and uplifted hands, the good folk will see that the King of Glory under the veil of bread is being borne through their midst, and that one of their neighbors is about to embark on his journey from the world."

The gathering around William's bedside was visibly stirred by the sounds of the approaching procession. When his hand was gently squeezed, William opened his eyes.

Master John halted the procession outside the darkened room where William lay. He asked for the shutters to be partially opened, and, as the last rays of the sinking sun streamed through the gap, he entered bearing the crucifix before him. The priest positioned himself at the end of the bed facing William, with the light shining behind him, and said, "I have brought thee the image of thy savior; look upon it and draw comfort for yourself, in reverence of him that died for you and me. In this image adore your redeemer and have in mind his Passion, which he endured for your sins."

Smiling at William, Master John placed close before the dying man's eyes the carving of the crucified Christ, with its gilded hair stained by droplets of bright blood trickling from the green crown of thorns, and its ivory white torso savagely rent with a gaping wound of stunning red. He encouraged William to focus on the image and say after him, as best as he could, "I know well thou art not my God, but thou art imagined after him, and makest me have more mind of him after whom thou art imagined. Lord Father of Heaven, the death of our Lord Jesus Christ, thy son, which is here imagined, I set between thee and my evil deeds, and the desert of Jesus Christ I offer for that I should have deserved, and have nought."

In a comforting voice the priest inquired of those gathered around whether William had set all his worldly affairs in order and passed on his property, carefully explaining that this was essential in order to demonstrate that William had willingly severed his links with this material world. They nodded that William had settled his affairs, although two of the neighbors whispered that some of William's bequests had caused many angry words to be exchanged between his three sons and his daughter.

The priest sighed and turned his mind to putting the dying man's spiritual estate in order. Seeing that William was now conscious and attentive, he began the Seven Interrogations: "Do you believe fully all the principal articles of faith as well as all the Holy Scriptures, in all things according to all the teachings of the holy and true doctors of Holy Church, and forsake all heresies and errors and opinions condemned by the Church?"

William nodded assent.

"Do you know how often, in what ways, and how grievously you have offended the Lord your God who created you from nothing?"

Another nod.

"Are you sorry in your heart for all the sins you have committed against the high majesty and love and goodness of God, and of all the goodness that you did not do but might have done, and of all the grace that you have rejected, not only for fear of death or any other pain, but rather for love of God and righteousness?"

William responded weakly, "Yes."

"If your life be spared are you resolved to amend your life so that you may never commit mortal sins intentionally again?"

"Yes."

"Do you forgive fully in your heart anyone who has done you harm or caused you grief, either in word or deed, for the love of Lord Jesus Christ from whom you hope to have forgiveness yourself?"

William scarcely moved his head.

"Would you have all things in your possession given back, and leave and forsake all your worldly goods if you cannot make satisfaction in any other way?"

William nodded, but somewhat reluctantly.

"Do you believe fully that Christ died for you and that you will never be saved but by the merit of Christ's Passion, and do you thank God with your heart as much as you may?"

"Yes."

Master John had spotted a momentary reluctance and, for the sake of William's soul, that it might forever live in Heaven with Almighty God and with his holy company, he pressed the dying man further. Had he always honestly calculated the tithes that were due to the Church and rendered them in full? Should he not make provision for the payment of a few shillings to make amends for those tithes and other dues which he had withheld unwittingly?

William wearily signaled his agreement, but the priest did not relent. William was wealthy and one of the more powerful men in the village, despite being a villein by blood and therefore of lowly legal status. William and his fellow villeins had never been, as the letter of the law would have it, at the mercy of their lord's whim, since custom rather than caprice governed relationships in Walsham, as elsewhere in Suffolk. William possessed substantial landholdings, for the bulk of which he paid little rent in money to his lord, though somewhat more in labor and other dues. He had inherited most of his land from his father, but throughout his life he had systematically acquired more land by astute purchases, sometimes from poorer peasants who could not repay money he had lent them. Some of his land William farmed, with the help of his sons and hired laborers, but he also leased out some of it and cottages at high rents, taking advantage of the scarcity of plots and living accommodations in the bustling village.

As one of the prominent tenants, William had often acted as the landlord's agent by serving as reeve, and as hayward and rent collector on the manor, which had brought him profit as well as power. In exercising the considerable authority these offices gave him, William had sometimes clashed with villagers and treated them harshly. Although not an unpopular man nor thought of as unjust, Master John knew from stories in the village that William had on occasion taken advantage of his position to profit from the weakness of others by lending them money at very high rates of interest, by delaying payment for goods that he bought from them, and by paying some folk less than the goods were truly worth. It was also firmly embedded in the folk memory of the village that, when a young, talented, but recklessly ambitious man, William had been involved in a spectacular dispute with a rich Ipswich merchant, John Baude. Spotting William's talent and energy during a trading trip to Walsham, Baude had entered into a business venture with him. This involved Baude entrusting William with the huge sum of £8 to invest locally on his behalf. However, some of the speculations William made in grain and wool were risky and went seriously wrong when the price of the commodities fell. A sizable part of the money was lost, and William was found guilty of failing to provide proper accounts.

Nevertheless, despite these past sins and misdemeanors William waved the priest away and obstinately denied that there was any serious wrongdoing during his life for which he needed to make recompense. Resisting the urgings of his anxious sons, William became angry and murmured, "Far more people have treated me badly than have been mistreated by me, and there are some who have so wronged me that I can never forgive them." He began to name names, but the priest stopped him and urged, "Put aside anger against those who have offended you and remember that you cannot rely on your own good works, but only on the love of Christ."

At this point William closed his eyes and refused to respond. Instead he lay back on his bed, groaning and sighing. Everyone in the room became concerned. William had come very close to avoiding damnation by confessing his sins, affirming his faith, abandoning the false treasures of this world, and placing himself in Christ's hands, but now his soul was once again in jeopardy.

The priest motioned to the family, friends, and neighbors who were crowded around the bed to draw close to him and said, "Men that are dying, in their last sickness and end have the greatest and most grievous temptations, such as they never had before in all their life. The hard storm of the perilous assault of the fiend is upon them! And we should assume that these fiends are most eager to tempt men and women in the hour of their death, to encumber men at the last stand, to make them have an evil end and so be damned."

Master John went on to his rapt audience: "There are invisible demons here in this room, perched even on the pillow by William's head, who will fight against Holy Church for his soul, prevent wishes being put into words, encourage despair by showing all the sins that have been committed, and threaten to drag his soul to Hell with them. But with the rites of Holy Church and the succor and refreshment of Our Lady, and the prayers of the saints and all the faithful, including you here today, the demons cannot do their will and they shall be sent flying away."

With that he gave the brightly painted wooden figure of the Madonna and child to William's youngest son to hold by his father's head. With healthy red cheeks, flaxen hair, kind blue eyes, and gently smiling red lips, Mary seemed almost to be present beside William in the flickering half-light of candles and setting sun. Her sympathetic authority and composure, combined with the sumptuousness of her swirling scarlet gown, decorated with gilded and sapphire roses and crosses, imparted both compassion and majesty, as Master John intoned, "For the Mother of Mercy will pray her Son to give him a place in Heaven and, as the empress of Hell who has power over demons, command them to harass his soul no longer. Go your way and let him have rest" (see figure 6).

With this Master John took his sprinkler and scattered holy water into the four corners of the room, and almost at once the atmosphere seemed, to those gathered around the dying man's bed, to become much calmer. With prompting from his anxious sons, William grudgingly admitted that there might have been fault on both sides in the violent quarrel that had erupted years before with the Packards over unpaid debts, which had led to the ongoing feud between the families. However, try as he might,

Master John could not get William to forgive Alice Packard for assaulting his wife and splitting open her head, saying it was for his dead wife to have forgiven Alice while she was still alive. But his eldest son prompted William to remember that he had dealt harshly with Adam Syre more than ten years before by refusing to pay him the barley he owed, and that the Syres had suffered through the winter and their young daughter had died. William then nodded in agreement that 12d should be paid to Adam's widow in recompense. Finally he affirmed, with Master John's prompting, that he expressly asked pardon from God and also from all those he had wittingly or unwittingly offended.

With evident satisfaction at having done all he could to save a soul, Master John quickly pronounced absolution: "Ego auctoritate dei patris omnipotentis et beatorum apostolorum petri et pauli et officii michi missi in hac parte absoluto te ab hiis peccatis michi per te confessis et ab aliis de quibus non recordaris. In nomine patris et filii et spiritus sancti, Amen."

Family and friends sighed with relief that William had made his peace, and he sank back with exhaustion. To the satisfaction of those present, William, though silent, was able to seal his contrition with a gift of 2s toward the costs of keeping the light of the Blessed Virgin Mary burning perpetually in the church, a donation of 12d for the repair of the rear door of the church, where the oak had splintered and the wind whistled through, and alms of 4s to be given to twenty-four poor people of the village on the day of his burial, and the same amount seven days later.

"Into Thy hands O Lord I commend my spirit. You have redeemed me O Lord, thou God of truth." The priest encouraged William to repeat the words of Psalm 31 after him, but William did not stir. The priest and his assistants now moved swiftly as William lay as if in a deep sleep. Observing from experience the signs of imminent death, Master John began commending William into God's hands by quietly but resonantly saying, "In manus tuas," while the chaplain, subdeacon, and servers chanted psalms. Pouring small quantities of oil into his palms from the flask hanging on his belt, John anointed William on his forehead and on the back of his hands and his feet, thereby sealing the forgiveness of sins and protection for the soul. Then, turning to the window with his back to those present in the room, he raised the precious ivory box above his head, saying softly, "Hoc est corpus meum. This is my body." Handing the box to an assistant, he turned back to face the room and broke off a small fragment of the wafer. Once again saying, "Hoc est corpus meum," he placed it into William's mouth and shook him gently to rouse him, while those gathered around fell to their knees.

Master John placed the rest of the wafer in his own mouth and swallowed it, but William's jaws did not move and he did not swallow. After waiting a few moments, the priest pushed the fragment farther into William's mouth with his finger. But, to the horror of the assembly, William coughed and fragments flew from his mouth and settled around his lips and chin. The priest remained calm and carefully gathered all the sodden fragments together and crumbled them into a small chalice into which he had poured a little wine. Prompted by a server, he found another trace on William's chest and added it to the wine, which he stirred. He motioned for William's head to be raised slightly and his mouth to be opened. Swirling the chalice, he poured the wine and fragments of wafer into his mouth, which he then held firmly closed while William gently spluttered. When he was satisfied that William had ingested the wafer, he took up the chalice himself and drained it.

Less than an hour later William died. After a straw and then a feather had been placed across his nostrils and mouth to confirm he had stopped breathing, William's body was stripped and washed, with great care taken not to remove any of the holy oil. It was then lifted onto a clean white sheet on which a cross had been traced with ashes from the kitchen fire. William's arms were folded across his chest and the sheet was wrapped tightly around him and tied, showing, as a neighbor remarked, that he was "clean shriven and cleansed of his sins by contrition of heart and by absolution."

The shrouded body was lifted onto the large table that had been brought from the kitchen and, as William had wished, lighted tapers were placed at the four corners. Through that night William's sons kept watch, and the next day a flow of villagers came to pay their respects and say prayers for him. It was agreed with satisfaction that William had died a good death.

Arrangements for the funeral and burial had been made sometime before William's death, and a chaplain came to the house to confirm that the body would be taken to the church the next day and buried the day after. It was expected that many would attend. There would be a large procession from William's house to the church and a grand feast after the burial. Candles were bought, the carter for the funeral cart was hired, and the purchase and preparation of the food and drink was begun.

Shortly after noon William's body was placed in a coffin on the fine cart that was often used in Walsham as a hearse, and the coffin was covered with a purple pall. Many paupers, for their pennies, lined up around and behind the cart, dressed in clean smocks, some bearing torches or candles, others simple wooden crosses. A server stood before the horse with a bell that he rang with somber peals, and another carried a large latten cross. Gathered behind the cart was a group of clergy from Walsham and nearby Gislingham, and these were followed by a crowd of family, friends, and neighbors. As the procession moved off, the sound of St. Mary's bells could just be heard in the distance. It was a loud, emotional, and dramatic procession, with much lamentation, many prayers, and the solemn chanting of the penitential psalms. In this way William was once again joined with his kin and with the whole village, and the village with the church.

On reaching St. Mary's, the coffin, draped with the hearse cloth, was carried by six paupers down the aisle and placed on a trestle table before the altar with burning candles at its four corners. William's body lay there through the day until at evensong the service of the Office of the Dead was begun by the reading of the seven penitential psalms. The air thick with incense, the coffin was sprinkled with holy water by a priest using a sprig of hyssop plucked from the bush in the churchyard.

"Purge me with hyssop, and I shall be clean: wash me, and I shall be whiter than snow."

This reading was followed by the Placebo Domine in Regione Vivorum, in which the clergymen were joined by three of the paupers, who each received an extra penny for being able to recite at least part of it from memory. A vigil over the body was kept overnight by a priest whom William's sons had hired for the purpose, and soon after sunrise at matins the Dirige Dominus Meus in Conspectu Tuo Viam Meam was recited and then the Psalms of Passion. Following breakfast a solemn requiem Mass was celebrated for the repose of William's soul.

In conducting each of the services, Master John was assisted by the lesser clergy of Walsham and a couple of acolytes from a neighboring parish, and in the congregation members of the Wodebite family were joined by a throng of parishioners. When the time of the burial drew near the church bell was rung, and two young boys were sent with handbells to inform the whole parish that William was being buried and exhort people to pray for him.

It was a fine day, and the coffin was carried into the sunlit churchyard where a grave had been dug for William immediately adjacent to the spot where his father and mother were thought to lie. The open coffin containing William's body wrapped in a shroud was laid beside the grave. The congregation had swelled, and Master John cast his head around to survey them all—conversing, weeping, and praying—and called to them, "The sight of corpses and weeping maketh a man to think on his death, and is the chief help to put away sin. Wherefore each man and woman should make themselves ready; for we shall all die, and we know not how soon."

Having raised his arms to hush the assembly, the priest began his sermon: "William lived close to the span of three score years and ten, but whoever might have lived a hundred years, when he comes to the death, he shall seem that he has lived but the space of an hour. Very seldom does any man, even among the religious and devout, prepare himself for death in advance, as he ought. For every man thinks he will live long and does not believe he will die soon. William had land and money and a large house, but he shall now have a hall whose roof touches his nose, and a garment of earth and worms.

"Here is a mirror for us all, a corpse brought to the church and then to the burial ground. God have mercy on him for his mercy and bring him unto his everlasting bliss. But, good men, you should understand that this corpse is brought to the church for three principal reasons. The first is to show us that he was meek and obedient during his life to God and to Holy Church. But since he oftentimes did wrong against God through pride, as we all do, therefore at his death he bequeaths his soul into God's hands and his body to Holy Church. Just as a mother does not forsake the child who is obedient to her, so Holy Church receives each man who will obey and acknowledge his guilt with a purpose of amendment.

"The second reason is that mankind was made of the slime of the earth, and when a man dies he soon takes on the smell of death. Therefore, bodies are brought to be put in earth that is hallowed; for each corpse is earth and comes from the earth and lives on the earth and is, in the end, buried in the earth."

At that moment William's body was lifted from the coffin and lowered into the grave, while Master John sprinkled it again with holy water. Master John, ever willing to instruct his flock, pronounced, "He has a white sheet on him to show he has been cleanly shriven and cleansed of his sins by his heart's contrition and by the absolution of Holy Church. His head is laid toward the east so that he will be more ready to see Christ who will come out of the east on Doomsday. He also has a wooden cross at his head, showing that he has the full right to be saved by Christ's Passion, who died for him on a wooden cross. So that devils will have no power in his grave, I am sprinkling it with holy water. For it often happens that devils have the power to trouble a corpse which has not had the full sacraments of Holy Church, as William has had."

As the earth was shoveled into the grave, Master John continued, "And the third reason for bringing William's corpse to Holy Church is so that it can be helped by the prayers and sacraments of Holy Church. For we pray intently for all whose bodies rest inside the church or in the churchyard, and all who are brought to the church, and the joy of Our Lady also gives them great succor and refreshment. Then the demons shall go flying away yelling, for they cannot do their will.

"Thus you shall know, good men and women, that for these three reasons corpses are brought to Holy Church to be buried. Therefore, each man and woman who is wise, make yourself ready. For we all shall die and we know not how soon."

Solemnity soon gave way to jollity as trestle tables had been laid with copious quantities of ale, bread, roasted meats, and offal on the grass against the wall of the church for all who wished to come and to remember William in their prayers. It was a splendid feast, but the older guests spoke in awed tones, as they often did on such occasions, of the wondrous banquets that were thrown for the funeral and anniversary of William Lene, the richest villein ever seen in Walsham, who had died sixteen years before. Six wethers, four piglets, twelve geese, twenty cockerels, and a whole bullock had been roasted and flavored with rare spices, the finest ale had flowed like water, and the wheat for the bread alone had cost 9s.

Over two hundred people had attended, and almost five hundred pennies had been given to the poor on the day of Lene's burial and at the Mass held a week later. It was equally as wondrous that he had left no less than 60s for a Mass to be said for him every day for a whole year after his death, and had given careful instructions that a pilgrim should be sent to the shrine of St. Thomas of Lancaster, who had been beheaded for treason at Pontefract Castle in 1322.

Soon the conversation of the old men and women turned to stories of Lene's support for the rebellious earl when he had fought unsuccessfully against the previous king, and how he and other villagers had given aid to the army of Queen Isabella and Mortimer four years later when it had overnighted close to the village on its march across Suffolk to depose the wicked monarch.

High as he stood in wealth and prestige among his contemporaries, William Wodebite inevitably paled in comparison with such a legendary villager as William Lene. Nonetheless, Wodebite's death was an important event in the village, and his funeral feast was judged a fine affair. So too was the dinner seven days later for family and friends, after a service to commemorate his death had been held in the church. In between the two services William Hawys, the manor reeve, called at the Wodebite house to collect one of William's draft horses that the brothers had agreed to surrender to the lord as the death duty on his estate, and a servant called on behalf of the priest to collect a steer as a mortuary payment to the church.

As Master John had often said, "Souls are drawn up out of Purgatory by prayers," and William's soul was repeatedly succored by the prayers of all who attended the parish church. His sons had paid for special daily Masses to be said for their father for a month after his death, and for many weeks after that William was specifically named in the collective prayers regularly said for the souls of all departed parishioners. Prompted by the priest, William's children had also paid a small sum before the funeral for a special obituary Mass to be held on the anniversary of their father's death the next summer. They also outlined plans to hold an obit feast after this service for friends and neighbors who attended the service, and for some of the poor and sick of the parish. In such ways William's soul would continue to be aided by the prayers of the living.

Autumn 1345 to Winter 1347

There are thousands of surviving records of the proceedings of late medieval English manor courts written on parchment rolls, each of which contains masses of information. Although much of this information is selective and partial, and suffers from the many obvious drawbacks of legal proceedings, it does provide a unique window into the lives led by ordinary people. The proceedings of the courts of the large manor of Walsham, held by Sir Hugh and Lady Rose de Saxham, and the small integral manor of High Hall, held by Nicholas de Walsham until his death in 1347 and then by Edmund de Welles and his sister, Margery, survive almost continuously through the 1340s and early 1350s, and they can be used to recall something of the individuals who inhabited this part of rural Suffolk more than 650 years ago.

Details of the yields and prices of all types of grain grown on the demesne farms of landlords are recorded in manor account rolls, which survive in their thousands. They show that the harvest of 1346 was disastrous and prices rose sharply. According to national statistics, only once in the previous twenty-five years had yields been lower, and the shortage of food forced the price of wheat up by more than 70 percent. As a consequence poverty worsened and many small-holders who had borrowed money to tide them over, expecting to be able to repay their debts by selling grain, had little left over when the harvest failed, and they were forced instead to sell their land to survive. Hardship was compounded the next year when the harvest was again significantly below average.

More happily, 1346–1347 marked some notable English successes against the French and their Scottish allies. On August 26, 1346, Edward III and his son, the Black Prince, won a decisive victory over a much larger French army at Crécy, and in October David Bruce's invading forces were confronted in Durham by a superior army raised by the lords of northern England and routed at Neville's Cross. Spurred by these successes, Edward III raised a huge army and laid siege to the leading northern French port of Calais, which fell in the summer of 1347.

Although the precise origins of the Black Death are disputed by historians and medical scientists, there is fairly common agreement that it must have originated among the rodents in the high steppe of the central Asiatic plateau, centered on present-day Mongolia. The eruption of the disease may well have been connected to the long series of major ecological disasters, including earthquakes, floods, and famines, which are recorded in a variety of Latin and Arabic sources as occurring in the East during the 1330s and early 1340s. More definite is the manner and timing of the spread of the pestilence west toward Europe, which is attested by numerous contemporaries. During 1346, we are told, it was raging around the northwestern shores of the Caspian Sea and the estuary of the River Don, and in the latter part of the year it reached out southward to the Caucasus and westward to the Black Sea. In the succeeding months the epidemic launched multipronged assaults to the west and south, striking Constantinople in late spring 1347 and spreading into what is modern Turkey, Macedonia, and Greece, and down into Syria, Iran, and Iraq. By late autumn, it was raging in Alexandria and along the southern coast of the Mediterranean.

Naturally, western chroniclers were primarily concerned with the progress of the pestilence toward their own lands, and by popular agreement the first outbreak occurred in Sicily, where signs of the infection showed themselves in early October 1347. According to one of the most famous accounts, written by Gabriele de' Mussi of Piacenza, the pestilence was carried to Sicily on a fleet of Genoese galleys fleeing from the port of Caffa, now Feodosia, on the Crimean coast of the Black Sea. The pestilence had been brought to Caffa by a Mongol army that laid siege to the city. When large numbers of the besiegers began to die of the fatal disease, the bodies of the dead were lobbed over the walls, thereby infecting the city and its colony of Genoese merchants.

The folk of Walsham did not lack for reminders of how their actions in this world would determine their life in the next. Sin, Hell, and Purgatory loomed large in their thoughts, and the fate of souls which departed this world stained with unpurged transgressions and wickedness featured prominently in the teachings of the clergy. For those who might forget, the brightly painted scene of the day of doom emblazoned across the chancel arch of St. Mary's served as a perpetual ghastly vision of the wages of unpurged sin to all who entered the church. At the apex of the arch, astride a world crowded with people and fine buildings, sat God in all his majesty on a magnificent throne, with the twelve apostles at his feet. Larger than life-size, God held his arms outstretched, signifying his awesome power over the world, with Heaven to his right hand and Hell to his left. On the right, the artist's vision of Heaven was portrayed by green fields, blue sky, sun, water, and flowers. To this idyllic land, angels with trumpets summoned souls that had served their time in Purgatory to reside in perpetual bliss, and they were seen all around emerging, naked, cleansed, and smiling, from dark holes in the earth into bright sunlight. By horrific contrast, the scene of the gateway to Hell on the left was dreadful to behold. Demons gathered tormented and abandoned souls into despairing bands, then chained them together and dragged them toward the gigantic gaping mouths of hideous dragons, or cast them into everlasting sulfurous fires (see figure 7).

Yet powerful as they were, the forces of faith and fear were not sufficient to cow the villagers into leading blameless lives. Walsham's inhabitants, like people everywhere and in all ages, argued, lied, cheated, stole, and fornicated; they reneged on debts, charged exorbitant rates of interest, misrepresented the quality and quantity of goods they sold and falsely denigrated those they bought, repeatedly cut their lords' and their neighbors' hedges for firewood, encroached on the property of others, and carelessly or maliciously allowed their cows, sheep, pigs, and geese to stray. Some of these multitudinous crimes and misdemeanors were recorded in the manor rolls. That of the Walsham court held in November 1345 contained a hundred and more items of business, including Walter Fuller's wandering cow, which had caused extensive damage to banks of earth in various parts of the manor, and Robert and John, the sons of Robert Farmer from Ashfield, who had been caught in the lord's rabbit warren, using dogs and setting nets and other traps.

Much to Master John's frustration, villagers often failed to behave charitably toward each other, and quarrels, deceits, and injustices, real and imagined, continued to flourish despite his best efforts to mediate between them. Acrimony between Walter Cooper and Thomas Bec, close neighbors and former friends, had been brewing for months before William Wodebite's death. The main cause of their quarrel was the damage they each alleged had been done to their land by animals owned by the other. Their relations deteriorated further when Walter went to the court of July 25, 1345, to sue Thomas for trespass and damages. The court duly awarded Walter an interim judgment, and fined Thomas 3d. But Thomas was determined not to let the matter rest there and counterclaimed against Walter; the court reluctantly set up an inquiry to examine their trivial dispute. When the members of the inquiry, who all knew Thomas and Walter well, reported back to the court in November, they attempted to apportion blame equally by fining each litigant 4d—Thomas for letting his sheep trespass onto Walter's pasture, causing Walter 9d worth of damage, and Walter for letting his animals stray onto Thomas's cornfield where they did 15d worth of damage. Thomas was outraged that he had been fined the same amount as Walter, although Walter had caused him greater loss. So he immediately accused Walter of refusing to return two old barrels he had lent him some time ago and succeeded in getting Walter fined another 2d. However, at that point, the hayward and Master John decided that enough was enough, and, under pain of further fines, the combatants were forced to reach a binding agreement with each other to end their litigation before the court adjourned.

Few quarrels, however, were as remorselessly bitter as that carried on between William Wodebite's surviving children over the division of their father's property. Since William was unfree, the villein of Sir Nicholas de Walsham, the transfer of his sizable landholdings to his heirs had to receive the formal approval of the lord and be recorded in his court. Therefore, it was duly read out to those assembled at the court of September 24, 1345, that at his death William had held from the lord of the manor three separate blocks of land, amounting in total to sixteen acres, together with two houses and their garden plots. Since a death duty of a draft horse had already been collected, all these lands were allowed to pass in equal shares to William's three sons, John, Walter, and John Jr., in accordance with local custom. The brothers were then summoned by the steward to swear fealty to their lord, and the two Johns, on bended knees, pledged allegiance and subservience to Sir Nicholas and Lady Rose. As Walter was living some distance away from Walsham and had not yet returned to take up his inheritance, the steward ordered that for the time being his share should be managed by the manor reeve with any profits going to the lord.

The next arrangement made by the court was more controversial and concerned a messuage and five acres of land that William had leased from Richard Gothelarde for the term of his life. William's death meant that the lease terminated. But since Gothelarde had not come to the manor to repossess his land, the lord gave his approval, on payment of a fee of 2s, that the land should be granted to John Sr. and Walter Wodebite, thereby excluding their younger brother.

It was widely known in the village that all had not been well between the Woodbite children in the days before their father's death, and their enmity had grown more bitter since. But the ears of those attending the court pricked up when it was reported that just after William's death, Agnes, his sole daughter, had gone to her father's house with a cart and taken away a great deal of valuable property which should have passed to her brothers. Furthermore, it was alleged, Agnes had subsequently transported this property outside Walsham manor against the express orders of the lord's bailiff. After hearing the evidence, the court decreed that her elder brother John was entitled to retain the corn and livestock belonging to Agnes that he had seized in retaliation and to take more of her goods if necessary, until she replied to the charges and the matter was settled.

The reason for Agnes's behavior became clearer later in the proceedings that day, when the court learned that she had been upset that all her father's property and land had gone to her brothers. Her grievance was transformed into rage when she learned from the bailiff that he had witnessed a gift her father had made a few days before his death of an acre and a rod of land to the two daughters of her eldest brother, John.

Early in the new year, Walter Wodebite finally arrived back in Walsham to take up the land he had inherited from his father. When he found that the door of the cottage in which he wished to live had been sealed by the lord's bailiff, he broke it and moved in without approval. For this he was duly fined 18d for contempt in the next manor court. Perhaps because the three Wodebite brothers were preoccupied with the death of their father and sorting out their inheritance, none of them turned up to work for the lord on his demesne farm, despite being repeatedly ordered to do so, and they were heavily fined for their misbehavior.

Over the ensuing months the Wodebite family was rent by further quarrels as the brothers wrestled without success to share their sizable inheritance in an amicable manner. By April, young John had decided that he no longer wished to carry on farming alongside his brothers, and he agreed to lease Walter his share of his father's lands in return for 5s a year. Family arrangements were rarely formally recorded, but because John did not trust his brother, he insisted not only that their agreement be registered in court but that it should contain the explicit requirement that Walter follow all normal practices of good husbandry, including spreading dung, and keep the land in as good a heart as when he received it.

Any hopes that Master John might have had about reconciliation between the Wodebite brothers were spectacularly dispelled at the obit feast after the special Mass held in St. Mary's church on the anniversary of the death of their father in late August. All present at the memorial were scandalized when a bitter row flared up between the brothers on the top table, to the great shame of the family. The community placed the blame for the incident squarely on the shoulders of young John, whose misbehavior was deemed to be so serious that he was hauled before the next High Hall court session and fined for making false accusations against his brothers.

Further months of wrangling produced yet another attempt at a settlement between the three brothers. This time they decided to split their father's lands in such a way that they would not have to cooperate in farming them. Once again, the breakdown of trust between the brothers had gone so far, and the amount of money and land at stake was so great, that the brothers decided to have their agreement registered in the manor court. At the session held on April 21, 1347, at a cost of 18d in legal fees, it was recorded that John the elder had taken the croft called Chesinees, Walter the one called Aprilles, and John the younger, Alwynes. These lands obviously had an abundance of cottages on them, for the lord took this opportunity of extracting a pledge from each of the brothers that they would keep all of them in a good state of repair. However, it soon became apparent that Walter had no intention of farming all of his lands himself, and he set about leasing small parcels at high rents to villagers desperate for land; his elder brother John took a couple of acres of pasture.

Life was habitually harsh for the majority of Walsham's villagers in the 1340s as the overcrowded land struggled each year to feed all the mouths that depended on it. Harvests needed to be good to avoid distress, but that of 1346 was exceptionally poor. The growing season had been extremely dry, and the lack of rain meant that grain did not swell in the husk. In late August and early September the baleful shadow of a hard and hungry winter loomed ominously ahead as the meager sheaves were gathered in. Farmer after farmer reported yields around a quarter to a third lower than normal, and by October the price of wheat, which for many years had averaged little more than 4s a quarter in the local markets, had reached 6s. Villagers sought to make their pennies go further by baking their bread and making their pottage from cheaper, coarser, and less appetizing grains such as rye, barley, oats, and peas, but the prices of these rapidly followed suit. Since few in Walsham had landholdings sufficient to grow all they needed to eat, low yields meant that the majority were forced to buy more of their food and pay more for it. Making matters worse, people sought to save money by putting off nonessential expenditures. Consequently those who offered themselves for hire in order to supplement their meager incomes suffered reduced earnings, while the cost of bread, beans, pottage, and ale soared. Those wretched folk with only tiny amounts of land or none at all, who had only the labor of their hands to live off, were driven deep into poverty and wracked with hunger, and those who were too old or sick to work had to rely on the charity of neighbors, many of whom were themselves suffering hardship and deprivation.

Harvest was normally a time when substantial bonuses could be earned, but this year the depleted crops in the fields required less labor to gather in and to thresh and winnow over the winter. More insidiously, low yields and high food prices ate into the disposable income of even the more affluent villagers. More money spent on food, which was essential, meant less to be spent on cloth, pottery, wooden and leather goods, building work, repairs and maintenance, and suchlike, which could be put off until later. As villagers deferred many purchases until better times, the drop in expenditure made it more difficult for their poorer neighbors to find casual employment as carders, spinners, weavers, potters, turners and woodcarvers, carpenters, leatherworkers, tilers, thatchers, carters, carriers, and, of course, common farm laborers.

As the price of bread rose still higher over the winter of 1347, the smallholders and landless of Walsham often went hungry. Many of those who possessed animals were forced to sell them to raise money or slaughter them in order to feed themselves, and many of those who had goods to pledge, however meager, were forced to borrow against them and seek charity from their richer neighbors. Particularly badly hit were poor villagers who had previously pledged their smallholdings as security for loans, on the expectation that they would be able to repay their debts from the proceeds of the harvest which had now failed. As they now had little or no grain to sell, they were forced instead to dispose of land, their main source of livelihood.

However, even when facing a cold and hungry winter, the villagers enjoyed some welcome diversions, none more so than the news which reached Walsham in late autumn of a glorious victory in the war against the king of France at Crécy. Sturdy English longbowmen, rustics like themselves, had slaughtered a host of mounted and armored nobility and knights, the flower of French chivalry (see figure 8). Amid much rejoicing, the valiant King Edward and his son, the Black Prince, were toasted by rich and poor alike. Englishmen and women were delighted to hear that God had been on their side, not just by bringing the victory but by sending heavy rain, thunder, and a terrible eclipse of the sun just before the battle, which both frightened the French and their Genoese allies and hampered them in their preparations. And then God had sent the most brilliant sun, which shone directly in the eyes of the enemy while warming the backs of the English.

Tales of the battle, its tactics, its feats of heroism, the manner in which the enemy was dispatched, were told and retold in the parlors of cottages, the bars of alehouses, the halls of manor houses, and the refectories of the local monasteries. Villagers listened intently as they were told how the English archers shot their arrows with such force and speed that it seemed to be snowing, and how those arrows struck down first the Genoese crossbowmen and then pierced through the armor of the mounted French earls, barons, knights, and esquires and brought them crashing to the ground, where they had their throats slit by the knives of Cornishmen and Welshmen.

For a time, all who came into Walsham found themselves the center of attention and treated to generous hospitality of drinks, meals, and even lodgings, as they were encouraged to disclose every scrap of information about Crécy, so that it could be assiduously added to that which had already been heard. In the alehouses and at markets and fairs, much pleasure was derived from recreating the chaotic battle scenes in which the French knights, and those who rode with them, had trampled down the fleeing Genoese crossbowmen in a series of mad charges at the thin but unyielding lines of brave English longbowmen and pikemen. Time and again the enemy had been repulsed and routed and finally killed in the thousands. The flower of French knighthood had been slaughtered, including many of the very highest nobility: the king's brother, the count of Flanders, the duke of Lorraine, the king of Majorca, and, most renowned of all, the blind king John of Bohemia. In the weeks that followed, the practicing of archery at the butts on Walsham village green became very popular, and a number of competitions were hastily arranged for holidays and festivals.

Walsham was also brought in touch with the wider community when Lady Margery called Master John to High Hall and insisted, against his protestations, that her private confessor, a Franciscan friar, should preach the first of the series of Lenten sermons, which was due to be given on Sunday, March 5, the first Sunday in Lent and the festival of Quadragesima. Rumors had been circulating in the village for some time about the sway this friar held over Lady Margery's life and how he lorded over the household staff. Master John was distraught, for he considered the sermon at the beginning of Lent to be one of the most important of the year, when he explained the meaning of Lent to his flock and set the spiritual tone for the forty-day period of fasting and confession. As far as John knew, this vital sermon had always been given by the parish priest, and furthermore the friar was no friend of his. In fact, he deeply resented his presence in the parish. For the friar preached coarse sermons full of demons, torments, and carnal sins, and he also frequented the taverns and told bawdy tales, gave easy penance to sinners for money, and bartered with his flock by offering them cheap deals on all his services, from burying loved ones to blessing marriages and barren cows. By undercutting the fees on which the poor assistant clergy of the parish relied to scratch a living, the friar was taking food out of their mouths. More important yet, the Franciscan was depriving his parishioners of spiritual sustenance. It was the sacred duty of Master John and his carefully chosen and schooled chaplains to hear the confessions of his flock, to make them feel genuinely ashamed for their transgressions, and to heal them by exacting an appropriately painful penance. Yet many of the sinners in the parish avoided this pain and shame by fleeing to the friar, who imperiled their souls by selling them easy forgiveness for a penny or two.

There was no denying the friar's popularity among parishioners, who were excited when they heard that the theme of his sermon was to be games rather than Lenten abstinence. More than that, it was rumored that Lady Margery, who was particularly fond of playing chess, had chosen the central message of the sermon: the similarity of the world to a game of chess. Then, during Mass performed before a packed congregation, when the time came for the friar to give his sermon, he theatrically leaped up from behind the rood screen where he had been crouching. The congregation gasped and some laughed nervously. But they fell silent as the friar approached the pulpit and, cupping his hand to his ear, said with heavy sarcasm in his voice, "Listen how quiet the church now is, how lacking in idle chatter and gossip. See how devotedly you all concentrate on my every word and movement and on every stone, every colored window, saint's image, brass ornament and fine cloth in this church. Yet when your own priest appears before you he can scarcely hear himself speak for the babble you make, though he offers you the route to eternal heavenly bliss. Devils and demons are with us always, and Tutivillus, prince among demons, is delighted to note down all your misdeeds and evil thoughts on his roll of sins, to be read out one by one on the day of doom. Should it take many a day to do so. You must go to the great church of Ely, just a few miles away, and see there the pew seat, which was carved a little while ago as a warning to those who like you keep up a constant babbling of voices during services in the cathedral. On it the master woodcarver has depicted Tutivillus in the shape of a pig, hugging with pleasure two women who are gossiping during Mass. This devil can also be seen stretching his long roll with his teeth and noting down their every word, which will be used against them later when the women are dispatched to be tormented by devils for their careless sins. See there too, how one of the women plays with her rosary, as if that will save her from the boiling cauldron and the venomous worms that will gnaw her body without ceasing. Ah! See how quiet you have all become, and how attentive to my every word. Ha! See how my words are already turning you from sin! Are you believing the tales you are hearing of the coming of the end of the world?"

Having gained the rapt attention of the packed congregation, the friar settled down to give one of his favorite sermons: "The world is like a chessboard, which is checkered white and black. The colors show the two conditions of life and death, or praise and blame. The chessmen are men of this world who occupy different stations and hold different titles in this life, although every one of us finally has a common fate which levels all ranks. You know the saying that you cannot tell a knight from a peasant in the charnel house, and I tell you that the king himself often lies under the pawns when the chess pieces are in the bag. In chess, the king's move and powers of capture are in all directions. This is because the king's will is law. The queen's move, however, is aslant only, because women are so greedy that they will take nothing except by rapine and injustice. The rook stands for the itinerant justices who travel over the whole realm, and their move is always straight because the judge must deal justly. The knight's move is compounded of a straight move and an oblique one; the former betokens his legal power of collecting rents and such rightful things, the latter his extortions and wrongdoings. The bishops are prelates wearing horns, and they move obliquely because every bishop misuses his office through cupidity. The pawns are poor men like you. Their move is straight, except where they take anything; so also the poor man does well so long as he keeps from ambition, because it is hard for a poor man to deal rightly when he is raised above his proper station.

"This game of chess is also like life because the devil says 'Check!' when a man or woman falls into sin; and unless the sinner quickly covers the check by turning to repentance, the devil says 'Mate!' and carries him off to Hell, from which there is no escape. The devil has as many kinds of temptation to catch different types of men as the hunter has dogs to catch different types of animals."

Master John had absented himself from the sermon by announcing, somewhat ostentatiously, that it was a mere *exemplum*, and that he would be visiting the sick on foot in the farthest corners of the village. However, he was amused to learn a few days later that Lady Margery had taken offense during her confessor's homily at the reference to women being rapacious and unjust, and then accused him outside the church, in the full view and hearing of others, of putting in this reference only because she had refused to buy him another fur-lined cape.

The harvest of autumn 1347 brought no respite to the poor of Walsham, for once again it was miserable (see figure 9). This time it was spoiled by torrential rain, which came just when the ripe corn was ready to be gathered in. The villagers had prayed while they scattered the seed that they would reap at least four times as much as they sowed. To this end Master John dispensed many gallons of holy water for sprinkling on the land and led numerous processions to bless the fields. Many villagers, in addition, sought the assistance of the powers of natural magic, as they had always done, by buying charms from wise old men and women who promised to boost the fertility of their soil and guard their livestock against pestilence. But the lack of sunshine in August led to dampness in the grain, and repeated heavy showers beat down the stalks so that they were difficult to cut, gather in, and dry. As a result the yield was not much better than the previous year, and far short of what was needed. Food shortages and high prices persisted, but now the problems of survival for poorer villagers, both financial and physical, were grievously aggravated because their scanty reserves had been twice depleted. Smallholders who earlier in the year had borrowed against the yield of their land in order to eat, now had their hopes dashed by the poor harvest and instead found themselves pressed for the repayment of loans at the same time as they struggled to find enough money to put food in the stomachs of their families. This rising inability to repay debts was reflected in the courts of Walsham, where the number of creditors seeking redress against defaulting debtors multiplied. With the heavy hand of the law behind them, bailiffs distrained the goods and livestock of those who could not pay what they owed, and many small but vital pieces of land were prised from their needy owners as creditors foreclosed and gobbled up their half acres, rods, and pightles.

As winter approached in late 1347, times were as bad as most villagers could remember they had been since 1339. But old men and women with longer memories, sometimes aided by overfertile imaginations, recounted how the present scarcities were as nothing compared with the horrendous famines that had struck England and Walsham three decades before. Then, they claimed, it had rained almost nonstop for two years and the land had flooded until there were lakes the size of seas all around Walsham. The village fields were so wet that it was scarcely possible to plow and sow them, for the seeds they scattered were washed away in the mud and water; if any sprouted, the shoots were beaten down by the rain and the cold. And when it came to harvest time, lucky indeed was the farmer who gathered in as much grain as he had sown. In those days of dearth, the old folk recalled, the price of all types of corn had soared fivefold, and it was said that a quarter of wheat had sold in London for more than 40s. Starving people had been forced to eat dogs and cats, not merely the roots and berries that some of the poor were eating these days. And, they whispered, in those evil days some had been driven to such madness by the pangs of hunger that they had devoured their own children. Then, the old folk recalled while their young audience listened in horror, as if crop failures and starvation on an unimaginable scale were not enough to bear, the famines were followed by a series of devastating murrains and plagues of their sheep and cattle. In the end it was difficult to say which had been the greater number: the death of livestock from plagues or of their owners from starvation and disease.

The people of Walsham, like everyone else, had a great love of stories and a vast appetite for news about important events and the doings of important people, which circulated in the humblest of places. And when there was little of note to talk about, even the most trite and trivial of tittle-tattle would find a ready audience, at least for a short while. It was always worth listening to the gossip of the servants who overheard conversations in the manor houses of their lords, and the reports of the monks who regularly shared company with visitors to the abbeys at Ixworth and Bury, and sometimes journeyed to London or even Rome. The carters who carried goods from place to place were an additional source of copious, if not always reliable, information, and news spread rapidly whenever people gathered in markets and fairs. Even those who did not travel far could hear in the alehouses and lodging houses of Walsham something worth listening to from the most lowly of wayfarers.

The progress of the war with France, the actions of the king, lords, knights, and parliament, the behavior of bishops and archdeacons, the price of wool, pigs, and barley, all were reported and recounted time and again. So too were exotic travelers' fables of sea monsters and dragons, man-eating half-human savages, and cities made of gold in far distant lands. These and more besides had long been a source of amusement and amazement, even in the quiet lanes of rural Suffolk. But from the early 1340s such long-lived tales were joined, and eventually surpassed, by even more fantastic stories that came from the edge of the world in the East— from the lands of the Great Khan, hard by India, and from Persia and Cathay. Thence came stories of torrential rains that turned vast plains into lakes or even seas, of massive earthquakes that consumed cities, mountains that rained down fire falling in flakes like snow and burning up the land and all who dwelled on it. Passed on by successions of travelers to places near and far, these fabulous stories crossed Europe and then England, and finally arrived in Walsham. Soon they had been brought to the village many times and in many different forms.

It may have been the harsh routine of daily life and the exhausting struggle that many faced daily for mere survival that stifled villagers' interest in wondrous happenings in the East, on the edges of the world. At first the reports were merely added to the feast of tall stories and legends that came from remote places, which fed the appetites of those who hungered after mystery, wonder, and entertainment. Eventually, however, the more curious and thoughtful residents of Walsham, assisted by their scholarly priest who was always willing to discuss and interpret, began to note how the mixture of myth and miracles, which on first hearing could so easily be dismissed as entertaining fantasy, was gaining a measure of credibility through the persistence and repetition of key elements.

As time passed, the provenance of these tales was becoming ever firmer. At first they had no known authors, but now they were confidently ascribed to Italians who, sailing the Mediterranean and venturing beyond the Black Sea, had heard them from the Arabs, Persians, and Tartars with whom they met and traded. By the early spring of 1347, men from Lynn, Ipswich, Cambridge, and London could be encountered in Bury, Thetford, and occasionally even in markets close to Walsham, who insisted they had spoken to the very merchants or seamen who had heard these tales from the infidels who had actually witnessed these fantastic events, or at least had told them that they had.

So often in the past, news that at first had seemed amazing had eventually become more prosaic, as more convincing testimonies successively stripped away the wonders and bizarre trappings. But this news was different. By the summer of 1347, the sources of the tales from the East were both multiplying and increasing in authority, and as this happened their contents were becoming more, not less, fantastic. Further, the tellers of the tales were becoming ever more deeply troubled by what they had to report. Now the center of the stage was not floods, eruptions, and earthquakes, but a pestilence of unprecedented ferocity and mysterious form, whose coming had been preceded by a series of awful omens, including rains of frogs, serpents, lizards, scorpions, and venomous beasts. This pestilence, it was said, was borne by the wind in clouds of poison, and was contaminating all those it touched, bringing sudden death to thousands upon thousands of Tartars and Saracens. The pestilence was moving hither and thither without warning, and as it did so broad regions were destroyed and far-spreading provinces, magnificent kingdoms, cities, towns, and settlements swiftly stripped of their inhabitants, who were ground down by sickness and devoured by dreadful death.

Yet even these latest reports caused little deep concern, except perhaps among a few devout parishioners who eagerly drew attention to parallels they found in the Bible, which included the floods of the time of Noah, as well as the hails of fire and blood, swarms of locusts and pestilences which God had visited in ancient times on grievous sinners. But Master John calmed the zealots, telling them that the sins in their community, though hurtful to God, were not sufficiently heinous to drive him, in his mercy, to smite them as he smote the citizens of Sodom and Gomorrah. "Why do you have so little faith in God's mercy? Do you not see that he is striking down infidels and not Christians?"

Then in late autumn, a London merchant visiting Bury to buy cloth to export across the North Sea claimed to have heard from a frightened Genoese trader, while on a recent voyage to Bruges, not only the familiar stories of a mysterious sickness destroying numerous provinces in distant parts of the world and leaving them covered with unburied dead bodies, but that the sickness had been carried westward by the Tartars and had reached the shores of the Black Sea. The London merchant explained that many of the fine silk cloths and rare spices that were sold for high prices in London, and were from time to time bought by the richest citizens of Bury, had been traded through ports on the Black Sea. But to the countryfolk of Walsham, such a sickness, if it could be believed at all, was occurring in strange places at the very ends of the earth, where no Englishman had ever been. There had never been rains of fire or serpents in Walsham, in Suffolk, or in England. And the wisest people in their village were certain that not even the most learned of monks and doctors, with all their books containing wisdom from the beginning of time, had any knowledge of pestilence striking England or Europe which bore even the slightest resemblance to the disease raging in the East.

So they turned instead with relish to the latest gossip circulating in their community about the doings of Idonea Isabel, a young single woman who had been waging a remarkably feisty struggle against her lord, Nicholas de Walsham, and his wife, Margery. The year before, Idonea had made a fuss by publicly refusing to turn up at harvest time to reap on Sir Nicholas's land, as required by her tenancy obligations, and had instead accepted higher wages from Robert Hovel to cut his corn. For this Idonea had been fined 3d, and her father was forced to act as a pledge for her future good behavior. But the young woman persisted in her rebelliousness and, although unmarried, had then become pregnant. What is more, Idonea, a skillful weaver, repeatedly refused to weave cloth for Lady Margery. And, as if that was not enough, she openly told all who would listen that she refused to weave the cloth because Lady Margery was a cheat who had failed to pay her mother, Olivia, for the linen cloth she made six years before. Then, to compound her contempt for her lord and lady, at harvest time she once again failed to turn up at their demesne farm to reap. But this time Idonea had an excuse, for she had recently given birth. However, Sir Nicholas decided that he had to make an example of Idonea, and at the manor court held after the harvest he fined her 3d for failing to reap for him, 2s 8d for producing a bastard, and 3d for not fulfilling his wife's order to weave cloth. Still Idonea was not cowed, and she boasted in open court that she had no intention of paying the fines or working for the de Walshams for nothing, either in their fields or at her loom.

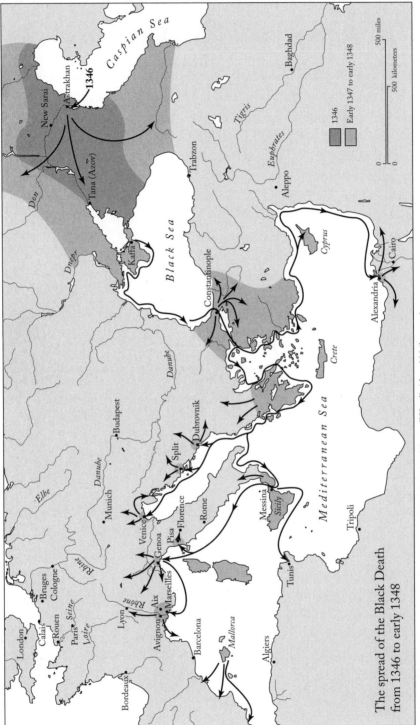

The spread of the Black Death
from 1346 to early 1348

Source: Ole J. Benedictow, *The Black Death, 1346–53: The Complete History* (Woodbridge, 2004), map 1.

Christmas and
New Year, 1347–1348

The spread of the pestilence into Europe depended primarily on the traffic of people and goods and for a time may have been restrained by the limited number of trade routes from the East. By the closing months of 1347, however, it had reached the Mediterranean Sea and was advancing with considerable speed in a multitude of directions. The dense networks of regular contacts between the ports and cities around the Mediterranean saw Sicily hit by October and Marseilles by November; multitudes were dying in Sardinia, Corsica, and Genoa before the end of December. Thence the pestilence began to strike up the west coast of Italy and inland into southern France, and during January it was reported to be raging in many more cities, including Pisa, Venice, Aix-en-Provence, Arles, and Avignon. There are a number of detailed accounts of the havoc wrought by the pestilence in Avignon, where the papacy had resided since its move from Rome in 1309. One of the best descriptions of the symptoms of the disease is given by Pope Clement VI's physician, Gui de Chauliac, who lived through the epidemic in Avignon and observed it firsthand. Chauliac commenced his account: "The mortality began with us in the month of January [1348], and lasted seven months. It had two phases. The first lasted two months; with continuous fever and the spitting of blood, from which victims died within three days. The second lasted for the whole of the remainder of the time, also with continuous fever, and with abscesses and carbuncles in the extremities, principally under the armpits and in the groin; and death took place within five days. The disease was extremely contagious."

In contrast to tiny Ixworth priory adjacent to Walsham, the abbey of Bury St. Edmunds was one of the greatest and wealthiest abbeys in England. Before the Black Death it housed a community of some seventy to eighty Benedictine monks, as well as numerous chaplains, servants, and lay residents. Only scanty physical traces of its former glory survive, but in the fourteenth century the abbey church was over 500 feet long with an aisled nave of twelve bays, and the east end was formed by a transept almost 250 feet long. Bury St. Edmunds abbey was one of the foremost centers of learning in fourteenth-century England with a particularly fine library, comprising more than two thousand volumes at its peak, acquired by purchase and gift as well as by the copying carried out by monks in the scriptorium. Henry Kirkstead was a notable abbey librarian in the late fourteenth century. Over the centuries many of the abbey's monks wrote chronicles that recounted historical and contemporary events. Like every large monastery, Bury St. Edmunds abbey had its infirmary for the care of sick monks and an infirmarer who dispensed medicines, supervised the care of the sick, and organized the regular bleeding to which the brethren were subjected.

❧ ❧

In the week before Christmas 1347 Master John returned breathless from what should have been a routine visit to Ixworth priory. As he arrived at St. Mary's, it was bustling with parishioners making preparations for the supreme feast and the great midnight Mass. His eye briefly alighted on a group decking the interior of the church with holly and ivy, but in uncharacteristic fashion he hurried past them; nor did the priest seem to hear the little choir practicing a particularly difficult carol. Despite calls to come and look, he scarcely acknowledged an excited huddle in front of the altar assembling a large, brightly painted wooden model of the stable at Bethlehem. Master John had gone to Ixworth to give the prior one of his regular reports on the state of his parish and the revenues it was producing, but just before he left he was given a letter sent by his good friend Richard, the keeper of the infirmary at Bury St. Edmunds abbey. It was the letter that caused his agitation.

Master John summoned his two chaplains, who were reluctant to leave the altar just as the life-size wooden figure of the Christ child was placed in the arms of an adoring Mary, and hastily ushered them to a quiet place to read the letter to them (see figure 10). The letter was brief and to the point. After a few words of greeting, his friend, who was most expert in medical matters, informed him that the pestilence from the East was moving swiftly westward across Europe. According to a number of unimpeachable sources, it had now crossed the Mediterranean Sea and was raging in many of the seaports of Italy and France, and possibly Spain too. The letter concluded ominously, "Nothing it seems can halt its progress; we can only pray that God's infinite mercy will cause him to stay his hand before it reaches our shores."

Master John was anxious that his flock should not be unduly alarmed and swore his chaplains to keep this terrible letter to themselves. But in the days and weeks that followed there was such a flow of unnerving news into Walsham, and from such a variety of sources, including the monastery at Bury, that even he found it increasingly difficult to sift fact from fiction. The priest resolved to travel to Bury to visit his friend early in the new year to hear more of the truth and hopefully dispel some of the wilder rumors. But he found his departure continually delayed by the pressures of work arising from the ever-mounting concerns among his parishioners, as well as the heightened demands for confessions and absolution which flowed from them. In addition, he was confronted by constant questions and requests for detailed explanations of the most complex and taxing kind, which even with his learning and long experience he found difficult to answer in an appropriate manner. John was constantly left without sufficient time for his own prayers and contemplation, and each night he was physically and emotionally drained as he retired late to bed. For these reasons, but perhaps also because he feared that his sober and learned friend might confirm the inexorable approach of the terrible pestilence, it was not until the third week in February, long after Candlemas had been celebrated, that he set out for the short journey to Bury.

John arrived at the abbey close to noon, which was dinnertime and the high point of the day for most of the monks. Despite his ascetic leanings, he was looking forward to some fine food and wine, congenial company, and stimulating conversation. After the exchange of exceptionally warm but unusually brief greetings at the gate, however, Richard hurried John past the refectory to the library to meet one of the most learned monks in the community. He was an elderly man, renowned throughout England as a scholar, who had held the office of librarian for many years and had spent most of his life delighting in the study of the renowned collection of old books housed in the great library of the monastery, which were stuffed full of the deeds of long-dead kings and knights, of descriptions of invasions, conquests, and battles in far-off days. But the librarian was also the abbey chronicler, and he took great pains to keep an accurate and comprehensive journal of contemporary as well as historical events, assiduously acquiring every piece of news about happenings in the wider world. As Master John readily appreciated, since the abbey of Bury possessed a magnificent library and hosted a constant stream of travelers from all parts, many of whom were welcome to stay and enjoy the lavish hospitality of the brethren for as long as they entertained and informed their hosts with the latest news and gossip, this learned monk was well placed for pursuing both of his special interests.

Richard breathlessly explained to John, as they drew toward the old man writing at an oak table at the far end of the vast room, "This abbey's librarian not only has a great talent for gathering information, he has a rare ability for grading and sorting it into order. He is singularly adept at prompting guests to divulge all they know, or think they know. But he also probes them deeply, to discover how much reliance he should place on their stories. Always he takes care to ask those with significant news to tell him how they have come by their knowledge, and then he rejects from it what is trivial or unreliable and raises to prominence what is not. Most importantly, he is always searching for connections and confirmations between the many stories that reach his ears."

John readily accepted that all this praise was fully deserved. It was for these very qualities that the librarian had been chosen to continue writing the great chronicles for which the abbey had been famous since the late twelfth century. But he was shaken when Richard took his arm and stopped him just before the table and whispered urgently, "You must trust the word of this man above all others on how the great pestilence has been spreading its poisonous tentacles across Europe in the past few months."

"Come and sit down," the old scholar said to John, as he beckoned a stern welcome with his hand. "What I am about to tell you is shocking. But it is not mere gossip designed to excite simple minds. It is carefully distilled essential information that I must pass on so that as many souls as possible can be saved in the little time that remains to us. I have agreed to inform you of my carefully researched findings because the infirmarer has assured me that you are a sober and learned priest, a man who can be trusted to make good use of what you will hear from me. In order that there should be no doubt about the importance of what I am about to impart, I will begin with the conclusion I have reached through deep study and calm and careful deliberation.

"As you know well, a pestilence of unprecedented ferocity started some time ago in the far east of the world, in the heathen lands of the Great Khan and the Golden Horde, and then, having grown in vigor in Turkey and Greece, spread from there over the whole Levant and Mesopotamia, and into Syria and Chaldea and Cyprus and Rhodes and all the Greek islands. This much is common knowledge, but what I am about to tell you is not. Although many travelers are claiming to know more than they do, and some are prone to falsify what little they actually know, I can confirm that last Michaelmas the dreadful scourge leaped to Sicily and then to Sardinia, Corsica, and Elba. You may be unaware of the existence of these places, but I can tell you that, beyond any doubt, this terrible plague is at this very moment spreading along the shores around the Mediterranean Sea. Not only this, but from there it is already starting to penetrate inland to strike many great cities in Italy and France."

This appalling news the librarian imparted in a calm and confident manner, but his voice grew weak and tremulous as he leaned toward John and confided, "In all of this time, from its very beginnings at the ends of the world in the East, this scourge has never weakened nor ceased its movement northward and westward toward our land."

John attempted to interrupt with an urgent question or two, but the librarian recovered his composure and impatiently hushed him: "Ordinary folk are gullible and unable to tell truth from fiction; they delight in fancies and superstitions. So we, as intelligent and literate men, have become accustomed to dismiss most of the dreadful stories we have heard as suitable only for the amusement of drunken peasants in alehouses. As mere tales that have grown massively in the telling as they passed from one careless mouth to another across countless countries. I have scorned them, and you have too. But I must confess to you that we were wrong. Now even the most remarkable of these fantastical accounts are daily being confirmed as true by those who have returned from neighboring countries and seen these terrible things with their own eyes, or spoken to those who have. Even more dreadful still, all those who have fled in the wake of the plague have spoken with one voice: nothing can stop its progress of destruction, neither the actions of city councils who close their gates against all outsiders nor the breadth of the sea. As it spreads through region after region, in towns and cities where there had once been twenty thousand people scarcely two thousand now remain, and in many villages and settlements fifteen hundred people have been reduced to barely one hundred."

Once again Master John made as if to disagree, but he hesitated and was then shocked into silence as the wise chronicler, holding up the palm of his hand and shaking his head sadly, signaled that he had even more horrific matters to tell him: "This was the news that I sought to impart urgently to priests like you, so that you might instruct your flock to call on God's mercy to avert this tragedy. But you hesitated to come to see me, and during the delay that you created I have learned much more. Just four days ago a young clerk lodged in this abbey as he made his way to Norwich to report to his superiors in the household of the bishop. He told us that he had just fled in terror from the city of Avignon, where he had been part of a delegation of churchmen from our country to the papal court. We all found him to be a man of the utmost intelligence and probity, and we offered him rest in our abbey. But he could not sleep, and for hours he held our brothers awestruck with detailed accounts of how the most sacred city, with its abundance of holy men, including the most holy of all, was suffering the ravages of a mysterious and most lethal plague, which nothing could assuage, not even the pope himself.

"I have his precise words here." With that the librarian took up the parchment folio on which he had been writing and scanned it as he continued: "It was last November, he told us, when news was first brought to the papal court that thousands were dying in the port of Marseilles about two or three days journey to the south; just before Christmas the sickness reached Aix. But still the residents of the holy city believed that God would spare them. As soon as the pestilence threatened, the young visitor told us, the pope commanded devout processions with the chanting of litanies, and these were attended by at least two thousand people from all the region round about, men and women alike, many barefoot, others wearing hair shirts or smearing themselves with ashes (see figure 11). As they processed they wailed, tore their hair, and thrashed themselves with cruel whips until the blood ran. The pope himself took part in some of the processions, as did our young clerk. But sadly, their lamentations scarcely affected the work of pestilence."

The old man then put down the vellum on which he had copied the words of the young clerk: "God knows what the end will be. The most powerful prayers and penitential processions proffered in their multitudes have not yet been sufficient to stay the hand of an angry God. The holy city is being destroyed as we speak, just as multitudes of Christian and pagan cities have been destroyed before it. There can be no doubt that our suffering will begin very soon."

Master John had fallen silent. His questions no longer seemed so pressing, and the prudent skepticism that he had so carefully nurtured over the past months now seemed merely willful. He just listened intently as the abbey chronicler, whose words resounded with truth and wisdom, went on to explain how he had arrived at his awful conclusions. "The plague cannot be halted or diverted. Time and again city authorities have sought to stop the plague entering their cities by shutting their gates and banishing visitors, but always without success. No doctors know how to cure it, neither present experts nor ancient masters.

"On careful examination of what has been reported, the infirmarer and I have found that God is scourging the world with a variety of pestilences, the likes of which have not been seen before. The clerk fleeing from the papal curia saw with his own eyes, just days ago, that the disease now raging in Avignon is an infection of the lungs. Its victims cough and spit up large amounts of blood almost immediately after they become infected, and they all die very soon. This young man swore that he had not seen or heard reports of anyone in Avignon being afflicted with the hideous swellings in the neck, armpits, and groin that, according to a multitude of witnesses, devastated the populations of lands in the East.

"But," the librarian cautioned, "one should not take any comfort in this. In fact, the reverse. For this new bloody pestilence is even worse than the other, if that could be true. All who catch it die within three days, and nobody recovers. It is also far easier to become infected with this affliction. From Avignon there is clear evidence that anyone who looks on a sick person is immediately infected. And so certain is it that all who catch the disease will die, without any hope of recovery, that in order to preserve the healthy in the holy city, all those who are known to be suffering from the sickness are at once borne off to the pit and buried, many of them while still alive. But still the deaths mount without ceasing."

The three pious men sitting in the great library of the abbey of Bury St. Edmunds in late January 1348 asked themselves whether there could be any doubt that this pestilence, or another no less terrible, would be stalking England in a matter of weeks, just as mercilessly as it was now stalking France (see figure 12). They concluded that it would surely come to pass. As they contemplated what they might do or what this might mean for their community and the realm, even the sober librarian, who knew well all the great events, catastrophes, and mysteries of the past, became agitated. Richard the infirmarer, who had seen countless diseases during his many years caring for the sick, eagerly voiced his acceptance of every dismal judgment that had been uttered. John could remain silent no longer, and he vainly attempted to stem the tide of pessimism by pointing to the protection that would be offered by the sea, which set England apart from its neighbors. But his weak objection was swiftly dismissed. He was told sternly that the pestilence had moved through Europe from the East across far bigger seas than the one separating England from France. Sicily was an island, but the infection was carried there in the ships and on the persons of the Genoese merchants and seamen who had fled from Caffa when it was besieged by the Tartars.

"Far from offering protection," the librarian sternly maintained, "the Mediterranean Sea is the prime means by which the plague has been spread across the world. Have you not understood what you have been told? The plague is spreading its fingers across the world carried by the sea, striking first in the coastal cities and then moving inland. Our only hope lies in cleansing our souls from the sins which stain them, for surely God is seeking by these plagues to turn us from our sinful ways."

"But, lest you lose all hope," the librarian assured John, "the finest minds in the monastery are being devoted to uncovering the mysteries of this merciless threat. We have a brother who has an unsurpassed knowledge of the planets and the stars, and he is working ceaselessly at his astrological charts. And our dear infirmarer here, who bows to nobody in his understanding of medicine, has joined with me in a search of all the ancient treatises in our library. I am certain that somewhere within these texts, which contain much of the wisdom of the world, lie the secrets of how to cure, avoid, or at the very least, God willing, ameliorate this sickness. And, of course, we are all praying ceaselessly for mercy."

As Master John rode slowly back to Walsham, he knew that, whatever the monks might discover in their charts and ancient texts, he and his assistant clergy had to redouble their already considerable efforts to encourage his flock to confess their sins and walk in the paths of righteousness. This is where salvation lay. Piety was superior to medicine. A sick man had to be cured of sin before he could be cured of his physical malady. This most important task was the responsibility of the clergy, not the doctors.

John resolved to make the forthcoming Eastertide a time of especially great shriving, when all would be exhorted, far more vigorously than ever before, to confess their sins and receive Communion. It also occurred to him that his parishioners must urgently bring their infants to church for baptism and christening. In Walsham as elsewhere, parents had often dallied in carrying out this duty, but in these days the souls of their children were in unprecedented peril.

Despite the awful knowledge burning within him, Master John resolved to say as little as possible about what he learned in Bury, not wishing to add to the fear already gripping his parishioners.

Spring and
Early Summer, 1348

Pilgrimages were incessant in the fourteenth century. They were undertaken as penance for sins committed, as thanks for good fortune or recovery from illness, or simply as an expression of devotion or a desire to travel. There were an almost infinite number of small shrines that enjoyed only a local reputation, as well as numerous venues that were celebrated throughout the realm. The latter included the shrines of Confessor Cuthbert at Durham and King Edward the Confessor at Westminster, the holy thorn tree at Glastonbury, and the tomb of the decapitated rebel against Edward II, Thomas of Lancaster, at Pontefract. But none could bear comparison with those of St. Thomas Becket at Canterbury and Our Lady of Walsingham in Norfolk, both of which attracted hundreds of thousands of pilgrims each year. Walsingham, the most revered Marian shrine in England, housed a miraculous bejeweled statue of the Virgin in a chapel that was reputedly modeled on the Holy House of Nazareth. The cult of Walsingham, which may have been founded by a local nobleman who visited the Holy Land in the twelfth century, flourished in the later Middle Ages on the strength of many royal visits and numerous stories of the powers of the shrine and Mary's milk to cure the sick, reward piety, convert the wicked, and work many other wonders. Pilgrims avidly collected souvenirs from the shrines they visited, many of which were cheap and shoddily made. In 1348–1349, despite the perceived risks of contagion, terror of the pestilence led soaring numbers to go on pilgrimages in search of the expiation of sins and protection from death and disease which saints and shrines might afford.

Although there are problems in charting the spread of the pestilence and uncovering the epidemiology behind it, the disease generally moved faster along the major routes of trade and communications, where it was carried by large numbers of people and possibly by the goods they transported. By spring and early summer 1348, the pestilence was not only raging throughout the Mediterranean but moving steadily northward through Italy and Spain. It struck Florence, Bologna, Pistoia, Perugia, and Padua in March and April, and had reached Siena, Ancona, and Naples by May, when Perpignan, Barcelona, and Valencia had also been infected. After the initial eruption in and around Marseilles and Avignon, however, progress in France was patchy. By the end of April the plague had arrived in Lyons, some two hundred kilometers up the heavily trafficked Rhone valley from Avignon, but it then began to slow down, and progress westward overland was sluggish. Transmission by sea was of great importance, and it was by this means that the plague arrived in Bordeaux and the coastal towns of Normandy, just across the Channel from England. The date the pestilence broke out in Bordeaux is disputed, but on September 2 Edward III's daughter, Princess Joan, followed the fate of many in her entourage when she died there on her way to marry Prince Pedro of Castille. Mortality did not begin to rise in Bruges until July 1349 and the disease did not spread northward to the Low Countries, Germany, and Scandinavia until long after it had landed in southern England.

⊰⊱

In the weeks that followed his visit to Bury abbey, Master John took care to reveal to no one the depths of his despondency about the inevitability of God's terrible scourge striking England and Walsham. Enough alarm, he believed, was already being sown in the hearts of his flock by lurid stories of the devastation wrought in neighboring lands, and the waves of dire prophecies that repeatedly washed through the parish. Yet he had to confide some of his private terror to his assistant clergy in order to spur them to ever greater efforts to purge the sins of their flock, for he was true to his resolve to spare no effort in ministering to his flock. In pulpit, confession, and conversation, John tirelessly encouraged his parishioners with the certainty of the blessings of repentance and, somewhat less frequently, he warned them of the dire consequences of remaining obdurate in the face of divine punishment.

News had always spread rapidly through the towns and villages of England, even when there was little to report. The desire to learn and the desire to tell were almost universal, and so it was no surprise in this time of mounting dread that almost every visitor to Walsham brought new details of the horrific pestilence, whether true or false, plausible or implausible. When the folk of Walsham traveled to nearby villages and towns, and especially when they ventured farther afield to fairs and markets, they returned with their fevered imaginations recharged by sensational accounts of terrifying carnage. Thus it was only a short time after Master John had returned tight-lipped from the abbey of Bury that surprisingly full and accurate accounts of much of what he had learned there began circulating in the village. Many details of the reports the young clerk had given to the brethren of the ravages of the pestilence in Avignon had been leaked, not just by monastery servants but by a number of garrulous monks. And it was not long before this relatively untainted testimony was embroidered and extended by constant and careless repetition.

In spring and early summer, as the pestilence continued to spread northward from the Mediterranean ports of France, tales of the desolation of foreign lands and cities that had recently come third and fourth hand to the village were now being supplemented by eyewitness reports, or at least by reports delivered by those who swore they had spoken to eyewitnesses of dreadful events. Testimonies emanating from merchants and sailors in Ipswich, London, and Lynn began to find their way by the mouths of carters and carriers, peddlers, travelers, and traders into the cities, towns, markets, fairs, and villages of Suffolk and neighboring counties. The sheer numbers of sources that fed these stories, the increasing familiarity of names of the places where the plague was now said to be wreaking its havoc, and the credentials of the people who were said to have experienced it firsthand combined to sow anguish in the phlegmatic and religious hysteria in the fervently pious. There was relatively little protest when it was decided to stop holding wrestling matches in the churchyard of St. Mary's because they might be an affront to God.

Mindful of the advancing plague, the pious and the petrified feverishly sought the protection bestowed by the worship of saints and relics. As acts of piety deserving of divine mercy, numerous little pilgrimages were organized, such as walking a few miles to the west to pray at the shrine of St. Edmund in the great abbey at Bury or considerably farther west to the popular shrine of St. Etheldreda in the cathedral at Ely. Not many miles to the northwest lay Thetford, where the villagers could pray before the magnificent altarpiece in the newly built Blackfriars priory and venerate the image of the Virgin, renowned for its miraculous cures, at the Cluniac priory close by (see figure 13). More conveniently, the well and chapel of Our Lady at Woolpit, which was just down the road, provided a regular supply of restorative and curative waters, and whenever the monks of Ixworth permitted it, large groups walked barefoot the short distance from Walsham to the priory, to worship before the high altar. William Lene, however, was far more adventurous. In remembrance of his long dead father's devotion to St. Thomas of Lancaster, who had been executed for treason a quarter of a century earlier, he decided to ride his mare a couple of hundred miles northward to visit St. Thomas's tomb before the high altar of Pontefract priory, in fervent hope that the saint would work one of his many miracles for him and preserve his family from harm.

Though most households in the village had their favorite saints, whose images were found in little shrines in their cottages, it was generally appreciated that the most efficacious pilgrimage by far was that to Our Lady of Walsingham, one of the most famous and holy shrines in the whole realm. To the great fortune of the folk of Walsham, this sacred site lay less than thirty miles away, close to the coast of north Norfolk. So venerable was this shrine and so powerful were the miracles that the milk of Our Lady could work, that kings of England had worshiped there on many occasions. Edward III had repeatedly journeyed to the shrine in the early years of his reign, and one of his first acts on returning to England from France, just a few years before, had been to ride to pray before Our Lady. Thus it was in late May that Margery Wodebite, sister-in-law of John Wodebite and one of the most vocal and ferociously devout of all Master John's parishioners, began persuading a group of prominent Walsham villagers to organize a pilgrimage to Walsingham, to draw succor from the milk of the sweet Virgin Mary, some of which was preserved there in a vial, and to see her fabulously bejeweled wooden image, which time and again had worked the most wondrous miracles (see figure 14).

The pilgrims would entreat the Blessed Virgin to stay the hand of God and spare them all, and they had faith that she would not fail them.

Within a short time a host of men and women had offered to join the pilgrim band and were busily making arrangements with their families, friends, and neighbors for the care of their households and farms during their absence; promising in return to pray for them and bring back a precious souvenir, a waxen image, a pewter badge, or a little palm leaf blessed by the monks who cared for Our Lady. Most of the pilgrims proudly swore that in penance they would walk the whole way instead of riding, and a few vowed to trudge barefoot or with their feet covered only in rags. All agreed to follow custom and remove their shoes at the newly built chapel, which had been swiftly named the slipper chapel, to trudge unshod over the final mile or so to the shrine itself.

Reluctantly, Master John decided that neither he nor any of his assistant clergy could be spared from their duties in the parish, but he urged his employer, the aging Robert Shepherd, to go. Despite being the official incumbent of the benefice of Walsham and still drawing a stipend from the prior of Ixworth, Robert was now performing scarcely any religious duties in the parish. Master John was delighted that Robert responded so readily to his encouragement that the pilgrimage would be good for his soul, and purchase for Robert some pardon for all the years he had devoted to the love of money rather than the spiritual welfare of his parishioners. But in truth, Robert saw it as an opportunity to seek the Virgin's help in finding the key to his strongbox, which contained a great deal of money and many of his property deeds; he had mislaid it some weeks earlier.

Master John willingly lent his expertise to the very careful planning which went into determining which route the pilgrims would take to Walsingham. This was to be no ordinary pilgrimage, but a spiritual journey lasting well over a week, perhaps even two. The itinerary would start with prayers before the altar of Ixworth priory. Then the band would proceed to the shrine of the Virgin at Thetford and include worship at many more churches and shrines along the way. There would be abundant opportunities for venerating the relics, rood screens, images, and veils to be found in numerous churches, and for looking with adoration at the holy scenes carved on their fonts and portrayed in the colored glass of their windows. All this would be done with the certain prospect that each sacred object and image would extend the depth of their devotion and raise the intensity of their rapture.

On a sunny morning in mid-June a band of more than fifty pilgrims was met by a further dozen or so villagers who had decided at the last minute to go with them. Even as they headed north out of Walsham toward the road to Thetford, a few more people gave way to their emotions on seeing the procession pass by and came hurrying to join, though poorly prepared for the journey. Young and old, men and women, moved off slowly, chanting prayers and psalms in unison. Their clothes and hats were adorned with many tokens, and in their hands they carried small palms or branches with newly sprouted leaves, and held strong staffs, some of which were embellished with silver or pewter. Margery Wodebite took up a prominent position toward the head of the band, clothed entirely in white, as if she were as pure as a maid. Her husband had died many years before, and, as she was fond of telling anyone who would listen, she had engaged in no carnal relationship with any man since, and was instead wedded to Christ.

When the Walsham pilgrims came to Thetford the next day, they were surprised and delighted to find themselves among many such bands making their way on the main route northward. Gaining strength and optimism from their shared purpose and from the intensity of the repeated demonstrations of spiritual passion among their fellow travelers, they flowed confidently and expectantly along the ways to Walsingham. Wondrous to behold, the crowds swelled still further as they drew nearer to the shrine of Our Lady. The faithful and the hopeful thronged in their hundreds through the streets of Fakenham where the roads to the shrine from the south, west, and east converged. So many people were gathered together that food and drink became difficult to obtain. But rather than being discomfited, most pilgrims rejoiced in the opportunity for fasting and drinking simple water. Accommodation was impossible to find, except for the elderly and infirm, but inconvenience and hardship became a welcome penance. Long queues formed at all the stalls and little shops along the way that sold wax, palms, and tokens, brooches and badges of lead and tin, and, most precious of all, the tiny sealed lead flasks containing holy water and a drop of milk from the breast of the Virgin. Though it was tempting to buy such precious mementos and sacred objects while they were still available, since the vendors warned that supplies were running perilously short, wiser and more experienced heads advised waiting to make purchases in Walsingham itself, where they could be sure that they were genuine and of better quality.

Later the next day the Walsham band reached Houghton St. Giles, where they found excited, agitated crowds of pilgrims gathered around the church, mingling with those returning inspired from the shrine. It seemed to those who came from country districts that the whole population of England must have been on the move, and even those who lived in the bustling towns of King's Lynn, Norwich, Bury, Cambridge, and London professed themselves amazed by the unceasing flow of humanity backward and forward. With a flourish the Walsham party removed their shoes at the slipper chapel, kindly provided by the monks of Walsingham for the pilgrims. Walking barefoot and chanting in unison, they slowly made their way the short distance to the priory and its shrine, ostentatiously carrying money in their hands for offerings, as well as candles and wax to place at the shrine, some of which had been fashioned into the image of absent loved ones.

On drawing close to the priory gates, they found their way barred by servants who sought to direct them to the rear of the buildings, there to form orderly queues. Those who had not been to Walsingham before were greatly disappointed at the small size of the priory, which despite its fame was tiny compared to the massive abbey of Bury, and scarcely bigger than their own little priory of Ixworth. Their hearts sank further at the size of the crowds ahead of them, and the prolonged wait they would have to endure before they were admitted into the shrine.

Word had long been circulating among the pilgrims that they would not be permitted to view the milk of the Blessed Virgin Mary, and the priory's guards confirmed that the milk was kept on the high altar of the priory church, to which only the most important visitors were admitted. At this, Margery Wodebite, who had been seeing visions of Our Lady and the Passion of Christ nightly in her dreams since leaving Walsham, waking her neighbors with her convulsive weeping and loud lamentations, became greatly distressed and swooned, appealing loudly to God as she collapsed. This brought monks running to her side, who were quizzical rather than sympathetic. They demanded to know why she was dressed all in white when she was not a maid, and why she, a simple rustic woman, proclaimed to have visions sent to her by God that were not sent to learned clerics, monks, and other men who were clearly more holy than she. Margery replied that God had chosen her, and they had not chosen God. For the monks had long since failed to obey the orders under which they were founded, and St. Benedict in Heaven had appeared to her in a vision and entreated her to do all she could to put them back on the paths of righteousness. At this the monks became angry, and the eldest in the group warned that if her companions did not keep Margery quiet, he would have her fettered and imprisoned in a stone house nearby where she would be unable to speak with any man. Her brother assured the monks that she would cause no more disturbance, and meanwhile Robert Shepherd created a diversion by asking each monk in turn for evidence that Our Lady of Walsingham had a special talent for finding lost keys. He was disappointed to learn that this ability was reserved to St. Sithe, who had no connection whatsoever with Walsingham.

Soon after, as had happened frequently in the past, Margery became subdued and compliant, and she was content to be led on a tour that included the Gate of the Knight, which had miraculously stretched itself to shelter a noble fugitive on horseback who found himself pursued by enemies and in need of sanctuary. Because of the unprecedented press of people making the pilgrimage in recent weeks, the monks of Walsingham had opened up a small chapel dedicated to St. Laurence, in which a number of holy relics had been housed, including the finger joint of St. Peter. But the first stop of the Walsham pilgrims was at a well filled by a spring sacred to the Holy Virgin, which long ago had burst forth at her command. The water was renowned for its ability to cure pains in the head and the stomach, and they found it wonderfully refreshing and cleansing as they eagerly gulped it down. Believing that it might also protect against the pestilence, they filled leather flasks to carry back home for their loved ones.

Then the Walsham folk joined the queue for admission to the Lady Chapel, which inched forward at an unbearably slow rate. While they waited, peddlers and hucksters walked up and down bearing trays of badges, brooches, and tokens of the shrine, which pilgrims eagerly purchased to pin on their hats and breasts. Among the favorites were a square cast picture of the Annunciation and, though more expensive, the representation of the Virgin seated with a fleur-de-lis scepter resting on her right shoulder and the Holy Child to her left. This, they were assured by the young woman selling them, was a perfect copy of the sacred image which they were about to see in the shrine. Yet more desirable were the versions of these badges bearing the name "Walsingham" along the base. Perhaps most popular of all, however, were the miniature lead flasks made in the form of brooches and badges, each guaranteed to contain a droplet of the Virgin's milk diluted by holy water from the Virgin's well, and each inscribed with a large W to signify the authenticity of their origin. Also irresistible for many in the party were the meat pies sold piping hot by vendors from handcarts with clay ovens on them.

When, after a very long wait, they had shuffled far enough forward to catch their first glimpse of the Lady Chapel, they could scarcely believe that this modest building housed the Shrine of Our Lady. Despite having been told about its modest dimensions, those visiting Walsingham for the first time were still expecting a magnificent edifice, radiating with the glory of the Virgin. But what they saw was a building of strange design, in some ways less impressive than the High Hall manor house in Walsham, and in fact not much bigger than Lady Rose's barn. It was built largely of undecorated stone, and barely twenty feet in width. However, their spirits were soon lifted by the bliss and contentment which they observed on the faces of all who were leaving through the far door, and by the frequent shrieks of delight and spiritual ecstasy from within which could be heard above the continuous chanting of prayers by those who queued. When at last they entered through the arch, all were entirely overcome by a profusion of gold, silver, and jewels, brilliantly lit by an abundance of shimmering candles. Then their eyes were swiftly drawn to the Blessed Virgin. Although it was of no extraordinary size, material, or workmanship, the image of Our Lady was overpowering. It visibly glowed as if illuminated from within by a hundred candles, and it radiated the love and compassion of the Blessed Virgin herself to all who looked on her.

Set all about the Virgin's image was an abundance of gold and silver statues, dishes, cups, candlesticks, paintings, brooches, and ornaments of all kinds and shapes. These in turn lay on cloths of gold and the finest scarlet that were not merely decorated with threads of gold but also set with a profusion of precious jewels of prodigious size and wonderful colors. Beside these treasures, hundreds, perhaps thousands, of coins were piled high, with a few stacks soaring almost to the rafters. As the pilgrims inched along the display, servants of the priory pointed out some of the finest and most famous items: a solid gold statue in the likeness of Henry III, given by the king himself, a gold brooch given by his son when he ruled as the first king Edward. Of special interest to the pilgrims were the many fine gifts donated by the present king Edward when he worshiped at the shrine, including the collection of exquisite cloths and a gold brooch set with jewels, which he had laid by the Virgin in September 1328. All gasped when told that these gifts were worth 83s 4d.

Standing in the most holy of shrines, in the very place where kings and queens must have stood before, and with such examples of generosity before them, the Walsham folk were encouraged to offer up their own pittances to the attendant monks, who took them and placed them at the side of the heaps. Somewhat more reluctantly, the monks also took the wax images of loved ones that some of the pilgrims had brought, and placed them on the floor at the foot of the shrine.

Margery Wodebite, of course, had spent most of her time in Walsingham in a trance of spiritual ecstasy. But there was not a member of the party who was not transformed by the visit to the shrine, whose spirit was not greatly inspired and strengthened by being in the presence of the Blessed Virgin, drinking from her water, and praying for her assistance. On the journey back to Walsham, excitedly talking and praying among themselves, the pilgrims were for a time able to push from their minds the news that they had repeatedly heard on their journey of the ravages of the pestilence overseas and its inexorable advance toward the shores of their land.

During their holy pilgrimage the humble rustics of Walsham met with other pilgrims of all ranks of society, drawn from many parts of the world, including gentlefolk, rich merchants, and high clergy. They sat spellbound while a wizened old lady told them of the pilgrimage she had made by herself, on the death of her husband many years before, from her humble cottage in Norfolk to the most holy city of Jerusalem. At the same fireside gathering, the miraculous story told by this frail and venerable pilgrim was immediately followed by one from a middle-aged man of obvious substance, who described his religious journey to Rome. The audience had next gasped in admiration at the sheer number and variety of badges and tokens which one seasoned old palmer, a tall, thin man from Leicester, wore on his cap and cape, and at the incredibly long list of holy shrines that he proudly claimed to have visited in person, which he subsequently verified by the intimate knowledge he displayed of every one of them. The palmer claimed to have devoted himself full-time to God's service many years ago, and since then to have lived entirely from the alms freely given by pious folk. With no further prompting, the pious folk gathered around the fireside gave him their pennies to support him on his next journey, which was to pray for the sixth time at the tomb of the blessed martyr St. Thomas at Canterbury.

But there were few occasions when the conversation and storytelling at resting places did not turn to the pestilence. Among the people journeying to and from Walsingham many recounted personal experiences of the horrors they had witnessed or narrowly escaped. Indeed, as they eagerly explained, it was for this very reason they were making the pilgrimage. So, they lost little time in apprising their fellows of what fate awaited them, saying such things as, "So great a plague has never been heard of from the beginning of the world to the present day," or "It is more awful than any ever heard of or to be read about in any books." Nobody had any hope to offer, saying instead, "Doctors know no remedy," and "Those who fall ill last little more than two or three days, many die suddenly, as if in the midst of health." While those who professed knowledge of overseas told the same story of how, "Despite all the efforts to halt the plague made by the rulers of towns and villages, such as barring entry to outsiders and cleaning the streets, and all the advice offered by the most learned doctors on avoidance and cure, and the supplications of the most holy clergy, and even by the pope himself, beseeching God to be merciful, the death moves unhindered from place to place, as if it were an invisible cloud of infection blown on the wind."

Gathered together for the night in a large barn near Thetford, two days after leaving Walsham, the pilgrims heard an account that was to alarm them more than any of the multitude of tales they heard on their journey. It was delivered with calm authority and great eloquence by Sir Robert de Godington, the clerk and auditor of the household of the bishop of Ely, who had been in the papal curia in Avignon when the pestilence broke out there. This gentleman, and his three attendants, displayed an intimate grasp of the ravages of the pestilence in Avignon, and he expressed himself so clearly and so powerfully that the fears imparted from hearing second- and third-hand versions of the testimony of the clerk who had lodged at Bury St. Edmunds abbey some weeks before were immediately multiplied, and the hazy outlines of the terrible images which had formed in their minds on first hearing were flooded with color and precision. The audience sat in awed silence as Sir Robert addressed them.

First, this lord set out his credentials: "I can assure you that the information I am about to impart is both accurate and up-to-date, for I have seen all these terrible things with my own eyes. Not only was I in the holy city when the pestilence erupted, I remained there for many weeks, and since my return to Ely I have been in frequent correspondence with friends who are still there concerning a future visit that might be made by my lord bishop to Avignon."

He stopped for effect and then proclaimed, "Whatever else you might have heard or hoped, the plague has indeed killed tens of thousands in the city, and left many thousands of houses entirely vacant, with nobody at all living in them."

When Sir Robert announced that the pestilence had recently abated in the holy city and that few of its residents were taking sick and even fewer dying, there were gasps of relief. But he immediately stifled the tremors of hope in his audience with a dismissive wave of his hand and went on to report that, having ruined this great city and destroyed the greater part of its people, the plague had moved on with renewed ferocity, and was at this very moment spreading northward through France toward Bruges and Ghent, eastward toward the Holy Roman Empire and westward toward Bordeaux and Calais, and thence perhaps to England. With his arms held wide before him, as if to symbolize how the pestilence was encompassing the whole world, Sir Robert intoned, "Wherever it goes, just as it did in Avignon, it is leaving thousands and thousands dead in its wake, with rotting bodies overflowing the churchyards and even the hastily consecrated new burial grounds, so that an infinity of good Christians end up being cast without ceremony into pits dug in the fields."

With cold detachment, Sir Robert reported his conclusions: "Nothing can halt the progress of the pestilence; it will continue to ravage unchecked. In Marseilles, we are told, all the gates of the city except two posterns had been closed, but there four out of five of the people died. In Avignon, not even the pope could halt it or even weaken its force. We must abase ourselves and ask for forgiveness. In Avignon while I was there, devout processions were held frequently at the behest of the pope, attended by two or three thousand people, chanting litanies, many barefoot, others wearing hair shirts or smeared with ashes, beating themselves with cruel whips until the blood ran. But I cannot deny it, all these lamentations scarcely affected the dreadful work of pestilence. God knows what the end will be or what the beginning was."

At this point, Sir Robert was finally overcome with emotion and ceased to speak. But his audience, after listening in total silence, except for occasional gasps or groans, burst into life with a torrent of questions: "Cannot people save themselves by fleeing from the plague?"

"No," replied Sir Robert, "flight did not help, for the pestilence reigned in every settlement and city in Provence, and strangers were not welcome anywhere. And besides, what would those who fled live off? Only the rich could afford to flee, and many of those hesitated to leave their goods behind, fearing that they would be stolen and their houses ransacked."

Another member of the audience called out, "We heard some time ago that the pestilence in Avignon was of a new and previously unknown type. Is that true?"

Sir Robert responded, "I am no medical man, but I can tell you from what I saw that not one but three types of pestilence struck the city, each of which was new and terrible. The first visitation was an infection of the lungs, in which victims suffered continuous fever and the coughing of blood. No one who had this corruption escaped death; all died within two or three days. What is more, the victim passed the sickness on to everyone who saw him during his illness. All who visited a sick person or carried his body to burial immediately followed him to the grave. A few weeks after this type of plague had taken hold of the city, another form struck. This also caused fever, but this time great boils as well, which erupted suddenly in the armpits. Then yet another form appeared, in which victims of both sexes were attacked by boils and carbuncles in the groin."

It was then that John Wodebite, one of the leaders of the Walsham villagers, stood up and with bowed head said, "We heard in our village that a young priest who had fled from Avignon told the monks of Bury abbey that the sick were deserted by their families and friends and left to die alone. And that there were even some priests who refused to visit the dying, thus leaving their souls in peril. Surely such stories cannot be true?"

At this the senior cleric looked down at the floor and said simply that unbearable burdens had been placed on the clergy by the vast numbers of people who were infected and dying. "Priests were not spared by the pestilence, but died in numbers at least as great as lay folk. And so, at the height of the deaths and sickness, it was not always possible for those priests who remained alive to provide sufficient spiritual care for everyone in the city who needed it. That is why the pope gave permission for confession to be heard by laymen when there was no other alternative."

The spirits of the party were doused by these revelations, and a couple of days later more blows were inflicted on their inherent optimism. While the bulk of the Walsham pilgrims were settling down to spend the warm night in a field on the outskirts of Fakenham, a small number decided to walk into the town to find an alehouse. There they were regaled in exuberant style by an Ipswich sea captain who had just returned from a voyage to Bruges, the great Flemish port where ships from all over the world berthed, and merchants and seamen traded, relaxed, and mingled with traders who had journeyed to the city across land and by river. The captain enjoyed informing his audience, most of whom he guessed had never seen a great city, that in Bruges he had met a multitude of merchants and seamen from Genoa, Venice, and Florence, and from the great northern cities of the Hanse, including Cologne, Dinant, Magdeburg, Hamburg, and Lübeck. Indeed, he boasted, he had also recently mixed with men from all parts of France, as well as the occasional Spaniard selling wine, iron, and rabbit skins. With this lengthy prologue he thoroughly convinced the alehouse audience that no one could have better or more up-to-date news on the current state of the pestilence than he.

"My news comes not from letters or distant recollections," he said, "but from my own experiences just a couple of weeks ago." Having gained everyone's attention, the captain curtly announced, "What I heard in Bruges was so dreadful that I forthwith abandoned the plans I had to buy more goods to sell in England, and instead I boarded my ship and sailed it as fast as I could back home to Ipswich." With a satisfied smile he continued, "That is not all. The future of the world looks so short and so dreadful, that as soon I arrived in port I set out on a pilgrimage for the very first time in the whole of my sinful life."

Having frightened his listeners in this manner, he then cunningly soothed them with words of reassurance. "You can believe me that the pestilence has not yet reached the North Sea or any of those countries closest to England. There is no sign of it in Bruges, nor in the whole of Flanders or Normandy. Nor even, in the lands of the Holy Roman Emperor to the east. What is more, I heard it reliably reported on a number of occasions that the far northern lands of Denmark, Norway, and Sweden have not been touched.

"But," he warned, "do not believe that you have been spared. As every day passes Death is coming ever nearer, and it is only a matter of time before he arrives in this kingdom. This most awful pestilence is spreading rapidly toward us, like a fire out of control. I was planning to sail from Bruges to Bordeaux, to buy some tuns of good red wine that I could sell at a fair profit in Ipswich. But as I prepared to put to sea, I was warned that many people in that fair city had started to die from a strange new disease. So beware of drinking any wine, it carries the plague!" His audience laughed as it downed draughts of good English ale.

"Do not laugh, but pray instead," the captain bellowed. "When the pestilence comes to us, as it surely will, it will crush us all to dust. It has left the greatest cities of southern France and of all of Italy in ruins, and their people totally destroyed. In Bruges I met a merchant from Florence who had been rich and powerful when he had arrived a few months before to sell his luxurious wares, but was now reduced to poverty and forced to live in exile. For fear of the plague he could not return to his mansion in his native city, and he had learned that his family, friends, and business partners had all been killed. As we were talking, we were interrupted by a rough seaman who hailed from a town near Rome, who told us, 'When the plague had done its work in my birthplace there was not a dog left pissing against the wall.'"

With this the shipman launched into a torrent of words, each uttered with total conviction. "Nowhere will be spared, everywhere will be struck and probably in a very short time. It was first thought that Jews and lepers were spreading plague by poisoning the wells, but the well poisoners have been burned and still the plague drives onward. Jews and lepers, and Saracens too, have all died in their thousands at the hands of angry crowds believing they were deliberately spreading disease, but many more have died in agony stricken by the disease itself.

"Now it is believed that the terrible infection is carried in ships. People tell how Genoese carracks, fleeing from the Tartars at Caffa, first brought the plague to Messina and thence to Genoa. In Genoa scarcely one in seven survived, and the carracks sailed on and the plague next seized Venice, where seven out of every ten perished. Nobody in Bruges will now eat, or even touch, freshly imported spices from those regions, and they hesitate to eat fish because they fear the infection is carried in the sea. Scarcely anyone sails to places where the pestilence rages, just as I was too afraid to sail to Bordeaux. A fleet of fine Genoese and Florentine carracks, laden with wares they long to sell in the East, remain anchored in Bruges harbor because their crews are too frightened to return home.

"You must realize that this terrible disease cannot be stopped. It is carried by the fish in the sea as well as by the ships that sail on it, and it is borne invisibly in the air by the wind. As I speak the fatal infection continues to spread toward us, and there is no way of halting or avoiding it.

"Nor is the disease itself the worst thing to be feared. I have heard the most terrible tales of human cruelty when the plague strikes. The sick are often treated like dogs by their families who put food and drink next to their bed and then flee the house, leaving the poor creatures to die alone, uncared for, and unconfessed. Few doctors visit the sick for fear of certain infection, even if they are promised riches. Many frightened priests fail to perform their sacred duties, denying their parishioners the last rites of shrift, housel, and annealing, and so abandon their souls trembling on the edge of everlasting damnation. So contagious is this pestilence, and so fearful are people of being infected by it, that fathers will not visit their sons, mothers their daughters, brothers their sisters, friends their friends. Thus it is that an uncountable number of people have died without any mark of affection, piety, or charity. And, if truth be told, many of those who have died might have escaped if they themselves had refused to visit the sick.

"So it is that everyone who is still healthy looks after himself. And even when a rich man dies, he is fortunate if his body is carried to a pit by a gang of vagabonds, with no mourners and only a few lights. While the corpse is borne along the street, neighbors and friends hide away indoors instead of accompanying the funeral procession. But perhaps they are wise, for in a short time the ruffians who are not afraid of carrying the bodies to burial die themselves."

The brave sea captain then prayed loudly and fervently, professing himself to have been a sinful man with frail beliefs throughout most his life. But now, he assured the Virgin Mary, he had been transformed into a pious pilgrim. He was going to Walsingham to wash all the stains of sin from his soul with her milk and to gain shrift and housel. For the short time remaining to him he would live as blamelessly as he could. When the pestilence came for him, as it surely would, there would be no priest to confess to, and he would die alone in agony without comfort or support from family or friends.

The captain was a good storyteller who had a frightening tale to tell, yet the more positive spirits among his audience soon pointed out that he had actually brought them good tidings. A stocky miller from near Lincoln, while not questioning the truth of the captain, urged that what he had said was of comfort to Englishmen and women. "This new and terrible pestilence is ravaging hot lands in faraway places, where the sun always shines and the rain does not fall, where fabulous creatures and strange diseases have always abounded." As the old lady who had journeyed to Jerusalem nodded her head vigorously, there was a murmur of agreement that nothing like this pestilence had ever been seen in England.

Encouraged, Robert Shepherd turned to his companions and confided, "The captain has told us the pestilence has definitely not reached as far north as Bruges. If we believe these tales, it may have killed large parts of the populations of such hot and distant places like Genoa, Marseilles, and Avignon, but it has failed to take hold in Flanders or in

any of the lands of our neighbors across the North Sea that have cli-
mates like ours."

On the journey back to Walsham a warm glow of optimism bathed the
pilgrim band. Uplifted by having been in the presence of the Virgin,
drunk copiously from her water, and prayed fervently for her assistance,
the pilgrims were in good heart. The spiritual refreshment they had im-
bibed in the holy places they had visited mingled with the warmth they
had drawn from companionship and shared experiences. As they returned
to their homes, they had renewed faith in the ability of the kindly Virgin
to stay God's hand, persuade him to be merciful, and spare them and
their loved ones. And if she should not hear at once, the precious mementos they had purchased would afford them protection.

Midsummer and Autumn, 1348

As the pestilence drew ever closer to England in the summer of 1348, the Church naturally took the lead in giving advice on how to ameliorate God's anger. Many bishops wrote letters to be read out in English, in words that all could understand, in all parish churches in their dioceses, urging confession and ordering penitential processions and Masses. The earliest of these letters were written by the archbishop of York and the bishop of Lincoln in the last days of July, and in mid-August Edward III asked the archbishop of Canterbury to arrange for prayers, Masses, sermons, and processions throughout the province of Canterbury "to protect the realm of England from these plagues and mortality." Since it was believed that all significant events took place at God's behest, these responses were highly appropriate. They were also the traditional reactions to times of distress, such as war or famine, and had been used seven hundred years before during the great plagues of the sixth century. Significantly, the episcopal letters often explicitly state that the progress of the plague across Europe, as well as its imminent threat to England, was common knowledge, and the archbishop of Canterbury goes as far as to say that "there can be no one who does not know."

Understandably, Church leaders struggled to formulate a coherent and convincing message in the face of the sheer scale and horror of the impending disaster, and there was often only a thin veil of confidence behind their public statements. The pestilence was described as "savage" and "cruel," and the letter written by the prior of Christchurch in Canterbury begins, "Terrible is God towards the sons of men." Leading ecclesiastics sometimes admitted that even the most learned of them only had an imperfect knowledge of God's will, and the bishop of Worcester wrote, "it is not within the power of man to understand the divine plan." In the proliferating discussions of the meaning of the Black Death and its later outbreaks, it could not be denied that God was inflicting pestilence as a response to the sinfulness of mankind, and parallels with biblical plagues were frequently drawn. But the most insightful thinkers framed the scourge not as an act of revenge or even a just punishment inflicted by an angry God, but as a merciful means of turning people from their sinful ways so that they might eventually be saved.

The profound dilemma faced by those who sought to explain why such a deadly pestilence was being inflicted on mankind recurs constantly in contemporary writings. Boccaccio, the author of The Decameron, *who lived through the plague in Florence, wrote, "Some say that it descended upon the human race through the influence of the heavenly bodies, others that it was a punishment signifying God's righteous anger at our iniquitous way of life." Giles li Muisis, abbot of the monastery of St. Giles in Tournai, drew attention in his chronicle of the plague years to the temptation he felt "to put more trust in the sayings and prognostications of astrologers and mathematicians than faith allows." But as a chronicler based in Neuberg, southern Austria, wrote, "When prayers failed to prevent it, when indeed the misery increased daily to a pitch never before recorded in the history of the world, and when the efforts of physicians proved unable to cure or avert it, then all they could do was to commit everything to God."*

There is a broad consensus among chroniclers that the Black Death made its first appearance in England in Weymouth, a seaport in Dorset on the southern coast, although the date given varies from the feast of St. John the Baptist (June 24) to early August. A number of sources claim that the pestilence was brought to the Dorset town on ships sailing from Gascony, at least one of which was said to have been a Bristol vessel. The wine port of Bordeaux seems the likeliest place of origin, and according to Geoffrey le Baker's chronicle, on August 15 the pestilence erupted in Bristol, England's second city. The place and date of the earliest outbreaks in England is important, but without detailed records of actual deaths it is not possible to be certain whether the dates given by chroniclers are for the day when the ships identified as plague carri-

ers docked, *the first appearance of plague victims in the location, or the dates by which the plague had taken firm hold. This is an important matter, since the range between the first and the last of these events would have amounted to a number of weeks and may well account for some of the confusing differences in dating.*

The early infection of ports in the south and west of England is in keeping with the presence of plague in the second half of 1348 in many places their traders visited along the Atlantic coast of Spain and France. It was not until much later in 1349 that plague reached northern France, the Low Countries, and Scandinavia, which were the main trading areas for the ports of eastern England. However, because London was the focal point for inland as well as overseas trade and communications, the capital was struck by November 1, if not before.

⊰ 吕 ⊱

"Almighty God uses thunder, lightning, and other blows which issue from his throne to scourge the sons whom he wishes to redeem. Accordingly, since a catastrophic pestilence from the East has arrived in a neighboring kingdom, it is very much to be feared that, unless we pray devoutly and incessantly, a similar pestilence will stretch its poisonous branches into this realm, and strike down and consume the inhabitants. Therefore we must all come before the presence of the Lord in confession, reciting psalms." (See figure 15.)

It was a hot summer's day in St. Mary's church, Walsham, and the parishioners who packed the great building listened in silence to their priest reading a letter from the bishop that he had sent to all parishes in his diocese. The prior of Ixworth, who had received the letter on behalf of his priest, immediately forwarded it to Master John, anxious to lose no time in following the bishop's strict instructions that his message, which he had written in Latin, should be read aloud to all parishioners in English, in words they could understand, and that its content should be carefully and fully explained to them.

When Master John hesitated for a moment to compose himself before delivering the rest of the letter, his assistant clergy, unprompted, broke out in unison chanting passages from the Psalms. With sonorous voices which resonated around the lofty stone building, they sang spontaneously but with an uncanny coordination, hot with emotion yet precise in their diction:

O Lord God, to whom vengeance belongeth, show thyself.
O God, to whom vengeance belongeth, show thyself.

Let us come before his presence in confession.
For the Lord is a great God, and a great king above all gods.
In his hand are the deep places of the earth; the strength of the hills is his also.
The sea is his, and he made it: and his hands formed the dry land.
O come, let us worship and bow down: let us kneel before the Lord our maker.
For he is our God; and we are the people of his pasture, and the sheep of his hand.

As the chanting subsided, the sound of low groaning from the congregation made itself heard. Master John swiftly continued reading the bishop's letter. "Since it is now public knowledge, there can be no one who does not know how great a mortality, pestilence, and infection of the air are at this moment threatening various parts of the world, and especially England. Unless the holy clemency of the Savior is shown to his people from on high, the inevitable human fate—pitiless death, which spares no one—now threatens us. The only hope is to hurry back to him alone, whose mercy outweighs justice and who, most generous in forgiving, rejoices heartily in the conversion of sinners. Therefore, we should all humbly urge him with orisons and prayers that he, the kind and merciful Almighty God, should turn away his anger and remove the pestilence and drive away the infection from the people he redeemed with his precious blood."

Struggling to make himself heard above the whimpering and lamentations of the congregation, Master John proclaimed, "Do not despair. All is not yet lost. Remember the ruin which was justifiably prophesied to the people of Nineveh—but who were then mercifully rescued from the extermination threatened by God's judgment after they had performed penance. For they, like you, said, 'Who can tell if God will turn and forgive and will turn away from his fierce anger, and we shall not perish?'

But as the Bible tells us, 'God did see their works, and that they were turned from their evil way, and God had mercy on them.'

"And therefore the most kindly Lord mercifully and wholesomely translated his anger into mildness, and destruction into construction, for the sake of a penitent people. But he has done the opposite for obstinate men and hard-hearted people unwilling to repent, as is proved by the stories of Pharaoh, of the five cities of Sodom, and of others who, impenitent to the end, perished eternally.

"To secure God's forgiveness, we shall say a special prayer every day in Mass for the allaying of plague and pestilence. And, as our lord bishop, trusting in the mercy of Almighty God and the merits and prayers of his mother, the glorious Virgin Mary, and of the blessed apostles and all of the saints, urges all of us, clergy and parishioners, we will gather for devout processions every Friday. We must abase ourselves humbly before the eyes of divine mercy, be contrite and penitent for our sins, and expatiate our guilt with devout prayers, so that God, for his kindness sake, turn away this pestilence from his people."

Then turning to the crucifix which hung behind the pulpit, Master John begged, "Remember not our former iniquities. Let thy mercies speedily succor us for we are becoming exceeding poor."

Having finished reading the bishop's letter, Master John went through it again slowly picking out the main points and explaining them to his parishioners. Then he stated baldly, "If the latest rumors are true, then the plague has already arrived in the far south and west of England."

Thus on that sunny August morning everyone who lived in Walsham learned that the pestilence was no longer confined to far-off places but was raging close by; they all faced an awful and imminent threat that it would soon be among them. The impact of the news, which had been predicted for some time, was all the greater because it came from Master John, who from the beginning had assiduously fostered a healthy skepticism of the wilder tales of pestilence in far-off lands, and had persistently counseled his flock to concentrate on living their lives from day to day. At once a vision began to form in the minds of the common folk of Walsham of imminent chaos, cruelty, despair, and death in their own village and the lands about, penetrating their own lives, entering their own houses, and destroying their own families.

The silence that was maintained as the priest spoke suddenly gave way
to an urgent rumble of agitated sound, as neighbor spoke to neighbor and
as questions were shouted at Master John and his assistants:

"Why has God sent this terrible pestilence?"

"Where is the pestilence now?"

"What has caused this pestilence?"

"Can penitence and prayers stop it coming here?"

The priest told them that he had no final answers, and that the wisest
and most pious men in the Church were seeking to explain why God had
called down this scourge. "All things are subdued to God's will, and it
may not lie within the power of man to understand God's divine plan."
Speaking rapidly, Master John went on to present them with the sentiments he had carefully prepared over the previous two days since he had
received the bishop's letter: "However, we must believe that the pestilence
is a sign of God's righteous anger at our iniquitous way of life, for the
Bible teaches us that God has in the past often visited many plagues on
sinful people. But you must also believe in your hearts that he is not
doing this out of cruelty but out of kindness. He is using the pestilence to
scourge those he wishes to redeem. He is punishing us in this mortal life
so that we may be turned from sin and not condemned eternally."

As Master John tried to continue with his carefully prepared exposi-
tion, a voice from the congregation interrupted him: "I have heard that
one of the monks at Bury, an astrologer who knows much about the planets and the stars, has said that the cause lies up there, as with most things
that happen in the world. It was the conjunction of ill-fated stars and
planets that corrupted the air and generated the sickness. It must be true,
because it is written in ancient books that conjunctions of Saturn and
Jupiter cause great pestilences in the air, and we know that just such a
conjunction happened a few years ago. And we all know that Mars is a
malevolent planet breeding anger and wars, and that it has recently been
in the sign of Leo."

The priest interrupted this surprisingly learned discourse from an illiterate peasant. "My son, while what you say may be true, it is even more
true that God controls the planets. They do not move of their own will."

Then Master John was interrupted by a female voice, shouting and
trembling with emotion. "If that is so, and if everything that happens in

the world happens because God wills it, why is he moving the planets so as to cause such a terrible poisonous plague to punish his people? Why is God so angry? What have we done to deserve such cruelty?"

The priest looked perplexed, and repeated that it was not for him to interpret God's will. "But," he added, "as far as we are able to judge, God must be sending the pestilences to chastise his people for their grievous sins. But not simply to inflict pain and suffering upon us. He is scourging us in order to redeem us."

From the back of the church a thin, tremulous, yet piercing female voice called out. Master John recognized it as belonging to an elderly healer and midwife of great skill, who had often accompanied him on visits to the sick and dying: "Our damnation is foretold not only by the stars but by the death of the two-headed child monster in Hull a short time ago. Last winter you all heard the sailor from Ipswich tell us about this creature. You heard him say how he had seen with his own eyes that it was joined in the lower part but divided from the navel upward, and was both male and female. He told us that when one part ate, drank, or slept or spoke, the other could do something else if it wished, and how very sweetly they used to sing together. This creature lived for almost twenty years. But I was told at Botesdale market that a short time ago one half died, and that the other half held it in its arms for three days, and then died itself. This has to be an awful omen."

Master John waved his hand impatiently and went to speak dismissively, but Margery Wodebite called out, repeating speculation heard on the pilgrimage: "It is said in Avignon that God is scourging the world with these evils as a punishment for the death of King Andrew of Hungary, who was butchered by his wife. Despite her grievous sins, the city of Avignon took her in when she fled there, and she was forgiven by the pope and permitted to marry again. It was for this that Avignon was deservedly devastated."

Before Master John could answer, another voice called out, "But the sins of the pope in Avignon should not mean that we who are innocent should also be killed? This is not justice and mercy!"

At this a stern carpenter and a woodworker named Robert stood up. He was a prosperous artisan, one of a few in the village who gained his living almost entirely from the skill of his hands rather than from farming or laboring, and a man well-known for his ability to read and write a little, as well as his austere way of life and condemnation of frivolity. "No, you are mistaken," he pronounced with absolute conviction. "The pestilence that threatens us is a punishment for the scandalous behavior of ladies, matrons, and gentlewomen with their outrageous and immodest manner of dress. At tournaments, which are now being held all over our realm, these shameless women attend without their husbands and fornicate with strangers. They dress themselves in extraordinary clothing, some attired like men, as if in a play. They ride to tournaments on chargers with elaborate trappings, wearing belts thickly studded with gold and silver, and daggers in pouches. They are the most beautiful of women but the least virtuous, for they abuse their bodies in wantonness and scurrilous licentiousness."

His friend, a tailor called John, then added, "And God has also been offended by the extravagant and unseemly dress of the courtiers and the nobility, which began when the Hainaulters and their grotesque fashions came to England with Queen Philippa, when she married our king. They now have new outlandish fashions that they change yearly, and these have supplanted the old decent style of long, full garments which covered the body. Instead, courtiers are wearing short, tight clothes, which are laced, buttoned, or strapped, making them look like torturers and demons. Even more shameful, women sometimes wear gowns so tight that they have to put a fox's tail inside the back of their skirts to hide their arses!"

A burst of ribald laughter momentarily lifted the tension. Then William Warde, who had a reputation as a troublemaker, called out, "Why should we humble poor folk be punished so cruelly for the sins of the rich and the immoral actions of the nobility in others parts of the realm and world?"

For once Master John had no answer to give this rebellious villein. Affecting a commanding voice and drawing himself to his full height in the elaborately carved oak lectern high above his congregation, he strove to bring order: "We all have sin, and to avert God's just judgment we must present ourselves before God and make full and proper confession of our sins, and make due satisfaction through the performance of penance. We must make humble procession as we are bid, and then God, being benign and merciful, long-suffering and above malice, may avert this affliction and turn it from us."

Once again John Tailor interrupted from the congregation. "Processions did not halt the pestilence in Avignon. Despite the pope himself joining them, and despite those who processed beating themselves till the blood ran. Still the great plague continues to come toward us. The solution lies inside our hearts and not in fanciful parades and shows of shallow emotion."

"Yes, but the pope in Avignon is French and he matters little, since Jesus has now become English!"

This last remark was uttered by a laborer who had served with King Edward and his chivalrous son on successful campaigns in France and regularly claimed in the alehouses of the village that he had faced far worse dangers on these campaigns than any pestilence could pose. "When I was in France," he went on, "we pasted up notices after our victories telling the French that Jesus was English, because he was on our side." He drew a momentary nervous titter, but soon frightened voices began shouting again, demanding firm answers to impossible questions. Master John was also frightened, but of losing control of the congregation in his own church, and he called for silence and discipline. He shouted above the chatter, gesturing toward the set of glass windows to his left, lit brilliantly by the sunlight, which portrayed the seven acts of mercy. "We must give alms for our sins. We must feed the hungry, give drink to the thirsty, clothe the naked, visit the sick, relieve the prisoner, house the stranger, and bury the dead. We must also gather for a procession this coming Wednesday, when the great bell will be rung to summon you all. My three clerks and I will hear confessions now, beginning with those who have the most to confess. And we shall continue until we have heard you all. And you shall all fully confess, and with the greatest contrition, and willingly perform the penances you are given. And God may protect us."

With that Master John turned and climbed down from the lectern. Some people began to leave the church, but the majority wished to make their confessions at once, and loud voices were heard as the assistant priests attempted to turn most of them away to return another day.

Outside, a huddle of the more prosperous and sober villagers gathered together in the churchyard, a little apart from the press of anxious people.

They discussed in urgent whispers how best to save their bodies and their souls, and resolved to meet together soon to take steps to provide themselves with the spiritual assistance they craved. When a score or so of these men and women met a couple of days later, they immediately discovered deep concerns they had in common. All were greatly perturbed by stories they had heard about the chaos that reigned while the pestilence raged in foreign Christian lands. It filled them with dread that the dying had been abandoned by friends and family, bereft of a priest and the sacred rites that only he could bestow. Instead of solemn funeral processions led by clergy carrying candles, crosses, and banners, bodies had been collected and piled on carts by wretches who neither knew nor cared to observe any of the essential ceremonies. These pious and prudent villagers, visibly anguished, repeated stories of corpses carted to patches of unconsecrated ground and cast into common pits, sometimes without a single priest being present and never with more than a cursory mumbling of the funeral rites. They resolved then and there to act collectively in a similar fashion to a guild and fraternity, of which a number of them had knowledge from their dealings with towns. Acting together in a community with rules and a common purse, they would do all they could, in both personal actions and gifts of money, to ensure that each and every one of their number who might die should have a good death, from the onset of their illness to their demise. In addition to pledging that they would each visit every brother or sister who fell sick, regardless of the perils, they eagerly agreed that every member who died would have a fitting funeral procession and burial in consecrated land, attended by priests and mourners, with candles and the full rites. They also agreed to provide for Masses to be said thereafter for the benefit of all departed souls.

To these ends they swore a solemn oath and collectively resolved to contribute generously to a common fund in order to supply a sufficient number of wax candles for the funeral processions and to burn in the church afterward, and to pay for a priest to give the last rites, conduct the funeral, and say a weekly Mass for the souls of any of their number who should die. In witness of their oath each of their names was carefully inscribed on a roll of parchment. Then they all freely handed over money to be held by their treasurer in a common purse, each paying such as was appropriate to their wealth and status. In addition one member pledged an image of the Blessed Virgin, another a fine cloth, another a pewter chalice; the richest member dedicated the finest room in his house for meetings. They all agreed that they would hold an annual feast to celebrate the founding of their fraternity. The only note of dissension arose when some members objected to the admission of Margery Wodebite, on the grounds that her swoonings, loud lamentations, and ecstatic visions would be too much to bear. But her brother-in-law, John, won them over with assurances that he would keep her under control, as well as make a gift of a fine large latten candlestick.

Soon afterward one of the older members, Catherine, the widow of a prominent free tenant, Peter Pynfoul, pointed out that the day when they had first thought of forming themselves into a society was very close to the feast of Corpus Christi. This caused much excitement, for Corpus Christi was a new and exhilarating feast that was already being celebrated in many places, although not yet in Walsham. Encouraged, she spoke enthusiastically of a fraternity in the town of Cambridge which had recently adopted the name and emblems of this feast of the Eucharist, and this led another member to report that there were plans to endow another such society in the great port of Lynn.

The celebration of Christ's Passion was most fitting at that time of glowering menace, and its contemplation brought comfort, as did the cleansing of their sins by the shedding of his blood. Without delay the fraternity started a fund to pay for a stained glass window to be made of a pelican in its piety, pecking its breast to feed its young with droplets of its own blood, just as the guild in Cambridge was said to have done (see figure 16). A short time after, Catherine Pynfoul commissioned a carving of a pelican and its young at the end of one of the pews in St. Mary's church where members of the fraternity might sit (see figure 16).

Pious Pelican, Lord Jesus
Cleanse me the impure, in your blood
Of which one drop can save
The whole world of all sin

The reading of the bishop's letter in church by Master John had a desolating impact on the villagers, not simply because it brought fresh and shocking news of the progress of the pestilence, but because it confirmed some of the wildest rumors that had been circulating in Walsham and its environs for the last year or more. In the days which followed there was always a stream of parishioners queuing in St. Mary's for confession and trooping into the church or to the prior of Ixworth's barn to donate cash or produce for tithes forgotten or evaded in past years. The volume of prayers, recited aloud and in silence, multiplied in church and in homes, and the poor, the old, and the sick, and many who were neither, received unprecedented charity in the form of doles of money and food and personal assistance of every sort. Few could remember a time when holy days had been more scrupulously observed as times of rest and worship. Everyone longed to perform good works, but they were forced to choose carefully from among the seven acts of mercy, which included such perilous exhortations as visiting the sick, sheltering strangers, and burying the dead. Protection against the advancing plague and forgiveness for past transgressions were avidly sought from saints and holy relics, and groups of villagers continued to go on pious pilgrimages to local shrines or venture as far as Walsingham, though the risks of contracting plague by traveling to distant places and mingling with crowds of strangers were now more cautiously weighed against the spiritual rewards that such journeys might bring.

So assiduously did the clergy encourage parishioners to examine their consciences, that folk of a naturally hotter disposition were driven to express their fear of imminent death or, as they would have it, their devotion to Christ's mercy, by a constant feverish striving for spiritual cleansing and religious experience. Even worldly and pragmatic souls were moved to engage in inward reflection. Attempting to meet such urgent demands all but exhausted the ministrations of a parish clergy already stretched by the heightened duties demanded of it.

Nonetheless, despite all the abasements and alms, the pilgrimages and prayers, and the holding of solemn processions on Wednesdays as well as Fridays, assiduously attended by most of the villagers in a state of true devotion, Master John searched in vain for a sign that either the power or the advance of the pestilence had been halted or even slowed. On the contrary, stories that the pestilence had crossed the sea and had taken hold in the southwest of the realm became ever more credible. While some folk rejected these stories, preferring to believe that the sea lying between England and France was a barrier the plague could not cross, there were others who cited what had happened elsewhere in Europe and the East, and feared that no physical barrier could resist the infection because it was carried in a cloud blown hither and thither by the wind. They cried that only God could offer protection, and why should he save Walsham when he was destroying the rest of the world?

To combat pessimism and despair, Master John from the pulpit of his packed church constantly taught his parishioners the lesson from Ezekiel that the Lord God was a merciful and not a cruel God, and that he was striking in order to reform mankind and not to destroy it: "As I live, saith the Lord God, I desire not the death of the wicked, but that the wicked may turn from this way and live."

Much as the dread of what was to happen in the future pressed on the present, ordinary life did not cease in Walsham. Most villagers had neither the leisure nor the inclination to dwell perpetually on the heightened imminence of the pestilence. Of course, some became extremely distracted, and some devoted themselves to hours of prayer each day, and to fasting and to mortifying their flesh by wearing sackcloth, lying on stone and earth floors instead of mattresses and straw, and going barefoot in all weather. But the majority of the residents could not allow such regimes to dominate their daily existence, for the simple reason that they had to fend for themselves and look after the needs of their families. Animals had to be fed and tended, fields weeded, money earned, and goods bought. Except for extra time spent on devotions, the bulk of their days continued to be taken up with a mixture of work and welcome relaxation. Nor did the trade of the village alehouses and alewives fall off, because for every Christian soul who forswore drink as a penance, there was another who saw it as a means of blotting out his fears.

At the same time, though villagers had little choice but to continue about the everyday business of their lives, the veneer of normality was fragile. Any fresh news of sickness or death in Walsham or a neighboring village caused waves of panic to roll through the community. Notably fewer friends and neighbors came to offer support and comfort at the sickbed, and funeral processions and burials were markedly less well attended. In order to secure a measure of calm and to encourage reluctant mourners to pay respects, the priests who gave the last rites were repeatedly forced to confirm publicly that the deceased had died from old age, accident, or some familiar ailment, with no sign of a strange pestilence anywhere on their bodies. Yet these assurances often failed to work because simple folk chose to be safe rather than sorry. When Mansur Shucford died suddenly of old age around harvest time, a rumor spread that the pestilence had arrived, and only a handful of people paid their last respects at the cottage he shared. In order to quell fears, Mansur's body was inspected by the hayward and shown to be free of any strange marks. At Mass, Master John urged both private prayers and public shows of mourning for a venerable and well-respected villager. Yet shamefully few dared attend his funeral, and scarcely any more turned up at the free dinner that followed it.

When news of the pestilence across the seas had first reached Walsham, the cowardly and heartless actions of foreigners who had left the sick to die alone and the dead to be buried without funeral rites and ceremonies were scorned. Such behavior was un-Christian, unforgivable, and a risk to the eternal peace of the soul. From what they had heard, once this new scourge had arrived in a place it seemed to spread everywhere like a fire in a wood stack, and death followed surely and painfully in its wake. There was nobody who had not listened with horror at descriptions of victims lying prostrate with pain in their heads and chests, coughing up great quantities of blood, or afflicted with huge black growths in their groins and on their necks, or simply dropping dead without warning. But even so, as they trembled on the brink of imminent danger, the villagers continued to believe that, if the pestilence should come to Suffolk, they would act with selfless compassion and charity.

But in the meantime, there was general agreement that it was only common sense to keep a distance from the sick and the dead. The lesson that the sick could transmit the deadly new pestilence by sight alone, or by touch or breath, had been quickly learned, and so too had an awareness that even the houses and clothes of the victims could kill. This all made good sense, for throughout their lives they had seen that many common sicknesses, such as coughs and colds, spread easily from person to person, just as scab did from sheep to sheep. No sensible person was going to take unnecessary risks, and it was only prudent to avoid all who might have the pestilence or be capable of passing it on.

Harvest time meant long hours of hard labor for almost every member of the community, but also a welcome source of additional income. While the weather held fine, the normal routines of craftsmen, traders, and even the clergy were abandoned for more pressing work in the fields. Despite the heavy rain that had fallen in midsummer, the yields of corn turned out to be pleasingly good when the fields were reaped and the sheaves bound during early autumn, and prices tumbled by a third or more, making bread, pottage, and ale far more affordable than they had been for many years. As was customary, those working at the harvest had been fed plentiful food and ale to encourage greater efforts. Now that the harvest had been gathered in and the barns were full, the villagers turned to celebrating their good fortune and the end of their intense labors. With coins jingling in their pockets from their bonus earnings, leisure followed on from labor in a succession of feasts and celebrations.

It was a week or so after Michaelmas, September 29, when most tenants had managed without too much difficulty to pay the rents due on that quarter day, that an extremely tall, gray-bearded, and wild-haired preacher came to Walsham. The arrival of a wandering preacher was not an uncommon event, for the number of strangers traveling the countryside ranting about the coming of the Apocalypse had grown in concert with the threat of pestilence. But even the most skeptical villagers were transfixed by this stranger's extraordinary appearance and burning black eyes. Word quickly spread that the preacher was a true prophet, a most holy man, who had lived alone for many years in the wilderness, with only a cave for shelter. So the stories went, that he had lived off berries, roots, and fruits, and occasionally animals he trapped and killed with his bare hands. Only in the harshest months of winter had he occasionally been brought small bundles of the most basic foods—barley bread and beans—by the servants of a nearby community of devout Carthusian monks.

With a thunderous voice that shook the air and a great black cloak that billowed around his shoulders, the prophet gathered a large crowd around him in St. Mary's churchyard after the first Sunday Mass. He had with him a band of devoted disciples who accompanied his sonorous words with the rhythmic banging of drums, clanging of cymbals, and wailing of tormented souls. Fired with unchallengeable conviction, he announced that the death-dealing pestilence, which the pitiful sinners gathered before him believed was still overseas, was in fact slaughtering Englishmen, women, and children in their thousands: "As I speak, Death is scything his way through the decadent coastal cities of the south of England. The inhabitants of these cities, that only yesterday were thronged with ships loaded with trifles, delicacies, and pleasures, all shamelessly brought from the godless lands of the infidels in the East to indulge the gluttony and vice of the rich, are now lying in narrow pits in the earth rather than in scented baths, and providing feasts for worms. At this very moment, the poisonous fingers of pestilence are stretching swiftly and irresistibly toward London. This city has for too long been offending God. It will be utterly destroyed. The Bible tells us that an angry God destroyed those sinful cities of Sodom and Gomorrah which had offended him long ago, and in like fashion he will now destroy London and with it Cambridge, Thetford, Bury St. Edmunds and its sinful abbey, Walsham, and all the rest of the world which is sullied with sin."

Drawing himself to his full height, he bellowed, "I saw under the altar the souls of them that were slain for the word of God, and for the testimony which they held. And they cried with a loud voice, saying, 'How long O Lord, holy and true, dost thou not judge and avenge our blood on them that dwell on the earth?'"

As he declaimed these terrible words, every few sentences he stopped and repeated alternately, "And I looked, and beheld a pale horse: and his name that sat on him was Death, and Hell followed with him," and then, "For the great day of his wrath is come; and who shall be able to stand?"

As his audience stood transfixed in the presence of this awesome man, and as the drumbeats accentuated his horrific message, he began to recite from the book of Revelation: "This was prophesied, and this has come to pass." (See figure 17.)

> And when the Lamb had opened the seventh seal, there was silence in heaven about the space of half an hour.
> And I saw the seven angels which stood before God; and to them were given seven trumpets.

The first angel sounded, and there followed hail and fire mingled with blood, and they were cast upon the earth; and the third part of trees was burnt up, and all the green grass burnt up.

And the second angel sounded, and a great mountain burning with fire was cast into the sea; and the third part of the sea became blood, and the third part of the creatures which were in the sea, and had life, died; and the third part of the ships were destroyed.

And the third angel sounded, and there fell a great star from heaven, burning as it were a lamp, and it fell upon a third part of the rivers, and upon the fountains of the waters; and many men died of the waters because they were made bitter.

And the fourth angel sounded, and the third part of the sun was smitten, and the third part of the moon, and the third part of the stars.

And the fifth angel sounded, and I saw a star fall from heaven unto the earth; and to him was given the key of the bottomless pit. And he opened the bottomless pit; and there arose a smoke out of the pit as the smoke of a great furnace; and there came out of the smoke locusts upon the earth and in those days shall men seek death and shall not find it.

And the sixth angel sounded, and the number of the army of the horsemen were two hundred thousand, and out of their mouths issued fire and smoke and brimstone. By these was a third part of men killed.

But the rest of the men who were not killed by these plagues, yet repented not of the works of their hands. Neither repented they of their murders, nor of their sorceries, nor of their fornication, nor of their thefts.

The preacher halted for a moment and slowly scanned his shocked audience, catching the eye of many with his fierce gaze. "A third part, a third part!" he scoffed. "The Bible tells us this, yet I tell you that sinfulness in our times is so great that God is killing with this present plague not the third part but the second part of man, and sometimes even six men out of every seven. Nor yet do we repent of our sins, and so the seventh angel shall not sound his trumpet that can open up the gates of Heaven, and they shall be forever barred to us."

"For God has said, 'At my command, let the planets poison the air and corrupt the whole earth; let there be universal grief and lamentation. Let the sharp arrows of sudden death have dominion throughout the world.

Let no one be spared, either for their sex or their age; let the innocent perish with the guilty and no one escape.'"

Then, when the hearts of his audience were collectively gripped with anguish and horror, he launched into a description of the Hell they would all be facing in a matter of weeks, when the pestilence came to their village and the time came for them to die.

"You have heard that those sick with the pestilence die agonizing deaths, but your death agonies shall be but nothing compared with what awaits you when your miserable life finally expires. You might be forgotten on earth after you die, but you will be remembered by the devil. For those that shall be damned in Hell shall have divers pains and tormenting, some with small devils, some with great devils, and so shall be in sorrow and care without end. And some in Hell shall burn in the great flame of fire, which is nine times hotter than is any fire in this world. Yes! And some shall be hanged by the neck, and devils without number shall draw their limbs asunder, and smite their bodies through with fiery brands. And some shall be hanged by the tongue, and some shall be hauled into the fire, and their bowels drawn out (see figure 18).

"I will show you what pain is ordained for your sins in Hell by this example. If there were here a barrel that was hammered full of long and sharp nails, with the points inward and the nails fiery hot, I trust there is nobody here before me that would be willing to be rolled a mile in this barrel for all the realm of England. And yet this were but a mile. Ah good Lord! How great pain there be eternally in every part of man's five wits, not only a mile's way but all the while God is God in Heaven."

As if this were not enough, his followers, as a chorus, began to chant a well-known verse on the agonies of death, and many in his audience, knowing the words, joined in:

When the head quaketh
And the lips blacketh
And the nose sharpens
And the sinews stiffen
And the breast panteth
And the breath wanteth

And the teeth clatter
And the throat rattles
And the soul has left
And the body is nothing but a clout
Then will the body be thrown in a hole
And no one will remember your soul

Anguished folk in the crowd cried out to the preacher and his followers to sell them pardons for their sins. And they begged for a sight of holy relics that he must have carried with him to Walsham. They proffered pennies to buy from him pottery and bone charms against the plague. But he laughed scornfully and said he had none of these, and that salvation was not for sale. He tossed their money aside, mocking them for their belated groveling and telling them that God's mind was already made up. It was now far too late to buy exemption from his dreadful will.

"In Hell a man shall weep more than all the water in the earth—alms, Masses, and prayers shall not avail him. Heaven is for those who serve God."

With that he turned his back and walked away out of the village on the road toward Bury, followed not only by the band of disciples and musicians he had arrived with, but by several villagers beating their breasts and crying pitifully.

The next day before a huge spellbound crowd in the Great Market of Bury St. Edmunds, the prophet pointed contemptuously to the soaring Guildhall and the rows of fine houses surrounding it, asserting that there was nothing the city leaders and the rich could do to save their city or themselves. The crowd visibly wilted as he swept his long arm across the skyline to encompass the towering churches of St. Mary and St. James, and beyond them the magnificent abbey of St. Edmund. Outside that very abbey while the monks looked on in horror, he proclaimed that the church with all its wealth, earthly authority, and majesty was powerless to protect its flock, or even its own clergy, from God's awful punishment.

This preacher made as profound an impression on the sophisticated citizenry of bustling Bury as he did on the simple folk. But it was not his oratory alone that had so shaken his audience. For among the crowd were some who had hotter news than even the prophet. The day before two carters from London had arrived with packs of groceries, and they had chatted freely about the terrible pestilence from France that was raging in the ports and towns in the south and west of the realm. And later in the evening, when they had been plied with drink, they confessed to having been told rumors of strange deaths in parts of London just before they departed on their northward journey to Bury.

7

Autumn and Winter, 1348

The pattern of plague dissemination is difficult for historians to unravel and must have appeared mysterious and unpredictable to contemporaries. Certainly information about its spread did not always flow smoothly. For example, the letter known as "Terribilis," urging the power of prayer against the invasion of plague, which Edward III wished to be circulated in the southern dioceses, took a long time to reach its recipients. The king had originally asked John Stratford, the archbishop of Canterbury, to write it, but Stratford died on August 23 and the task was devolved to the prior of Christchurch, Canterbury. A copy of his letter written to the bishop of London survives that is dated September 28. Nor did bishops always reside within their dioceses. When the bishop of Winchester wrote a letter on October 24, in which he expressed "anguish . . . that this cruel plague has now begun a . . . savage attack on the coastal areas of England," it was from what he thought was the safety of Southwark, a suburb of London. But the plague was fast approaching there as well.

Knowledge of the plague in London is frustratingly thin for such an important city, which had a population of around 100,000. The diocesan registers have been lost, and there are no equivalents of manorial court rolls. Being such a large settlement, the capital experienced a duration and pattern of the epidemic differing from that seen elsewhere. From analysis of surviving wills, the disease appears to have persisted for at least six months as it spread across the city, which is considerably longer than it lasted in smaller settlements. It is also possible that the death rate experienced considerable fluctuations, plunging for a time after the initial flare-up in late autumn 1348, only to soar to fresh peaks in the opening months of the new year. This is indicated by the announcement in early January of the prorogation of the forthcoming parliament at Westminster, because "the plague of deadly pestilence has suddenly broken out . . . and daily increases in severity." Twenty-five of the monks of the abbey of Westminster, out of a usual complement of around fifty, died in 1348–1349.

There was a great deal of magic in fourteenth-century orthodox religion, and a great many survivals of pagan beliefs besides. Such beliefs and practices were naturally resorted to with mounting fervor under the threat of the approaching pestilence. In addition to the powers attributed to saints and holy relics, in the minds of theologians as well as simple folk, God was called on to bless the holy bread that was given away on Sundays in place of the Eucharist, "so that all who consume it shall receive health of body as well as of soul," and thus was regarded as providing medicine for the sick as well as protection against plague. It was commonly thought appropriate for the faithful to sprinkle holy water to drive away evil spirits or pestilential vapors, as well as to drink it as a cure for disease or a protection against it. The wearing of wax amulets, originally made out of Easter candles blessed by the pope, was extremely popular for the benefits they bestowed on the wearer.

Priests alone had the power to administer the seven sacraments, of which penance assumed particular significance at the time of the Black Death. Three conditions were necessary for the forgiveness of mortal sins, which were more serious than venial sins: penitents had to be truly contrite, confess their sins to a priest, and perform the penance they were given, which was appropriate to the sin that had been committed. Those who died with sins that were unconfessed and unrepented could, or would, go to Hell. But a dilemma arose if, through no fault of their own, the dying were denied the ministrations of a priest, and for this reason sudden death was especially feared throughout the Middle Ages. In early January 1349, at the height of the plague in the diocese of Bath and Wells, the bishop, acknowledging that "priests cannot be found for love or money," ordered his clergy to "make it known speedily and publicly . . . to everybody, but particularly to those that have fallen sick, that if when on the point of death they cannot secure the services of a properly ordained priest, they should make confession of their sins . . . to any lay person, even to a woman if a man is not available." He further urged them "to let it be known at the same time that confession made in this way can be wholesome and of great benefit to them for the remission of their sins."

⊰ ⊱

Amid the gathering fear and despair, two young people in Walsham—Robert, son of William Cranmer, and Alice, daughter of John and Amice Terwald—decided to marry. The match met with the warm approval of their families. Robert's father and grandfather, being generous and relatively wealthy by Walsham standards, set about providing the couple with the resources needed to support themselves in their independent life together. Robert had two older sisters, Olivia and Hilary, who had already been set up in married life, and an unmarried brother, William. His father and grandfather decided to treat both of the brothers equally, and soon after the announcement of Robert's betrothal, William Sr. purchased a piece of land in Brookfield from William Wither to give to his sons, and added to it an acre of his own land in Hulkescroft. The relatively comfortable independence of the young married couple was assured when their grandfather generously gave a further three acres to the two brothers, together with a house where Robert and Alice might set up home.

Though some aspects of life in Walsham in the autumn and early winter of 1348 might have appeared on the surface to be proceeding very much as usual, residents noted some disconcerting signs of change. For example, a trickle of people had always drifted off the manor never to return, but of late there had been a sharp increase in the numbers of departures. What is more, the migrants were no longer drawn merely from the landless, rootless, poor laboring folk who had little to give up. Now significant landholders were to be found among those deserting Walsham, including a few from long-established families who were selling their lands and stock in return for ready cash. A disconcerting unease lay just under the surface, which strained social relations and made formerly calm people act in excitable and unpredictable ways. This was certainly the case with the eleven tenants who refused to turn up when summoned by the reeve to harvest crops for Sir Hugh de Saxham and Lady Rose. When they were challenged to fulfill their obligations, the rebels openly boasted that if the end of the world was coming they were not going to spend their last days working for nothing for grasping lords. The manor had never seen such large-scale defiance, but, surprisingly, the lord and lady decided to respond in a cautious manner and simply warned the default-ers that they would be dealt with at the next meeting of the manor court, where they were eventually fined a few pence.

Try as the villagers might to push aside the horrifying threat they faced in the near future in order to deal with the prosaic routines of the present, their efforts were consistently undermined. The terror engen-dered by the fiery preacher had barely subsided when word spread quickly through Walsham that Master John had received another official message to deliver from the pulpit. This time it had been sent on the or-ders of the king himself.

"I have a message which comes from our most excellent prince and lord, Edward, by the grace of God the illustrious king of England and France. Your valiant king, ever mindful of the welfare of his subjects, tells us that he has given serious consideration to how Almighty God, of his infinite mercy, might save and protect his realm of England from these plagues and from death. To bring this about, on his orders, the bishop of London has written to all churches urging devout prayers and Masses, so that God, pacified by prayers, might yet snatch the people of England from these tribulations, and of his grace show help to them and, of his in-effable pity, preserve human frailty from these plagues and mortality.

"Terrible is God toward the sons of men, and by his command all things are subdued to the rule of his will. Those whom he loves he cen-sures and chastises; he punishes their shameful deeds in various ways during this mortal life so that they might not be condemned eternally. He often allows plagues, miserable famines, and other forms of suffer-ing to arise, and uses them to terrify and torment men and so drive out their sins. And thus, indeed, the realm of England, because of the grow-ing pride and corruption of its subjects, and their numberless sins, has on many occasions stood desolate and afflicted by the burdens of the wars which are exhausting and devouring the wealth of the kingdom, and by many other miseries." The priest stopped speaking for a second or two, and then added with special emphasis, holding the letter up so that all could see: "The king, through his spokesman the lord bishop, tells us, 'It is now to be feared that the kingdom of England is to be oppressed by the pestilence and wretched mortalities of men which have flared up in other regions.' But the arrival of this letter has been long delayed, and in the time it has taken to reach me it has been overtaken by even more somber news. What the king and the bishop of London feared is now a reality."

There was turmoil among the tightly packed congregation, as their trusted shepherd, on the authority of the king himself, confirmed their worst fears. Master John paused, but he waited in vain for silence to return. So he continued above the hubbub in a loud, deep voice that he unsuccessfully tried to keep from shaking: "It is with great sorrow, and I am myself struck with terror, that I must tell you that people are at this moment dying in great numbers from a new and mysterious disease in towns and villages in the south and west of the realm, and in the great city of Bristol in the far west near Wales. I cannot confirm rumors that the pestilence may already be in London, but it is likely to be far closer to us than we know."

The priest continued, trying to make a message of hope heard above the din of lamentation that rose from his distressed parishioners: "So, we must redouble our efforts to appease God's anger, both by refraining from sin and by begging for his mercy. In accordance with the wishes of the king, I will organize more Masses and special sermons, as well as put the greatest efforts into our regular penitential processions on Wednesdays and Fridays. I have been asked to announce that the bishop, with the blessing of the archbishop of Canterbury, will grant generous indulgences to remit pains and sufferings in the afterlife to all who perform these things. Faith and hope must rest with these actions."

Many wept, pleading for God's mercy, while others questioned whether prayers and processions were any use, and whether the instructions of bishops and even the king would have any effect at all on God's anger. To the despair of the prudent, pragmatic, and sensible villagers, who with commendable self-control for the past few weeks and months had remained calm, and had given reassurance to their neighbors of the mercy of God and the unreliability of rumor mongers, it was the fantasists, the pessimists, and the hysterics who were shown to have grasped the truth more firmly.

Though inwardly aware that he was scarcely hanging onto coherent speech, Master John doggedly explained to his flock what they all must do. He urged them not to lose faith, but to throw themselves willingly into yet greater depths of devotion and contrition, and he made a bold show of ordering the clerics around him to organize new encompassing acts of worship.

"As we have been directed, every Wednesday and Sunday all the clergy of this parish will assemble in our churchyard, or in the church if it is wet, and humbly and devoutly recite the seven penitential psalms and the fifteen psalms of degrees on our knees (see figure 19). And every Wednesday and Friday all the people of the parish, regardless of the weather, will go solemnly in procession. They will sing these psalms and the great litany that the fathers of the church have instituted against the pestilence, and also perform many other acts of devotion. At various stations along the route, myself and my assistants will conduct readings or give short sermons. You will all abandon your worldly tasks and accompany these processions with bowed heads and bare feet, fasting. With a pious heart and lamenting your sins, you will set aside all idle chatter. And as you go devoutly, you will say as many times as possible, the Lord's Prayer and the Hail Mary. And when the procession returns to this church you will remain in earnest prayer until the end of the Mass, which I will celebrate immediately after each procession.

"And we will believe in our hearts that if we persevere in our devotions with faith, rectitude, and firm trust in the omnipotence and mercy of the Savior, we will soon receive a remedy and timely help from Heaven. And you will each be granted an indulgence by our bishop of forty days for taking part in the procession and Mass and for praying there for the safety of the king and his subjects, and all Christians, and for the end of the plague. And if you cannot join us for the best of reasons but say these prayers elsewhere, you shall receive an indulgence of thirty days."

Again a torrent of voices arose from the congregation, but the priest felt helpless to hush or answer them. Not wishing to sow doubt where faith should prevail, he turned toward the altar, saying that he had to pray for forgiveness and guidance, and he suggested that they all do the same. The gathering fell silent and, as if in one movement, all fell to their knees, except those who threw themselves prostrate on the floor. A few beat their heads on the flagstones until the blood ran.

The time now being devoted to prayers and processions cut deep into the working week of almost all residents, but the steward of Lady Rose and Sir Hugh de Saxham was at pains to make it clear that all of his lord's and lady's unfree tenants were required as usual to attend their court, which was scheduled for Friday, October 24. He saw no reason why conjectures about the pestilence should deflect him from carrying on as normal, especially as there was a particularly heavy load of business to conduct and some substantial fines to collect. During the proceedings, which lasted a good part of the day, an exceptionally large number of transfers of land were registered, including the gifts to young Robert and William Cranmer by their father and grandfather, and the formal passing of dead Mansur Shucford's half a cottage and six acres to his son John, on payment to the lord of a cow in calf as heriot. As usual, small fines were levied on those who had broken bylaws by grazing animals on the common fields without right, and the steward took special delight in ordering that the goods of Roger, the prior of Ixworth, should be attached because his sheep had been grazing unlawfully, although, of course, he had no intention of taking any such action. Various manorial officers presented evidence of a spate of minor but worrying thefts, reporting the servants of eight tenants for stealing small quantities of the lord's straw, for which they were each fined about a day's pay. Another seven persons were fined twice as much for helping themselves to small quantities of the lord's corn while it was growing in the field just before harvest time. Then the court found Peter Gilbert guilty of the more serious theft of half a bushel of unwinnowed wheat from the lord's barn, for which he was fined a hefty 6s 8d, more than ten times what it was worth. And the lord's officers also pursued, in a time-honored fashion, the trespasses of villagers who had carelessly damaged their master's and mistress's crops by failing to keep under adequate control a variety of animals, ranging from cows and foals to geese. Equally mundane, but no less pressing for the litigants, was the continued refusal of John Robhood and Thomas Fuller to settle a dispute over where the precise boundary between their lands should lie, Richard Qualm's obstruction of a watercourse, and Thomas Julle's pursuit of John Man for the repayment of an overdue debt.

However, when the steward moved on to deal with tenants who had sold pieces of land without license, those present at the court immediately realized that this particular misdemeanor had grown into a matter of considerable consequence. Many times in recent weeks they had witnessed long-standing residents, people of some substance, offering their land for sale, but the number of cases now being presented to the late October court was even higher than expected. More unusually still, they were told that the heirs to three tenements had not come to Walsham to take up their inheritances. In order to preserve the veneer of normality, the steward had been advised by his master and mistress to pass quickly over the conspiracy of the eleven tenants who had refused to work on the demesne farm, and reluctantly he fined them each only the 3d which his bailiff had to pay to hire substitutes. But no such concession was allowed to newly-weds Alice Terwald and Robert Cranmer. They were charged a hefty fine of 20s for having their marriage approved because they both came from wealthy families who could afford to pay.

Soon after the court session ended, one of the missing heirs, Richard Man, turned up to claim the acre and rood of land that his sister had left him on her death. He gave the steward the convincing excuse that he had been forced to make very careful inquiries before setting out to travel to Walsham to ensure that the village and its environs were free of plague.

While there were no signs of plague in the region around Walsham, news came almost daily of pestilential deaths spreading across the far south of England. In early November a monk from Ixworth reported that his prior had received a letter informing him that twenty-three of the twenty-six monks in the Cistercian abbey of Newenham in Devon had died, and a few weeks later the dreadful news reached Walsham from many sources that multitudes were dying in London from a new disease. Then a Walsham carter who had set out on a journey to London hurried back in panic to the village. He had turned around before reaching Chelmsford because he encountered so many travelers with tales of strange deaths occurring in towns and villages farther along the route into the capital.

Wayfaring preachers, however, were not deterred by the spread of the pestilence but were inspired to wander the country with ever greater frequency. When they visited Walsham, which they did in ever increasing numbers, Master John frequently expressed his disapproval because they were unlicensed and displayed little knowledge of the Scriptures. But his condemnation did little to prevent these itinerants attracting large audiences and collecting many pennies, as they declared, with fevered relish and redoubled confidence, that the villagers faced the same terrible fate as that being inflicted on London and other fine places in the south. One claimed he was hot-foot from Hampshire and had the bishop of Winchester's own writ to proclaim what was happening to town and country there: "These cities, castles, towns, and villages, which until now have rejoiced in their illustrious residents, their wisdom in counsel, their splendid riches, their great strength, and the beauty of their womenfolk, have been suddenly and woefully stripped of their inhabitants by this most savage pestilence. Until recently crowds of people have flocked from far and wide for succor, pleasure, and comfort to these fine places, and they have rung with the abundance of joy. But now no one dares to enter these places anymore. Instead all flee from them, as if from the caves of wild animals, so that all joy ceases, all sweetness is dammed up, and the sound of mirth silenced. And they have become places of horror and desolate wastelands."

London, the finest and largest city in the realm, with the most splendid riches and most illustrious residents of all, lay a little more than eighty miles to the south of Walsham. It was an easy four-day journey on foot and could be comfortably reached in less than half that time on horseback. It was a place of wonder, by far the leading port and trading market in England as well as the center of court and government. Although few Walsham residents had ever ventured to the capital, they had frequent contact with people who had. Direct travel between Bury and London was commonplace for traders. A wide range of goods were brought up from London to Bury and thence to nearby towns and markets on an almost daily basis. Fine cloth, wines, fruits, spices, as well as mundane haberdashery and hardware, all made their way on carts and packhorses from London to the stalls and shops in Bury's market places. In return, Bury acted as a collecting center for the wool, corn, and livestock of the region, which

together with some of the cloth produced along the Stour valley in Lavenham and Clare, went southward to the capital for redistribution within
England and export overseas.

It was in mid-December that a man and a pregnant woman arrived in
Walsham, carrying a few packs of possessions on a small horse. They quietly moved in with relatives in a cottage tucked away toward Alwood and
kept to themselves. The man was a journeyman pewterer who specialized
in making chalices, and with his wife he had lived happily in a garret over
his master's pewter workshop near Cheapside. That was until his master
died suddenly, coughing up blood. They had helped bury him the next
day but, with signs that the sickness was spreading in the crowded streets
round about them, they then fled in terror from the city. The day after
they arrived in Walsham, inquisitive neighbors were told that they were
visiting close relatives for a short period over the coming holy days.
Though villagers had their suspicions, the newcomers were allowed to
stay, it being Christmastide and the uncomfortable resemblance they bore
to Mary and Joseph seeking shelter in Bethlehem.

Soon after Christmas a distracted stranger was found sleeping in the
church. When questioned by the village beadle, he said he was searching
for his wife's brother who he believed lived near Newmarket. He was sure
he would give him shelter, but in a week or two's wandering he had not
been able to locate him. He asked whether his brother-in-law lived in Walsham but was told he did not. On being pressed further, the stranger admitted fleeing from London and, without further prompting, unfolded, in
short breathless bursts, his personal experiences of the pestilence there:
"The great city is in the grip of a terrible and most powerful disease that
keeps growing in ferocity. When you catch it, you suffer unbearable pains
and cough and spit up cupfuls of blood, and then you die within a couple
of days, without fail. I know what I am talking about, for I nursed my sick
wife and my three young sons for two days until they had all died in agony,
without a priest or even a neighbor to comfort them or help me."

Thinking that his sufferings would arouse the spirit of charity in those
confronting him, the stranger went on. "Then I carried them to the
cemetery on my shoulders at dead of night, when nobody else was about,
and laid them side by side in a narrow, shallow grave which I dug with my
own hands in the corner of the churchyard. As I left their graveside just

after dawn, I caught sight of a score or more of bodies being unloaded from carts and hastily piled into four open graves, with only a single priest to say brief obsequies." Asked what he did next, he recalled returning to his lodgings and spending a couple of days in his room praying for the souls of his wife and sons. But soon others in the house and in properties up and down the street were also struck with the pestilence, and so he had fled the city hoping to escape from its clutches.

By now an excited group of parishioners were quizzing the stranger, for he was the first person they had met who admitted to seeing the effects of the pestilence with their own eyes. Eager to please, he willingly responded to their questions and told them how he had seen victims without number stricken with fever, prostrate with pain, spitting and coughing up blood, and also heard that a few were afflicted by great boils. Others had dropped dead without warning or any outward signs of illness, though he admitted that he had only heard about such sudden deaths and had not himself seen this happen. But he had seen many bodies lying in the streets, both alive and dead, abandoned by their families and friends.

The villagers demanded to know whether the pestilence had taken hold in any of the villages and towns that he had passed on his way up from London. Sensing their growing hostility, he assured them that he had seen no trace of it anywhere and that he would surely be dead by now if he had been infected in London. Then he coughed loudly and spat on the ground to show that there was no blood in his sputum. But they chased him from the church and then from the village, and threw stones at him until he was running in fear of his life. At a meeting that evening the villagers decided to split into groups and take turns in guarding the roads to see that he did not return. Those who had met the Londoner and felt his breath on their faces as they interrogated him spent the next days waiting in terror lest they had caught the pestilence from him. But they had not.

Nor in the following weeks did the pestilence appear to draw any nearer to Walsham and its region. In fact, during a particularly frosty spell in mid-January encouraging rumors began to circulate that the plague was waning in London. But these hopes were soon disappointed when the Bury burgesses who had been summoned to attend a Parliament in

Westminster in late January received notice that the king had abandoned it because "the plague of deadly pestilence had suddenly broken out, and was daily increasing in severity." The grave fears for the safety of the nobles, knights, burgesses, and bishops if they were forced to travel to Westminster were also shared by the common folk, who were well aware that nothing seemed so certain to lead to infection than to go into places where the pestilence was raging and mix with people afflicted by it.

The terror raging less than a hundred miles from the doors of Walsham's residents combined with their beliefs and the teachings of their priests to feed an almost obsessive concern with sin. Many of those remarkable people, who through feats of self-control or indifference, had managed until now to continue to lead normal lives, finally succumbed to the pervading spirit of heated anxiety, and a few who had formerly appeared unmoved swung to the opposite extreme of scarcely controlled hysteria.

Everyone now knew that the sinful would be punished, but they hoped God might still avert his anger for those who deserved mercy. It was not for man to know the mind of God, but deliverance from death might follow from the speedy confession of those sins and misdemeanors that had been unwittingly committed, if accompanied by the expression of sincere contrition, the dutiful fulfillment of penance, and the avoidance of new transgressions. So the clergy of the parish redoubled their fervent exhortations to all those who might have committed sin to perform acts of public and private abasement, and they repeatedly pronounced that none should believe themselves exempt. Time and again parishioners were urged from the pulpit to "beseech all the saints in heaven to pray for you to Christ, that he will have mercy and pity on you as he bought you on the cross." This the faithful did with great fervor and stamina, having been taught that "confession cleanses one's heart, enlightens one's senses, sanctifies one's soul, and prepares one to receive Christ." The flock was repeatedly warned by its shepherds, and by each other, of the evils which awaited those who delayed confession or, after confessing, returned to their sin "as a dog returns to its vomit" and by so doing "crucified the Son of God a second time."

At the end of a particularly emotional Sunday Mass, during which everyone in attendance prostrated themselves on the stone floor of the church publicly confessing their sins and begging forgiveness, Master John stood in the porch of the church and told a story. It was about a very devout woman who had always confessed every sin she had committed since childhood, except one, which she held back for shame. "That night, as she was in a deep sleep, Jesus Christ appeared to her with his wounds wide open and showed her his heart, which was laid bare, bleeding and pierced. He spoke to her asking, 'Why are you ashamed of showing me your heart when I am not ashamed of showing you mine?' And he took her hand and put it in his side, saying, 'Take and touch my heart.' She woke up with great remorse and showed her bloodstained hands to all she met, and then she confessed that sin. For this confession, as a sign that her sin was forgiven, her hands became as they had been before."

Not wanting to add to the alarm that had already gripped most of his parishioners, Master John preferred to encourage rather than frighten, and he refrained from telling what awful fates befell unconfessed sinners. But his assistants, and a succession of wandering preachers and mystics, were not so reticent. His flock also used their fevered imaginations to conjure up their own terrifying visions of the Hell that awaited them if they were unfortunate enough to die a sudden death or a lonely one, or rendered insensible by the disease which struck them down.

Regular attendance and animated participation at Mass became a daily or even more frequent endeavor. To cater for the needs of many in their flock who desired to see the Host at least once every day, the clergy combined together with tireless commitment to offer a succession of Low Masses throughout the day. And, as if these ceaseless devotions were insufficient in number, groups of parishioners took to contributing money to common purses, from which they periodically drew to hire priests to perform additional Masses in private. Yet more comfort was available when needed from wayfaring friars, who found their reassuring words, easy confessions, and light penances in far greater demand than ever before, even though the clamor for their services encouraged them to increase greatly the fees they charged.

Frequent attendance at Mass was essential for collective as well as personal salvation, and neighbors and friends cajoled the recalcitrant and assisted the old and infirm to make their way to St. Mary's. Those who lived far from the church, in High Hall, Alwood Green, and Hartshall, expended much time and experienced considerable discomfort on their journeys in the cold, dark days of January and February, but were succored by the thought that the greater their sacrifices the more likely they were to be noted by God and to earn special dispensation from him. With Master John's encouragement, much time was devoted to learning the Creed, the Paternoster, and the Ave Maria, and to identifying the sacraments, the seven deadly sins, the works of charity, acts of mercy, and seven virtues. After much thought, Master John introduced additional Communions, where the most assiduous and knowledgeable were permitted to partake more frequently of the Body of Christ in the form of the Communion wafer. For the others, who hungered no less fervently after health of body as well as of soul, there was the comfort of a piece of consecrated bread, which was dispensed each Sunday from a large mound on a trestle table in the porch. The size of the mound grew larger by the week, until an additional table had to be provided to hold the quantities of bread that were demanded by the lengthening queues.

Less seemly were the struggles that had begun to take place among parishioners to grab the stumps of the candles that had been used at High Mass. Those who were successful rolled them into wax cakes, impressed them with the fingers of the right hand of the large wooden statue of the Madonna kept in the church, and wore them on a leather band around their necks. Much as the clergy strove, they had little success in controlling the trade in such charms, and the wax amulets were sold in the village for a day's wage. In the hysteria which bubbled just under the surface of everyday life, the demand for the protection offered by holy water also soared. Troops of villagers filed daily to the church with containers of all shapes and sizes, and the supply was supplemented by carriers who fetched more from the well of Our Lady in the nearby village of Woolpit. Holy water was drunk, sprinkled over food, loved ones, and animals, thrown over paths and fields, and used to moisten almost every doorway in Walsham by constant dousings.

Anyone with skill as a wood carver was able to earn extra money meeting the desire for carvings of the Madonna and of the saints, and those who could paint adorned them with colored vestments, raven and flaxen hair, and ruby lips and cheeks. The pewterer who had recently arrived from London found himself employed for long hours casting tiny bracelets and necklaces of brightly polished tin to adorn the images which stood in the shrines of most cottages and all houses. Master John had always loved a well-decorated church, and fervently believed that statues and pictures of the saints, and especially of the crucified Christ, were the books of lay folk. Just as the clergy got closer to God through reading his words, so those who were ignorant of letters should at least be able to see with their eyes what they were not able to read in books. But of late he had become concerned by the heightened emotional veneration of the mere images of saints, and he was troubled by the constant prayers and oblations offered to saints by name for the procuring of personal protection and benefits. He chided the most fervent of the worshipers to remember that the figures they treasured were only wood and stone and nothing else. "When you kneel before the images, you should utter your prayers not to these but to God and his saints." He also warned many times in church, "If we give offerings and worship to these images of wood and stone that should only be given to God, we not only offend God, breaking his behest, but also we offend all the holy saints of Heaven. For, as St. Austin witnesses, they hate if such things be done to themselves, for they do not wish to usurp to themselves such things that belong only to God."

Master John, however, was delighted to receive a collection from the parish amounting to 40s for the making of a large stone statue of the Blessed Virgin Mary to stand beside the high altar. He swiftly commissioned a mason from Bury to begin work immediately, and then set about finding the best painter to decorate it when the mason had finished.

Master John hoped fervently that the devotions of his parishioners would succeed in placating God, but he also took special note of everything he heard which might enable him to care better for his flock should the plague come. It was some time since he had first learned of the chaos in Italy, Avignon, and other distant places caused by the sheer multitude of sick and dying, with many left to face death without the opportunity of confessing to a priest. But he could not condone what he saw as the irresponsible actions of bishops and other church leaders in these stricken places, when they felt compelled to bestow the ability to hear confession, perhaps even to absolve sins, on the lowliest of clergy, including those who had scarcely begun their training for holy orders.

So he was deeply troubled to learn from the treasurer of Ixworth priory on one of his regular visits to collect money from John's parish, that the ravages of plague in the diocese of Bath and Wells had caused the bishop to go even further in diluting the sacred offices of the priest. "Apparently," he told John, "the huge numbers dying unconfessed in this western diocese because priests could not be found has panicked the bishop and his advisers into proclaiming that confession might be made to a layperson, even to a woman if a man were not available!" The treasurer looked at John to see the effect of his words, and was gratified to see John's face frozen in shock. "The bishop excuses himself in perpetrating this error, perhaps even heresy, by saying that he was forced to act because so many were dying without the sacraments, and here I use his own words, 'since priests cannot be found who are willing out of zeal, devotion, or for any stipend to visit the sick and administer to them the sacraments of the Church.' Can you believe what I am saying?" John remained shocked and silent. "And, as if this were not enough," the treasurer complained, "in the bishop's palace in Norwich, at this very moment, similar errors are being contemplated, and by the bishop of Ely too." When John recovered enough composure to question him further, the treasurer told him that the senior officers of the bishop of Norwich, left in charge of affairs while their lord was in France on the king's business negotiating a truce, had become so alarmed by a recent spate of untimely deaths in their city that they were urgently discussing the matter among themselves. Rumor also had it that the supporters of such a dispensation were gaining the upper hand by maintaining that the pope himself had already approved it and that they had found it was allowable according to the teaching of the apostles.

In truth, this news, far more than the daily tales of carnage in southern England and London, shook Master John's faith in his Church. He had always considered ministering to the sick and the dying to be among the most important of all his duties. What could be more vital than to wash the soul of sin and guard it with the prayers, rites, and litany of the Church and all its saints as life ebbed from the body? He accepted the customary practice that someone faced with sudden death might confess to whoever happened to be with him or her, but such desperate remedies should only be used in rare and extreme circumstances. A general rule should never be made that allowed the role of the learned, skilled, and holy priest to be cast aside. Inward contrition could be strengthened by confession to a layperson, but contrition could not slay mortal sin; it could only beat it down. Confession to a priest, who had the power of the keys and was in a state of grace, was the only way of slaying the most deadly sin. A priest alone could take out the root and destroy it, heal the wound, wipe out the pain, and make it as if it never had been.

Master John pondered the confusion and hysteria that such extreme and ill-founded responses from the leaders of the Church would provoke. When the world emerged from the pestilence, surely the standing of the clergy was bound to be irreparably damaged. What everlasting comfort could confession to a neighbor really bring? How could God listen as intently when confession was made to a woman? The bishops might hope that all lay confessors were bound by Church precepts to conceal and keep secret all they heard, forbidden by a decree of the sacred canons to betray such confessions, but John knew in his heart that only the clergy could be trusted not to reveal the secrets of the confessional. Moreover, those who thought themselves close to death did not always die, and confession to a layperson would leave the penitent open to blackmail, public shame, and derision.

Yet, despite his misgivings, from that moment on Master John began to turn over in his mind who among his parishioners might be capable of shouldering a few of the burdens and duties of the priest in the midst of a death-dealing pestilence. His flock included an abundance of willing and capable helpers, and, without informing them why, he began to instruct a chosen few on what should be said and done at the bedside of someone in their hour of their death, if they feared a priest might not arrive in time. He spent a long time without success pondering how to harness the energies and boundless devotion of Margery Wodebite for the good of the parish.

In early February an earnest young clerk scarcely out of his teens, with carefully tonsured thick brown hair, arrived at St. Mary's from Ely. Shortly after, another novice, dressed somewhat extravagantly for such a junior cleric, arrived from Norwich. They presented themselves to Master John for employment as chaplains, bearing letters from their bishops confirming that they had recently been ordained into the priesthood.

Their arrival confirmed what John had heard from many sources, that inordinately young men were being hurried through their orders in an unseemly fashion to bolster the ranks of the army of God in its battle against the inevitable onslaught of plague. The two young priests stressed to Master John that they were eager to assist in the cure of souls and gather small fees for their services wherever they might. They professed themselves ready, under his direction, to work tirelessly ministering to the parishioners of Walsham and, if necessary, to die in the service of God. When Master John tested their ability to recite Mass, matins, and hours, he found that they gabbled their words and skipped over parts of the text, and that their Latin needed considerable improvement. For these failings he told them he would refer to them as deacons until they showed satisfactory improvement. He also made a special point of reproving the young man from Norwich for the fashionable peaked shoes he wore, telling him they were a sign of vanity and gave out a signal that he cared too much for the worthless things of this world.

In former and more settled times, Master John might well have sent both of them away, deeming them to be boys in need of further education. But now, though professing an outward show of reluctance, he was inwardly grateful for their abundant youthful energy. Moreover, so great were his fears for the future that he continued with the meticulous training of his chosen lay helpers.

8

New Year, 1349

The monks charged with looking after the health of their communities were called infirmarers. They were chosen for their knowledge of medicine, and as they often served for lengthy periods they acquired exceptional working knowledge of the symptoms and prognosis of many ailments. In addition to responsibility for the health of the community and prescribing treatment for the sick, infirmarers consulted with a variety of medical practitioners, including leading specialists brought from a considerable distance and at substantial cost, if the need arose. Although based on many false premises, medieval medicine was to a considerable extent a logically constructed and internally consistent discipline, and therefore convincing to contemporaries. New diseases were expertly assimilated into the existing intellectual framework, and the manner in which the plague of the mid-fourteenth century, which had not been seen for seven hundred years, was incorporated into existing theory was particularly impressive. Academic medicine coexisted with pragmatic medicine, derived from long experience of the ailments of both humans and farm animals, and with a formidable array of pagan and Christian potions and charms.

A university-trained physician stood at the top of his profession. Like Chaucer's doctor of physic,

> *He knew the cause of every malady,*
> *Whether of hot or cold or moist or dry,*

And where engendered and of what humor,
He was a very perfect practitioner.

But the remedies from such expensive physicians were not necessarily more ef-
ficacious than those dispensed by local or itinerant herbalists, healers, leeches,
and quacks.

The nature of surviving sources, as well as their scarcity, means that very
little light can be thrown on disruption to the normal patterns of communica-
tions between towns, villages, and regions. We know from market tolls and cus-
toms accounts that trade as well as production plummeted during 1348–1349,
but it is extremely difficult to glean much hard detail on how people conducted
themselves in the surrounding counties as the plague raged in the capital. In the
circumstances it is reasonable to follow the more loquacious chroniclers and com-
mentators of Italy, France, and elsewhere, and surmise that people in England
were also fearful of contagion, sensibly tended to shun contact with strangers,
and tried to stop them coming into their settlements. But these sensible precau-
tions created tension, not only with the need to buy and sell goods and earn
money in order to survive, but with the desire for spiritual nourishment, which
might be sought from itinerant clergy as well as the local parish clergy and
church. The reprobates among such wayfarers have been immortalized in
Chaucer's portraits of the friar, summoner, and pardoner, with the former "an
easy man to give penance" for money, and the latter's bag "brimful of pardons,
come from Rome all hot."

⊰⊱

The two new young clerics soon began to provide welcome support to the two priests who assisted in ministering to the spiritual needs of Master John's large and populous parish, and this prompted him to reflect again on an invitation he had received a couple of weeks before to visit his friend Richard, the infirmarer at the abbey of Bury. The summons from Richard was urgent in tone, but out of tiredness and devotion to his parishioners, and perhaps fear of what he might learn, John had delayed responding to the entreaty. Now, however, he could be spared for a day or so. As soon as he informed his housekeeper of his plans, a rumor started to spread through the village that the monks of Bury had discovered a sure means of protection against the plague and a cure for those who were afflicted by it, and that Master John was going to collect the medication and bring it back to Walsham. The truth, however, was that his friend's letter contained no such marvelous tidings but simply urged him to visit soon so that Richard could inform him of the many discoveries about the plague found in ancient texts in the abbey library. While there were possibly some grounds for optimism in what Richard had written, try as he might John could not construe its words to imply that the secrets of the plague had been uncovered and a cure had been found.

Since travelers were likely to be treated with suspicion or even hostility, John decided to leave early and arrive at Bury before midmorning. Taking back paths and detours around villages, and keeping his horse at a trot when near any cottages, John had an uneventful journey until he drew within half a mile of the city. There he was forced roughly to a halt by a band of men armed with staves, knives, and a sword or two. They announced that they had been directed by the citizens of Bury to stop anyone entering who did not have lawful business that would be useful to the residents. When Master John told them who he was and protested at their rudeness, they told him to hold his peace, and that so far their actions had ensured that their city remained free of the plague. The men kept their distance while John explained why he had come to Bury, and then he unhooked his cloak to reveal his clerical chasuble. In further evidence of his good intentions, he offered his letter of invitation to the leader, a brawny miller wearing a dusty white coat with a blue hood, who told him to place it on the ground. Reluctantly, after walking around it a few times and peering for signs of the plague, the miller picked the parchment up with the ends of his fingers and held it at arm's length while he perused it. Perhaps he recognized the name of the monk who had signed it, for John began to sense that he might be permitted to enter the town. But first he was made to strip to his undergarments and turn about while holding up his arms and spreading his legs, so that he could show the motley band of sentinels that he had no signs of the plague about him.

Though he had demonstrated that he was a priest, was free of the pestilence, and on permissible business, Master John still found himself accompanied to the abbey by one of the men, who insisted that they take the most direct route and not stop on the way. Unusually, John found the gates of the abbey barred, and he was forced to explain his business to the gatekeeper at considerable length, even though he knew the face of his inquisitor on the other side of the grill well from previous visits. Eventually his friend Richard came to the gate, and it was opened for him to enter.

Richard had shown an interest in medicine from an early age and had been in charge of the infirmary for many years. It was his duty as infirmarer to supervise medical care for the monks when they were sick, arrange for the regular bloodletting of the whole community, supervise the herb garden, order medical supplies from apothecaries and grocers, and deal with the physicians and surgeons he summoned to treat monks he could not cure himself. Richard liked to spend much of his time in a small stone room lined with clay and metal jars of various sizes and colors, grinding up herbs and spices with his favorite pestle and mortar and preparing the potions and unguents he used to treat his patients. But he also had to find time to supervise the servants and young monks who nursed the residents and day patients, direct the gardeners who grew many of the herbs he used, and keep an eye on the cook who prepared a wide variety of meals, each one of which had to be appropriate to the particular patient's condition.

The infirmary occupied a large site in the monastery. In addition to a hall which sometimes accommodated as many as six beds, it had a number of private chambers intended for the more senior monks and those whose condition required them to be isolated from the rest of the patients. Yet to Richard's constant annoyance, much of this space tended to be filled with the old, the tired, and the lazy, rather than the genuinely sick. In recent weeks he had been trying especially hard to release vacant beds in preparation for the pestilence. But as they walked through the courts and corridors Richard muttered resentfully that he had just been forced by the abbot, William of Burnham, to give up his best chamber to accommodate a rich lay benefactor who wished in his old age to retire to a place where both his body and his soul would be well looked after.

As he journeyed to Bury, seeing no signs of disease anywhere, Master John had become somewhat optimistic. But he could see at once that

Richard had little good news to impart. As was his custom, the infirmarer began with a lengthy preamble, but this time in uncharacteristically hushed tones rather than the loud voice with which he usually broadcast his skills and learning. And alarmingly, he halted his discourse whenever anyone came within earshot.

"Since word of the great new pestilence first reached this abbey more than two years ago," Richard reported, "I have meticulously quizzed every visitor with any knowledge of how the pestilence raged in other countries, and how the great physicians of the world observed it. As it spread toward England and I became convinced that we would not be spared, I have sought to supplement these haphazard and sometimes untrustworthy accounts with a systematic understanding of the truth contained in the writings of the great masters of medicine. This superb library contains a score of books on medicine, including many written by ancient Greek and Roman scholars who knew all the secrets of the world. I have searched them all for references to plague, and I have made a number of journeys to view books in other libraries, in Cambridge, Ely, and Thetford. But what I found there added precious little to what I had gleaned in my own abbey's library. My eyesight has suffered from the long hours spent reading by candlelight, and my studies have been constantly interrupted by the entreaties of brethren who are forever finding suspicious marks on their skin or pains in their bodies, which in fear they foolishly take to be symptoms of the plague."

Richard laughed scornfully but John, who was by now displaying some impatience, urged his friend to reveal his findings. Although Richard resented being hurried, he soon arrived at his first major point: "In all of the works of the ancient scholars I have consulted, along with the multitude of lesser works written by more recent foreign and English writers, there is nothing to surpass the quality and authority of the great Greek master, Galen. Therefore, I have undertaken a most careful of study of all of Galen's works which I could lay my hands on; especially those in which the master comments on the achievements of Hippocrates, the greatest physician who ever lived. This has shown me that Hippocrates is the fount of all certain knowledge on diseases such as the present plague. But Galen took Hippocrates' understanding of these matters even further. He was able to do this, I believe, because many, many centuries ago, Galen might well have lived through an epidemic of the same diseases that are striking the world now."

These last words gripped Master John's attention, and he listened intently as the infirmarer went on with his analysis. "Galen taught us that the body has three crucial sectors, *emunctoria* he calls them, dominated in turn by the brain, the heart, and the liver. Now, from a study of all of the symptoms of these present scourges, I have found that in the type of pestilence that gives rise to great swellings, these swellings, commonly called buboes, form in one of three places on the body, each of which corresponds to one of the *emunctoria*. When a victim is infected, probably by breathing in foul vapors, the poison enters the body and goes to either the brain, the heart, or the liver. The body forces the poison out of these vital organs, so if it is forced from the brain it forms a swelling in the neck or behind the ears. If it comes from the heart it commonly forms a bubo in the underarm, and if from the liver, the swelling appears in the groin or on the thigh."

"See, I have one of Galen's treatises here," he said triumphantly, "in which these lumps are explained." And with that he took down a large text, strongly bound in dark brown leather, opened it at a place he had marked with a quill, and began to read from a section entitled "The Art of Medicine," asking John not to be offended that he was translating the Latin into English for him, because of the technical terms it contained: "'Unnatural lumps are to be divided into inflammations, indurations, tumors, and *erysipelas*.' I am still seeking guidance on how to translate this last word, which is Greek, but I am hopeful that Galen could be describing exactly the same lumps in the groin and the neck that swell up on victims of this present pestilence," he interjected, before returning to his text.

"A constant pain in a part indicates either a dissolution of continuity there or an overall change of the substance. Continuity is dissolved by cutting, erosion, compression, or tension. The substance is changed by heat, cold, dryness, or moisture." John's mind was already beginning to wander, but his attention was gripped by Richard's excitement as his finger ran down toward the bottom of the folio. "See here, 'Substances expelled may be divided into parts of the affected area, excretions, or matter contained within the part in its natural state.' Time and again we have been told that the swellings caused by the present pestilence excrete substances that are not part of the natural substance of that part of the body, like blood, but rather pus and bile."

"But what do your researches tell us about how we may cure or avoid the pestilence?" asked John eagerly. Richard laid the book down and closed it with some force. Then, at last, he began to explain all that he knew, gathered from the vast knowledge he had gained from all the books he had studied and the great skill acquired from his long experience treating the sick. Master John listened intently to the soft and occasionally wavering voice of his friend disclose the awful truth about the pestilence that was about to destroy them. As a priest, Richard first dealt with theological issues, and after a lengthy discourse he concluded that, while scholars might dispute whether the sinful and unrepentant will be more vulnerable than the confessed and contrite when the plague came to the place where they lived, everyone was in mortal danger. He further elaborated on how the pestilence invaded the body and then coursed through it. But, much to John's frustration, he refused to be rushed into disclosing how the pestilence might be cured or avoided. Finally, after many promptings, Richard conceded that he had little advice to give on cures.

"I have not so far discovered any cure that works once the victim is infected, and I am not convinced that any exists, although some victims do recover," he said flatly. "But for the avoidance of this pestilence, I am able to give some very useful advice, which is in addition to what we all know about the necessity of keeping our humors in balance." John looked up eagerly. "But you will not like to hear it," Richard said mischievously. "A host of doctors, now and in the past, have claimed to have found the means of escaping infection by using a miscellany of different remedies—taking this or that potion, avoiding this or that food, or this or that activity. However, I am not convinced that any of their advice will work with this present scourge, which is far more devastating than anything I have read about. But this much I do know for certain. The chance of infection for a healthy person is greatly increased by inhaling air breathed out by those who are sick, even if that healthy person is a priest administering the last rites. Further, it has many times been reported by learned doctors, and confirmed in the books, that an airy spirit of poisonous vapor is emitted by the eyes when someone is heavily infected and close to death, and that this vapor can pass on the sickness merely by striking the eye of a bystander."

John interrupted, "This must be how people have become infected even though they have scrupulously avoided any intimate contact with the sick. The clerk from Avignon repeatedly asserted that this had happened, in the face of your skeptical questioning."

Richard impatiently waved him quiet. "For these reasons, I conclude that the best means by far of avoiding catching the plague is not only to shun all contact with other people when plague is in your town or village, but to flee immediately from where the plague is. If you have sense you should flee even from where it is threatening to come. As the experts have learned across Europe: if you wish to stay alive, flee the plague quickly, go far away, and return as late as possible.

"But of course," the infirmarer added wryly, "all this expert advice so painstakingly gathered is of no use whatsoever to either of us. Because a priest cannot desert his flock nor a monk flee his cloister."

Notwithstanding his bleak conclusions, Richard later divulged that for some months he had been building up stocks of aloes, salt of Ammon, and myrrh, in order to provide protection for members of his community against the plague and offer them the best chance of survival. As he handed a tiny quantity of each to John and demonstrated with a small brass pestle and mortar how to pound them and infuse them in wine, he said, "These palliatives are already becoming very expensive, and when the plague strikes this region they will become impossible to obtain. But they are worth searching for, because Rufus of Ephesus, one of the most respected of the ancient physicians, never knew of a person dying of plague who did not recover after this draught."

John chuckled cynically. "Even I have heard of Rufus of Ephesus, and if the cure is that simple and that well-known why have so many physicians in so many countries confessed their helplessness to save victims from the pestilence?"

Richard rebuked him, but with a twinkle in his eye, saying that medicine was far too complex a field of study for even a clever man to understand without many years of study. And he quickly moved on to the other essential task, the spiritual healing of the dead as well as the living. The infirmarer advised Master John to buy as much oil as he could afford for annealing the dying, and to have stores of wax and candles put by for the torrent of deaths sure to follow when the plague arrived. John had already begun to stockpile supplies, but he promised he would not fail to visit the market in the city on his way home to make further purchases. "And, most important of all," Richard stressed to his dear friend, "do all that you can to welcome into your parish as many of the itinerant clergy as you can. Treat them in a friendly manner, and not too severely. Even if this means accepting those who in the past you would have had no hesitation in rejecting, and permitting them to charge higher fees than you would like or they will never stay."

As Master John rode slowly back to Walsham, his saddle bags bulging with wax, candles, and holy oil, he reflected ruefully that, for all the fine words and deep wisdom he had absorbed that day, running away from the plague was probably the only effective course of action. Any cures, however painstakingly based on the teachings of the ancient masters, were likely to prove far less effective than simply fleeing from areas where the scourge raged. This dismal conclusion fitted very well with all information he had previously acquired from the abundance of reliable and unreliable reports he had heard, that told of hoards of terrified people grabbing a few possessions and taking flight in the face of an approaching plague. Though he shuddered to accept it, the effectiveness of running away added weight to the infamous tales of priests deserting their flocks in their hour of greatest need. But flight was impossible for a good priest. He knew that he would have to take himself daily into the very heart of the sickness, minister to the dying in their infected houses, and bury their polluted bodies. Though he must remember not to look into their eyes.

Throughout the dark, wet days of winter Walsham church was brilliantly lit by a profusion of torches and candles, many made with the finest beeswax. All these lights had been eagerly donated by parishioners, both rich and poor, in numbers never before seen. Where there had once been chattering, gossip, and occasional laughter during services, there was now rapt concentration, complemented by the almost constant murmuring of prayers. Yet members of the flock were not content to be silent witnesses to the liturgy in St. Mary's, and they responded with fervent recitations of Ave Verum Corpus when the Host was elevated, piteous wailings when the sufferings of Christ on the cross were contemplated, and the chanting of prayers to the Virgin Mary whenever there was a lull in the service or a new act of ritual raised the level of excitement.

> *Hail be thou Mary full of grace;*
> *God is with thee in every place;*
> *Blessed be thou of all women;*
> *And the fruit of thy womb Jesus!*
> *Amen.*

The great majority of villagers took solace in these rituals and drew spiritual comfort and strength from the sense of participation and community. But there were a few grave and self-contained individuals in Walsham who, although extremely pious, took strong objection to all exuberant outward displays of religious emotion. These plain-minded folk complained that the ceaseless prayers and Masses, processions, genuflections, inclinations, censings, kissings, oblations, kindling of lights, and pilgrimages were a distraction from the contemplation of God, and apt to confuse and deflect people from the leading of a good life. Resting on their own convictions, they made few calls on the time of priests, praying largely in their own homes or in those of other like-minded people, silently confessing their sins. For they held that the path to salvation was primarily in their own hands, and lay strictly in leading a good life.

Contact with London virtually ceased in the weeks after Christmas. Scarcely anyone could be found who was willing to carry goods to the city, and even those who attempted to come to Walsham with commodities from more than a few miles distant were often shunned. So, with ample stores of food from the recent good harvest, and with the depths of winter confining mobility and the availability of work, Walsham closed in on itself and tried to shut off the outside world.

The craving for isolation heightened in late January as word filtered through that the pestilence was raging ever more fiercely in London, with tens of thousands dying and cemeteries so overflowing that new burial grounds had to be speedily consecrated. In this climate of fear even minor or common ailments in the village could panic the patient and his family, and induce near hysteria in friends and neighbors who had recently spent time with him. Although none of the more lurid reports of excessive and inexplicable deaths in the vicinity of Walsham, caused by such portents as the coughing of blood or swellings in the neck or groin, were confirmed, it made good sense to deter strangers and visitors, especially those who came from the south. Anyone who aroused suspicion or stayed too long was treated harshly and driven away. From time to time attempts were made to bar entry to all outsiders, but the numbers of roads, tracks, and paths leading into the village from all sides and crisscrossing its lands made this impossible.

Yet, rage as the plague might in London, there were no signs that it was stirring far from the capital, and the numbers of deaths in the towns and villages around Walsham did not show any reliable signs of increasing. Though some in the village counseled against placing too much reliance on the reports of commercial people who had much to gain by playing down the dangers of trade and travel, it was considered a most favorable sign that those who continued to bring essential commodities from the south all seemed to be in the best of health and repeatedly swore that they had encountered no signs of plague along the way.

Consequently, by early February, when a fragile confidence began to grow, some restrictions were relaxed. Among the many familiar faces who were once again welcomed to come and go from Walsham were drovers taking animals to distant markets, merchants and traders riding in carts loaded with goods or leading teams of horses with bulging packs, and peddlers and hucksters tramping on foot carrying bags of cheap goods. But certain unfamiliar faces were also greeted. Some of these, mainly men but a few women, belonged to the purveyors of medical, magical, and spiritual protection against the plague. The numbers of sellers of potions and charms mushroomed during this time of impending doom, but they all did good business among the fearful folk of Suffolk. A few of the quacks had visited Walsham before, but most had not; some had impressive qualifications and had acquired good reputations, but most had not. Pardoners, unlicensed as well as licensed, brought wallets stuffed with little rolls of parchment that were powerful enough, they claimed, to absolve all the sins which weighed heavily on souls and offended God (see figure 20). They brandished sacred documents hot from Rome which bore the signatures of cardinals or even the pope himself. If these lofty indulgences proved too expensive for the poor or too fanciful for the skeptical, the villagers were offered a cheaper but still attractive alternative obtained from bishops, priors, and archdeacons: pardons designed to suit the size of every purse.

Holy men came to Walsham bearing pieces of bone from the skeletons of saints, hairs from hallowed heads, fingers from sacred hands, and pieces of wood from the cross of Christ, or at the least a chunk of wood from the coffin in which he had been laid. If asked, they found it easy to produce from their packs a fragment of the veil of Our Lady, or perhaps her shoe, or the ring of St. John the Evangelist, or even the very finger which John the Baptist had pointed at Christ. Some of these holy relics were brought in glass bottles, so they could be seen but not touched; others were handed around and could be kissed for a halfpenny, or purchased for 4d. When the incredulous, or the simply curious, asked for details of the provenance of these objects, they were told long and mysterious tales of far-off countries and a series of providential survivals and fortuitous meetings, which had brought them from the Holy Land many centuries ago to the green fields of Suffolk in 1349. The arrival of these holy relics in Walsham was truly a miracle, and every step in their long journey over the centuries had been guided by God's own hand.

The pardoners and preachers often gave fiery sermons to announce their arrival and gather the largest number of people. These diatribes inspired fear and whetted the appetite for the wares they sold. The crowds who gathered were told of the coming of death-dealing pestilence and of the day of doom, and were captivated by biblical quotations such as, "Before him went the pestilence, and burning coals went forth at his feet"; and again, "there shall be famines, and pestilences, and earthquakes in diverse places. All these are the beginnings of sorrows." When Master John permitted them, which was but rarely, the pious wayfarers declaimed in church. And when, despite the entreaties of their supporters, they were refused entry, they freely gathered audiences together in the churchyard or in the road outside, in the market or even in the fields (see figure 21).

Almost all itinerant preachers and pardoners left Walsham with their purses far heavier than when they arrived. It was not that the simple folk of Walsham believed all they were told; time and again they saw through the masks of false piety to the greed and cynicism beneath. And they laughed heartily when hecklers claimed they had been shown in the last three months more wood from Christ's cross than would have been used to build Noah's ark. But so great was the terror of being struck down in a state of sin within the next few weeks or months that few dared to reject every opportunity to gain spiritual cleansing and divine protection. While there were some who eagerly offered up their last silver groats for a piece of bone which looked more likely to have come from a pig's carcass than from a saint's holy body, the more skeptical majority felt that it was worth some small change from their pocket to have the possibility of benefiting from the spiritual beneficence of a particularly convincing memento or document.

The arrival of a doctor or leech provoked a similar tremor of excitement in the village, as did the cunning men and women who plausibly claimed to have herbs, potions, or charms which would guard against infection, particularly that inflicted by the hitherward hastening pestilence. The clergy of the parish, of course, continually counseled that the surest way of surviving the plague was to be free of sin; through God's will, medicines would only be effective if they were taken by a blameless person. But most felt it foolish not to seek protection for the body as well as the soul.

Prominent among those who offered their services to all who could pay were the finely dressed doctors of physic who came to Walsham at the behest of the new resident of the fine moated manor house of High Hall, Edmund de Welles. Edmund, who had succeeded in 1347 to the joint ownership of the manor of High Hall with his sister Margery on the death of her husband, Nicholas of Walsham, was becoming increasingly obsessed with dread of the pestilence. Of late he had turned his attention to compiling every detail of the very best advice on how to avoid sickness and how to cure himself if he became infected. Naturally he interrogated Master John at length on what he had learned during his recent visit to the abbey of Bury, and these conversations helped focus his thoughts.

Edmund at first eagerly accepted the advice of his physicians who concluded that, since the pestilence was borne in the air in a cloud of infection,

blown hither and thither by the prevailing winds, and since it infected its
victims when they breathed in these poisonous vapors, sweet air should be
used to combat the infected air. This he did by holding posies of flowers to
his nose, especially when meeting anyone, and by ordering incense to be
burned continuously in all the rooms he frequented in the Hall. However,
Edmund was not inclined simply to follow the directions of his learned advisers, even the most eminent of them, and devised his own regime to protect himself against infection. Enthusiastically pushing the logic of the
recommended remedies further, he noted that posies and sweet smells had
not protected against the plague in Italy, France, and other parts of Europe.
Therefore it seemed obvious, he reasoned, that air poisoned by the pestilence must be more potent than sweet air, just as the stink of rotting fish or
bad eggs easily overwhelms the delicate fragrance of flowers and most
spices. Accordingly, Edmund decided to create a foul but harmless vapor of
his own to repel the pestilential air that might threaten him. This he did by
ordering his servants to gather together each morning the content of all the
privies in the hall, from his sister's bed chamber as well as from the grooms'
and scullions' piss pots, and tip them into a cavernous brass cooking pot
which he had brought up to his private chamber from the kitchen. Three
times each day he bent over the brimming pot with a towel draped over his
head and, for as long as he could bear, he took as deep breaths as his gorge
would permit. Then smiling with satisfaction, he would reflect that he had
gained double immunity. First, the vapors would provide a strong antidote
against the ingress of pestilence into his body, and second, the vomiting
that often followed directly afterward would expel any noxious substances
that managed to penetrate his defenses.

The doctors from Bury and farther afield who visited lord Edmund at
High Hall often tarried to conduct a little extra business among the richer
residents elsewhere in the village, but their fees were very high and few
were able or willing to pay. More affordable were the less exalted practitioners who eagerly tramped the roads and paths in search of new customers. Those with homemade potions from common herbs were the
cheapest, and those who could speak convincingly of the signs, points, and
positions of the constellations the most persuasive. With ease these aspir-
ing astrologers captivated their clients with fluent discourses on how the
planets rule: how some, like Jupiter, are joyful, and others, like Hercules,

are wrathful; how one planet is favorable when it is in the ascendant, and another when it is in decline. Also compelling were those who knew the secrets of the waxing and waning of the four humors of the body: blood, which was hot and moist and came from the heart; phlegm, which was cold and moist and came from the brain; yellow bile, which was hot and dry and came from the liver; and black bile, which was cold and dry and came from the spleen. It was obvious to all who listened that every ailment must be due to an imbalance between the humors, and that only those folk whose humors were in perfect balance could expect to resist the infection of the plague. Unsurprisingly, virtually all whom these quacks examined were found to have one or more humors which were either deficient or excessive, so they readily purchased the expensive potions which would right this dangerous imbalance before the plague arrived.

Who could afford not to do business with those who claimed to bring cures hot-foot from plague-stricken France or Italy, where they had just been discovered? Who could resist the means of deflecting the arrows of infection from penetrating the body, or of lessening their power should they strike? Finally, there were the tried and trusted local healers who had proved themselves useful in dispensing healing herbs to fight the diseases of people and animals in the past and could often be relied on to dispense cheap but powerful potions and charms to ward off all sicknesses.

As winter began to wane without any verifiable sign of plague appearing in the village or anywhere round about, the embers of hope were kindled. As far as could be discovered, plague did not appear to have strayed far from London. Naturally, caution urged against tempting fate by giving voice to optimism, and it was clearly unwise to place reliance on the word of tradesmen and merchants who had much to gain by playing down the dangers of trade and travel. But people could not stop themselves wondering whether it had been God's plan all along to select London for extreme punishment because of the extravagant luxury and unbridled sinfulness of that city's inhabitants. As each day passed, it began to seem ever more possible that all their prayers and processions, and their acts of mercy and contrite entreaties for forgiveness, were managing to secure a deliverance for simple, pious Walsham.

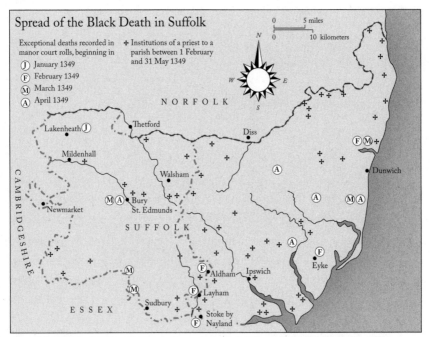

Spread of the Black Death in Suffolk

Exceptional deaths recorded in
maner court rolls, beginning in

Ⓙ January 1349

Ⓕ February 1349

Ⓜ March 1349

Ⓐ April 1349

✝ Institutions of a priest to a
parish between 1 February
and 31 May 1349

0 ____ 5 miles
0 ____ 10 kilometers

N O R F O L K

Lakenheath Ⓙ

Thetford

Diss

Ⓕ Ⓜ ✝

Dunwich

Mildenhall

Walsham

Ⓐ

Ⓐ

Ⓜ Ⓐ

Newmarket

Ⓜ Ⓐ Bury
St. Edmunds

S U F F O L K

Ⓐ

Ⓕ
Eyke

C A M B R I D G E S H I R E

Ⓜ

Ⓕ Aldham

Ipswich

Ⓜ

Ⓕ Layham

E S S E X

Sudbury

Stoke by

Ⓕ Nayland

Source: Mark Bailey, *Medieval Suffolk: An Economic and Social History* (Woodbridge, 2007), p. 178.

9

Lent and Easter, 1349

England is blessed with relatively rich collections of fourteenth-century records, both local and central, but it is very difficult to construct a precise chronology of the spread of the pestilence across the country. Manorial court rolls, which scrupulously record the deaths of the lord's tenants, are potentially the most informative of all, but the precise dating of the epidemic depends both on courts being held at the right time and the survival of records of the proceedings, a co-incidence which happens but rarely. Fortunately, however, we are exceptionally well informed about the region around Walsham. For example, it is known for certain that almost twenty tenants had died by the first days of February on the manor of Lakenheath, a village less than thirty miles west of Walsham. The early arrival of the plague in Lakenheath, which is documented in the parchment roll of the manor court held on February 11, was probably due to the direct river communications that it had along the River Ouse with the major port of Bishop's Lynn, now known as King's Lynn. The early onset of plague can also be revealed in a group of manors close to Ipswich in the far east of Suffolk, around twenty-five miles from Walsham. The manor of Eyke, some four miles from Woodbridge, held particularly frequent courts, and six deaths, an unusually high figure, are recorded in the roll of the session held on February 21, and a further eighteen in the next held on March 28. Relatively close by at Aldham, the manor court held on March 6 recorded ten deaths, while at Layham, a small manor less than four miles from Ipswich, a suspiciously high number of four deaths were recorded in the court held on February 20, and a further twenty-eight in that held on April 8.

The forty weekdays of fasting and penitence during Lent began on Ash Wednesday, which in 1349 fell on February 25, and culminated in Holy Week. The aim of Lent was to prepare for the celebration of the Passion, death, and resurrection of Christ by purifying the heart and mind, and it understandably took on a special significance with the threat of dreadful pestilence hanging over the country. Holy Week, the period from Palm Sunday to Easter Day, was punctuated by elaborate ceremonies, and the laity of the fourteenth century attached the greatest significance to the Palm Sunday procession, the Tenebrae services on Wednesday, Thursday, and Friday, when candles were snuffed out one by one to symbolize the abandonment of Christ by the apostles, the "creeping to the cross" and the ritual of the burial of the Host in the Easter Sepulcher on Good Friday, and the annual receiving of Communion by all parishioners after High Mass on Easter Sunday.

As far as it is possible to judge, the pestilence struck Walsham close to Easter Day, which this year fell on April 12, was fading fast by early June, and had departed by late June. Not a single tenant death was reported at the Walsham manor court session of March 6, but no fewer than 103 were reported at the next session, which was held on June 15. That the pestilence was virtually over by this latter date is indicated by the proceedings of the next Walsham court of August 1, in which a mere five further deaths were registered. Fortunately, additional evidence of the duration of the epidemic in the parish is provided by the proceedings of the courts of High Hall, where eleven out of the total of fifteen tenant deaths suffered on the small submanor occurred before May 25. It was in April and May 1349 that the plague in England probably reached its peak, in terms of geographical spread and number of deaths. At this time the pestilence not only raged in Walsham and throughout Suffolk and its neighboring counties in East Anglia, but over much of the country from Cornwall in the far southwest to Yorkshire in the north.

⊰⊱

C ruelly, the poisonous fingers of the pestilence began stretching toward Walsham at the same time as the sprouts of the wheat sown in late autumn were beginning to appear. And just as attention was turning to plowing the fallow land that had been set aside for the sowing of spring barley and peas and beans, hope of deliverance was all but crushed, even in the most optimistic hearts. Death was breaking out from the bounds of London and moving swiftest, not as villagers had feared along the tracks and roads which radiated northward through Hertfordshire, Essex, and Cambridgeshire, but seemingly carried on the ships and boats which transported goods and people around the coasts and up and down the navigable rivers.

The terrible news of the proximity of the pestilence was first delivered to the residents of Walsham by a young man who had lodged in the village for a couple of years, earning his living from casual labor. Hearing that his eldest brother had died, the young man set out at the end of the second week in February for Lakenheath, where his brother had a small farm. Lakenheath lay an easy walk away, a little more than twenty miles to the northwest on the far side of an expanse of sandy heath land. The young laborer, who like all his fellows yearned for land of his own, could hardly contain his excitement. He told his friends, as well as anyone else who would listen, that he was in line to inherit a cottage and a small plot from his unmarried brother, together with all its household possessions, livestock, and tools. But just a few days after setting off for Lakenheath, he returned considerably distressed to his lodgings in Walsham, saying that another brother older than he, long believed to be dead, had unexpectedly turned up to claim his inheritance. People were curious, however, and some of the replies he gave to the many questions that were fired at him, about his journey and happenings in the wider world, were thought more than a little odd and evasive. In the climate of fear which had recently gripped the village, suspicions soon multiplied, and it was decided that Walter Osbern, the reeve, and Geoffrey Rath, the hayward, should interrogate him further. After a few weak denials the young laborer blurted out that he had arrived in Lakenheath to find that it had been struck by an awful new kind of disease, and that huge numbers of men, women, and children were dying there.

Details were urgently demanded, and the young man readily recounted how the large and normally bustling village had been unexpectedly quiet when he arrived. The few people he encountered hurried away from him without speaking. Eventually he found his brother's tiny cottage sitting at the front of its couple of acres and went to enter, but the neighbors called to him not to go in because the owner had died of the pestilence and his body had only just been collected for burial. They told him that a pestilence had arrived in Lakenheath a week or so before, which was killing all who became infected by it. It had been brought, or so they thought, on one of the many barges that plied along the River Ouse carrying goods from the port of Lynn on the north coast of Norfolk, and now each day more people were dying than on the day before. More than fifty in the village had already perished, along with the bargee and his wife, and many more had been taken ill.

At this point the young man's tale was interrupted by the hayward, who accused him of exaggerating and spreading alarm. "No, this is all true," he protested. "My brother's neighbors told me of the court session they had attended only a few days before I arrived, where the deaths of a score of tenants had been sworn and registered. By my own eyes I could also see that people were sick and dying all about, and everyone was saying that it was the same in many of the other villages around. So, not wanting to die myself, I decided to leave after spending only one night in my brother's cottage. I sold his sheep, pigs, and chickens to the neighbors for a few pence, then I nailed the door of the cottage shut and hurried back here, carrying what I could with me. You can see the brass cooking pot, spade, and blanket over there, and I also have these three latten spoons which I am willing to sell."

The inquisitors nodded to each other as if they were convinced, and the young man was pleased that they believed him at last. But instead of offering the hand of friendship as he had hoped, they shrank from him in fear and shouted at him to leave Walsham immediately. They threw him out of the door and hurled his few possessions after him. He spent that night and the next few days hiding in a barn on the edge of the village, but he was soon discovered and driven out of the village.

It was not long before the story of the young laborer's encounter with plague little more than a day's walk to the west was confirmed. By the first week in March, even the most skeptical villagers were convinced that the plague was raging close by to the south and east of Walsham, as well as to the west. Carriers with packhorses whose itineraries included the cloth-making towns and villages to the south of Bury, such as Sudbury and Lavenham, reported that they were no longer able to go there to buy cloths because death had advanced from the southeast. Other travelers also revealed that the pestilence was traveling along the coast and being brought inland toward Walsham along the Deben and Waveney valleys.

A peddler who regularly visited Walsham selling trinkets and shoddy clothing told how he had been stopped a mile or so outside Stoke-by-Nayland near Colchester, where he was due to collect some combs and brushes, and warned that the pestilence was in the village. He had fled northward and soon learned that Stoke was far from alone in its suffering, and that a whole string of prosperous settlements close to Colchester had been hit by death. His audience solemnly noted this would have occurred around the same time as the pestilence had settled in Lakenheath. The peddler went on to tell them that he had come across a man, a woman, and two children huddled by an old handcart. He thought they were sleeping but on drawing closer, he found they were dead. Within just a few miles of that terrifying sight, he had seen many dead or dying people from a distance and encountered others acting very strangely, some almost dancing with agony, some seemingly fit but threatening to kill him if he came near. After that he had made his way back to Walsham across the fields avoiding the tracks and roads he normally tramped along.

News of the imminence of the pestilence provoked a fresh wave of hasty departures from Walsham, despite warnings from the peddler and other travelers that they would be safer if they remained where they were. Most of the manor court session on March 6, which was only sparsely attended, was taken up with the registration of large numbers of sales and exchanges of small pieces of land, which fearful people had hastily concluded before they left the manor. As few other items of business had been brought before the court, the steward soon called the proceedings to an end and allowed the tenants to return quickly to the relative safety of their homes and farms.

Faith among the pious that exemption would be somehow granted from God's punishment and hope by the worldly that good fortune might intervene to save them had helped Walsham sustain a grip on normality.

But now these comforts were being steadily supplanted by a broad spectrum of emotions ranging from extreme terror to calm resignation. The
particular emotion that each person experienced naturally depended on
individual character and circumstances. Although, in truth, as the days
and weeks passed, many people found themselves running through a
whole range of feelings. Yet much of the routine of life had to continue as
usual—land had to be plowed and sown, weeds pulled up, livestock
tended, produce bought and sold, and wages earned. However, a coldness
shrank the dealings that people had with each other, and sometimes also
with their families and closest friends. Most business was conducted
curtly, with conversations kept to a minimum and contacts restricted.

Except, that is, for those reckless folk who felt that, as the end of the
world was nigh and all would soon perish, they might as well live for the
present and spend what money they had on pleasure. Within the confines
of Walsham this usually meant passing long hours in the alehouses which
were liberally sprinkled across the parish. The wanton, both men and
women, drank excessively, gambled recklessly, and enjoyed each other's
intimate company. This crowd of seemingly carefree folk, who were more
numerous than might be imagined, even found it diverting to make jokes
about death and the pestilence. However, there was general agreement
among this dissolute crowd that fat Simon went too far when he cleared
Alice Pye's packed tavern by suddenly falling off his bench, screaming
and gesturing to a large swelling on his upper thigh. The horrified
carousers who glanced at him writhing on his back on the floor, and did
indeed see a great lump in his crotch, ran screaming from the tavern.
When Simon chased after them into the road laughing and exposing his
huge erect cock, he was given a sound beating and had the door locked
against him. For many years after the regulars at the Pye's alehouse took
grim delight in telling of the prank of Simon Greathorn, as he was
henceforth dubbed.

As each day of March passed, the plague spread ever more widely through
the towns and villages of Essex, Cambridgeshire, and Suffolk, and drew
ever closer to Walsham. As if it were an invisible cloud blown by the wind,
the deadly infection made its way, never ceasing to disperse itself despite
all the precautions taken to halt it. At the manor court held on March 6,

the steward, at the prompting of his lord and lady, uttered some words of comfort, but just two days later a violent mob raised the hue and cry against a band of travelers who had fled in fear of the pestilence from Aldham, which lay little more than a day's walk to the south. The fugitives had been spotted by a patrol hiding in a clump of trees close to the path which led to Westhorpe, and at least two of them were said to be bearing signs of the plague on their faces. Over the next couple of weeks desperate runaways were apprehended from towns and villages no more than ten or fifteen miles distant, and after just a few more days signs of pestilence began to make their appearance in adjacent villages to the south and east—Wyverstone, Wetherden, Elmswell. Then two Walsham carters who had taken grain and wool to Botesdale market returned in great haste. They had seen a young man dying by a hot pie stall. At first an angry crowd had surrounded the pie seller, blaming his pies for poisoning a customer. However, someone pointed out a large blue and black swelling on the young man's neck and they all ran off. Walsham was being encircled by an ever-tightening band of death.

It was too late to flee. During the remaining days of waiting for the death to come the last few miles to Walsham, the village lay under an eerie calm. Most felt helpless in the face of divine anger and found their resistance drained by the infinite power of the earthly terror which had cornered them. The pestilence was now everywhere all around, and there was nothing to do but suffer God's will.

So near was the Death, and so ineffective were the prayers, processions, and pilgrimages in halting or slowing its march toward their village, that even Master John found himself succumbing to the collective hysteria which repeatedly broke out in St. Mary's church. He had wracked his brains, read and reread all his sacred texts and guides many times, and searched every corner of his experience, but he could not identify any of the profoundly grave sins in the people of his parish which could justify this awful punishment from God. Perhaps it was indeed the end of the world, when the very last stains of sin would be washed from every soul before it entered eternal bliss.

Master John, though widely respected for his learning, wisdom, and compassion, was repeatedly made to feel hopelessly inadequate by his inability to give answers to the questions fired at him by anxious and often angry parishioners. Most folk seemed visibly strengthened by any-thing he told them, however ephemeral or labored it appeared to his scholarly mind. But try as he might, he was unable to find his words of comfort passably convincing. In one sermon he even found himself join-ing in the hunt for scapegoats by attacking the sins of dealers and traders in Walsham and nearby markets, who were certainly no worse than those found anywhere else. From the pulpit, Master John railed against the brew-ers, bakers, butchers, and cooks who, in addition to overcharging the poor, were so ruled by avarice that they used false oaths to swear to the quality of their products, weighed them with false weights and measures, and adulterated their wares.

"Do not the alewives mix thin halfpenny ale or even dregs with the good penny ale they charge you for? Do not the bakers add sawdust to their bread? The butchers sell meat and the fishmongers fish which are so rotten they would kill a dog? The hot pies you buy so willingly and con-sume so greedily are often stuffed full of unspeakable substances. At the moment, these traders spend their days in wealth. Yet as the prophet Job tells us, in the end they will go down to Hell because of their treachery and tricks." Master John added, almost apologetically and certainly un-convincingly, that so great was the divine displeasure aroused by such conduct that it might well be the cause of the sundry sorrows currently being brought down on the whole community.

The Walsham flock needed no special encouragement to enter the Lenten fasts and confessions with enthusiasm. When their priest, in his first Lenten sermon, reminded his congregation of the need to come to shrift, to lift the veils from the sins in their hearts, and to make amends in prayer and penance, abstinence and almsgiving, for the evil they had committed in the last year, they eagerly embraced his admonitions: "Good people, the time of Lent is entered, the time when we must cleanse ourselves of all misdeeds we have done before. And in this holy time we should abstain more from sin and wretchedness than at other times of the year. Now shall we resolve to fast, to come to the church, and to serve God in holy prayers, and shrive us of our misdeeds."

The Lenten fast this year was exceptionally well observed, and scarcely any villagers failed to make confession, in order to prepare themselves for receiving Communion on Easter Day and, as many felt, for their impending death. Those who were too old or sick to reach the church unaided were helped by family and neighbors out of charity, while the parish clergy tirelessly visited those unable to travel.

As Holy Week approached, there was no slackening of the intensity of devotion, but rather a quickening of fervor. The excitement of the imminent celebration of the Passion was swelled by chilling evidence that deaths were multiplying in communities within a few miles of Walsham. It rose to an almost unbearable crescendo in the scorching heat of an unseasonably warm spring when rumors began circulating that at least two or three families, and maybe even four or five, in the far southeast of the village were secretly nursing members who had been struck down by a mysterious ailment. In the Palm Sunday procession many fainted with ecstasy or with sheer terror of the horrors that surely awaited them. Despite the fears of contagion which wracked the community, it was the largest such assembly that could be remembered. So great were the crowds walking behind the cross that the procession slowed almost to a halt as it squeezed between the houses and hedges in the narrow parts of the road which led from the church up Jolycote Hill. Everyone clutched palms of yew, box, and willow that had been blessed by the priests, and at the end of the day they carried them home to serve as charms to protect their houses against the plague.

Good Friday was a day of immense grief and mourning, in which terror for the future, regrets for the past, and desperate pleading for forgiveness burst into barely controlled passion. For time out of mind, on the day of the crucifixion the clergy and people of Walsham had crept, barefoot and on their knees, down the aisle of St. Mary's to kiss the foot of the cross which was held in front of the altar by the youngest priest. But this year many walked barefoot from their homes while others crawled on hands and knees. Some wriggled forward prostrate on their stomachs across sharp stones and through muddy puddles. Such self-inflicted pain and humility was traditionally in remembrance of Christ's suffering, but this year it was also in fear of God's wrath.

From the pulpit, in his Good Friday sermon, Master John gestured dramatically toward the stained glass windows on the right of the aisle, where an assistant pointed with a long stick at the first in a series of vivid pictures devoted to scenes from the Passion.

"Behold, then, that good Lord shivering and quaking, all his body naked and bound to a pillar. About him standing the wicked men, who are, without any reason and without any pity, full sore scourging that blessed body. See how they cease not from their angry strokes, till they see him stand in his blood up to the ankles. From the top of the head to the sole of his feet, whole skin saved they none. His flesh they razed to the bone, and then out of their own weariness they left him almost for dead."

The pointer moved on. "Look then aside upon his blessed mother." Every neck turned and every eye strained to see the figure of Mary in the adjacent window. "See what sorrow she maketh for her dear son." The congregation sighed and began softly reciting prayers to the mother of Christ. The pointer moved on to the next window. "Turn again to thy Lord and see how they thrust on his head a garland of thorns, till the blood ran down his eyes, nose, mouth, and ears."

Thus far, Master John had begun his Easter sermon in the traditional St. Mary's fashion, making use of the splendid set of stained glass windows of which the church was justly proud. But then, aware not just of the threat of the pestilence from all sides but of the latest rumor, overheard at this very Mass, that it was already in their midst, he chose to stress the parallels between Christ's Passion and the scourging and suffering which was afflicting the world and awaiting his flock.

"Now is the time for our passion; for us to be struck by the terrible scourges of pestilence, as Christ was scourged with whips in his Passion." Master John told them how the dreadful mortification, which they almost certainly faced within weeks or even days, would help to cleanse their souls of sin. "You have only to ask God for forgiveness and it will be granted, however terrible your transgressions may have been.

"Omnis enim qui invocaverit nomen Domini, salvus erit." Summoning all the power of his voice, John let the Latin resonate around his throat and boom from his chest. He was deeply stirred by the manner in which his words resounded through the church as if they were a pronouncement from God himself. Latin had its special magic. "Omnis enim qui invocaverit nomen Domini, salvus erit." The message bore repeating yet again, and in the mother tongue: "Every man, whosoever he be, who calls the name of the Lord, shall be saved."

FIGURE I

A reconstruction of a peasant cottage

"the dwellings which peppered the landscape were of varying size and condition" (page 4)

FIGURE 2

A poor parson from the Ellesmere Chaucer

"a man who was 'rich of holy thought and work'" (page 13)

FIGURE 3

Celebrating Mass: raising the Host

"there was no shortage of clerics . . . conducting services, administering rites, and saying Masses" (page 16)

FIGURE 4
Derision

"in spite of his best efforts at mediation, arguments continued to bubble up" (page 20)

FIGURE 5
A deathbed scene

"family, friends, and neighbors clustered in his house and around his bed" (page 22)

FIGURE 6
Bust of the Virgin

"For the Mother of Mercy will pray her Son to give him a place in Heaven'" (page 28)

FIGURE 7
Painting of the Day of Doom

"God held his arms outstretched . . . with Heaven to his right hand and Hell to his left" (page 37)

FIGURE 8
The Battle of Crécy

"sturdy English longbowmen, rustics like themselves, had slaughtered a host of mounted and armored nobility and knights" (page 42)

FIGURE 9
Gathering in the sheaves

"The harvest of autumn 1347 brought no respite to the poor of Walsham, for once again it was miserable" (page 46)

A nativity scene

"an excited huddle in front of the altar assembling a large, brightly painted wooden model of the stable at Bethlehem" (page 54)

Pope leading a penitential procession in time of plague

"the pope commanded devout processions with the chanting of litanies" (page 59)

In fear of the plague

"The three pious men . . . asked themselves whether there could be any doubt that this pestilence . . . would be stalking England in a matter of weeks" (page 60)

The Thornham Parva Retable

"the magnificent altarpiece in the newly built Blackfriars priory" (page 66)

Miracle of the Virgin"s Milk

"a pilgrimage to Walsingham, to draw succor from the milk of the sweet Virgin Mary" (page 66)

FIGURE 15
Figure of God
"Almighty God uses thunder, lightning, and other blows" (page 83)

FIGURE 16
Pelican in her piety
"Catherine Pynfoul commissioned a carving of a pelican and its young at the end of one of the pews" (page 91)

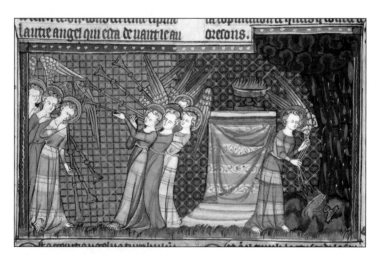

FIGURE 17
Scene from the Book of Revelation
"And I saw the seven angels which stood before God; and to them were given seven trumpets" (page 96)

FIGURE 21
**Preaching in
a churchyard**

*"they freely gathered
audiences together in the
churchyard" (page 130)*

FIGURE 22

**Lay communion with
houseling cloth**

*"helpers offered a long white towel
to each communicant" (page 147)*

FIGURE 23
Cemetery

*"it seemed that all
humankind would
perish" (page 148)*

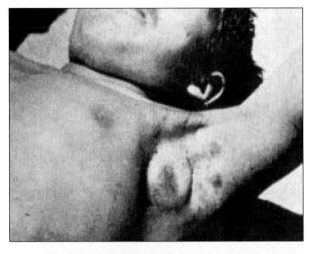

FIGURE 24
Patient with bubonic plague

"Within one or two days from the onset, a bubo develops" (page 150)

FIGURE 25
Death strikes

"As each hour passed, John Chapman's health deteriorated appreciably" (page 153)

FIGURE 26
**Demons seizing the soul
of an unconfessed man**

*"a crowd of grinning demons
striving with their infernal
claws to snatch away her
husband's soul" (page 157)*

FIGURE 27
Burying plague victims

*"From Easter Day onward
the bells of St Mary's steeple
sonorously proclaimed an ever
spiraling toll of deaths"
(page 165)*

FIGURE 28
Mass for plague victims

*"ministering to his flock in the
valley of death" (page 171)*

FIGURE 29
Holbein: Death drives the plow
"*We may as well die of the pestilence as of hunger*" (page 178)

FIGURE 30
Corpus Christi procession
"In a spirit of optimism, clergy and laity decided to . . . mount a procession for Corpus Christi feast day" (page 187)

FIGURE 31
Laborer digging
"scarcely any of the tenants were bothering to turn up on the required days to perform their work on the lady's farm" (page 192)

FIGURE 32
Plowman

"The plowman warned that if he did not get what he deserved, he would not stay around to undertake the plowing of the fallow land" (page 197)

FIGURE 33
A court scene

"Fearing a public defeat, the steward decided to move on, but only after threatening Fraunceys" (page 206)

FIGURE 34
Drinking game
"I would rather sit here on my arse drinking" (page 229)

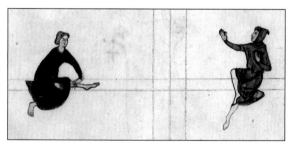

FIGURE 35
Man and woman dancing
"if the rustics should get the upper hand, God's creation would be entirely ruined" (page 231)

FIGURE 36
Man digging up a tree
"But only for light jobs, like digging up small trees, for which he asked 5d per day and two square meals" (page 244)

FIGURE 37
Harrowing

"Scarcely any acres received the benefits of double plowing, and the harrowing too was slipshod" (page 248)

FIGURE 38
Preaching to an elite audience

"The prior's audience, consisting largely of senior clerics, gentry, lawyers, burgesses, and merchants, nodded in agreement" (page 252)

FIGURE 39
Flagellants

"these bands processed through towns and villages along their way, chanting in unison and whipping themselves and each other" (page 259)

FIGURE 40
Reeve from the Ellesmere Chaucer

"So outraged was Sir Henry by the demeanor of Geoffrey Rath that he began asking around Walsham what the villagers thought of their reeve" (page 266)

FIGURE 41
Souls in peril and torment

"In Hell a man shall weep more than all the water in the earth" (page 267)

FIGURE 42
Two women driving cows and a bull

*"As Olivia and Hilary were quick to appreciate,
livestock could be bought very cheaply"* (page 274)

FIGURE 43
Death of a cleric

*"Master John collapsed,
breathless, with pains in his
chest"* (page 283)

But most members of the congregation were still dwelling on their priest's former words, and on the passion through pestilence they had been sentenced to. As despair threatened to engulf them, try as they might, there were few in the congregation who could envisage that any of the sins they had committed warranted such cruel and extreme punishment as God was about to inflict on them—just as Christ on earth had been tortured "without any reason and without any pity."

Mindful of his flock's bewilderment and fearful that they might grow more skeptical and lose faith, John reflected aloud that it was not within his power, or even that possessed by the most holy and learned prelates and scholars, to fully understand the divine plan. Rather than seeking to find reasons why their world was being subjected to such death and destruction, he urged his parishioners to place themselves completely in God's mercy and have faith that he would provide succor and salvation for those who were deserving.

With that Master John came down from his pulpit to perform the annual ritual of the symbolic burying of Christ, in the form of the Host which he bore aloft in the pyx. As he moved toward the wooden Easter sepulcher which had been constructed in a corner of the church, his way was temporarily blocked by a crush of people jostling for position and struggling to kiss the cross carried by his deacon. The intensity of devotion was so great that some fainted when Master John took off his vestments and sandals and wrapped the pyx containing the consecrated wafer and the cross, still moist from kisses, in linen cloths. While doing this he repeatedly intoned, "I am counted as one of them who go down to the pit." And when he stepped forward to place the sacred items in their symbolic tomb, the surge of the crowd caused him to stumble and others to fall.

As the congregation fell silent, with many reflecting on their own possible death and burial, Master John announced that he had something more to tell them. He put on his vestments and made his way back to the pulpit, his hand reaching into his pocket and touching the letter with which his fingers had absentmindedly played many times during the sermon. The letter had been sent to him a couple of weeks ago by his archdeacon, and he was meant to read it out in church and then nail it in the porch for all to see and for those who were able, to read. But John had delayed doing so, for he was deeply troubled by the archdeacon's message. It stated that the pope had given his permission for parishioners to choose their own confessor if a priest were not available in their hour of death, "in all the places in which the epidemic or mortality of people, which at present, by the Lord's will, flourishes in many parts of the world, now or will in the future." Since receiving it, he had been wrestling inconclusively to resolve the conflict between his humanity and sense of duty to his superiors, on the one side, and his theological conscience, on the other. But now he took the letter from his pocket and unfolded it. Even so, he could not bring himself to read it aloud to his congregation, as he had been instructed. Instead he gently informed them, in as matter-of-fact a manner as he could, that should the pestilence strike, and should its blows be as heavy as they had been in some other places, and should the occasion arise where a fully trained priest might not manage to reach the sick in time to hear their confession in their hour of death, then the pope, the bishop, and the archdeacon had each given their approval that a lesser qualified member of the clergy, or even a layperson, might be chosen instead to do so. With that John left the pulpit, as stunned as his congregation, muttering less than coherently that clarification of any arrangements should be sorted out with his assistants. He turned his back and walked away, closing his ears to the urgent pleas uttering from a hundred throats.

Soon after dawn on Easter Day, April 12, to commemorate Christ rising from his tomb, the clergy gathered to remove the pyx and the cross from the sepulcher while the choir sang Christus Resurgens. A huge throng of excited parishioners gathered around, some of whom had spent the night outside the church waiting for the resurrection. In unison they all recited the news over and again that "Christ dieth no more and Death hath no more dominion over him." At the Easter Day Mass Master John exhorted the folk gathered in the churchyard in their hundreds to enter the church and its precincts, "Arrayed in God's livery, clothed in love and charity, and not in the fiends livery, clothed in envy and deadly wrath."

Oppressed by the unbearable weight of responsibility which the advancing plague placed on his shoulders, Master John had spent many sleepless nights over the past two weeks or more trying to compose a relevant and appropriate message for his deeply troubled flock. But he had been unable to think of anything that came close to meeting the needs of the time and his own high standards, and at the last minute from the pulpit he gave them instead the traditional Easter homily. He counseled them to retain their newly cleansed state and cautioned them how the seven deadly sins would soon stain their soul once again if they did not learn the lessons of the Wounds of Christ. And he urged them not simply to refrain from committing sins, but to act positively by forgiving the trespasses of their neighbors and behaving with charity to all.

At the climax of the highest Mass, the crowd surged forward to peer through, round, or even over the rood screen to observe Master John at the altar, some placing their children or ailing relatives on their shoulders. The priest, as was usual, turned his back on the congregation as he raised the Host above his head in celebration of the moment of transformation from wafer into the Body of Christ. But with loud and excited voices the throng called for their priest to show them more clearly the Body of Christ. Half turning by instinct rather than by design, he granted them their desire. Then, with the help of his many assistants, order was restored and the communicants were lined up, row after row, before the chancel screen for their spiritual sustenance. With prompting, they pleaded that Christ's sufferings might be for them a means of mercy and salvation, and not of death and eternal condemnation. As they drew close to the altar, helpers offered a long white towel to each communicant, who clutched it in anxious hands to prevent any fragments of the Host falling to the floor. And when, having partaken of the Host, they moved on to grasp the proffered chalice to wash down the fragments of the Host with a draft of wine, they fervently desired that wine to be the most holy dear blood of Jesus Christ shed for their redemption, although the priest had told them it was unconsecrated and no sacrament. They were also most careful to wrap their fingers in the houseling cloth as they held the chalice to avoid contaminating it with their bare hands, for they knew in their hearts that the power of his blood leaked even into the cold hard metal (see figure 22).

Scarcely had the ingestion of the Host begun to provide the comfort and protection that was so desperately sought, than half a dozen villagers, who had been feeling listless for a few days with chills and aches, began to develop high fevers and suffer a rapid deterioration in health. When these sick folk were visited by cautious neighbors, fearful of the worst, they were found either lying prostrate in bed, unable to stir, or in the grip of a frenzied delirium. Within a further day or so large swellings appeared in the groin of four of them and on the neck of the others. As the swellings grew and blackened so the pain intensified, and in a short while some other members of their households began to feel unwell with aches and fevers. At the end of six days all the original six victims were dead, and at least another score of people in the village, including one of the newly arrived young priests, were showing the deadly symptoms. In the time it took for these new victims to pass from health to death, a further and much larger group had become sick and commenced their short and agonized journey to the grave.

The pestilence, feeding ever more greedily, grew stronger by the day, until its black shroud encompassed the whole village and, as far as anyone in Walsham had knowledge, all areas in the country around. Within little more than two weeks the mysterious contagion had broken all bounds of precedent and reason. Behaving with merciless ferocity and gargantuan energy, it proved quite beyond the capacity of prayers or medicine to resist or to heal. As the bells of St. Mary's tolled almost without ceasing, it seemed that all humankind would perish and the whole world would soon come to an end (see figure 23).

Mid-April to Early May, 1349

The accounts of the sickness and deaths of John Chapman and Robert Helpe in this chapter are based on the best fourteenth-century descriptions of the signs, symptoms, and prognoses of the pestilence which was the Black Death, and on modern medical knowledge of the characteristics of bubonic plague and its progression in patients. Given the vast distance in time and expertise between the two sets of sources, they are reassuringly compatible. Gabriele de' Mussi, a lawyer in Piacenza, wrote in one of the more detailed of surviving descriptions, "So that the conditions, causes, and symptoms of this pestilential disease should be made plain to all, I have decided to set them out in writing. Those of both sexes who were in health, and in no fear of death, were struck by four savage blows to the flesh. First, out of the blue, a kind of chilly stiffness troubled their bodies. They felt a tingling sensation, as if they were being pricked by the points of arrows. The next stage was a fearsome attack which took the form of an extremely hard, solid boil . . . as it grew more solid, its burning heat caused the patients to fall into an acute and putrid fever, with severe headaches. As it intensified, its extreme bitterness could have various effects. In some cases it gave rise to an intolerable stench. In others it brought spitting of blood, for others, swellings near the place from which the corrupt humors had arisen . . . Some people lay as if in a drunken stupor and could not be roused. Behold the swellings, the warning signs sent by the Lord. Some died on the very day the illness took possession of them, others on the next day, others—the majority—between the third and fifth day."

While some of the symptoms given by de' Mussi are not unique to plague, their presence in conjunction with each other is highly significant, as are genuine buboes, the large and exquisitely painful swellings of the lymphatic glands. As modern medical texts tell us, the first symptoms of bubonic plague are chills, headache, and backache, restlessness and high fever, followed rapidly by prostration. Within one or two days from the onset, a bubo develops, which is often followed by secondary, smaller swellings elsewhere on the body (see figure 24). Vomiting and delirium are common, as is a strange stench. Death usually follows in a further three to four days. Though de' Mussi devotes most of his description to symptoms and prognosis that fit the bubonic form of plague very closely, references to "the spitting of blood" and to death "on the very day the illness took possession" fit well the two other variants, pneumonic and septicemic plague. Fourteenth-century authorities tell us that no one who vomited blood survived, which is the case with untreated pneumonic plague. Victims who are reported as dying suddenly during the Black Death, often within hours of the onset of illness and without exhibiting external signs, could well have been victims of the rarer but equally lethal septicemic variant, in which the plague bacteria pass directly into the bloodstream.

It is probable that it was primarily bubonic plague which ravaged Walsham from early April to early June, killing half the population. If so, it would have been introduced into the village a number of weeks before the human epidemic flared up. The epidemiology of plague indicates that it often took more than two weeks for the enzootic and epizootic phases to run their course, that is, for plague-bearing fleas to infect and then decimate the rat population to such an extent that the fleas could no longer feed. Then a further two weeks for the endemic phase, when the infected rat fleas began biting human hosts, and those human hosts incubated the disease and began to die. From the first sprinkling of human deaths to a full epidemic with multiple deaths might take a further two weeks or even longer. Of course, if human fleas, or the fleas carried on birds and animals other than rats, were also effective transmitters of plague in 1348–1349, the process of dissemination might have been considerably faster.

⊣⊢

The cottage of John and Agnes Chapman, which lay in the far east of the parish, was among the first to be struck by the pestilence when it showed its terrible face in Walsham. John was taken sick just after

Easter Day, April 12, almost four years to the day since their wedding. It was the second marriage for both of them, their former spouses having died, and Agnes became pregnant soon after the wedding had been blessed. They now had a three-year-old daughter who was also named Agnes. The Chapmans lived in a tiny cottage and cultivated a small field to the rear, which they rented from Edmund de Welles, the lord and lady of the submanor of High Hall. John was in his early fifties, of modest means but well respected, and over the years he had been entrusted with a number of supervisory posts in the village. Agnes, who was significantly younger than her husband, came from a large and modestly prosperous villein family. She was the daughter of Gilbert Helpe, who had died suddenly in spring 1338 at almost the same time as his father. In keeping with the customs of the manor, her four brothers—Robert, John, Gilbert, and Henry—had inherited the eighteen acres her father and grandfather held in Westhorpe, and they farmed it together until the spring of 1347, when Henry sold his share to his brothers and left the manor.

Immediately on hearing that a number of villagers who lived close by had been taken ill with a mysterious affliction, John and Agnes retreated into their cottage. They left it only to tend their animals and crops, and then only when no one else was about, and they were especially careful to keep their daughter always within sight. Despite these precautions, John began to feel unusually weak and listless one late afternoon while pulling up the first crop of weeds, and the next morning he returned unexpectedly early from spreading their cow's manure onto the vegetables in the croft at the back of their cottage. He complained, with slightly slurred speech, of tiredness and an unusual tingling sensation in his painful arms and legs. Agnes put him to bed, praying that it was simply a heavy cold. But her instincts told her this was unlikely. John had been perfectly well the previous morning, and he had become too weak too quickly, and now he was slipping into a fever and was strangely disoriented. She feared that he had caught the pestilence and would soon die.

Agnes did not sleep much that night, being overcome with fear and disturbed by the tossing, heavy sighing, and sporadic moaning of her husband beside her, as well as the intense heat he radiated. At first light, as he slept, Agnes began to explore for signs of the pestilence. She put her hands gently around John's neck and thought she felt a slight swelling, and when she touched the inside of the thigh that was pressed against her knee, her fingers traced the contours of a very small but distinct hard mound close to the groin. With that she leaped to her feet, pulled on her clothes and shoes, and ran from the cottage.

Agnes hurried through the early morning mist and was soon banging on the door of the ancient midwife, Juliana Denys, who had helped her when the birth of her daughter became complicated. With calm efficiency the midwife had probed inside Agnes, and when her fingers touched feet rather than a head, she swiftly turned the child in the womb, with the result that she had been born without further stress. Juliana was also a successful healer. For a penny or two she would help the sick with advice and medicines derived from her wide knowledge and extensive collection of herbs and potions, and she happily dispensed cheap charms that worked well against ill fortune or curses. The two women had struck up a form of friendship, so Agnes was surprised when she was refused entry into the cottage. The midwife insisted on speaking through a window, and despite Agnes's pleas, she could not be persuaded to visit John. Anxious to see Agnes depart, the old woman hurriedly made up a potion with secret ingredients, which she passed through the window in an old clay bowl. A little of this, Juliana instructed, should be fed to John, mixed with his pottage, and also rubbed into his swelling thrice a day. She refused to take any money from Agnes, not wishing to handle it, but as Agnes was leaving she tossed her a polished stone attached to a leather string to wear around her neck at all times. Wishing Agnes and her husband well, Juliana slammed the shutters closed.

When Agnes returned home, she found that John's condition had worsened. He was extremely agitated and tried to get up and walk, but fell to the floor. Agnes struggled to get him back into bed, but there was no reasoning with him, and he would not respond to her pleadings. Eventually he tired and she managed to get him to bed. Agnes then took the little rough wooden carving of St. Katherine from its place in the alcove near the window and put it under the covers for his protection. She fetched some water to bathe her husband because he was so hot and feverish, and began by mopping his brow and wiping his face, while John clasped her other hand tightly. When she bathed his abdomen, she was relieved to find that the swelling she had felt on the inner part of his right thigh was no more pronounced. But then she was startled to notice a patch of blackened skin close to his right ankle and quickly rubbed it with the potion from the midwife. When Agnes finished, she moved quickly to the corner of the room and grabbed her sleeping daughter from her bed and ran to her eldest brother's cottage.

When Agnes banged on Robert's door, it was her brother John's voice which answered from inside, saying that Robert was unwell and it could be the plague. Now in a state of panic, Agnes ran to the house of John Wodebite, which stood about half a mile away. As the eldest son of wealthy William Wodebite, John had inherited the fine dwelling from his father four years before, and Agnes had often worked for him, as she had for his father, cleaning and cooking and looking after his livestock. John opened the door but did not invite Agnes in, and he quickly waved her back when he heard the reason for her visit. She pleaded with John to care for her daughter for a few days while she nursed her husband. Though fond of Agnes, John was at first very reluctant to agree. But seeing that neither Agnes nor her child appeared to be at all ill, he eventually relented. When Agnes had gone, John waved the little child round to the back of his cottage and ushered her into a small barn. There little Agnes was left to be looked after and fed by his servant girl for the next two days, before she showed by her abundant energy and absence of marks on her skin that she was completely free of the pestilence and was allowed by John into his house.

Agnes walked slowly home, relieved that her daughter was safe. But as she neared her cottage, a dread seized her. She suddenly realized that she had many times looked directly at her husband's face since he had become ill, completely forgetting that to look into the eyes of a victim was the surest way of catching the pestilence.

As each hour passed, John Chapman's health deteriorated appreciably (see figure 25). He became increasingly distraught with physical agony and mental terror, and intermittently seemed to be possessed by demons or to have lost his senses. His condition alternated between violent ravings, during which he would rise from his bed and stagger around the cottage, and comatose prostration, during which he seemed to be scarcely breathing. Though the blackened pustule on his ankle did not get much worse, the lump on his inner thigh swelled ominously and became luridly inflamed and exquisitely painful. The medicinal potion was clearly having no effect, nor was the holy water Agnes sprinkled on her husband. The image of St. Katherine she had placed in his bed had been kicked by his restless legs across the room, and Agnes retrieved it and placed it at the base of the bed. Despite her exhaustion and despite the impossibility of avoiding looks from her husband, whose wild eyes often stared at her, Agnes felt no symptoms of illness. Gratefully, she gently rubbed the stone amulet around her neck, which was still protecting her from infection.

Soon after sunrise on the fourth day of John's illness, Agnes shouted to passersby that her husband was dying and begged them to go to the church and fetch a priest. She also asked her neighbors to call again on the midwife. When neither the priest nor the midwife had arrived by the afternoon, Agnes went the mile or so to the church, which she found deserted except for a single lay helper. He told her that so many people were sick in the parish that the priests were able to respond only to those who were very close to death. Having asked Agnes when John had first fallen sick and what was his present condition, he assured her that a priest would call in good time, well before John's death.

By the following morning the carbuncle in John's groin was the size of a duck's egg, blackened and leaking pus, and John was delirious and only sporadically conscious. As Agnes nursed him through the day, she began to dread the brief periods of consciousness when she had to hold him down as he struggled to rush from the house to throw himself in the river to cool his pain. Once he grabbed a knife intending to slice open his festering lump. By dusk, as John lay exhausted from his struggles and seemingly close to death, Agnes decided to run again to the church, to beg for the priest or one of his chaplains. To her relief she soon encountered Master John on a tired mare trotting slowly along by Cranmer Green, returning, physically and emotionally weary, from visiting the sick, administering the last rites, and arranging funerals. When Agnes stopped him and begged him to come to her husband's deathbed, he smiled weakly, patted her on the shoulder to comfort her, and then turned his drowsy horse around and gestured for her to lead the way.

The priest found John half conscious, breathing heavily, sweating profusely, and wracked by intense pain. Agnes lifted the cover to show him the angry black and purple swelling in his groin that had grown to the size of an apple, and John nodded gravely. He quickly left the room to unpack his saddle bags and asked Agnes to help carry candles, a crucifix, a Madonna and child, and various boxes and cups to the bedside. Master John paused for a moment breathing heavily and wiped away the sweat trickling down his forehead and into his eyes. As they settled by the bed, he told Agnes that, from his experience, he feared her husband was going to die soon, and he asked her if John had confessed his sins. Agnes shook her head and explained that she had not thought to do this.

"Have you forgotten already the letter from the bishop permitting lay confession *in extremis,* which I read out in church only a few weeks ago?"

"I remember, but I do not understand. Can it really be true?" she replied.

Master John patted her arm sympathetically. "Then I will hear his confession now," he said.

Despite Agnes's repeated attempts at soothing, John remained distracted, failing to respond to any of Master John's questions and refusing to look at the image of the Madonna placed before his eyes. When asked to kiss the cross, he pushed it violently to one side, almost wrenching it from the priest's hands. After many attempts to offer a Communion wafer to John's lips, only a few crumbs were ingested, and those only with Agnes's assistance, holding his mouth firmly closed until saliva dissolved them. Agnes was in a state of despair at her husband's inability to confess, and at his sacrilegious violence in the face of death and Master John. He was surely possessed by devils and his soul was bound to be lost if he would not relent and accept Christ's salvation. But the priest remained calm and tried his best to ignore John's agitations and occasional blasphemies, while resolutely continuing through each stage of the sacred ritual.

When he had finished, Master John comforted Agnes: "I am sure it is the pestilence and not devils that have taken over your husband's mind. Deep inside he was struggling to participate." Then he gestured for Agnes to remove the sheet so that he could anoint John's body. John screamed with agony and the priest recoiled from the blackened skin and engorged bubo which looked set to burst. He hurriedly dabbed a few droplets of oil on John's forehead, hands, and ankles, explaining that the

amount of oil was not important, and that he had to save as much as pos-
sible in case the pestilence spread. Then Master John pronounced, "Into
Thy hands O Lord I commend your spirit. You have redeemed John, O
Lord, thou God of truth."

It had been a brief and methodical procedure rather than the elaborate
and emotional ritual Agnes had witnessed many times before at the
deathbed of loved ones. With apologies for her insolence, she begged
Master John to do more. The priest assured her, "I am certain your husband has confessed inwardly. Yet, should he regain his senses, however
briefly, you must help him confess further." He then hurriedly rehearsed
with her a few key phrases, but Agnes's mind was whirling and she stum-
bled over the words as she repeated them to herself and forgot some of
them altogether. When Agnes suggested fetching her brothers to support
her and pray for John, the priest shook his head and urged her not to
leave her husband for any length of time, but to stay with him so that he
could further confess his sins if he was able.

As Master John rode off into the night, his mind was deeply troubled.
Almost all the victims of the pestilence that he and his colleagues had so
far ministered to had been incapable of responding to the questions put
to them, and unable to confess adequately or to express sufficient contrition. In fact, few on their deathbeds had shown sufficient awareness of
the rites being performed on their behalf. John vowed that somehow he
and his clergy must try to see the sick earlier in the onset of their disease,
when they were still conscious and rational. But, he also mused, visits
must not be made too early, for confession must take place when close to
death, and certainly no one who might recover should knowingly be
anointed. Moreover, however vigilant he and his clergy might be, it was
the family or neighbors who had to decide when to send for a priest. He
determined that his clergy should act on the experience they had accumulated over the years, and had absorbed from their predecessors, rather
than on fear of the pernicious progress of this horrible new scourge.

What was happening in Master John's parish was entirely without
precedent. The numbers of dead and dying were already almost unman-
ageable for the clergy, and yet were rising daily. Yesterday there had been
five burials, and these had stretched the resources of the church almost to
the limit. A backlog of funerals was building up, to which Master John

made a mental note to add John Chapman's, as so much time was being devoted to the administration of the last rites. Furthermore, there were processions to organize and attend, an abundance of Masses to be sung, and the confessions of the healthy to be heard. And, added to all this, he had been told that morning at the bedside of his most trusted church-warden that the newly ordained assistant who been taken sick a few days ago had died, and that one of his most experienced chaplains had fled to a neighboring parish thought to be free of plague.

Though Master John had promised to tell friends and neighbors of her husband's impending death, no one called on Agnes during the night. She became increasingly distressed that, in his pain and delirium, her husband had not openly confessed his sins. As dark thoughts whirled around her head, she began to grasp the full awful meaning of the words she had heard many times before: "Death gives no certain respite to departing creatures, but takes them suddenly." Seared into her mind was the terrifying vision of the fate of the damned painted on the chancel arch of St. Mary's, which she had seen more than once every week of her life. As a child she had been horrified by the depiction of the damned, for their faces looked just like her family and neighbors. Falling beneath God's right hand, naked and chained, they were being dragged by tormenting demons and cast wailing and weeping into the huge fetid mouths of monsters or the everlasting fires of Hell. Nor could Agnes keep from recalling words that she had heard many times before about the souls of unshriven sinners being cast into darkness, and from the pulpit Master John had often proclaimed, "Without confession the just man is judged to be graceless, and the sinner is held to be dead." Her husband had not been a bad man, but she had been well taught that even the smallest sins can stain the soul.

Agnes sat up with John all night, intermittently mumbling prayers and falling into fitful and troubled naps, only to be confronted by a crowd of grinning demons striving with their infernal claws to snatch away her husband's soul; once she thought she saw them bearing off her beloved daughter as well (see figure 26).

John did not regain his senses, and soon after sunrise he stopped breathing.

Agnes arose and looked vainly around the bare room and peered out of the window and door for the support of friends, family, and neighbors, for herself as well as her dead husband. She lit the candle the priest had sold her and recited the Placebo as best she could. But the words of the prayer, which she had known well since she was twelve, kept slipping from her mind. As she washed John's body, she was shocked to see that much of his skin was now blotched and blackened, and that there were a number of swellings as well as the carbuncle in his groin. She folded him into a clean sheet, just as she had her former husband, John Cristmasse, after his death. Then she fetched some sticks of wood that she washed and dried, and placed them at the edge of the embers in the hearth and waited till the ends blackened and burned to ash. Taking them up, she allowed them to cool and then carefully traced a cross on the shroud, and smoothed and shaped it with her fingers.

As Agnes was leaving to tell her brothers of John's death, Margery Wodebite called to offer comfort and a candle. Margery, who lived close by, was renowned as the most devout and intense of parishioners, whose eyes had rained tears of grief at the remembrance of Christ's Passion at the Easter Mass a few days before, and whose body shook convulsively with emotion at any religious experience. But today she was unusually calm and announced that her well of tears had run dry. Agnes could not help but note that even Margery was taking great care not to go near John's body, and instead prayed with Agnes from the outer hallway, shaking quietly with fear and apprehension.

"I am sorry that I have taken so long to call on you," Margery apologized, "but I have been visiting the sick and dying all around High Hall. The pestilence is spreading so quickly around here, and also into the rest of Walsham, that it seems to me as if the end of the world might be coming."

Margery then reeled off a list of a dozen or more names of people she had visited on their deathbed, and many more than a score who were dying. The dead and sick included some of the richest farmers in the village as well as their servants, the poor, the landless, and the totally indigent.

"Most terrible of all," Margery said, "is the fate of the children. There are so many young orphans. Even as we speak, I fear there must be young ones who are the only live beings in houses of death. We cannot leave things like this, despite the dangers of infection. Did you know that both the Goche brothers are dead, and one of their wives also, and the other sick? Their five children, all under ten years of age, have been left entirely alone to fend for themselves, for their servant girl has fled. I am doing all I can to help, but I am old and I have to spend a long time each day praying for forgiveness and begging the Blessed Mary and Christ to make sure that God does not forget me or my good works."

Seeing Agnes in tears, Margery hesitated to confirm that her brother, Robert Helpe, was dying. Instead, she assured her that she had seen her daughter the previous day and that she was in good health, adding that God had seen fit so far to spare the Wodebites from the pestilence. Agnes gratefully accepted Margery's offer to arrange for John's funeral when she visited the church for matins that evening.

Agnes was not expecting to meet many people on her walk to her brother's farm, but as she came to Market Way she noticed in the distance a small group standing outside old William Cranmer's house on the green. As she drew nearer she saw they were gathered around a funeral cart. Just a week or so before, William's death would have been major news in the village, and Agnes, although not a close acquaintance, would have joined the procession to St. Mary's churchyard. But now she just hurried off, worrying about her own safety and the health of her brother. As she walked, Agnes touched the stone amulet around her neck and silently prayed for protection for herself and her daughter and for the soul of her husband. On the rest of the way to Westhorpe she saw only a handful of other people, most in the distance, and those who saw her hurried away before she drew near.

As Agnes approached her brother's cottage, she heard loud shouting and saw John and his wife, Alice, struggling with Robert near the door. She ran forward and helped restrain him, which was not a difficult task as he was desperately weak. She was told that he had jumped from his bed and run from the house naked, and that after a lengthy search had been found a quarter of a mile away lying in Harteshall Brook. Robert had been sick for four days now, and Agnes recognized that he had the same sickness as her husband and that it was following a similar course. As they looked down on him, lying motionless on the bed and scarcely breathing, Agnes gently suggested that he might be close to death. John agreed, saying that a couple of hours ago Gilbert had gone in search of a priest, but nothing had been heard from him since. Recalling her own desperate experience, Agnes urged John to go and help his brother to find a priest.

John Helpe returned in midafternoon accompanied by one of the laymen Master John had trained to hear confession. Agnes and Alice recognized him as the kind old man who helped clean the church and polish its sacred metalwork. However, they were disappointed to learn that he had brought nothing with him but a vial of holy water and a small painted image of the Madonna and child on an oak board. To their dismay the old man explained that he did not have any of the powers of an ordained priest and was not permitted to administer the last sacraments of Communion and annealing. However, he assured them that he was trained to hear her brother's confession and would do so in case he died before a priest could come. Then he ushered them from the room. A few minutes later the old man emerged and, after offering some brief words of encouragement, hurriedly departed saying that he had to rush to another sickbed.

In all this time there was no sign of Gilbert, but it was a great relief that a chaplain arrived later that evening, apologizing profusely for his tardiness which he excused by the extraordinary numbers of sick and dying in the parish. By now Robert was close to death in a half-conscious state of delirium and oblivious to all attempts to encourage him to participate in the struggle to guide his soul to salvation. The chaplain stayed only a few minutes, and Robert died shortly afterward.

Agnes, exhausted and tormented by grief at the death of her husband and her brother within a day of each other, insisted on walking back to her cottage in the gathering darkness to pray over her husband's body and tend her poultry and animals. The news of the rapid spread of the pestilence rekindled her fears for the safety of her daughter, and she worried whether John Wodebite's household had been infected. As she walked along the lane to her cottage, she expected to find that the elderly couple next door had milked her cow for her, leaving the milk in a wooden bowl by her doorway, as they had often done in the past. But as she drew near she heard the distressed bellowing of the animal and then the desperate cries of the old lady next door, who pleaded for help as her husband was sick and she had become too weak to look after him.

Agnes lowered her head, closed her ears, and mumbled an apology while hurrying past. As she entered her cottage and lit a candle, she shuddered, partly with sobs but partly with fear at the sight of the shrouded body lying across the bed. Agnes gathered the carving of St. Katherine from the bed and reverently placed it in the niche by the window, and lit a tiny fragment of candle on a metal tray. Her heart jumped as the light flickered across St. Katherine's face. Could it be that her dearest saint was crying? Holding the candle close to the rosy cheek on the left hand side of the carving's face, Agnes peered closely and saw that there was indeed a tear where there had been none before. She felt it tenderly with her finger. The wood had definitely swelled, round and smooth, under the eye, in the shape of a tiny teardrop. Despite her entreaties to God, St. Katherine had been unable to stop the deaths and now she was crying for the world, and especially for Agnes and her daughter.

Urged by the old lay confessor who visited Robert Helpe's house again the next day, Agnes and her brothers agreed to combine Robert's and John's funeral service and burial. The old man apologized that their bodies would not be permitted to lie in the church for fear of contagion, a rule which Master John had been forced to institute because so many people had begun to avoid going to pray or hear Mass when there were bodies within. But the verger readily assured them that a full service would be held at the graveside, and many Masses would be said for the souls of the brothers on the day of their burial and for long afterward. However, it would be necessary for both bodies to be picked up from the same cottage. Reluctantly they agreed that the funeral procession should start from Agnes's home, since that was closer to the church, and John undertook to carry his brother's body to her cottage early the next morning.

The cart that arrived at Agnes's cottage to collect the bodies was not the usual clean and polished funeral wagon, for that was in use elsewhere. The cart also lacked the special pall to drape over the bodies, although in its place the carter produced a clean white linen cloth. A dozen or more neighbors and friends gathered with the families of the deceased, and two servers soon arrived, one with a bell and the other with a plain wooden cross, followed by a chaplain new to the village carrying a prayer book. Eventually, some time after the cortege was ready to leave, a small group of shabbily dressed poor folk, a number of whom were not recognizable as locals, turned up to serve as mourners and pallbearers. They did not apologize for their tardiness, and before they would agree to walk beside the cart to St. Mary's graveyard, carrying candles and wooden crosses and chanting psalms, their spokeswoman demanded an advance payment of three halfpence each, rather than the accustomed two. When Agnes returned to her cottage from the graveyard, she found her cow lying dead in the field behind.

Despite her own cares and grief, Agnes had been leaving her elderly neighbors a bowl of lentil soup at their doorway each morning. But the next morning she found the bowl from the previous day untouched, and she received no answer when she called out to them. A couple of days later, since she did not have her daughter to protect, Agnes joined a handful of mourners to walk to the church behind their coffin cart. Those who attended were shocked to find that among their little group they could compile the names of well over a score of villagers living in the east of the village who were already dead of the pestilence, and another score who were sick with it. While death was scything through her village without mercy, Agnes decided she would quietly tend her sheep, pigs, and poultry, and weed her little plots of beans and corn.

Mid-May, 1349

Precise death rates have been calculated for a large number of English manors during the Black Death, and the results are truly shocking. They indicate that around half of the rural population was killed in the epidemic. Although occasional manors can be found where only one in five of the tenants died, these are outnumbered by those with death rates in the region of two in every three, and on a few manors mortality may have reached three in four. Although the range of mortality between places could be wide, there was a pronounced tendency for it to cluster between 40 and 60 percent, with the greatest proportion of manors experiencing death rates of between 45 and 55 percent. The most recent attempt at an average mortality rate for the peasant tenantry of England as whole, calculated by Ole Benedictow, is close to 55 percent, and there are indications that the rural landless may have suffered to an even greater extent. Walsham is exceptionally well documented in the mid-fourteenth century, but it lacks the comprehensive listing of all tenants just prior to the epidemic that is essential for making a precise calculation of the death rate. However, close study of the excellent court rolls indicates that there were approximately 176 tenants on Walsham and High Hall manors just prior to the Black Death, of whom 109 were dead by June 1349, which produces a tenant death rate of marginally under 60 percent. There is also some evidence that mortality was particularly high among older adults, who were likely to be overrepresented among tenants. On the other hand, however, children were especially vulnerable to epidemic diseases, and it is likely that the adult landless also suffered disproportionately.

In common with other places at this time, there are no censuses that would make it possible to provide an accurate population of Walsham parish. However, from a series of indirect indications it is probable that Walsham contained as many as 1,500 souls in 1348. If so, then some 750 to 900 people would have died in the less than two months that the Black Death lasted. If deaths had been spaced evenly over this period, approximately one hundred would have died each week. But, given the behavior of most epidemics, including plague, the number of deaths in the village would have started relatively low, climbed rapidly in the early phases, peaked, and then declined in the latter phases. When the plague was at its peak, therefore, as many as fifty villagers may have died in a single day.

Because the plague was indisputably God's will, and caused its victims to die in a horrible manner and on a scale almost infinitely greater than anything ever seen before, contemporaries had great difficulty in explaining why God found it necessary to inflict it. Sermons are an especially informative source to the debates and confusions that raged, particularly when the preacher invented a dialogue with lay folk and used their supposed responses as a means of structuring his own argument. Thus Thomas Brinton, the bishop of Rochester, preached, "Let us not impute the scourges of God to planets or elements, but rather to our own sins . . . But you say, 'If sin was the occasion of the aforesaid, by the just judgment of God, the notorious sinners should perish, not children or the just who have not sinned in this way!' . . . I make the reply and say that the children are not dying for their own sins, but for those of their parents . . . But someone asks, 'Since sin is the outstanding cause of the pestilence, what are to be the remedies, that the Divine hand may cease?' I reply that the chief remedy would be the confession of the sinners. For how should the scourge of God cease at the people's prayers, while a third part of them are in mortal sin?" Yet for all the apparent dogmatism of the language used by church leaders and preachers, their reflections frequently betray a sense of bewilderment and an awareness that they were attempting to explain the inexplicable.

English chronicles are generally frustratingly laconic in their descriptions of the Black Death, and rarely provide more than the scantiest details of how people behaved during it. By contrast, there are many narratives written in Europe and the Middle East, by both clerics and lay folk, which contain extensive reports of what life and death were like while the epidemic raged. Although some were written many years, even decades, after the event, and some contain passages which bear a disconcertingly close resemblance to Thucydides' account of the great plague of Athens in the fifth century B.C., *others were written by eyewitnesses of intelligence and perception. Notably informative are the description of the plague in Florence contained in Giovanni Boccaccio's introduction to his* Decameron; *the account of plague in Piacenza in Gabriele de' Mussi's* Historia de Morbo; *a letter sent from the papal court of Avignon, by Louis Heyligen, a musician and friend of Petrarch; accounts of the plague in Tournai, written by Gilles li Muissis, the abbot of St. Giles monastery, in his chronicles; and the history of the Black Death in the Middle East compiled by al-Maqrizi, who was born in 1364. These and many other accounts have been drawn on in this chapter but, unfortunately, fourteenth-century commentators on the Black Death are overwhelmingly urban in their focus, and have relatively little to say about events in the countryside.*

࿓ ࿔

From Easter Day onward the bells of St. Mary's steeple sonorously proclaimed an ever spiraling toll of deaths to the folk of Walsham (see figure 27). By the last week of April the bells scarcely ever seemed to be silent, as the rhythm of the plague's blows quickened progressively, and each new strike was delivered with ever greater ferocity. In early May, however, they began to be heard less often. But this was not because the number of deaths had fallen, for they continued to spiral upward. On the instructions of Master John, for the sake of morale in his parish, as well as a lack of bell ringers, each peal now announced a multitude of burials. Though henceforth the numbers of deaths in Walsham were more difficult to count, no sensible villager had any doubt that they were on a scale that was likely to herald the end of the world. So great was the multitude of dead and dying, and the fear of infection among those who as yet remained untouched, that the fabric of routine daily existence threatened to fall apart and the comforting pillars of spiritual life to crumble. It was thus that the people of Walsham came to live out for themselves the most shocking experiences of death, devastation, and demoralization that over the last two years they had heard about time and again as the pestilence visited distant parts of the world.

The first victims were struck down in the east of Walsham around High Hall, but, with its poisonous emissaries dispatched in all directions, death was soon rampaging across the whole village. At first, people felt that far more would die in a month than the number who usually died in a year. However, such gloomy observations were soon proved wildly optimistic. As the distemper spread its arms ever wider to embrace the whole community, the numbers of its victims soared to unimaginable heights. Within a short time, the corpses of scores of men, women, and children were being cast each week into hurriedly prepared graves, and in mid-May villagers who lived close to the churchyard swore that as many as this were being buried each day, though few of those who witnessed these harrowing scenes lived to tell the tale. Certainly the hasty records kept by Master John and his assistants noted many days when thirty or even more corpses were packed into freshly dug pits in the churchyard. In the warm sunshine of early summer, the stench that came from the graves assailed the nostrils of all who came to pray and celebrate Mass.

So great was the ceaseless press of bodies that burials had to take place at night as well as during the day. It was not long before space for new corpses had to be made by digging up old graves, removing the bones, and piling them by the churchyard wall. Even though old graves were routinely excavated and fresh bodies packed ever more tightly into the ground, such measures gave only temporary respite, and plots of land adjacent to the churchyard had to be hastily consecrated and incorporated into the cemetery. Just as it was impossible to find enough room for a decent Christian burial for all parishioners who were entitled to one, so it became ever more difficult to find enough men and women to dig the graves and handle the corpses. Gravediggers died mightily from the pestilence and often swiftly followed their clients into the pit. Since those laboring people who remained alive and healthy had an understandable fear of contagion, the collection of the dead from the places where they had expired became increasingly hard to arrange, despite the offer of extraordinary wages and other inducements. Often the only people who were available to perform the solemn task of carrying departed loved ones to their final resting place were misfits, criminals, and outcasts. As a result some bodies were hastily buried in the fields near the location of death, although how many was not known because of the shame of those who carried out the deed.

The pestilence took many forms, just as the villagers of Walsham had been warned it would. Though the majority died, like John Chapman and Robert Helpe, with fevered minds and bodies, unbearable pains in their heads, and a large blackened boil or carbuncle in the groin, armpit, or neck, there were others who died without these telltale signs. These victims died swifter and, some say, even more horrible deaths, with intolerable chest and head pain, vomiting, coughing and spitting up large quantities of blood. Others were said to have collapsed almost without warning, with no visible signs of sickness, and expired within hours. Although catching the pestilence was at first thought to be a sure sign of imminent death, this was not always the case. While no one who coughed blood was ever known to have survived, a portion, perhaps one in five, who fell sick with carbuncles and buboes survived the critical days and slowly recovered, though often not to full health.

The good folk of Walsham had been brought up to believe that the last moments of life were of supreme importance in securing salvation, and they had been well taught that each stage in the elaborate rituals which confessed, cleansed, and reconciled the dying, and secured the safety of their departing soul, was crucial. But so cruel was the pestilence and so debilitating the afflictions of the dying, that few on their deathbed were able to respond to the urgings of their confessors, and many were incapable of even understanding what was said to them. Thus, unless God granted them special dispensation, their souls were not washed clean. But worse than this, in these dreadful times, at the very moment when the distraction, frenzy, or torpor of the dying required support from church, family, and friends it was not forthcoming. Instead it shrank, decayed, and frequently fell completely away, out of inability, fear, and selfishness. And, so it must be admitted, as the intensity of the pestilence grew ever stronger, an increasing multitude of Christian folk were left to perish alone, their souls abandoned, with scarcely a mourner or even a candle to accompany them to the pit.

Despite the best efforts of the majority of the clergy of Walsham and the lay folk who assisted them, extreme adversity rendered it impossible to provide the full traditional rites so beloved by all. Instead, the sheer scale of deaths and the terror which accompanied them forced many aspects of the observance of sacred ritual and liturgy to be curtailed or abandoned altogether, and often not in an orderly fashion. In the cruel chaos many major shifts in faith, custom, and practice were condoned as necessary and unavoidable. Accordingly, it became common for parishioners to be assured that the souls of their dear departed would not suffer if both they and their loved ones had done all they reasonably could to secure a Christian passage of death. Surely God would not punish those who strove to do their best against impossible odds?

Try as he might, however, Master John often found it difficult to accept such compromises with an easy conscience, being torn between a desire to offer comfort and aid to his flock and a firm conviction that most traditional practice was indispensable. Nor could ordinary people easily accept that making do was as effective in securing salvation as the age-old beliefs and ceremonies they had grown up with. In their hearts folks desired the old liturgies and meticulous routines they were accustomed to, and lamented the frequent lack of a priest at the bedside when they and their loved ones departed the earth.

Nor were they easily comforted, for there had been no such meddling with the truth before the plague. Instead, parishioners had been told many times by their priests, "The passage of death out of the wretchedness of the exile of this world was extremely hard, very perilous, and also very terrifying," and that it was essential for all Christian folk "to die in a state of true repentance and contrition." Deeply implanted in hearts and minds was the belief that "although bodily death is the most dreadful of all terrifying things, spiritual death of the soul is much more horrible and detestable, as the soul is more worthy and precious than the body." Therefore, even the most unlearned of parishioners understood that the attainment of a pure and contrite condition at the moment of death required free and full confession in the last breaths to a priest, as well as the making of amends for past transgressions, the aid of the power of the Communion Host, and the protection of the Virgin. It was no less a matter of fact that the safe passage of the soul required the sealing of the body anointed in holy oil, the collective prayers and candles of family and friends, the singing of psalms, the chanting of prayers, the solemn procession with clerks, the careful interring of the body in consecrated ground, and a multitude of Masses. How could it now be accepted that a lonely death in a state of near madness or stupor, unshriven and unhouselled, except perhaps by the stumbling efforts of family, with bodies cast with little ceremony into shared graves, could serve the same purpose? Guilt and despair as well as terror hung over the households of Walsham, and these emotions were fed not just by fear of the imminence of a horrific death, but also of the fate which awaited stained and abandoned souls in the afterlife.

Villagers knew well enough what was expected of them from the seven acts of mercy, as Master John constantly reminded them of their Christian obligations. But under the onslaught of death, decent impulses to self-sacrifice were strained and broken. Fear of the plague and the burdens of the spiraling deaths and sickness of loved ones and neighbors, forced most folk into a reordering of the priorities of their lives, and in others it precipitated blind panic. Dread of catching the pestilence by contact with its victims, which was just common sense as well as the advice of experts, meant that the sick were shunned instead of being cared for. As soon as lodgers or servants displayed any symptoms of ill health they were evicted from their rooms, and left to wander abroad. Where good neighbors would once have conscientiously visited the sick, now when a person lay on their deathbed even dear friends hid themselves away, weeping in shame. And, sad to relate, the scourge implanted in the heart so great a terror that it vanquished love, and some mothers even deserted their sick children, husbands their wives, and brothers and sisters their siblings.

Nor did this shameful neglect apply only to the living. Fear of the corruption which lay in corpses led to the abandonment of the souls which were waiting to depart from them. Instead of joining the unceasing flow of funeral processions, most villagers peered from behind doors and window shutters or from a distance thought safe, sorrowfully noting that the deceased they knew and liked had scarcely a candle to guide them to their resting place. Whereas before the pestilence even the poorest creatures were sent on their way with ceremony and a goodly gathering of the devout and the conscientious, now a good burial was enjoyed only by those villagers who had been fortunate enough to join together as members of the Corpus Christi fraternity.

In the rising temperatures of an unseasonably warm spring and early summer, the fear of infection and the need to safeguard the living led the less virtuous to resort to any means to get rid of the bodies of their loved ones without endangering themselves. Thus corpses were thrown into fields and ditches where they were collected like rubbish and cast without ceremony into common pits by rough hands. Yet there were also a multitude of instances of courage and self-sacrifice. It became not uncommon for good folk, sometimes sick with plague themselves, to carry their parents, wives, husbands, brothers, sisters, and children to the graveyard in their own carts and barrows, or even in their arms, rather than entrust them to uncaring and impious hands.

Priests, for good reasons and bad, often failed to come and administer the sacraments before death occurred, and when they did arrive in time few could stop their hands and voices shaking with fear. And, shame though it is to tell, among those clergy who continued to perform their divine vocation there were some who demanded payments far in excess of those deemed adequate in former days. Much of the cruelty, however, was caused not by the selfishness of the people but by the sheer scale of the sickness and death that tormented them. The lack of nursing pushed the death rate even higher, as those who might have survived died from want of nurture rather than an excess of infection. Whole households often fell ill at the same time, and so there was no healthy person left to provide food, drink, and basic hygiene. And the sickness and death of parents, as well as the sheer callousness of their guardians, repeatedly left young children to suffer and perish without food or care. Though cowardice and selfishness in these days frequently threatened to overwhelm courage, kindness, and charity, it was the sheer enormity of the pestilence which thwarted all but the exceptionally devoted. As Good Samaritans assisted a sick stranger at great risk to themselves, so they commonly found within a few days that two, three, or even more friends and neighbors became sick and demanded their attention. In this manner, even the most pious and selfless were physically and mentally drained by calls on their time and emotions. What is more, servants were scarcely to be found, whatever the wages that were offered.

Yet even the most helpless of young children did not always die for want of care, and tales were told of babies found alive and healthy, clutching tightly to their dead mother's breast. Margery Wodebite, without fear for her own safety because she enjoyed the protection of Christ, rescued the young orphaned Goche children from the house of their dead parents, and it was largely due to her charity that they survived the pestilence. Margery, however, succumbed to the sickness herself in mid-May.

It cannot be denied that, even under the stern and watchful eye of Master John, some of the Walsham clergy shamefully deserted their duties or made excuses not to attend the dying. One of the newly arrived chaplains, notable for his pointed shoes rather than his learning or devotion to his flock, fled from Walsham soon after the plague broke out and was not seen again. Another assistant hid himself away, from exhaustion or fear rather than sickness, only to be found by Master John, who roused him from his sloth and drove him to return to his duties. But the most devoted of Master John's band of helpers were repeatedly overcome by fatigue, and the better part of them succumbed to the sickness itself, with the most diligent among them seemingly the most vulnerable.

Master John, of course, was the most assiduous priest of all, in Walsham or elsewhere (see figure 28). He provided both a shining example and a relentless goad, leading and driving his clerical assistants and lay helpers to perform feats of courage and endurance. While ministering to his flock in the valley of death, he paid no heed to personal profit and little to the revenues of his patrons, the monks of the abbey of Ixworth. Though accepting all dues which were offered freely, John did not press for payment from those who had forgotten, were too poor, or were too distracted by grief. So, at the height of the plague he received an angry message from the bursar of Ixworth priory reprimanding him for not spending enough time keeping his accounts and chasing payments. Master John, however, ignored this missive, continuing to pay more attention to souls than to money. As there was scarcely time to comfort the dying and bury the dead, he neglected to press for mortuary gifts in the form of cattle, sheep, and pigs from the bereaved. Moreover, there was no space in his glebe to keep all the livestock that had been given, and there was no one to look after them. In desperation, he had them driven to Ixworth and left in a field outside the priory walls.

Physical exhaustion was not, however, the greatest weakness Master John had to confront in himself. From first hearing of the pestilence when it was in distant lands, he had found it difficult to understand fully God's purpose, and had relied instead on faith to carry him through. However, as time passed and the pestilence drew ever closer, John's doubts had multiplied. Now it was smiting Walsham, and his bewildered parishioners demanded answers to their urgent questions: Why is God scourging us with this cruel torment, and poisoning and destroying the blameless along with the sinful? What have we done to deserve such cruelty? Why does he permit the good to die and the evil to live? Why does God kill innocent children, even infants who have had no chance to sin? For Master John, providing satisfactory answers was much more challenging than ministering to the contagious on their deathbeds in plague-ridden houses.

Like many of his colleagues in the Church, including the bishops, archdeacons, and theologians who were charged with interpreting God's will, John did not feel capable of fully comprehending the divine plan. He was well aware that some of his betters believed that, since God's judgment was always just, the unprecedented scale of the present carnage must have been provoked by the unprecedented scale of sinfulness in the world. So he repeatedly scoured his memory and his conscience to uncover the immense weight of sin and malice in Walsham that would deserve the savagery of the pestilence now being visited on it.

But he did so without success. Master John believed, of course, that God was not using the pestilence out of vengeance as a punishment for transgressions, but in his mercy using it to turn men and women from their sinful ways on earth, so that they might enjoy eternal bliss. However, he found himself far too deeply disturbed by the sheer scale of the misery and suffering that he observed daily to accept that all would turn out for the best. And when he paused for prayer and contemplation, he found that the clarity of the faith in his heart was increasingly clouded by doubt, and its strength drained by uncertainty.

This doubt and uncertainty infected the parishioners of Walsham as well as their vicar. Master John, who had hitherto invariably been treated with great reverence, now often found himself being interrogated and his judgments questioned. When asked to explain why God's vengeance was condemning the best part of the people to an agonizing death, Master John hesitated to follow the example of other priests by berating parishioners with accusations that the evil in the world was now many times greater than it had been in the time of Noah. Instead he would say, "As the Bible tells us, God drowned the whole world in the time of Noah because the wickedness of men was great on the earth, and all the thought of their heart was bent upon evil. But I do not know what is the true answer today, and it is not for me or you to interpret the mysterious will of a kind and forgiving God." And he encouraged them to consider the offense caused to God by the lechery, greed, hypocrisy, and frivolity which abounded in their own village, even in the midst of death.

Sometimes, in a hostile or angry manner, a mother or a father who had lost a young child in agony would say, "If sin is the reason this plague is scourging us, and if God is just, then evil sinners should die, and even myself, but not my children who have not sinned at all, or so very little." In his response, John would refrain from repeating the harsh pronouncements favored by other priests and their superiors, such as, "God is punishing the innocent in order to chastise the most evil and guilty," or "God is punishing the children not for their own sins but for those of their parents." Nor did his belief that the guiding hand of God lay behind all things permit him to remark that fortune was to blame or that God made mistakes. Some popular preachers stated that "although God strikes the target when he seizes a sinner sleeping in his sin and gives him a terrible death, he is a wayward archer who sometimes shoots the arrow of death beyond the target by hitting an elderly mother or father, or short of the target by hitting a son or daughter, or to the side of a target by hitting a brother or sister." Instead, Master John preferred to comfort grieving parents with words derived from the story of the son of Bersabea: "Your children living in a sinful world would soon have wished to follow the sins of their parents and others had they lived, and as a consequence they would have suffered eternal punishment. So, by taking them while still pure, God does them no injury, but allows them to escape from the dangers of this world and go forth to glory."

It was most destructive of all to the faith of Master John that there were no signs in the bottomless pit of the pestilence that any of the measures that he and his trusty assistants were so assiduously performing were having any effect whatsoever on God's wrath. Nor did his parishioners fail to observe that the greatly increased numbers of Masses, confessions, processions, and prayers did nothing to weaken the pestilence, but rather it grew daily in ferocity. While Master John tried to answer those doubters who railed that "Prayers have no power this pestilence to halt. For God is deaf nowadays and deigns not his ears to open," he increasingly found himself uncertain of the truth of his own words. At no time more so than when he was brought news of the death of his best friend, Richard the infirmarer of Bury abbey.

An elderly groom who had been Richard's personal servant for many years fulfilled his master's last wish by traveling to Walsham to give John the sad news: "The plague has been ravaging Bury abbey for more than a month, and the Lord has already taken more than one in two of the monks, and the greater part of the servants and pensioners who dwelt there. As if that isn't enough for him, he shows no signs of being satisfied with this haul. He is still striking down those who loved him much more effectively than those who didn't." John was too shocked by the news of his dear friend's death to reprimand the messenger for his blasphemy, and he listened silently to details of how Richard had devoted himself selflessly to caring for the sick, until eventually he was too ill to rise from his bed. John nodded with assent when told that his friend, despite the danger he knew only too well he was exposing himself to, had tended both the physical and the spiritual needs of those who filled his infirmary to overflowing. And he smiled knowingly at his practical turn of mind when the servant reported how Richard had persuaded the abbot to cut the lengthy and elaborate funeral rites that the abbey had always followed on the death of a brother, because of the threat posed by pestilential corpses to the health of those monks and servants who remained alive. So, instead of bodies lying in the chapel for three days, Richard arranged for them to be interred the same day, after a brief but intense requiem. Then he personally supervised the adding of quicklime to the earth when the grave was filled, to rot the body swiftly. John mused that Richard would have been very satisfied to know that this was exactly how his groom had treated his own corpse immediately after his soul departed.

Even in the darkest days of the plague, when John was exhausted by the endless struggle to perform all of his sacred duties for all of his parishioners, and distraught by his constant inability to do so, he continued to inspire faith in others. But inwardly, time and again he felt himself in imminent danger of collapsing into despair. Then, one night in the depths of his depression, as he was agitatedly turning the pages of his Bible in a desperate search for advice and comfort, God had caused his fingers to rest and his eyes to fall on Psalm 91, and he read:

> *I will say of the Lord; He is my refuge and my fortress: my God; in Him will I trust.*

Surely He shall deliver thee from the snare of the fowler, and from the noi-
some pestilence.

He shall cover thee with his feathers, and under His wings shalt thou trust:
His truth shall be thy sword and buckler.

Thou shalt not be afraid for the terror by night; nor for the arrow that flieth
by day;

Nor for the pestilence that walketh in darkness; nor for the destruction that
wasteth at noonday;

A thousand shall fall at thy side, and ten thousand at thy right hand; but it
shall not come on nigh thee.

Because thou hast made the Lord, which is my refuge, even the most High,
thy habitation;

There shall no evil befall thee, neither any plague come nigh thy dwelling,
For He shall give His angels charge over thee, to keep thee in all thy ways.

John knew at once, with absolute certainty, that God was by his side and had guaranteed his deliverance. Thenceforth he went daily into the eye of the storm of the pestilence without fear in his heart or doubt in his mind. Although the pestilence struck down hundreds of his parishioners, henceforth John did not waver in his determination to minister to his flock in their time of need. He was indeed protected by angels.

Master John was not alone in regaining his faith. Indeed, despite all the horrors and tribulations that the pestilence inflicted, the light of faith burned constantly in some hearts, not least in the pious villagers who, eight months before, had formed themselves into the religious society they called Corpus Christi. These brethren and sistren remained true to the oaths they had sworn to assist each other in the time of their death, and now in the face of waves of adversity that washed over Walsham after Easter they spent from their common purse and also gave of their time and love to provide spiritual comfort and fitting funerals for their dying and dead fellows. Their ranks were culled time and again, and the survivors were repeatedly overwhelmed with the intolerable burdens imposed by sickness among their own family and friends, yet they found themselves miraculously refreshed and replenished with zeal. With strength derived from working together they strove to uphold impeccable standards of devotion and ritual, even in the most difficult of circumstances. If anything, the ardor of the members appeared to increase with their shrinking numbers to match the growing weight of their burdens and the perils of their obligations. This selfless devotion ensured that a succession of funerals were held which bore, for those dark times, a rare and fitting resemblance to those of old. Although wax was scarce and very expensive, the fraternity prided itself on always carrying a respectable number of candles of sufficient size to light the funeral bier of their fellows on its way to burial, though sometimes mourners were to be seen bearing makeshift torches made from wood and rags dipped in oil and fat. In this way, loyalty and piety provided a curing of the soul, a greater peace of mind, and a safer route to salvation for the brethren and sistren. And, it must not be forgotten, the whole community derived great benefit from the collective prayers which were said at their gatherings.

But while the members of the fraternity could offer each other protection for their souls, they had nothing to offer for their bodies. At their first meeting after the pestilence had finally ceased, almost a year to the day since the group of villagers had taken their common oath, the roll of parchment on which the names of founder members had been inscribed was read out. Then, with solemn ceremony, the names of each of the brothers and sisters who had perished were crossed out, to be carefully written again on the foot of the same roll, and it was noted that more than half of the original members had perished. The survivors decided that this list would henceforth be called the bede roll, and they swore an oath to keep the departed in perpetual memory and celebrate frequent Masses for the sake of their souls.

Yet piety and steadfastness was not the only story to be told. As person after person and family after family succumbed to horrific deaths, the capricious nature of the pestilence, which carried the innocent as well as the guilty daily to their graves, led some villagers to lose faith in their religion and abandon themselves to fate. Instead of quietly and obediently awaiting death, they chose to spend their remaining time and worldly wealth enjoying life to the full, seeking to satisfy every base appetite, spending their waking hours eating, drinking, and fornicating. In this way they squandered what little money they had, consumed their inheritances, and sullied their soul.

However, with the rich diversity that characterizes human society and is accentuated rather than dulled in times of crisis, there were others who appeared strangely indifferent to their fate. Or at least their senses had been so blunted by tragedy that they went through their days as if in a state of trance, concentrating on the basic tasks and seemingly unaware of the chaos surrounding them. Yet others shunned all worldly things and concentrated on the spiritual, leading lives of extreme abstemiousness and piety. Some folk of this disposition hid from all social contacts, praying ceaselessly, eating and drinking only the most simple fare, and daily mortifying their flesh.

But lest it be thought that the plague inspired all to extreme responses, the greatest numbers of folk followed what they understood to be the sound advice of doctors and of priests, adhering to moderate regimes to obtain spiritual as well as bodily health, trusting that sober and pious behavior would best ensure the resistance of their bodies to the pestilence and, if that failed, ensure salvation for their souls.

It was commonly agreed that there was no better defense against the plague than to run away from it. Some had fled before the plague arrived, and when it did come eventually to Walsham many more thought hard about following them rather than waiting to die. But where could they run to that did not also have the plague, or would soon be struck by it? How could they abandon their homes, property, livestock, lands, and livelihoods? How could they raise sufficient money to survive for long away from their native village, when they were offered so very little for their possessions and land when they tried to sell them? So those few who did leave were predominantly poor landless people with little to lose, and they soon discovered the awful truth that the plague was raging for scores of miles all around Walsham, destroying the fine cities of Bury, Cambridge, Ely, and Norwich, as well as innumerable market towns, villages, and hamlets. Wherever they turned, they faced dangers in strange places at least as great as those they had fled from in their home village. It was almost impossible to find shelter and food, except for the highest prices. What is more, even if these fugitives chanced to find a place where the plague had not yet arrived, they encountered the most violent hostility from the residents who feared that they were bringing the death with them. Consequently these wanderers soon drifted back to Walsham or died along the way.

From the cities of Bury, Ely, and Cambridge, with their narrow, crowded streets and their multistoried houses, came tales even more shocking than the events witnessed in rural Suffolk. Particularly disgraceful were the piles of corpses in the streets, which, for fear of infection, had been thrown by families from their doors or even from their upstairs windows. There they lay until they were collected up like foul rubbish by gangs of vagrants who promised for high fees to take them to the cemetery and arrange for a priest to supervise their burial, but more often cast them into the river or dumped them in fields.

In the spring and early summer of 1349, as plague ravaged central and eastern England and began its march to the far north and west of the realm, it seemed to even the most sober of men and women that the end of the world might be nigh and that, within the space of a few months, the whole of humankind would be wiped out. Vacant cottages, overgrown fields, and deserted farms abounded in Walsham. Families which had been present in the village since time out of mind entirely disappeared, whole lines of succession to wealthy inheritances were wiped out, and innumerable households were left with only one or two members rather than the five or six who had previously flourished.

Yet still the pestilence persisted. Weeds grew high in the fields and, because there was no one to care for them, sheep, cows, oxen, and horses strayed unchecked through hedges and closes, damaging crops, falling into ditches, and dying from hunger, accident, and neglect. The roads, paths, and tracks of the village were largely deserted, as strangers were repelled and most folk sought to avoid contact with others. In these days, only the poor continued to be out and about, for they had no choice but to seek work and the wherewithal to buy food and drink. "We may as well die of the pestilence as of hunger," they retorted when questioned about their reckless habits. And so they did in prodigious numbers (see figure 29).

Late May to Early June, 1349

The lords of the little manor of High Hall, Edmund de Welles and his sister Margery, were relatively poor by the standards of most medieval landlords, and even in normal years would have struggled to maintain their household and status on the income they received from the produce of their demesne farm and the rent from their tenants. Lady Rose was of a higher social rank and appreciably wealthier. For not only was Walsham manor many times more valuable than High Hall, but Lady Rose held a number of properties elsewhere.

The High Hall demesne farm lay close to the manor house and comprised around 150 acres of arable land, as well as pastures and some woodland on which cattle, sheep, and pigs were kept. Although the de Welles had more than thirty tenants prior to the Black Death, the majority of them held very small amounts of land, for which they paid little in rent. However, the modest amount of cash the de Welles received from their tenants was boosted by the work most of them were required to perform on the demesne farm, as well as the sizable fines and dues that had to be paid whenever a tenant died or a tenancy changed hands, and various other levies exacted through the manor's court. Labor services tended to vary in relation to the size of holdings, and in a rental of 1327 William Wodebite, one of the more substantial tenants, is recorded as owing three shillings, three pence, and three farthings in cash each year, as well as fifteen winter works and twenty-two harvest works, six hens and five eggs. The efficient farming of the demesne required substantial inputs of labor, and tenants probably supplied more than a fifth of the labor requirements through the year and a much higher proportion at harvest time. In addition, the de Welles employed a few full-time servants (called famuli) *on annual contracts, for whom they provided accommodation as well as quantities of food and clothing. Finally, because of the unevenness of the workflow in the course of the farming year, they would have relied on hiring casual labor by the task or by the day at busy times.*

By far the most important problem facing landlords in the aftermath of the plague was a shortage of people, both to refill the landholdings made vacant by the deaths of so many tenants and to work on their farms and in their households. The situation was made worse because the supply of laborers shrank even more dramatically than that of tenants, not simply because half or more of the former laborers had died, but many of the survivors acquired land for themselves and thus had less time and inclination to work for others.

Since there are no surviving account rolls for High Hall or Walsham for the period of the Black Death, we do not know for certain what wages were paid, but copious evidence from other manors shows that wages soared and many tasks went undone. The closest evidence comes from the manor of Fornham All Saints, just northeast of Bury, where additional day workers were being hired at enhanced wages from April onward because of the shortage of full-time servants. Farther away, at Cuxham (Oxfordshire), farm servants were given an extra shilling (12d) between April and June 1349, "to encourage them to work better," and in September the plowmen, carter, and shepherd were given further cash bonuses of 5s. On the estates of Westminster abbey, pressure from farm servants led not only to substantial increases in their cash stipends but to improvements in both the quantity and quality of their food rations. Casual laborers apparently fared even better, with their wages at least doubling in the year of the Black Death, and they were commonly given substantial additional benefits including food. Even the notoriously mean bishop of Winchester was forced to pay 4d a quarter to get his wheat threshed, rather than the 2d or 2.5d he had paid formerly. Yet, despite these very substantial increases in wages and perks, most employers still found it impossible to hire all the labor they needed, as the reeves of a number of Westminster abbey manors confirmed when they reported that the winter wheat could not be sown because it had proved impossible to find enough men to plow the fallow in the summer of 1349.

The fourteenth-century calendar was punctuated by the celebration of a host of saints' days, festivals, rituals, and holidays, many of which ordered or marked the ecclesiastical, farming, and communal years. The cycle of ecclesiastical feasts roughly coincided with the cycle of traditional popular festivals, which in turn often marked points in the farming year. The calendar continued to grow as new festivals were inaugurated and additional saints given their feasts. Corpus Christi was, perhaps, the most spectacular addition to the calendar. It was first observed in England in 1318 and grew rapidly in popularity among both Church authorities and the laity. The feast celebrated the Body of Christ in the Host, and through that evoked the whole body of true Christian people. Its emphasis on blood, suffering, and mutual assistance struck a chord with the pious in the midst of confusion and death.

⊱⊰

Sir Edmund de Welles, lord of High Hall, survived the pestilence, along with his sister Margery, although many of their household perished. Since well before the pestilence arrived in Walsham, Edmund had followed a strict regime of covering his head with a cloth, plunging his nose into cauldrons filled with excrement and urine from the hall's privies, and inhaling deeply. Although he suffered from repeated bouts of diarrhea and violent vomiting, and exhibited intermittent symptoms of extreme frailty, he did not fall victim to the plague. His escape was held by some people wise in these matters to prove that the lord of the manor had discovered the surest means of avoiding the infection. Edmund's private physician, initially skeptical about this regime, later began to reason that by adopting it, his lord had enjoyed twofold protection. First, the noxious vapors Edmund constantly kept around him and inhaled probably repelled or negated any air poisoned by plague that might come near; and second, any residual plague poison that did manage to enter his body was likely expelled by his violent shitting and vomiting. Yet the doctor remained puzzled that Edmund's valet, who inhaled the same vapors and experienced the same favorable emetic experiences as his master, had died of plague, while Margery, who had ridiculed her brother's antics and retreated to live in the far end of the house to avoid the unpleasant smells, had also been spared.

Whereas most folk were satisfied simply to survive from day to day while the plague raged, Edmund became increasingly anxious not just about his bodily health but about his financial health as well. He fretted over the turmoil on his little manor, the uncollected rents, the plethora of unpaid fines arising from the death of so many of his tenants, and the fate of the animals which had to be collected for death duties, looked after, and sold for the best price. And he was alarmed about the vacant holdings, the whereabouts of unknown heirs, and above all about the lack of proper written records or even accurate hearsay information as to what was happening to his lands and his tenants. Edmund was well aware that his demesne farm, with its ample fields, animals, and buildings, was suffering from severe neglect. He had prided himself that it was one the best-run farms in the area, but now it was deteriorating rapidly because there were so few people tending it. Most of his full-time and part-time farm servants had died or were ill, his tenants did not turn up to perform their customary labor services, and there were scarcely any laborers who could be hired for reasonable wages. Just as worrying were the serious and growing threats to his lordship and the respect in which he was held. If order and correct procedures were not restored soon and his rights and dues properly witnessed, written down, and accounted for, he feared permanently losing authority over his tenants, with his lordship irreparably weakened or even destroyed.

It was for these and other reasons that Edmund made up his mind in the middle of May, when plague was raging with extreme virulence in and all around Walsham and High Hall, that a session of his court had to be held. However, he wisely decided to change his normal practice of presiding in person over the court, a role he had always greatly enjoyed, and remain shut up safely within the walls of his hall. So he asked John Talbot, the parson of the neighboring parish of Rickinghall, to deputize for him. Though Talbot was at first reluctant, the fatness of the fee Edmund eventually offered was sufficient to persuade him.

Because High Hall manor was so small, with less than forty tenants, the normal attendance at the courts was far lower than at those of Walsham itself. In the early morning of May 25 less than fifteen people, all fearful of catching the plague from each other, gathered reluctantly in the courtyard of the manor hall. John Talbot was clearly ill at ease and anxious to get things over with as soon as possible. He had arrived in Walsham only the day before and, although he clutched some parchments in his hands, which he repeatedly referred to, it soon became obvious to all that he had not been able to brief himself adequately on the business before the court. Talbot began, as Edmund de Welles had instructed, by ordering that the cottage and plot of land of Henry Trusse, a freeman who had died, should be taken into the lord's hands until the heir came to court, and then he set yet another deadline for the Wodebite brothers to repair the vacant houses on their lands. Then, with a theatrical flourish, Robert Sare, a prominent freeman, galloped into the courtyard on a fine white horse, strode proudly up to the table where Talbot sat, knelt and swore fealty to Sir Edmund and Lady Margery for the lands that he held of them. Talbot was so taken aback at this fine show and so flattered to have such a wealthy man kneeling before him, that he quite forgot to ask the Wodebite brothers who they had secured to pledge to the court on their behalf that they would carry out the required repairs.

Rather flustered, Talbot announced that he was moving on to try and deal with the consequences of all the deaths among the lord's tenants, of which there had been eleven to his knowledge. A shout from the small gathering asserted that at least another five tenants had also died or would be dead in a couple of days, but Talbot responded by saying that he could only deal with those deaths of which he had prior knowledge and confirmation.

He began, "John Goche and Peter Goche, villeins, who held certain tenements from the lord, have died. It is ordered that these tenements should be seized until the heirs come." But before he could say more there were loud protests from the gathering. John Wodebite stepped forward and stated forcefully, "It is a breach of custom for the lord to seize these holdings. Everyone in the village knows who the heirs of the Goche brothers are, because they each have young sons who are alive and well." Another villager brusquely informed the parson, "If you don't know what to do, we can tell you. On the payment of a heriot and perhaps a small fine, their landholdings should pass to their sons, and the court should assent to the sons, and the holdings, being placed in the hands of guardians until these boys become of age."

Talbot attempted to compose himself, but at this point another more aggressive voice from the gateway informed him that he should not be in charge of the court at all, seeing that he did not know what he was doing, or even where the Goche brothers' holdings were, or how much land they contained. Talbot was shaken by the rudeness of the assembled peasants, and he attempted to quieten them down, first by rebuking them, and when this had little effect, by reassuring them: "Lord Edmund is anxious to identify the true heirs to all vacant holdings and has no desire whatso-ever to occupy these lands himself or to go against custom in any way. I can assure you that everything will be sorted in an appropriate manner in due course. But as the lord's agent and as steward of this court, I am re-sponsible for making sure that no mistakes are made. Therefore I can only accept properly authenticated statements, not hearsay and gossip shouted at me from the floor."

With a show of authority, Talbot attempted to move on to the next item of business, which was the death of William Isabel, another of the lord's villeins. But it soon became clear that he knew no more about this matter than he knew about the Goches. Once again, because he had not been told what lands Isabel had held, he was forced to use the same vague phrase about "certain lands" rather than the precise location and acreage. Once again, to hostile murmurings, he reported that Isabel's lands should be taken into the lord's hands temporarily until the true heir was found. However, this time there were no assertions from the gathering as to who this might be, just sad shakes of the head and soft confirmations that all the Isabels in the village had died, including the feisty Idonea who had caused the lords and ladies of High Hall so much trouble. Nor was there any dissent when Talbot stated that William Isabel's estate could not pay the customary heriot because William did not have any large animals when he died. Therefore the heir, when he or she was found, would have to pay a fine in money before taking possession of the lands.

Talbot was on firmer ground when he came to the death of John Chapman. He reported that Chapman had held a messuage and two acres of land, and according to the custom of the manor, John's three-year-old daughter, Agnes, was the heir, but that until she became of age, the land would be granted to his widow, Agnes. As the Chapmans' cow had died, he ordered that the heriot to be rendered to the lord was a ewe.

Agnes had come into court as she was keen to establish her rights, and kneeling before John Talbot, she swore fealty to Sir Edmund and Lady Margery. Talbot granted her possession on accepting 6d from her as a fine for formal entry into the land. John Wodebite stood up and confirmed that he would act as surety for Agnes. When she had completed the ceremony, Agnes hurried to John Wodebite and eagerly inquired of him how her daughter was faring. She was told that little Agnes was well, and they agreed that as nobody in John's household had been taken sick it would be best for her to remain where she was for the time being.

The full information Talbot possessed about the Chapman inheritance proved to be exceptional, and he was soon forced to revert to brief and incomplete summaries for the majority of the remaining deaths. However, he was able to note on his roll that John Helpe had given a mare to the lord and lady on the death of his brother, Robert, and that neither of Robert's other brothers, Henry or Gilbert, had turned up to claim their share of the inheritance. The death of Margery Wodebite was also noted with some alarm by the gathering, since, as her brother-in-law John mournfully remarked, "If God has not seen fit to spare so holy and devout a person as Margery, what chance has any of us of surviving?" Talbot called the meeting to order and announced that Margery had left no beast which could serve as a heriot, so her sister had paid a fine of one silver shilling to take possession of her four acre holding. By the time this part of the proceedings had been concluded, the deaths of eleven tenants in all had been recorded on the roll.

Finally, as the gathering prepared to disperse, Talbot proposed electing Adam of Angerhale as collector of rents and dues, to replace the previous officeholder who had recently died. To Talbot's great relief, both Adam and the assembly agreed. He knew that Sir Edmund would be delighted to hear that he had strengthened the manorial administration at such a difficult time, but he did not know that his lord would soon be hearing complaints that the court proceedings had been handled incompetently.

A rumor had been circulating that Edmund de Welles was holding his court because he had received word that the pestilence was coming to an end. But that hope was soon shattered. Death continued to rage without respite through the rest of May, and at times its ferocity seemed even to strengthen, if that were possible. Robert Sare, who had theatrically braved danger to swear fealty at High Hall court, expired soon after, and Adam of Angerhale accompanied him to the grave, not living long enough to carry out any of his new duties. In the ensuing weeks the sorely depleted ranks of the once populous parish of Walsham were thinned still further, and, to Agnes Chapman's alarm, John Wodebite's wife was taken sick.

For most villagers attendance at Mass was the only occasion when they took courage and willingly braved the dangers of exposure to disease by mixing with others. Surely, it was thought, God would not allow his church to become a place of contagion. Even under the darkest clouds of pestilence there were relatively few who allowed their fear of mingling to outweigh their fear of neglecting the service of God or missing his bless-ing. Even if they felt that God was deaf to their own pleas for mercy, they had the souls of their dear ones to pray for and, sad to relate, there were many who had to assuage the guilt of deserting their sick relatives in the time of their greatest need.

As the pestilence persisted, stoical resignation and even lethargy pro-gressively overcame panic and hysteria. Surrounded daily by death and the fear of imminent infection, many of those who had yet to succumb to the sickness welcomed the deadening of their senses and the dulling of their emotions that the enormity of their predicament brought. Though only a few would openly admit it, there was also confusion about what God's will was and what he wanted them to do. It was commonly ob-served in conversation that none of the prayers, processions, confessions, censings, kindling of candles, or ceaseless Masses had given protection against the pestilence or lessened its force. Rather, death had raged ever more fiercely. And secret doubts were harbored about whether it was worth trying to anticipate his demands or assuage his anger.

The Rogationtide and Whitsuntide festivals passed without much celebration, and far fewer people attended because there were far fewer people alive. In previous years large bands of enthusiastic and triumphal villagers had joined the Rogation procession. Led by priests with bells, banners, and the cross, they had progressed along each of the parish boundaries, beating the bounds of its territory, blessing the fields, bridges, crossings, and mills, enthusiastically driving out the evil spirits which brewed enmity between neighbors and sickness in man and beast. This year, however, the procession in the third week of May was a thin and mournful affair attended by a handful of the most zealous, and it had quickly assumed the aspect of a penitential procession. The Whitsun Communion on May 31 was also a subdued ceremony, and what had always been one of the leading sermons of the year was given by a young, recently tonsured clerk because the rest of the clergy were needed elsewhere.

But then, just as it seemed as if all might perish, there were slight, at first almost imperceptible signs that the scourge might be starting to wane. There had been disappointments before as the toll of deaths had fluctuated—first surging, then falling back, only to soar again with indescribable ferocity—but this time hope progressively turned into belief and conjectures into reality. By the first week of June there were indisputable indications the clouds of contagion that had rained death on Walsham were lifting. Not only were significantly fewer new victims observed day by day, but the battle between the frailty of the victims and the potency of their affliction began to become less unequal. A larger number of buboes began to break down of their own accord, more carbuncles shrank, more inflammations cooled and faded in color, more fevers abated and raging pains in the head subsided. As what they were witnessing bore relation to the knowledge they had that even the most devastating visitations of the pestilence overseas had eventually waned and then disappeared, and that the pestilence was no longer raging in southern England, the gloom slowly began to lift from people's hearts and smiles began to replace frowns. Villagers emerged from their houses, timidly at first but then with greater assurance.

In a spirit of optimism, clergy and laity decided to make a special effort to mount a procession for Corpus Christi feast day on Thursday, June 11 (see figure 30). Though it was too early to be confident that the present waning of the pestilence would lead to its total demise, people yearned to celebrate their deliverance and speed the contagion on its way. Master John strongly favored these optimistic sentiments, believing that the celebration of the Body of Christ would help lift morale and confirm the church in its rightful place in the center of village life. He hoped to create an atmosphere of wonder, excitement, and exultation, so that his parishioners could put behind them the disappointing festivals held since Easter.

Master John knew in his heart that no more than one in every two of his parishioners was still living, and he feared that some of the survivors would be reluctant to leave their homes and that some were doubting their faith. So he decided that the procession should be severely short-ened to the cluster of roads and paths in the vicinity of St. Mary's, in order to ensure that there were crowds of observers all along the route. In the early morning of the feast day groups of children went along strewing flowers, leaves, and rushes on the ground. Those participating in the procession were arranged in a strict order of precedence as they ar-rived, and as usual there was much squabbling among the lay folk as to who would occupy the best positions following the Host and clergy. At the head of the ranks were at least six clergy dressed in their finest cas-socks and copes, one bearing the great latten cross of the parish, another the painted wooden Madonna and child, and others holding books, handbells, and smaller crosses. In prime position came Master John, holding aloft the Host in its ivory casket, walking slowly under a red cloth canopy supported on poles held by choirboys. Following closely behind him was Margery de Welles with her friar confessor and two members of her household; Edmund had decided he was not well enough to attend. Then came the brothers and sisters of the pious fra-ternity of Corpus Christi, who had given 2s toward the occasion. Each one held candles, except for the two most senior guild members who proudly grasped painted wooden poles which supported a newly woven banner depicting a pelican feeding its young from the blood of its breast. The villagers who followed behind were carefully positioned according to wealth, office, and popularity, with the precise order of precedence being even more contentious than usual, owing to the multitude of holes that had been torn in the accustomed village hierarchy. It was the first procession for very many months that was not driven solely by a desperate supplication for mercy, and at times it resembled a celebration of deliverance.

But the mood in the service that followed turned somber. The liturgy was underscored by almost continuous low grieving moans from the body of the congregation, punctuated by howls of sorrow, as husbands mourned for their wives, wives for their husbands, parents for their children, children for their parents. The days and weeks of isolated grief swelled to a crescendo in its public expression, and Master John frequently paused during the liturgy and stepped back, nodding with understanding, till the sobbing subsided. He delivered only part of his usual Corpus Christi sermon. Severely abbreviating his lengthy account of the seven miracles of the Body of Christ by omitting most of the homilies and moral tales with which he normally accompanied it, Master John moved swiftly to pray for the souls of the multitude of departed. In the days before he had made a special effort to collect the names of all who had died from his assistant priests and lay helpers, and now he recited them for the congregation and God to hear. Even though he read more quickly than normal it took him fifteen minutes to reach the end of his list.

Rising to a crescendo of supplication, Master John beseeched God, "We pray that the pestilence may be brought to a speedy end here in Walsham and in the country about, just as we have heard that it has now ceased to kill in London and in many other parts to the south. Be merciful, O Lord, and spare your sorely scourged and pitifully enfeebled parish any further divine punishment." Fortunately, it was not long before these pleas were heard.

In early June, as the deaths in Walsham finally slowed from a flood to a flow and then to a trickle, Lady Rose thought it safe enough to instruct her estate steward to travel to her most valuable manor to bring its disrupted administration to order and hold a much needed session of the court; on the same journey he could also visit the other properties and interests that she held in the region. Although Lady Rose had always taken a close interest in the fat revenues that Walsham manor produced for her, she had never resided there for more than short periods, and in her advancing years she had relied heavily on her third husband, Hugh, and her estate steward, John Blakey, to keep the local officials, demesne farm, and manorial tenants in good order. Sir Hugh had died in the pestilence, and Lady Rose increasingly turned to her son, Henry, for advice.

Living with the rump of her household in a remote house deep in the country, Lady Rose found it almost impossible to obtain reliable

information about Walsham, and her estate steward, John Blakey, had
been too preoccupied with the death of his wife and two children to pay
much heed. But in recent days news had started to dribble through to
her, and it was unremittingly dire. Many holdings were lying vacant for
want of tenants, her demesne farm had scarcely been tended for weeks
on end and was now in a very poor state; the local peasant officials appointed to act on her behalf were apparently either dead or shirking their
duties, and her tenants were failing to perform their customary work. As
a result the fields were exceptionally weedy, and a fair proportion of her
livestock and draft animals were suffering sorely from a variety of ailments. Still, Blakey ruefully remarked to Lady Rose, "Since God decided
that he had to strike Walsham with a plague, he could have chosen a
worse time to do it." Spring lambing had been massively disrupted and
most of the young lambs had perished from lack of care, as had many of
the ewes which had borne them. But, more importantly, much of the
spring plowing and sowing had been completed before the plague arrived, and there were more than 250 acres of wheat, barley, oats, and
peas growing on her fields, and there was plenty of time to prepare for
the harvest, which was still many weeks away.

Since Lady Rose was reluctant to risk her son by sending him to Walsham, she would have to rely on Blakey to make decisions on her behalf.
From the conditions on the manor where she lived and the other she held
nearby, she knew that short-term compromises with tenants and laborers
would be necessary in order to get things back to normal in the shortest
possible time. So she told him, "My priority is to fill all the lands left vacant by the deaths of my tenants before the weeds take over and the cottages fall down. Therefore, you should use all my rights and powers to
compel reluctant heirs to take up their obligations. Set some examples;
punish some of them harshly to cow the others. Yet also offer some in-
centives where necessary. If either the land or the heirs are poor, you
should reduce the entry fines you ask them to pay, and you may also allow
them to pay in stages, if you think fit. I am not at all keen on reducing
their rents, but you can grant some allowances, as long as they are strictly
temporary, on the poorest lands, if they are impossible to let otherwise.
But be very careful. You must not be too generous, for that will encourage others not to pay their customary dues."

At this point Blakey sought to intervene with a question, seeking clarification. But Lady Rose raised her hand to quiet him and plowed on: "I
need to restore order and my rights, and I need to raise money. So I cannot
abide having lands left empty. If, after searching very diligently, there are
any lands for which you cannot find heirs or anyone else willing to take
them on the customary terms, then I will permit you to let them on short
leases of a year or so, until someone comes to take them on the old terms,
as they surely will when the world returns to normal. Or, if even that proves
impossible, then get my reeve to sell the pasture rights, animal by animal,
to those who would wish to put their cattle and sheep on it. Finally, but
only as a last resort, you must take any land that is entirely unwanted in
hand, and have it farmed for me at a profit. But again, do so only on a
short-term basis, so that I can take my full rights again when the world recovers to normal. Above all, be very careful not to allow any peasant to get
the better of you, or any of my revenues to be lost or my assets to be run
down, or my lands to be occupied for less than they are truly worth."

Blakey was becoming hopelessly confused as to whether he should be
harsh or conciliatory, but he had little time to ponder as Lady Rose went
swiftly on. "I know you will tell me it is difficult to hire good workers, but
I am determined that you should not throw my money away by paying
common laborers outrageously high wages. I am aware that you might
have to offer some small additional rewards to those of my full-time farm
servants who have remained loyal and hardworking during the pestilence,
but be restrained, show no sign of weakness. Most importantly, you must
force my own tenants to work for me all the days that they are required
to by the ancient customs of the manor. More than this, I rely on you to
instruct my tenants that when they hire themselves out as day laborers,
they must first offer themselves to me. I am their lady and I have the
right to first call on their labor, and at reasonable rates of pay."

Blakey assured Lady Rose that she could place absolute trust in him,
and that he would do all in his power to uphold her interests and rights
and would take full stock of the situation in Walsham before granting any
concessions on fines, rents, or wages.

When John Blakey arrived in Walsham at the end of the first week in
June, he was shocked to find conditions far worse than he or his lady had

imagined, and only one of the three major officers the community had
elected to run the manor was fulfilling his duties. The reeve, Walter Osbourn, who was responsible for managing the lord and lady's demesne
farm and its buildings, had perished, and so too had his deputy. Matthew
Gilbert, the manor woodward, had been too upset and too busy since the
death of his wife to carry out any of his duties, let alone offer additional
assistance in the running of the manor. Only Geoffrey Rath, whose responsibilities as hayward were to manage the tenants, collect their rents
and services, and ensure they behaved themselves, was there to meet him.

The steward sat in shocked silence as Geoffrey Rath told him that
scarcely any of the tenants were bothering to turn up on the required
days to perform their work on the lady's farm, in blatant breach of their
tenancy obligations (see figure 31). Blakey's mood darkened further
when he learned that shortly before he was taken ill, Walter Osbourn
had handed over an extra shilling in cash to each of the remaining full-
time farm servants in order to get them to carry on doing even a small
part of the duties for which they had been hired. And he had become almost incoherent with rage by the time Geoffrey admitted that, in desperation, he had been forced to pay almost twice the normal daily wage
to hire workmen and women to save the farm and its livestock from
complete ruin.

Blakey remonstrated with Rath, "There is not the slightest chance that
such outrageous and unsanctioned payments will be allowed as legitimate
expenses by her lady's auditors. In fact, not only will I not support them,
I will see to it personally that you are required to repay any excess above
the normal wages."

But rather than being cowed by these threats, Rath was defiant. "Your
eyes will soon be opened by spending a few days in Walsham," he told
the steward.

Later that day Blakey learned that the same farm servants who had received the unwarranted extra shilling were now demanding yet another
shilling to be paid at once, and an extra bushel of the best wheat every ten
weeks in addition to the eight bushels of mixed grains they had always
been given. If they did not get the money and the corn, they asserted,
they would all run away to be day laborers and be far better off. Blakey
immediately summoned the spokesman of the servants intending to dis-

cipline him, to make him aware of his obligations to the lady of the manor, and to inform him that they would henceforth be reverting to the precise terms of the contracts they had freely agreed to last Michaelmas, before the arrival of the pestilence. But the ringleader turned up with a group of his fellows, and the meeting broke up in disorder when Blakey was told by the plowman, "I don't give a pea for the lady's plow," and the men stormed off.

Before the spluttering steward could compose himself, Geoffrey intervened and drew John Blakey aside: "We must stop these men walking out. It would be a disaster for the lady if these servants break their contracts and cease working. There would be no chance at all of us hiring replacements, and even if we were able to we would have to pay them more than these men are demanding. There are simply too few people seeking work and far too many jobs for them to do."

Geoffrey went on to try and explain to the steward that most of the laborers in Walsham had died, and most of the survivors had been able to find land of their own and were busy farming it. Blakey tried to wave him quiet, but Rath pressed on, venting the frustrations that his post had brought him over the previous weeks. "What is more, because of all the deaths and all the vacant holdings that have to be filled, hardly any of the lady's tenants are willing to work in full the days of labor they owe on the demesne farm. I have tried bribes of food as well as the threat of fines or even eviction, but I have been unable to get more than a handful of these tenants to turn up and work. What can we do?" He did not wait for Blakey to answer. "There are far fewer people offering themselves for hire, but we still have the same number of acres to cultivate, and even more animals to look after than normal, because of all the heriots that I have carefully collected. I have offered wages that you see as outrageously high, and a good meal on top, but still I have not been able to find nearly enough willing to work, and fewer still who are willing to work hard. Most of those who have turned up and taken the lady's money have been lazy and obstinate, moving slowly at their jobs and sitting around idling or playing games for much of the day. I have to spend most of my time wandering round prodding them to get off their backsides. I have also been forced to take on women and boys to do men's work, but even they demand excessive wages."

John Blakey had been shocked into silence and eventually began to show more understanding by raising his hand in mild appreciation of his hayward's dilemma. But Rath would not be humored. "It is an impossible job that I have to do. And, anyway, I was not elected reeve but hayward. I am doing the work of the reeve, and much more besides, but I do not receive the stipend of a reeve, let alone all the extra money and perquisites I deserve for suffering abuse from almost everyone in the village for acting diligently in my lady's interests."

Rath had been serving as hayward for three years and had made a good income from the office. From Lady Rose he gained remission of the rent on his land and some other gifts of cash and corn but, more importantly, as an officer of the manor court he pocketed a host of small offerings from those who had to appear there, who had transgressed the village bylaws or sought some favor or other. For a halfpenny or so, Geoffrey had many times forgotten to present a case of trespass or report a missed labor service or the breach of the bylaw prohibiting the serving of ale in unmeasured cups and jugs. For a more substantial fee, he had always been willing to assist in the negotiation of lower fines for miscreants and act as a pledge in court for villagers in need of the formal support of a man of good standing. For the time being, he decided, he would remain in office. In the current disorder there might well be the chance of even greater rewards.

While the pestilence raged, Lady Rose whiled away some of the hours isolated in her remote manor house calculating the profits as well as the losses which the huge toll of deaths among her tenants might bring, in particular, the size of the windfall she was about to receive from the animals collected as payment of death duties. Before her steward departed for Walsham, she had given him detailed instructions on the necessity of accounting for every single animal that was due to her as heriot from the property of every dead tenant, and how to ensure that these were indeed the best animals. She also insisted that all the heriot animals be well looked after, fattened up, and then taken to a good livestock market to be sold for the highest price. She knew that a significant number of her Walsham tenants were wealthy enough to own some very fine cattle and horses indeed, and as she checked back over the court and accounts rolls of recent years, which she kept in a chest in the castle, she found that cows had generally brought her 8s or 10s each, and mares, calves, and steers around 4s each. Even if only two score of her tenants had died of plague she would receive very many gold pounds which would more than compensate for the loss of rent and the reduced sales of produce from her farm.

But now the steward sat in stunned silence while Geoffrey recounted at great length and, he had to admit, often in plausible detail, why Lady Rose's dreams were far from coming into reality. First, Geoffrey reported that it had proved impossible to collect all the heriot animals that were due, not just because he could not find the time or the help to do so, but because he could not always discover who had died. What is more, Geoffrey argued, although it was essential to collect the heriots quickly from unoccupied farms before they perished from accident or hunger or theft, it had often seemed best for the present to leave the rest with the new tenants since he had no means of properly looking after them. He couldn't hire a reliable herdsman, the manorial pound was full to overflowing, and he was having to dump animals in any available vacant field.

When the steward asked, "Why have you not sold them?" Geoffrey laughed. "I have tried, but I have only been offered ridiculously low prices that I knew you would not accept. At best half of what they fetched before the pestilence, but usually far less. There are so many animals for sale and so few buyers. Have a look round the village, and you will find sheep and even cows wandering around without owners." Blakey thought about interrupting but did not know quite what to say. So Geoffrey continued, "On the other hand, perhaps they should be sold for whatever we can get. For they are eating so much that the lady's own livestock are having to go short of fodder, and that will cause the milk yields of her cows to fall, the wool of her sheep to coarsen, and her oxen to lose strength. Anyway, many of these heriot animals are in poor condition, and likely diseased in some way or another, so they could infect her lady's stock."

The steward kept his temper and bit his tongue, but inwardly he refused to accept Geoffrey's word or his competence. For the next couple of days he toured the village with his hayward noting livestock prices and seeking to hire sufficient men and women to tend the lady's animals, weed her land, clean ditches, build new fences, and carry out essential repairs on the demesne buildings. When they went to the green opposite the church, where men and women had always gathered early each morning to offer themselves for hire, they found it was almost deserted. In desperation, they offered the customary wage of three halfpence per day without food to the poor specimens who were there, and were ridiculed and abused, and told that none of them was prepared to labor for less than 3d per day in good sound money, no clipped coins, and a good meal on top. The steward then marched Geoffrey off to the nearest alehouse, where they found a number of fit young men and women drinking and gambling. After announcing who he was and demanding that they all stand up, he offered the men 2d per day and a meal of bread and pottage if they would follow the hayward to the demesne at once. But none off them accepted. So he remonstrated with them, reminding those who were the bondsmen and women of Lady Rose that they had the obligation to work for her whenever she wished, and at the rate of pay she felt appropriate. Most gave excuses, but two of them reluctantly agreed to serve at two and a half pence per day, as long as they were given a hot meal at noon with generous slices of meat. Blakey agreed but made it plain he would only hire them for the one day on these terms.

As they walked back to the farm, Geoffrey praised the steward for getting workmen so cheaply and gently suggested that he should have secured them on a longer contract. "Times have changed. When the pestilence was raging, these humble folk saw that those who performed even the meanest of tasks were able to demand three, four, or five times what they had always been paid. They have tasted what to them are riches, and they have no intention of returning to the old wages. Why should they when they can get far more than we are offering from the bailiff of Edmund de Welles? Or indeed from any number of farmers, large and small, in this village and all those round about, who need help and are able to pay for it."

As if that was not enough, Blakey found the lady's truculent plowman waiting for him when he went exhausted to his lodgings. Tugging disparagingly at the dull russet tunic and dirty white shirt he wore, the plowman excitedly reported that Edmund de Welles had just given his plowman a brightly colored doublet and gown, and a girdle decorated with pewter, which had been the second best outfit of Sir Edmund's bailiff until he died in the plague. Then he reminded Blakey that Lady

Rose was a far greater lord than Sir Edmund, and her reputation could be damaged if her servants looked scruffy. So he brazenly demanded similar livery to encourage him to work harder for his lady. As Blakey ordered him to be thrown out, the plowman warned that if he did not get what he deserved, he would not stay around to undertake the plowing of the fallow land that would have to be done over the next few weeks if the winter wheat was to be sown on time (see figure 32).

The sleepless night Blakey spent worrying about what he had seen and learned since he arrived in Walsham was not wasted, for in the morning his mind was made up. Since the lady's farm and its buildings were in sore need of repair and enormous amounts of work had to be carried out urgently to save them from ruin, he would have to make concessions in the short term, which could easily be reversed when the world returned to normal. He would not do anything that would permanently diminish his lady's rights, but he would do what was necessary to stop immediate decline. So, first thing, he gave the hayward permission to reach agreements with a small number of workers at whatever wages it took to secure them, as long as he was careful to note their names, the number of days they worked, and the pay and other perquisites they were given. He told Rath that under no circumstances would he be drawn into negotiating with rustics himself, and he privately vowed to get his own back on each and every one of them who overcharged him, when conditions returned to normal. In the afternoon, as a show of strength and in order to frighten the others, he gave orders to sack the young assistant dairymaid when she asked for an additional shilling in cash to be paid to her at the Michaelmas reckoning. It was only later that evening he learned that the senior dairymaid had run away with a young laborer the day before to seek her fortune elsewhere.

John Blakey had already spent far too much time bickering with laborers and now needed to sort out the tenant farms. In all the years he had worked for Lady Rose, he had never had to cope with anything remotely like the task that faced him. During his time as steward only about five to seven tenants of Walsham had died each year, and he had never before dealt with the inheritance of more than a handful of holdings in a single court session. Yet now he reckoned that many scores of tenants had died, and some people he remembered as sober and reliable witnesses were claiming that less than one person in every two had been left alive.

As a matter of urgency, the steward needed accurate evidence to be gathered on each and every holding that had become vacant or changed hands. This had to include the name of the former tenant, the rent and other obligations that were due from the tenement, whether or not the best beast had been taken as heriot, who the correct heir was, whether or not the heir had been found and whether or not he had taken possession of the land, and what entry fine should be paid. This information would have to be obtained through a multitude of systematic, detailed inquiries in the village, beginning with Master John, who would know all of the deaths. Being a practical man, Blakey had brought with him a rental of the manor compiled many years ago that listed one by one the landholdings, their tenants, and the rents and obligations due from them. He had been pressing for some time for a new rental to be drawn up, but Lady Rose and her husband had never got round to agreeing the expense. Even though the record at his disposal was long out of date, it would still prove an essential tool in his struggle to compile an accurate and complete record of the manor and what had happened to it. He had been amused to learn of the crude mistakes made when John Talbot had presided over the High Hall court a few weeks ago, and he was determined not to repeat them.

But everywhere the affairs of the village were in turmoil. The discontinuity and confusion caused by the sheer scale of deaths among villagers, which had time and again slashed through many of the lines of succession to landholdings and cottages, made the correct identification of heirs a monumental task. Each tenement had to pass down the bloodline in a precise sequence, and where wives, sons, and daughters had died along with the father, then the brothers, sisters, and grandchildren of the deceased had to be identified. That was only going to be a relatively straightforward task if they were close kin and living in Walsham or nearby. But, if there were none, then nephews, uncles, or cousins had to be found, wherever they might be living. Finally, even if distant but rightful heirs were eventually identified by the testimony of villagers, if they were not living in Walsham there would be little chance of discovering in time whether they were alive or dead.

Knowing that he needed assistance, Blakey decided to appoint a panel or jury composed of the most prominent men in the village. They would be chosen with the approval of community leaders for their wisdom and honesty, and would ask questions and pool their knowledge of the manor and its families, and of the horrendous events of the last couple of months. But when he set about doing so, he soon discovered that finding appropriate members for the panel was an unexpectedly difficult task. Although Walsham manor had always been well administered during the steward's time, the pace of change had been relatively slow and it had never been difficult to find experienced and generally capable men available to fill its main offices, inquisitions, and juries. But now, many of the usual reliable and knowledgeable candidates for such posts had died, and the few wise and able men who had survived the plague had many other preoccupations. Therefore, it was only after considerable effort that the steward and Geoffrey Rath managed to get together a panel of fifteen men. In this task they were helped by the eagerness of a number of relative newcomers to serve, since they were flattered by being asked to exercise such power for the first time, and by the desire of a number of long-standing residents to serve in order to ensure that order was restored and custom strictly followed. Further, one or two boasted that they would use their position to keep an eye on the behavior of the steward and his lady.

Over the next few days the jury spent a great deal of time gathering information, and Master John was most helpful in providing the names of the dead. But when the steward met with the jury, he found that far too much of the evidence to hand was conjectural, hearsay, or partial. Reluctantly, he decided that there was no alternative but to try to firm it up using the villagers who attended the court session, which he would do by asking the assembly to confirm or amend the record. Blakey was also beginning to appreciate that even a successful court would leave a substantial amount still to be done. The jurors tried to impress on the steward the truth of the remarkable rumors circulating the village that a good number of peasants were refusing to take up the lands they had inherited. But he dismissed them contemptuously: "Rustics always take whatever scraps of land they can get, even if it is of the very worst quality, and at whatever rent I choose to ask. In any case, I will show them what is good for them, if they are too stupid to know it for themselves. I have the legitimate means to compel heirs, and indeed any of my lady's serfs, whether they are the kin of the deceased or not, to take up any tenancy my lady wishes, and to pay the rents and obligations due from it. I will not stand by and let even the smallest of my lady's rights and authority be gainsaid."

He then instructed them to tell all tenants of Walsham manor that the court would be held soon after sunrise on the following Monday, June 15, and he sent a message to Master John asking him to announce the meeting in church on Sunday.

June 10–20, 1349

Such momentous mortality naturally had the potential to create confusion and disorder, but equally striking is the speed and power with which forces within society and economy moved to restore stability. The compilation of commendably accurate and complete records within days or weeks of the ending of an epidemic of phenomenal ferocity is a testimony to the efficiency and durability of the procedures that were entrenched in many administrative structures, from humble manors up to the extensive bureaucracies of the Crown. One such record is the roll of the proceedings of the session of the manor court of Walsham held on June 15, 1349, when the pestilence had barely ended. In this roll the deaths of 103 tenants are recorded in entries that, with few exceptions, provide the name of the deceased, details of the tenancy, whether a death duty (called a heriot) had been paid, and if so what it was, who was the heir and whether they had taken up possession, and if so what fine they had paid for entry. Walsham was a sizable manor, but neighboring Redgrave was even larger, and the roll of the court held there in July 1349 recorded the deaths of 169 tenants in similar fashion. We know little for certain about how all this information was collected and presented with such commendable speed and accuracy in such difficult circumstances, but the identification of heirs must have proved an especially formidable undertaking when so many lines of succession were repeatedly broken by sudden deaths, and so many heirs were distant kin who did not reside on the manor.

In the weeks and months after the departure of the pestilence there was considerable potential for severe disruption or even chaos, but, against all expectations, the great majority of the landholdings made vacant by the deaths of probably around half of all English tenants were speedily filled. Detailed study of manor court rolls, including those of Walsham and High Hall, reveals that although the huge mortality caused the proportions of holdings that passed to sons and widows to fall substantially, since close kin were also frequently killed in the plague, a plentiful supply of new tenants was usually to be found among more distant kin, as well as from unrelated people seeking to acquire land for the first time or add to their existing holdings. Also, of course, a substantially increased number of daughters were able to inherit because they had no surviving brothers.

The speed and completeness of recovery on each manor depended to a considerable extent on the quality of the responses of landlords and their officers, as well as the attractiveness of the lands on offer. In general, lords responded with commendable flexibility, quickly realizing that it was often in their interest to make concessions in rents, fines, and other conditions of tenure, rather than risk existing and potential tenants leaving to seek land elsewhere on more favorable terms. The shift back toward normality was also assisted by the culture of peasant communities, in which the landless were rooted at the bottom of the social hierarchy, and wealth and status were measured in terms of the amounts of land that were held.

But whereas the historian is struck by the continuities, contemporaries would have been overwhelmed by the scale of the changes. In the days, weeks, and months after the Black Death there was understandably much confusion as both lords and peasants struggled to comprehend what had happened and determine how to react. The sheer scale of deaths had resulted in a massive shift in the relative scarcity of land and labor, and set in train powerful forces that threatened to alter permanently the balance of political and economic power between lords and peasants. But in the short term, in the village of Walsham, ordinary people were more interested in enjoying their new freedom to make choices about whether to take possession of a relatively unattractive piece of land or when and for what wages they would agree to work.

The tenants of Walsham drifted hesitantly into Lady Rose's large barn not long after first light on Monday, June 15, glancing anxiously around to see who of their friends and acquaintances had survived and who of their enemies had perished. Though many, for fear of infection, had withdrawn from community life while the pestilence raged, news had still managed to spread quite effectively, and even the most reclusive could not have failed to be aware of the scale of the changes which had taken place in the village. Nonetheless, it was still deeply traumatic to witness the absence of so many who had been present at the court held a little more than three months before, and bewildering to see the abundance of the young and often unfamiliar faces of those who had come to take up the lands of the departed and assume their place in the community. At first sight it seemed that most of the prudent and wise old figures who had always guided the court and the community through the multitude of decisions it had to take each year were no longer there. Who would now determine farming routines on the common fields, adjudicate on customary practices, enforce law and order on the manor, conduct dealings with the lady and her officials, and regulate relations between villagers when the need arose? The ranks of the men of substance and experience who filled the manorial offices, acted as pledges on contracts, guarantors on the ability of lesser people to meet their obligations, mediators in disputes, and who could be relied on to interpret what was right and proper from long memory, old customs, and repeated practice, had been mercilessly thinned. Moreover, many, perhaps most, of the richest residents had perished, and their fine houses, ample acres, and plentiful livestock were now in the hands of young sons, daughters, grandsons, or even total strangers who eagerly awaited to be confirmed as the legitimate possessors of these enviable assets.

The clerk of the court sat at his table against the east wall of the barn and ceremoniously unfurled the longest parchment roll that had ever been seen at the court, fully four feet in length, that he had specially extended in anticipation of the unprecedented amount of business to be written down. Then John Blakey, the steward, entered with a considerable flourish, carrying a large bundle of rolls and scraps of parchment, and sat down in a high oak chair next to the clerk's table. He immediately called the gathering to order and announced that Sir Hugh de Saxham, the husband of Lady Rose, had died, and that Lady Rose was now the sole holder of the manor. He asked them to pray for Sir Hugh's soul and then moved swiftly on. He stressed to the gathering, most of whom were there for the first time, that a huge amount of business had to be conducted in order to deal with consequences that flowed from the multitude of tenants who had perished in the pestilence.

As those present began to murmur among themselves about who had perished and who survived, Blakey sharply silenced them: "The number of deaths that we have to deal with today is probably more than a hundred. For each one, it will be necessary to identify the rightful heir, and for me and my clerk to account for the payment of death duty and entry fine. Note will also be taken of whether the heirs have already acceded to their holdings, and if they have not, arrangements will be made for the custody of the land." Then, with great solemnity, the steward pronounced, "Henceforth the great roll made in this court will serve as a perpetual record of landholding on this manor, so the information it contains has to be accurate, and I require all of you to ensure that it is."

Blakey had decided in advance that the best way to proceed was to read out the name of each tenant who had died, the tenement he had held, and the animal or sum of money due or already taken as a heriot for the lady. This having been settled, he would invite the jurors to move on to deal with the more difficult issues of who was next in the line of succession to take over the farm, and whether or not he was in court to be confirmed as the legitimate heir. If he was, he would be required to swear fealty, and if not the jurors would be ordered to make further inquiries to find the person obliged to take the holding, backed up with the threat of force and the distrainment of property if necessary. Usually the steward was strict in keeping people from chattering during the session or from interrupting while court business was being conducted, and he had been known to fine them heavily for doing so. This time, however, he urged those attending not only to listen very carefully to each announcement but to have no hesitation in letting him know if they believed any part of any statement they heard was not correct. He also encouraged those who were knowledgeable to respond without fear when asked a question. But, he warned, they should offer information only if they knew it to be correct, as he would punish ignorant or mischievous people who interrupted with a large fine for wasting the court's time.

The momentous proceedings then began with the jurors formally opening their presentments through their foreman, Geoffrey Rath: "John Syre held from the lord on the day he died a messuage and twelve acres of land by services and works, and after his death the lord took a cow in calf as a heriot." When the steward asked what the cow was worth, the hayward replied that it was impossible to say because there were so many animals for sale, and he did not know whether he would be able to sell it at all. This statement met with nods of approval, and Geoffrey went on to report that John's son, Adam, was the nearest heir, and that Adam was of sufficient age and entitled to have entry to his father's land by the payment of that heriot, following the custom of the manor. Blakey then beckoned Adam Syre forward. Kneeling before the steward with his hands clasped together, Adam swore an oath of fealty to Lady Rose, commending himself to her as her loyal and obedient bondsman.

"Success!" thought Blakey. "If only all the business could progress as smoothly as this." But he knew it would not. The next presentment of the jurors related to the death of Adam Hardonn, who had held a cottage and a garden. A mare had already been taken from the premises as a death duty, but the heir, Adam's brother William, had not entered into possession of the holding and was not in court. In response to the steward's questions about William's whereabouts, claims were made that he was living only a few miles away and knew about his brother's death, but would not come.

"This cannot be tolerated," the steward pronounced. "Let it be ordered that William Hardonn be found and distrained to come to Walsham to take possession of his brother's holding, and pay all the required fines to do so."

The next succession went smoothly, commendably so since the jurors had been especially conscientious in not only identifying Alice Fraunceys of Bury St. Edmunds as the heir to Nicholas Fraunceys's landholding but getting her to take it up. Alice was the daughter of Margaret Fraunceys, who many years before had done well for herself by marrying John Hammond, a freeman of the borough of Bury. Now, through an attorney, the young woman formally accepted possession of Nicholas's messuage and a little over three acres, and agreed to pay a cow as death duty, but only after it had calved.

This success, however, was swiftly reversed, for neither of the next two heirs identified by the jurors had so far taken up the landholdings they were obliged to occupy. The first, John Robbes, had simply failed to appear in Walsham to take possession of his sister Matilda's bake house and half acre. Robbes's absence was troublesome to the steward but not altogether unexpected, for he did not live in the village and few of the people present had ever met him. It was possible that he had not heard of his sister's death or that he was not alive. However, John Fraunceys's point-blank refusal to take possession of his dead sister's cottage and garden posed a different problem. Fraunceys resided in Walsham and was sitting right in front of Blakey at the court as a member of the jury that he had appointed to assist in finding heirs to holdings. His behavior was a direct challenge to Lady Rose's authority and flew in the face of all custom and practice. Blakey was beside himself with anger and decided to challenge Fraunceys directly in open court, hoping to assert his authority by cowing him into compliance. So he asked the rest of the jurors to swear that John Fraunceys was indeed the legitimate heir to his sister Emma's tenancy. This they did, and Blakey then ordered him to occupy it immediately and render all the appropriate rents and dues. But Fraunceys repeated his refusal to accept the holding, although now in an evasive rather than an openly defiant manner. Fearing a public defeat, the steward decided to move on, but only after threatening Fraunceys that he would regret having gone against his lady in this matter (see figure 33).

Blakey was relieved that in the next item of business, John Deeth's little cotland, passed to his daughter Catherine without delay, though because her father had no animals she was required to pay only a token fine of 3d to have possession. The court then turned its attention to the shocking series of deaths that had struck down several branches of the Deneys family. Walter Deneys had died in the early days of the plague, and the jurors reported that his five acres of land had passed immediately to his son, Robert. However, shortly after inheriting Robert had also died. Robert's son John was the next in the bloodline, and as he was present in court, he was formally acknowledged as the legitimate tenant of this land and also of an additional cottage and garden.

The villagers had been gossiping for some time about the good fortune of Nicholas Deneys, a moderately wealthy landholder who stood to gain handsomely from multiple deaths among his close relatives. The jurors first reported that Nicholas was the heir to the estate of his brother, William Deneys, and he gratefully accepted possession of the eight and a half acres that William had held in Walsham, and added them to the acre in High Hall he had already inherited when his brother's death had been noted in that manor's court in late May. Then the jurors moved on to formally identify Nicholas as the sole heir of his recently deceased mother, Avice Deneys, and he was duly admitted to the five acres of land she had held. The next death to be reported was that of Juliana Deneys, a distant relative of Nicholas. But such was the mortality suffered by this unblessed family, Nicholas was again identified as the next in line to inherit, in this case a cottage with just over an acre attached to it. To the consternation of the steward, however, Nicholas stood up in court and declined to take over the rundown cottage and garden. When asked to explain himself, Nicholas said that he already had enough land to be going on with and had no need of a derelict hovel and weedy garden, especially since his wife had died and he had to manage everything on his own. It was not only Nicholas's effrontery to go against custom and refuse a kinswoman's land that set the tongues wagging, for it was widely known in the village that Nicholas had already found himself another partner, Agnes Fraunceys, to share his bed.

The steward immediately stood up to quell the chatter and bully Nicholas into accepting responsibility for the cottage and garden. "Do you not know that from time out of mind it has always been the lady's right to compel her unfree tenants to accept holdings which descend to them through the bloodlines of their kinsfolk?" he asked sarcastically. "Do you not know that you are obliged to take this property, keep it in good order, farm it competently, and render all that is due by custom for it?" Nicholas, however, refused to be cowed and replied excitedly, "There must be other heirs more directly in line than me. I hardly knew the woman. I simply cannot manage anymore land. If I am compelled to take up this rundown cottage and weedy plot, I may be forced into poverty and driven to abandon the holdings I have already agreed to accept."

The steward glowered at Geoffrey Rath for not solving this problem earlier, but once again he reluctantly decided not to prolong a confrontation in front of the full and unruly court. He passed on, saying, "This matter is not settled. It will only be settled according to my lady's will, after further inquiries have been made."

Irritated by these setbacks, Blakey called a short break, during which he made a pretense of checking up on Nicholas Deneys. But his mind soon began to reflect on the enormity of the task that faced him, and how the world of Walsham had been utterly transformed. For as long as anyone present at the court could remember, custom and precedent had invariably guided the land market. But the pestilence had thrown this orderly world into turmoil, and now villagers were struggling to make sense of the new situation by choosing the course of action that suited them best. Blakey recognized that what suited the interests of the tenants often did not suit those of Lady Rose.

For time out of memory, the swift and smooth succession to a tenancy on the death of its holder had never proved a problem. Land had always been eagerly sought by rich and poor alike. There had never been enough land in Walsham to meet the needs of its resident population. Land provided essential food, employment, and income, and there had always been a press of people seeking the social and economic benefits it bestowed. Vacant holdings and cottages coming before the court had always passed swiftly into eager hands, which almost invariably belonged to the close family of the deceased—usually their wives, husbands, and adult sons, sometimes their daughters or, very rarely, their grandchildren. Until the pestilence had struck, that is. Just a few weeks ago no heir in Walsham would have been unwilling to assume his inheritance. On the contrary, so strong was the tie to family holdings that those who left the manor to settle elsewhere invariably kept in touch, so that they could be readily found if a close relative died. And those who did not wish to live in the cottages or farm the acres themselves could draw a generous income by subleasing them either to substantial folk seeking to supply the market with yet more quarters of grain and heads of sheep or cattle, or to landless persons and cottagers. Yet now there was an abundance of acres and cottages left vacant because those who had been in line to inherit them had died too, because distant kin could not be traced or had not turned up to claim them, and, most remarkable of all, because those to whom they were offered had refused to accept.

Calling the court to order after a few minutes, Blakey pressed officials to hurry on. But however hard they tried, dealing in an orderly and appropriate fashion with the multitude of deaths and the almost interminable list of landholdings in need of tenants was an impossible task. The successor to Walter Norys was the next item to be decided. It was deemed to be his son, Walter, who had died just a few days ago, and no other heir had turned up to claim the holding. Then John de Broke's desirable freehold farm of seven acres should have passed to a cousin with the same name, but he did not come to claim it. However, Adam Pidelak gratefully accepted the lands of his uncle, Jericho Bartholomew.

As the holdings continued to be processed, the steward noted gloomily that in many instances, even when the rightful heirs were found and were willing to take up their inheritance, they were ill equipped to farm efficiently on their own account, being short of experience, equipment, or capital, or simply too young. In the coming months and years this would continue to create problems for the community, and almost certainly for him as well. Another burden was created by the untimely deaths of both parents, which frequently left young children and heirs as orphans. As the court learned, John Gooch was just four years of age when his father and mother died in the plague; the death of both Cecilia and John Typetot left their nine-year-old son, John, orphaned; and when John Pynfoul died, his five-year-old daughter Hilary was named in court as the sole heir to her father's fifteen acres. The heirs of Robert Springald, whose brother Walter also died in the plague, were found to be his young nieces, Isabel and Hilary Stonham, and Agnes, the three-year-old daughter of his sister Mabel. Suitable guardians had to be found by the court for all these orphans, who would look after them and their inheritances until they were considered to be of a sufficient age to manage for themselves, which in Walsham and High Hall was usually when they reached their midteens.

Within the past two months Walsham had witnessed the extinction of many households, and some wealthy families that had lived for generations in the parish had entirely disappeared. The evidence presented by the jurors on the succession to old William Cranmer's holding revealed that this ancient family had suffered particularly grievously. In the early days of the pestilence soon after Easter, Agnes Chapman had seen the funeral procession of old William Cranmer while her husband was dying, and shortly afterward his only son, also called William, had followed him to the grave. William Cranmer the younger had two sons, Robert and William, and two daughters, Olivia and Hilary, and in accordance with the custom of the manor the two sons had inherited their father's lands in equal shares. But, the jurors went on to report, Robert, who had recently married Alice Terwald, was now also dead, leaving young William as the only surviving male member of the Cranmer family and so the sole heir. However, when Blakey called for William to come forward to swear fealty, a number of his neighbors said that he had been taken sick with the pestilence a few days before, and a voice from the back called out that the court might as well save itself the trouble and admit Hilary and Olivia to the estate now, as young William was so sick he was certain to die.

The steward was alarmed to hear further evidence that the pestilence remained far more active in Walsham than Lady Rose had told him, and he began to wish he had delayed his visit for a few weeks. But for the time being, he stifled his fears and pressed on with the registration of young William Cranmer as the lawful tenant, and made a point of confirming with Geoffrey Rath that the three heriots due on the death of his grandfather, father, and brother had all been duly rendered. Rath proudly confirmed that he had indeed collected two stotts and a cow, only to be told sharply by Blakey that he should be ready to take yet another fine animal from the farm if William did not survive.

At this point Blakey decided to adjourn the proceedings for dinner, although it was not quite midday. He needed to compose himself and ponder further how to deal with the problem of large numbers of legal heirs dwelling in Walsham refusing to take on the landholdings and cottages that were offered to them, which had astounded not only him but all who gathered in Lady Rose's barn on this tumultuous day. As the seriousness of this situation had unfolded during the morning, Blakey had switched tactics, albeit reluctantly, from uttering threats to offering concessions. But, despite saying on many occasions that Lady Rose had empowered him to allow reluctant heirs to take possession without paying the customary fines in full, refusals continued to mount. Moreover, the open defiance shown by the recalcitrant soon began to infect the behavior of others at the court. Even those who were pleased to inherit repeatedly expressed discontent with their conditions of tenure, complaining that the rent was too high, the entry fine too large, or the amount of labor that the lady required them to perform on her demesne farm was too heavy. Almost all those present murmured in assent when complaints were made of poverty, the poor state of the buildings, the weediness of the land, the sad, neglected livestock, the lack of decent farm equipment, or the money to buy it. And they made much of the difficulties caused when the best animals on the farm were taken by the lady as heriot and by the Church as mortuary.

During the course of the morning John Blakey had become increasingly uncomfortable with having to negotiate with these lowly and ungrateful people, and he bitterly observed to his clerk, in between slices of pork and drafts of ale, "These lowly rustics who just a few weeks ago were condemned to a miserable life of hardship and toil for others, have now suddenly become rich in land and prospects. But instead of thanking God for their good fortune, they do nothing but complain to their betters and demand conditions even more favorable than those they have so undeservedly and unexpectedly come to enjoy. God will not forgive them, and nor will I. Make a special note of all those who defy and displease me. I will make amends when the world returns to rights."

In the afternoon session, which soon became the longest-sitting Walsham court in memory, or in the huge collection of court rolls held by Lady Rose, the steward, his clerk, Geoffrey Rath, and the panel of jurors continued to process death after death, case after case, as methodically as they could. For most of the time, the tenants, new as well as old, sat listening attentively to confirmation of who had died and who was succeeding to holdings and becoming their neighbors, farming partners, and fellow members of the community. Master John was delighted to learn that John Kebbil, a favorite protégé who had been ordained a few years before, was returning to Walsham to take up his inheritance on the death of his father, Richard. Gasps periodically greeted extraordinarily rapid promotions of wealth and power, and bemusement attended the complexities that flowed from the failure to find heirs among close family. All were envious of William Alwyne, a man of little ability and no consequence who was fortunate enough to be distantly related to both Agnes and Nicholas Goche, from whom he inherited a cottage and twelve acres and a cottage and fourteen acres respectively.

Few lines of succession proved more complex for the jurors to sort out than that to Walter Rampoyle's messuage and four acres, which he had purchased from William Taylor a short time before he died. On his death Walter had left no surviving wife or children, so the property should have been divided equally between his brothers: Robert, Simon, and William. But since Simon and William had also died of the pestilence a week or so before, their shares passed in the court to Simon's daughter, Alice, and William's sons, William, Robert, Walter, and John. This meant that six people had an interest in the four acre holding. But then, to Blakey's annoyance, two of William's sons, William and Robert, came forward to decline to hold the tenement. In frustration the steward refused to spend any more of the court's time on this case and adjourned it until the next court.

Resentful and skeptical muttering, fueled by the strong ale that many villagers enjoyed during the noontime break, greeted the occasional announcement that yet another nobody, who for years had been scraping a bare living from laboring and begging, had fortuitously come to inherit a prized piece of land, thanks to the death of five or even ten distant kinsmen and women. Many of the older male villagers became alarmed at the unprecedented surge in the numbers of daughters and nieces who became landholders because of the death of their brothers, nephews, and cousins, fearing change and speculating that they would struggle to look after their farmland adequately and play a full role in community affairs. When William, John, and Roger Rampoyle died in swift succession, their sister Alice inherited the entire holding they had farmed together while Alice Patyl first inherited her father's cottage and landholding, and then acquired a further half a messuage and its land from Edmund and Walter Patyl when they died shortly afterward.

When the clerk finished recording the entry that John Hereward had succeeded to a tiny parcel of land held by his dead father and should pay a heriot of a cow after calving, he laid down his goose-feather quill. He had almost filled both sides of the four-foot parchment roll with records of every death and every changed tenancy that had occurred in Walsham since the last court, held three months before. The villagers took this as a sign to rise to their feet to leave, but the steward called them to order: "Stay where you are for a little longer. There is still some important business to be conducted on behalf of Lady Rose. This pestilence has struck some mighty blows but it has not brought the world to an end. There are misdemeanors to be punished and customary laws to be enforced."

During the course of the afternoon proceedings, the steward had become angry at the increasing truculence displayed by many of the tenants who appeared before him, and at the necessity of accommodating the demands of even the meek among them. Reluctantly he had accepted that for the time being it was wise to compromise on many issues, as his lady had urged him to do, but there were limits. A stand had to be made. So, with great ceremony he put on a show of enforcing the lady's rights, just as if it were a normal court instead of the most exceptional the village had ever seen. The hayward and Master John had informed him that two women had produced bastards since the last court, and he decreed that one of them, Olivia Cook, should be fined 2s 8d for childwyte. Then, in a show of vindictiveness as well as strength, he fined Alice Patyl, who had provoked his envy by her good fortune in inheriting so much land, twice as much, for giving birth to twins out of wedlock. This unprecedented fine provoked anger and hilarity in equal measure, and in the general hubbub that followed it could scarcely be heard that John Lester was fined 2d for baking bread which did not come up to the agreed standard and 3d for brewing and selling substandard ale. A fine of 6d, imposed on Alice Pye for selling bad ale in her tavern, was greeted with a small ironic cheer by a group of her regulars. Finally, in a further attempt to assert some of the authority which had been so undermined in the course of the day, the steward issued a warning to the departing tenants that they would soon be required by the lady to come back to another session of the court, which he intended to hold in a few weeks.

As the villagers left the meeting and walked to their cottages or fields, they reflected on the empty homes and farms they passed, the torrent of deaths that had caused them, and the absence of relatives, friends, and neighbors. It seemed that the greater part of the village, rich and poor,

pious and profane, had passed away and the world had been turned upside down. Similar sentiments were expressed that evening by the steward and his clerk as they set about preparing their report for Lady Rose.
As they pondered over the mass of entries they had made on the great
roll, they counted that just over a hundred of the lady's tenants had died
since the last court had been held before Easter, only three months before. Obviously the roll was far too messy and incomplete to be presented to Lady Rose as it stood. The sheer weight of business and
difficulty of gaining enough accurate information meant that the record
of the day's proceedings was littered with gaps, messy corrections, and
marginal notes. There remained such a multitude of loose ends to be
sorted out, forenames corrected, heirs determined, and details filled in
that the steward would have to stay for some days making inquiries and
interviewing the jurors and Master John. The clerk would have to stay
with him to take notes and find time to produce a fair copy of the court
roll on new parchment. But, they gloomily reflected, they would be unable to complete a final record because the pestilence had still not finished its work in Walsham, and an unknown number of villagers were
sick and dying.

John Blakey felt utterly exhausted and bemused as he prepared for bed.
Despite his best efforts he knew he had lost respect at the court. He was
overwhelmed with problems that urgently needed to be solved, yet almost
everything he tackled was far more difficult than it had ever been before.
He found himself having to bargain with the most lowly of rustics who
were not only insolent but ignorant and irrational, and would not be told
what to do. The old ways were not working anymore, but the new were
inconstant and unpredictable. Through no fault of his own (although
Lady Rose might think otherwise), a score of empty holdings lay in his
hands that nobody was willing to take up, despite urgings and threats, yet
he could not hire anyone on reasonable terms to look after them or the
lady's fields and livestock. Only a couple of months ago he and his officers could take their pick of the strongest and most willing laborers, and
rely on them to work well for long hours and fair wages. Blakey longed
for the present turmoil to end and normality to return, when any available
land would once again find a host of willing takers and the men and
women seeking employment would far exceed the numbers he needed to

hire. Instead, however, things were daily going from bad to worse. Substantial landholders and landless paupers alike were making unreasonable and uncustomary demands which he could not and would not meet. At least not until he had had further consultations with Lady Rose and her son, and received new orders.

The pestilence had chastised John Blakey dreadfully with terror and the loss of loved ones. It had also burdened him with guilt for his cowardice, when fear of infection had driven him to neglect his own dying children during the worst days, and he had fled his house leaving them in the care of servants. And now that the pestilence, God willing, was drawing to a close, he found that looking after his lady's estate, which had always given him so much prestige and pleasure, as well as profit, had turned into a wretchedly uncomfortable and immensely difficult task. If he did not give in to at least some of the unreasonable demands of greedy and disobedient tenants and laborers his lady's lands would lie empty and untilled and her estate would be wasted, and if he carried on making concessions to them they would soon get the taste of power and destroy his lady's estate anyway.

Blakey took some comfort in the rumor that the king and his nobles were already devising a means of putting the world to rights and thrusting the rustics back into their proper place. But this would not happen for some time, and meanwhile he had to persuade the very reluctant Geoffrey Rath to serve as reeve of the manor. Despite the substantially improved offer of cash and perks he had already made, as yet Rath had not been willing to commit himself. Much as it grieved Blakey to admit, Rath was indispensable to the recovery of the manor. He knew the residents well, having served many times as hayward, and he had acquitted himself tolerably over the last few days, even if he had been far too profligate with the lady's money. Perhaps, Blakey mused, he would be tempted with an offer of some of the vacant land that lay in the lady's hands on a short-term basis at very low rent. Perhaps the lady could find an outfit of smart clothes to give him from among the liveries left by the deaths of so many of her household servants and retainers. Fine clothes would flatter Rath's vanity and endow him with greater authority to deal with rebellious rustics. Of course, the steward realized with a jolt, any apparel Lady Rose gave Rath must be much inferior to the fine outfit he himself should receive as a reward for the truly exceptional service he was rendering in the most troublesome circumstances.

Then, just as Blakey was pulling back the coverlet on his bed, a servant knocked and entered his chamber bearing news from the priest that the last remaining male member of the Cranmer family, William the younger, had died. There had scarcely been a court in Walsham since Blakey had become steward when a Cranmer had not made a prominent appearance in the proceedings. The family had lived in Walsham for as long as anyone had recollection, or the ancient rolls of the manor extended. There was even a green named Cranmer Green, at the eastern end of Church Way, where they lived. Now this family had been destroyed, its male line completely wiped out—father, sons, and grandsons—and its ancient and substantial estate would pass into the hands of women.

Were the deaths never going to cease? Blakey was frightened and made up his mind to leave Walsham the next day. First thing in the morning he would give final instructions to Geoffrey Rath and stress yet again how important it was for him to keep pressing those rustics who were unwilling to take up their lands and to get the community to make more determined efforts to track down the heirs to vacant holdings. Once more, he would threaten the officers of the manor with hefty fines if they did not start enforcing the lady's rights and the village bylaws more effectively, and all the lady's servants with diverse punishments if they did not manage her farm more efficiently. Then, before noon, he would begin his journey back to his lady's household that, mercifully, lay in a region which for a little time had been completely free of pestilence. Blakey knew his lady would chide him for his early departure, and he would have to come back sometime soon to tackle the mass of unfinished business. But he was determined to return only when he had definite news that the pestilence had finally departed Walsham and its hinterland.

Summer, 1349

The alarm that elites felt at the empowerment of the lower orders by the massive mortality is clearly expressed in the Ordinance of Laborers, issued by the king and his councilors on June 18, 1349, while the plague was still raging in many parts of the realm. This legislation, which was reiterated throughout the late fourteenth and fifteenth centuries, sought to compel the common people to work when required and accept wages no higher, and conditions of service no better, than those current in the five or six years prior to the Black Death. In letters addressed to all English bishops, the king and his council requested that this ordinance be proclaimed in all churches, and that the rectors and vicars of these churches should "beseech and persuade their parishioners to labor and to keep the ordinances, as instant necessity demands." Naturally, attempts to enforce the ordinance provoked considerable discontent and resistance among the peasant, laboring, and artisan masses, who saw it as an act of oppressive lordship which threatened to restrict their freedom and snatch away unprecedented opportunities for boosting their income. Wage inflation was not restricted to the peasantry, and every bishop was urged to do all within his power to "constrain the wage-earning chaplains of [his] diocese, who refuse in like manner to serve without excessive salary."

The medieval world was steeped in custom and precedent, and change generally occurred at a slow pace. Society was rigidly stratified, and its highly unequal distribution of wealth, status, and authority was reinforced by a powerful ideology. For centuries the world had been divided conceptually into three estates—those who labored, those who fought, and those who prayed—

and the members of each had essential tasks to perform to the best of their ability, for the good of the whole community, and in accordance with God's will. In the eyes of the elites, an efficient economy, social stability, and the maintenance of civilized life depended on the masses performing the manual toil for which they had been divinely ordained. If the masses at the bottom of the social pyramid did not perform their allotted role, the world would collapse. As Thomas Wimbledon wrote in the late fourteenth century, "If laborers work not, priests and knights must become cultivators and herdsmen, or else die for want of bodily sustenance."

Before the Black Death the shortage of land and work had helped keep the great mass of the laboring poor subservient, but now the population had been sliced virtually in half the social and economic order was gravely threatened by what was seen as the greedy, selfish, and sinful demands of the lower orders. The great pestilence let loose powerful forces that threatened upheaval in the social order, affecting not just peasants and laborers but clergy and lords. But change of this kind was interpreted as sinful and likely to antagonize an already angry God, who might react by inflicting further plagues on mankind. The dreadful paradox was highlighted by a rapidly emerging awareness that the inordinately harsh penalties God had apparently exacted for sin had not led to the improvement in the behavior of any social stratum, which instead had become worse.

There are excellent series for the prices of a number of major commodities in fourteenth-century England, and they show that all kinds of food were exceptionally cheap at the time of the Black Death and in the months following. The low prices in the spring and summer of 1349 must reflect the severe disruption to trade and travel caused by pestilence and the fear of it, as well as the sharply reduced demand from the shrunken population. The price of all grains plunged at the same time, and barley, rye, oats, and peas were the cheapest ever seen, and the same was true of cheese. The fact that wheat, although cheap, did not fall in price as much as the other grains was probably due to survivors using their improved income to eat more wheat bread at the expense of loaves made out of inferior coarser grains. Manorial accounts show that the price of all types of farm animals also slumped dramatically, in many cases to levels not seen since the early thirteenth century. By contrast, the price of manufactured items such as cloth, clothes, nails, and wheels soared, pushed up by the substantially enhanced wages of the people who made them.

The reader is reminded again that the narrator of this book is an educated person writing soon after the Black Death, who tells the story from the perspective of the literate and religious elites, and gives voice to their fears and resentment about the new order, and especially the threat posed by assertive peasantry and laity.

-ᴴᴵ ᴵᴴ-

The great mortality had raged in Walsham for little more than two months, but during that brief time it scythed the village's population by half. At the height of the carnage in late April and early May, it had seemed to any sensible villager that all humankind might perish. In those dark days, only the knowledge that the pestilence had ravaged but not entirely destroyed other places in England and overseas nurtured the faint hope in those who had not yet perished that the world might not end. This proved to be so. During the second half of May and into early June, the torrent of deaths slowed, imperceptibly and irregularly at first and then more evidently. When stock was taken of the victims in the epic court session of June 15, the terrible power of the pestilence was ebbing fast, and by mid-July the deaths had ceased. God had ordered the pestilence to leave, and obediently it moved on to devastate the north of England.

As the villagers emerged from the thrall of God's cruel purging, they blinked like prisoners liberated from dungeons into the sunshine. But the blessed relief was mixed with profound loss, and when they had time to think of their new predicament, with bewilderment and guilt. After the joy of survival had subsided somewhat, the shock of the loss of loved ones and the absence of so many familiar faces intensified, as did concern over why they were spared when so many others had perished. Cherished and trusted family, friends, and neighbors were no longer there when they were needed, whether to loan food, money, or a farming tool, or to make a gift of time and friendship. Many leading members of the community had also been destroyed, along with familiar figures of authority, officials of the lord and the parish. And, of course, some families counted themselves unfortunate indeed if they had not lost a rival, an enemy, or a creditor or two.

The sense of shock in Walsham was compounded by the news pouring into the village of the ruin of all other towns and villages around, as well as farther afield. No community, it seemed, had escaped the scourge; all had been struck severely. The streets of Bury were said to be deserted, many of its fine houses uninhabited, its markets sparsely attended, its stalls and shops lacking both customers and commodities. The great monastery had lost forty of its monks, and the greater part of its chaplains and servants, and was now said to be urgently seeking permission from the pope to allow mere schoolboys to take vows of profession to enter the community to fill the places of the venerable wise and holy men who had perished. But St. Edmundsbury had fared better than the Dominicans of Norwich, who had been wiped out almost to a man.

Bewilderment followed from the shifting or transformation of so many landmarks of village life. In this new world, people repeatedly found themselves unprepared for the positions they found themselves in, and often lacked the experience to exploit fully the opportunities which now presented themselves. Not a few of those who now had sizable farms to run had little knowledge of farming or the skill to carry out its variety of tasks. New occupiers were often inadequately accomplished at plowing or mowing, or shepherding or harrowing, and they did not know enough about judging the quality of soils, selecting seeds, or caring for sick animals. Many had never possessed more than a garden plot before, and had earned their crusts by doing odd jobs and what they were told. Now they were giving orders and having to manage not only their own affairs but those of others too.

Frustratingly, those who were now rich in land often lacked the ready cash to exploit it adequately. Money had leaked away in the weeks before the pestilence arrived, as fear of infection disrupted patterns of work, travel, and trade. And while the pestilence raged, survival, prayer, and care of the sick rather than money making absorbed the hours of day and night. Then, when they came to inherit, the heirs found that the two best animals the family possessed had been taken by the lord and the Church. The loss of these cows, horses, oxen, and even sheep meant a loss of milk and cheese to eat and to sell, and often also the means of drawing a cart or hauling a plow. On top of this, the lord and lady demanded that they pay large fines to have their tenancy confirmed.

Many of the poorest sort had, of course, already derived some benefit from the high wages they could get for doing even menial jobs during the pestilence, but their earnings did not amount to much when it came to meeting the costs of equipping a farm and its cottage for efficient occupation. While the baser sort, who had robbed their betters by demanding outrageous fees for tending the sick or disposing of their bodies, soon wasted most of their ill-gotten gain in the alehouses and on prostitutes.

Walsham began to experience a loosening of constraints as villagers enjoyed the taste of new freedoms. However, it was early days for the new world, and there was much disorder and confusion. The unprecedented speed of the changes sweeping through the dazed community presented formidable challenges as well as an array of choices and opportunities, both to lowly folk accustomed to a life of dull and harsh routine and to more fortunate villagers who possessed greater wealth. The departure of the sickness liberated the survivors from the stifling fear of death, but the harsh experience of a lifetime could not be unlearned in weeks or months. Survivors, lords as well as peasants, found it difficult to grasp the significance of what had happened and to distinguish reality from illusion, prospects from pitfalls.

Life had never been busier for the distracted villagers of Walsham. There had never been more things that needed doing and so few people to do them. As the village struggled to right itself, everyone craved assistance. Only a fortunate few had not lost the invaluable help of partners, parents, sons, daughters, brothers, and sisters in carrying out a multitude of tasks in their houses, on their farms, and in their daily lives. Men who had lost their wives found that household and farmyard duties took them away from their work in the fields, and if they had children to look after, these added greatly to their burdens. Widows, though experienced with managing a wide range of household and farm tasks, were now forced to struggle alone with the heavier work in the fields. Jobs took longer to complete because there were fewer people to do them, and those folk who were forced to work alone found that many tasks were impossible to accomplish single-handedly. But scarcely any who craved assistance were able to hire sufficient workers, and certainly not at an acceptable price.

The numbers of people seeking work in Walsham had shrunk alarmingly. Smallholders who had previously been pleased to accept a penny or two for any day's work offered to them now had enough acres and animals of their own to care for, and most of the landless folk who had swelled the ranks of willing laborers before the pestilence had disappeared. Half were in the graveyard, and many others had left the village. Of those who remained, a good number acquired land of their own, some by inheritance and some by leasing the surplus furlongs, pightles, and acres of other tenants. In this way the cultivation of their own plots now took up much of the time they had previously spent laboring for others.

There were, of course, villagers who remained landless by choice or ill fortune, and they continued to live off the labor of their hands. But they were no longer the tireless and subservient toilers they once had been. In days just past they had begged for hire and sweated ceaselessly when they were fortunate enough to obtain it. Now, in the summer of 1349, with wages higher than they had ever been and food of all kinds unusually abundant and cheap, these lowly folk could choose when and for whom to work, and how much effort to expend. Whereas, just a couple of months ago, such men and women would have been delighted to win the security of an annual contract as a farm servant with board and lodging, now they frequently chose freedom and spurned the opportunity to be bound by such contracts, believing they could earn far more for less effort by taking casual work as and when it suited them. In the weeks and months after the pestilence this proved to be true. All about there were rustics who, finding that they could keep themselves by laboring just three or four days a week, refused to sweat for five or six. In desperation householders and farmers, deprived of the services of full-time adult servants, sought to replace them with girls and boys. But in contrast to what had happened before the pestilence, parents now usually chose to keep their children at home, where there was much for them to do. In any case, those who did manage to find a child to serve them learned that the young were no more willing to work hard than their elders.

Everywhere, therefore, jobs went undone. Not just those that could reasonably be postponed, such as fencing and ditching, but tasks essential for getting the best out of the land and its livestock, such as manuring, hoeing, weeding, and tending the ailments of sheep and cattle. And this lack of sufficient attention took place not just on the great farms of lords and ladies or the large farms of richer villagers, but also on the small-holdings of ordinary people. Due to a shortage of time and hands, land that could have raised decent crops was often turned over to rough pasture, and the crops growing in arable fields and plots did not receive anything like the close care previously paid to them.

The lives of those who lived through the pestilence had been rent asunder, and the accustomed patterns of daily existence recast. Nor did the fear of infection cease when people stopped dying in Walsham. It was not known for certain what was happening in places round about Walsham, and gloomy rumors repeatedly sprang up, fed by the fact that the plague continued to rage to the north and west of the realm for many months. In the summer and autumn of 1349, therefore, the recovery of trade between people and places remained fitful, disrupted by both a reluctance to travel and the loss of so many familiar merchants and carriers. Markets that had previously thrived now attracted few buyers and sellers, and it was no longer possible to rely on finding all the goods that one sought, or the dealers and merchants ready to buy the items one wished to sell. This meant that much of the food that would otherwise have been sent for sale outside Walsham remained on the manor, and since the number of purchasers had fallen it was possible to eat extraordinarily cheaply. Even in late summer, just before the new harvest, which was normally the dearest time of the year, there was an abundance of grain. So, with so much work available at unprecedented wages, there were few in Walsham whose bellies were not full.

But cheapness and plenty was far from true of all items. Anything which required labor to produce, such as shoes or boots, or even the leather to make them with, quickly became very expensive. A multitude of craftsmen—cobblers, weavers, tailors, tanners, and suchlike—had perished in Walsham and the surrounding villages and towns, and those who had come through the pestilence were only willing to sell their wares for excessive rewards. But it was also vanity that drove the prices of clothing ever higher. For lowly folk, who now had a little spare money in their purses, eagerly sought to acquire things beyond their station, and ape the attire of their betters. As a consequence, a pair of quite ordinary shoes formerly to be had for a few pence now cost 10, 12, or even 14d, and the price of ordinary cloth at least doubled.

The new life, however, was not simply a matter of work, money, and goods. The absence of dear and trusted partners, family, friends, and neighbors left painful gaps in the lives of the survivors. The need for love and companionship, as well as practical support, prompted a multitude of recent widows and widowers hastily to seek new partners, and the months after the pestilence saw a huge upsurge in marriage and in couples cohabiting, openly but illicitly. This impulsive behavior offended both the lords of Walsham and High Hall and the clergy. The former because many unions were contracted without the permission or knowledge of the officials of Lady Rose or of Edmund and Margery de Welles and thus escaped the payment of marriage fines, and the latter because marriage was a solemn sacrament only to be entered into after due personal and spiritual consideration. Now, however, time-honored formalities and blessings were being thrust aside in a selfish or sinful manner.

Many routine aspects of village life became more difficult in Walsham because so many experienced and prudent men and women had died, and so many unknowing newcomers had arrived. Organizing essential communal activities, in the church as well as in the fields, was suddenly far more difficult than it had ever been. Manorial and parish business was impeded, and the accustomed hierarchy of wealth and power upset. Not only were there half as many people to call on to fill the gaps left in the administrative offices in the village, but many of those who now lived in Walsham and occupied her farms were strangers, whose strengths, weaknesses, and motives were unknown and untried. The setting up of the sheepfolds on the commons, the allocation and supervision of grazing rights, the selection of crops, the planning of the harvest, the enforcement of good standards of husbandry, the maintenance of pathways, and much more besides, now involved extended discussions with newcomers, and greater persuasion and education than ever before. And, despite best efforts, what with goodwill should have been simple and amicable to organize all too frequently became the subject of rancorous disputes.

Although Master John lived through the pestilence, Walsham suffered severe losses among its other clergy. By the twin blows of desertion and death during the pestilence and promotion to fat livings soon afterward, the parish was for a time reduced to its priest, a single clerk, and a handful of lay helpers. Master John lost his housekeeper and had to make new arrangements for his cooking and the washing and repair of his vestments. Two of the best bell ringers had died, along with his favorite choirboy. Most of all Master John missed his sexton, who knew every detail of the liturgy of every Mass and every festival throughout the Christian year, and unfailingly anticipated his master's needs for the books, vestments, plate, sacred vessels, and furniture that each one required. Eager new helpers came forward, of course, and the priest was pleased to welcome them. But they needed time to learn their tasks properly and, in Master John's mind, many of the assistants and servants he had lost were irreplaceable. Moreover, three of the four women who had faithfully cleaned the church were no longer in Walsham, and the old man who looked after the brass and latten plate and candlesticks, and kept them clean and in a good state of repair, had passed away just after Easter.

Though there were far fewer people in the parish, the weight of spiritual guidance they required seemed heavier than ever. Master John was well aware that the appetite for spiritual sustenance provided by Masses and confessions, and all sorts of rites and censings, had scarcely diminished since the pestilence, but, confusingly for him, it now existed alongside a rampant decline in morality and in the observance of the teachings of the Church. Everywhere he looked he saw people acting from selfish motives, not just in the pursuit of money but in the pursuit of lust. He was especially concerned with the unseemly haste with which his bereaved parishioners rushed into new emotional attachments, and he constantly warned them that they would repent at leisure. A marriage was for life and had to be founded on love and respect, but now people were rushing into matrimony because they were desperate for help in running household and farm, for a parent for their children, or, worst of all, because they were attracted by the possessions of a wealthy widow or widower.

In fact, Master John worried more about his parishioners' loss of respect for the traditional teachings on matrimony than the manorial lords did about the loss of marriage fines. During his tenure of the parish of

Walsham, Master John had always encouraged the formal and public betrothal of couples, which usually involved the exchange of gifts as tokens
of mutual love and trust and their commitment to marry, and he had been
remarkably successful in cajoling even the most reluctant of them into
having their marriages sanctified by him in St. Mary's church. So he was
sorely troubled that a large and growing number of couples were living
together, not only without solemn betrothal but lacking due consideration and notice. While he had always condoned sexual activity between
couples who had solemnly pledged themselves to each other, he did not
believe that true marriage took place until a ceremony was held in his
church. Now, however, couples were sharing houses and beds out of con-
venience and self-indulgence, without exchanging binding vows in public
or even to each other, without the reading of banns in church, and certainly without having their union blessed.

Such sinful behavior was certain to anger God and had to be stopped,
but Master John found himself unable to halt it. Try as he might, he
could not exert sufficient persuasion or coercion on the majority of offenders to cause them to desist. Not only were there too many who were
misbehaving, he frequently encountered among them a new spirit of independence which he called stubbornness. In these matters, as well as in
many others of which he disapproved, Master John felt himself losing authority. And it was not just because so many of his parishioners behaved
with blind and stubborn willfulness, it was because the deaths and departures among his junior clergy had left him unable to perform adequately
all the spiritual duties and moral teaching that were essential for the cure
of souls in his parish. There were far fewer people in his flock, but the
heavy routine of Masses and other offices he had to celebrate in St.
Mary's church, as well as the distances he had to travel visiting parishioners, were undiminished. Before the pestilence many good priests seeking preferment were willing to work for small stipends in every parish,
but now they were scarce and expensive everywhere, and Walsham was no
exception. The pestilence had taken two of Master John's chaplains, another had fled, and now another, born and brought up in Walsham,
Robert Terwald, had just been appointed rector of Herringswell, a few
miles away, near Newmarket and Mildenhall. Master John liked Terwald,
but the young man still had much to learn; it was far too early for him to

assume such heavy responsibilities and so fat a stipend. He grumbled publicly that the rectorship of Herringswell was a most unsuitable promotion for such a young cleric.

In the world as it was now the scarcity of priests was every bit as severe as the scarcity of laborers. Not only had almost one in every two priests in the realm perished in the pestilence, the demand for the services of the survivors had grown rather than diminished. What is more, so had the number of positions, both in the Church and outside. Every gentleman's household now sought to have its personal confessor, and even the miserly Edmund de Welles paid freely for the services of a young clerk who traveled from nearby Ixworth to conduct private Masses in a room in High Hall manor house that had recently been consecrated as a chapel. Each guild and fraternity, however humble, sought its own priest, and the fraternity of Corpus Christi in Walsham risked the ire of Master John by taking his only assistant away from parish duties three evenings a week. Since the pestilence had created a multitude of new souls awaiting assistance in their journey to salvation, there was a fast growing need for chantry priests who were required to do little but sing Masses for inflated stipends. In consequence, many clergy who should have been serving parishes opted instead for this easy life.

Master John heartily condemned all of these developments. What he found most difficult of all to bear was that priests, even the most inexperienced and incompetent chaplains, eagerly followed the example of common laborers by selfishly demanding outrageously high wages. In midsummer, John was at last formally appointed to the benefice of Walsham by the prior of Ixworth on the death of old Robert Shepherd. The stipend the prior decided to pay John was little more than the pittance he had received from Shepherd, and a small part of what young Terwald would enjoy from the tithes at Herringswell. But the prior knew that John was far too devoted to his vocation and his parishioners to be tempted to seek a more lucrative benefice or run off to Bury or London to sing Masses for sweet silver. However, Master John's asceticism did not make him an attractive superior. In these times of unprecedented opportunity and ambition, all John could offer prospective chaplains considering settling in his parish were the customary low fees, strict discipline, and hard but spiritually rewarding work tending his vulnerable flock. Sadly, but not surprisingly, John found that all that he was offered in return were the services of the illiterate and the uncommitted, the vain and the perverse. Thus far he had refused to allow any of them to serve his parishioners, fearing that they would do more harm than good. But this left the large parish of Walsham with just one priest and a young chaplain to perform the divine services, Masses, matins, vespers, and sacraments essential to save the parishioners from further chastisement by an angry God.

It did not take long for prelates, barons, knights, and lesser lords to turn to the king and the law for a remedy for the ills caused by the pestilence. And so the king and his councilors, mindful of the damage being caused to the realm and the livelihoods of all great people, deliberated in haste on how best to boost the supply of workmen and women and curb their greed and malice. Even before the pestilence had departed from Walsham, stories were circulating that King Edward was going to pass laws that would force the idle to work for their lords and whoever else wished to employ them, and at the accustomed wages. The bishops too, it was rumored, were going to issue edicts to curb the excessive salaries that chaplains and priests were demanding.

It was in the last week of June that a carter returning from carrying grain to Stowmarket confirmed the truth of these rumors. He told a rapt audience in John Lester's alehouse that he had been present when a squire retained by the sheriff of Suffolk read out a new ordinance from the king in the marketplace of the town making it illegal for any man or woman to refuse to work for anybody who might ask them, and at wages set by the lawyers. The carter reported further to his incredulous audience, "You will all soon find yourselves having to accept any kind of work that is offered, women as well as men, and for whatever pittance the lord or rich farmer chooses to give you. It'll be less than half what you can now get. What is more, no one will be given dinner at work, on the king's order. So you can bid farewell to all that lean meat and strong ale. And if you refuse, you will be thrown in jail."

This was all too much for a number of sturdy laborers in his audience, and they began jeering and laughing, but the carter quickly responded with disconcerting authority, "You can jeer all you like, but I was there when the squire warned us that anyone who refused to accept work on these meager wages and oppressive terms would be immediately hauled off to the stocks or jail, and held there until they changed their minds."

On hearing this astounding news, a mixture of disbelief, resentment, and anger filled the noisy room, and a host of questions and responses were flung at the carter. "Why should I have to work for someone else when I have plenty to do farming my own land?" said Nicholas Deneys, who had recently inherited more than he ever dreamed of owning. "I am willing to work for anyone who pays me well enough," said William Warde, a well-known troublemaker, "but I will not sweat for a penny halfpenny or tuppence a day and no dinner. I would rather sit here on my arse drinking, with my only work being pissing the ale out again" (see figure 34). Some laughter greeted this protestation, but soon troubled voices called out, "How can they force us to work? How can they stop the people who are desperate for our work paying us what we ask? Have they got enough soldiers to compel us? How will the work get done if we are all in jail? What if we flee to other places where the king's writ doesn't run?" Warde piped up again at this last remark and urged them all to become mobile: "Why stick in one place where your lords can oppress you with the old customs and charges, and the king can find you and fine you for working, and tax you to pay for his wars? The country outside of Walsham is full of opportunities for those who can find them and grab them."

The carter had no answer to most of these questions and assertions, but he remembered hearing something about lords being fined if they paid wages that were too high, or if they enticed a worker to break their contract with another employer. As an afterthought, he added to the consternation by telling the throng in the alehouse that they would also be imprisoned if they gave alms out of pity to anyone found by the lawyers to be capable of working for their living. This provoked waves of derisive laughter. Even the king could not presume to punish pious folk for following the teachings of Christ by giving money to the poor. Finding himself suddenly transformed from the fount of important news into a teller of tall stories, the carter attempted to explain that the squire in Stowmarket had said that the king was doing this because he was troubled that too many idle people were making the scarcity of laborers worse by feigning handicaps and living off the charity of others. But his words were drowned in a tide of scorn, as well as anger at distant lords who threatened to interfere in their lives.

Soon their worst fears were confirmed. For it was no more than a week later that a copy of the king's ordinance against rebellious laborers and servants was delivered to Walsham, on the orders of the bishop of Norwich, for Master John to read out in the church. In the letter which accompanied the writ, John was urged to "beseech and persuade his parishioners to labor and to keep the ordinance, as instant necessity demands," and also to do all he could to constrain the excessive claims of wage-earning chaplains, and to use threats of suspension by the bishop if they refused to take the accustomed pay. John, of course, was fully in agreement with the latter request, and the former caused him only a moment's hesitation. Until the last few months, John had always urged compassion for the poor, and he had repeatedly instructed those who hired servants and laborers to pay them promptly and fairly for their work. Ever since his arrival in Walsham he had preached from the pulpit of St. Mary's that lords should not oppress the weak with unjust rents and taxes, and that those who had wealth should be charitable to those who had not. But the world had been tipped upside down, and he was becoming alarmed that the hearts of many of his humble parishioners were waxing stout with greed and defiance. While part of him welcomed the fact that the lords of Walsham had lost some of their power, he was dismayed that lowly peasants and laborers were openly defying their betters, and so soon after God had given them the most terrible warning.

Since the beginning of time, God had ordained a social hierarchy and had allotted to each stratum its own particular duties and responsibilities, so that the world might be well ordered and the needs of the whole community met. This divine system prescribed that the common folk were required to labor diligently to provide the food and other wherewithal to maintain those born into more elevated estates: the clergy, knights, and nobility. If the peasants did not labor, their superiors would have to leave their divinely ordained vocations in order to cultivate the land, and then who would pray for the world and provide the protection, law, and order that it needed? Master John acknowledged that there was much that needed improvement in this sinful world, and that many lords and clergy persistently failed to live up to the highest standards demanded of them, but God had taught that men should live not by turmoil, anger, and defiance but by love and obedience and the fulfilling of obligations. Every man and woman of whatever estate, from the abbot of Bury to the most junior acolyte, from Lady Rose to John Lester, one of the least honest bakers and ale brewers in Walsham, were charged by God to carry out the duties of their calling to the best of their ability. Then and only then would the world be well ordered in its estate. But the world was currently in disorder, and in his heart Master John knew that if the demands of the common people were allowed to rise unabated, contrary to God's ordinance as well as the king's, the world would go from bad to worse. And if the rustics should get the upper hand, God's creation would be entirely ruined (see figure 35).

Summer and
Autumn, 1349

*The small-scale disputes and hard bargaining between the villagers of Wal-
sham and their landlords and employers were repeated in thousands of manors
across England as the survivors of the great pestilence struggled to gain some
control over their dramatically changed circumstances. Although these squabbles
might appear trivial and local, and often involved clashes of personality as well
as interest, they were symptoms of what was to prove a long-term and dramatic shift of the balance of power in perhaps the most important economic and
social relationship in the Middle Ages, that between lords and their tenants, between land and labor. But in the early days after the world was turned upside
down, as contemporaries put it, the future was anything but clear for the survivors of the Black Death. Nor is it easy for historians to distinguish the general from the particular, as lords, their officials, and peasants were individuals
who often reacted in different ways when facing the same or similar choices.
Overall, however, the majority of lords acted with surprising flexibility, swiftly
recognizing that it was better to offer concessions, albeit often of a temporary
nature, than risk having large numbers of vacant holdings and untended fields
and livestock.*

*From manorial and legal records, as well as the complaints of contempo-
raries, we can also see that lords, though unanimous in their support of legislation designed to control wages, disregarded these laws and competed with each
other for laborers and tenants when it suited them. They commonly paid cash*

wages well above the levels prescribed by the ordinance and statute of laborers, routinely provided food and other perquisites prohibited by law, and rarely displayed any compunction about hiring workers who had broken contracts with former employers. When strangers appeared who were willing to take up land, the local stewards, reeves, and bailiffs who were charged by their lords with filling vacant holdings rarely bothered whether they had fled illegally from another lord, though they usually took steps to satisfy themselves about their creditworthiness.

There is abundant evidence of extraordinary wages being paid by landlords to harvest their crops in August and September 1349. According to Henry Knighton, author of one of the leading fourteenth-century chronicles, it was not possible to get reapers for less than 8d per day plus food or mowers for less than 12d plus food, whereas the customary rates had been 2d–3d and 5d respectively, and "therefore many crops rotted in the fields for lack of people to gather them." Unfortunately, there are no reeves' accounts for Walsham or High Hall, but close by at Fornham All Saints the costs of harvesting and mowing hay in 1349 were double what they had been in 1347 and 1348. Nor were landlords compensated by good yields. On the contrary, yields of all grains and pulses were exceedingly poor, doubtless due to the combination of neglect during the growing season (lack of weeding, trespass by animals, and so on), an acute shortage of labor during the harvest season, and extremely wet weather. There is much evidence of heavy and prolonged rainfall in late summer and that the harvest was consequently much delayed. Little can be discovered about yields on peasant holdings, but they may well have suffered less than those on the lords' farms as their owners gave priority to their own lands over working for their lords.

⊣⪦ ⪧⊢

Although their world had been badly shaken, Edmund de Welles and his sister Margery were determined to rise to the challenge, and as the pestilence waned so their administrative efforts waxed. Before the pestilence, things had moved more slowly, and conservative and cautious management had carried far fewer penalties, and less harsh ones too. But in the new age a host of complex problems arrived each day that directly challenged their lordship and threatened to drain their purse. Worst of all, few of the problems could be solved by applying the old methods. Who before ever had to deal with the loss of half of their tenants, an acute labor shortage, and querulous rustics seeking to usurp the authority that belonged to their betters?

Since they resided in High Hall, Edmund and Margery were able to keep a close eye on all that was happening on their little manor, and they urged their officers to keep them informed about every issue, however trivial. They interfered directly in many small matters, but the times demanded it. Observing with their own eyes what was going on, they learned much faster than the absent Lady Rose that advantages could be gained from compromising with the new power of the peasantry, if their demesne farm was to be run with some semblance of efficiency and their rent rolls secured.

Edmund and Margery did not have a hoard of cash to cushion them against hard times, for they had always spent as much, and sometimes even more, than they received in income. It was not that they were particularly profligate, as the gentry went, rather that their revenues were relatively modest and their lifestyle costly. Even in good years, they usually had little to spare after the personal and household expenditures essential to feed their appetites and support their status had been met. Taking one year with the next, High Hall usually provided less than £7 in cash, clear of expenses, which did not go very far, given the price of fine clothes, wines and spices, the costs of maintaining buildings, and the wages of household servants. Thus even in normal times the de Welles had been acutely vulnerable to shortfalls and interruptions in the flow of money and produce that their steward delivered to them, and now they were terrified that their harvest would be utterly ruined for want of labor, and that their tenants would carry out their threats to abandon their holdings and seek their fortunes elsewhere.

So, painful as it was, they felt they had no choice but to use all means to try and minimize the fall in their revenues, even if it meant temporarily weakening their customary rights and principles. Margery soon persuaded Edmund that it was better to pay out extra money in high wages than to risk the corn being choked by weeds or left rotting in the fields. With the help of her reeve, she calculated that the additional outlay in wages would easily be recouped by higher receipts from the sale of corn,

just as she knew instinctively that it was better to receive a lower rent or
a reduced fine than none at all. Thus they gave leave for their officials to
reach compromises with tenants, servants, and laborers over the levels of
rents, fines, services, wages, and many other things, believing that these
concessions would be temporary and could be revoked when the world
returned to normal.

Shamed by the chaotic court session held in late May, when John Talbot, vicar of Rickinghall, had presided on their behalf with unforgivable
incompetence, Edmund and Margery were determined to restore their
reputation for good governance. To this end, they thoroughly prepared for
the court they intended to hold toward the end of July, and they were
greatly helped by the fact that only four of their tenants had died since the
end of May. The pestilence was now definitely over. They knew that business had to be attended to in a particularly systematic fashion during these
uncertain times, and so they decided the first task was to check all the information which had been noted at the May court, in order to rectify that
which was inaccurate and supply that which was missing. Edmund and
Margery spent long hours carefully going through the records of the last
court, instructing their clerk to place marks against incomplete entries or
matters, as reminders that all major items were to be followed through to
a conclusion. It was essential for their officials to continue finding and
confirming heirs, vetting guardians for those children who were too young
to occupy their inheritances, and establishing precisely what land each
tenant held and what payments and services they ought to render.

The initiatives by Edmund and Margery met with some immediate success. Almost all of the heirs missing from the May court were identified,
most of them without too much difficulty. But the lord and lady soon discovered that naming heirs was one thing, ensuring that they took up their
tenancies on acceptable terms was quite another. William Isabel's ten acre
farm had been unoccupied since his death sometime after Easter, and the
search for his heir was complicated because the pestilence had killed all the
immediate family members living in Walsham. Finally it was shown that
Sarah Flintard, living some distance away, was next in the bloodline. But
when the hayward summoned her, she refused to come to Walsham. A
large number of other successions on their small manor also proved troublesome, often because both husband and wife had died and their surviving

children were too young to assume their inheritances. It was also frustrating for Edmund and Margery that not one of the successions to the holdings made vacant by the four deaths since the last court proved to be straightforward. Robert Banlone was a particular nuisance, for although he was quite prepared to farm his father's smallholding, he adamantly refused to pay an entry fine for doing so. As for the other three holdings: the heir of Robert Sare, a free tenant, had not yet paid the 19d due as relief; the heir to Adam Angerhale's ten acre holding was his four-year-old nephew, and for the time being the farm remained vacant; and nobody had been found who was willing to take Walter Osbern's tiny enclosure.

The court, which was held on Thursday, July 23, with Edmund de Welles presiding and his sister sitting beside him, did not get off to a good start. They had hoped to intimidate Robert Banlone into paying an acceptable entry fine by having him appear before them in full court, but when called by the hayward he once again refused to pay anything whatsoever. Asked by his lord to explain himself, Banlone repeated that he was perfectly willing to take the land but would not pay an entry fine for doing so. Edmund, acting on Margery's advice, loudly asserted that Banlone was in contempt of his lords' authority and the ancient customs of the manor, and ordered the hayward to evict him forthwith from the holding in question. This action shocked Banlone, and he attempted to protest but was curtly dismissed. This show of seigneurial strength made an impression on the skeptical tenants who were gathered in the manor barn, and soon the fruits of Edmund and Margery's administrative hard work became evident as many of the gaps and inaccuracies in the proceedings of the previous court were systematically rectified. Whereas in May the court had been told only that John and Peter Goche "held certain tenements from the lord in villeinage," now it was reported that they had each held half of a messuage and six acres of land before their death, that a calf and a young unsheared ewe had been taken as heriots, that John Goche's heirs were his sons Walter and John, ten years old and two years respectively, and that Peter Goche's heir was his son John who was four. It was further reported that Robert Man and his wife Catherine were willing and able to act as custodians of Peter's holding and guardians of his young son, and they were formally appointed to occupy the tenement until the boy was old enough to assume his inheritance.

With pedantic attention to detail, Edmund and Margery insisted on the precise terms of tenure of an acre of land, made vacant by the death of young William Cranmer, the grandson of old William Cranmer, being read out, so the hayward recited that each year a hen, twenty eggs, a day's plowing, a day's harvesting, and 2d in cash were due. The brother and sister smiled with satisfaction as the acre was accepted with enthusiasm by Hilary and Olivia Cranmer, who added it to the plentiful lands they had inherited from their father and grandfather within Walsham manor. Next, it was the turn of Alice Helpe, who had come with her sister-in-law, Agnes Chapman, to have the court formally register her accession to her recently deceased husband John's holding. Alice was comforted by Agnes as she swore fealty to her lord and lady. But administrative efficiency alone could not fill holdings that nobody was willing to occupy, and Edmund and Margery reluctantly had to take Walter Osbern's small enclosure into their hands as no heir could be found. Finally, after it was confirmed that the reeve and the hayward were to take what profits they could from the other vacant holdings, an announcement was made that John Wodebite had been granted a license to remarry. This was the first that Agnes Chapman had heard of John's betrothal, and she found it difficult not to show her distress.

Although the court had been a great improvement on its predecessor, Edmund and Margery were far from satisfied when they met with their clerk and the hayward the next day to complete the fair copy of the proceedings. Although all the outstanding items of business from the previous court had been raised as planned, many still awaited an acceptable resolution. The rent roll had shrunk appreciably, there were far too many vacant acres going to waste, and too many empty cottages were falling into disrepair. Most of all, Edmund was distressed at his inability to control events. It took much reassurance from Margery to persuade him that, until the world was righted, as it soon must surely be, it would be best to follow the path of conciliation and compromise. However painful it might be to barter with rustics, she said, it was preferable to risking an even sharper fall in their income by demanding the last penny from them when they were in no mood to give it. Reluctantly Edmund agreed to accept his sister's advice, and that of the hayward too, when he asked permission to continue paying whatever it cost to hire enough farmworkers to keep the demesne in reasonable shape and to make small advance payments to good and reliable workers to ensure that they would turn out promptly to gather in the harvest in a few weeks' time. Margery nodded her assent when the hayward proposed that he should listen to any reasonable offers for the vacant farms, and that his lord and lady should be prepared to make significant further concessions on their rents and services in order to get them occupied. Margery further assured him, to his surprise, that he also had permission, if there were no other offers, to let vacant holdings on very short leases or even to use them as rough pasture if there were no better alternative.

In the event, the hayward soon found the latter option to be the most popular. Demand for pasture was rising in Walsham as many farmers were choosing to increase the numbers of livestock they kept. Cutting back on arable made good sense, for not only could livestock be bought very cheaply and looked after relatively easily, they were capable of producing better profits than ever before. Peasants with money in their pockets were eating more meat and cheese, and drinking more milk. No villagers showed greater initiative than Hilary and Olivia, the Cranmer sisters. The pestilence had made them wealthy by endowing them with an abundance of land on the death of their father, grandfather, and all their brothers. Now they created a stir in the village by seeking to make even more money, instead of mourning. On their extensive lands they pastured large numbers of good cattle that they purchased cheaply, and it proved such good business that they rented additional acres from the hayward. Alice Pye was no less entrepreneurial, and eagerly used the proceeds from the booming trade in her alehouse to build up a large flock of sheep, knowing there would be a ready market for their wool and meat.

Rose de Saxham, lady of Walsham manor, fretting in her manor house many miles away, was made of sterner stuff than the de Welles siblings, and was considerably wealthier too. In spite of losing her second husband and two of her sons in the pestilence, and having lived more than seventy years, she was determined to continue to take a close personal interest in her financial affairs and the running of her estate. At home she had been struggling, albeit without much success, to fill the gaps in her household staff caused by the death of pages, maids, grooms, esquires, scullions, and cooks, as well as trusted advisers. And she found it extremely irksome having to train inexperienced and ill-educated replacements to do jobs they were not well equipped to carry out. So she had come to rely more heavily on John Blakey, her long-serving steward, for a range of household as well as estate duties.

Lady Rose did not like what she learned from her steward about the condition of Walsham, her most valuable manor, any more than she liked what her treasurer told her about affairs in her own household. Much as she was loath to spare Blakey, she knew that he was needed urgently in Walsham to supervise the harvest, as well as attend to a host of other pressing matters there. So, in late July, after hearing that Edmund de Welles was about to hold another court, she dispatched him with detailed instructions on how to improve the running of the manor and appoint a competent reeve and hayward. Before he departed, Blakey took great care to gather information confirming that Walsham and its locality were entirely free of pestilence, and on his arrival in the west Suffolk village he was pleased to learn that his informants had been correct. The deaths had petered out soon after his last visit in mid-June, and none had occurred since the first week of July.

There were other things that pleased Blakey when he was briefed. Geoffrey Rath and his assistants had been making considerable progress in clearing up matters left outstanding when he had hurriedly departed more than five weeks earlier. Acceptable tenants had been found for four of the holdings left vacant on his last visit, and willing heirs had been found to take up the farms of all the five tenants who had died since his departure. It was a particular triumph that John Frunceys, who had refused Blakey's direct order to take over his dead sister's lands at the last court, had finally agreed to do so, and that he had paid a small but symbolic fine for entry. John Terwald, a prominent villager, was also helping the situation by mopping up various plots of vacant land. But even more successful was the policy agreed between the steward and his lady of encouraging outsiders to take over holdings for which heirs could not be found. During Blakey's absence, three residents of neighboring villages had come forward to occupy holdings in Walsham which were proving difficult to let, including two villein holdings burdened with all the customary works and services. Since these outsiders were not well known in Walsham, they had to be carefully vetted, and the hayward had to be persuaded to act as a pledge for their good behavior. Having passed these tests, William, the son of John the smith of Ixworth, moved into Adam Hardonn's cottage and garden, Roger Hamund of Langham moved into Juliana Deneys's cottage and garden, and Alexander the baker of Thurston took up residence in John Taylor's former tenement called Chequers.

But things took a turn for the worse when Blakey viewed the demesne farm the next morning. His first task was to inspect the stacks of hay mowed in the meadows a few weeks before. Despite his low expectations he still found them disappointingly small. But it was the sorry state of his lady's cornfields that shocked him most. He had taken care to warn Lady Rose that she should not expect the forthcoming harvest to be anything but poor, because of the turmoil and neglect caused by the pestilence, but when he inspected the fields he realized it would turn out far worse than feared. The weather had been very wet throughout the spring and early summer, and exceptionally heavy downpours in the last few weeks had left the corn beaten down and slow to ripen. However, it was not just the rains that had damaged the crops. Neglect had allowed weeds to flourish, and in many parts they entirely crowded out the corn or left it thin and wispy. Furthermore, because broken hedges and fences had not been repaired, large numbers of untended animals had trespassed onto the fields, trampling the shoots. After a quick appraisal, Blakey estimated that much of the crop was already lost, and the remainder could only be saved if the weather improved and prompt and plentiful supplies of labor could harvest the fields after a decent spell of warm sunshine. But, judging by his recent experiences trying to hire decent workers on reasonable terms, that was not likely to happen. Moreover, the prospects of the next year's crop of wheat had already been severely damaged because, as Geoffrey Rath explained, the scarcity of farm servants had made it impossible for the summer plowing of the fallow to be completed.

The steward was furious that the good advice and stern instructions he had given on his last visit about obtaining sufficient labor for the lady's demesne farm had not been followed. Neither the full-time farm servants on annual contracts nor the casual laborers hired by the day or week nor the days that her tenants owed had been managed well. In fact, all had fallen far short of what was required and what should have been delivered. Angrily, Blakey accused the remaining manorial officers, including Geoffrey Rath, of incompetence or fraud. But to his surprise, they made a spirited defense, claiming that none of them carried the responsibilities or the status of reeve. Although they had ordered the lady's tenants to labor for her and no one else whenever she required them, on pain of the loss of their tenancies as the law of the manor required, and threatened laborers who demanded excessive wages or simply would not work with the force of the king's ordinance, few had heeded them.

"Have all humble rustics become rebels overnight?" Blakey queried, sarcastically. Rath responded immediately, "For a brief time a few workmen were cowed by news of the king's command, but most were angered, and the former soon gained the strength to resist by seeing others continuing to break the law with impunity. And who is to stop them? Everywhere you look in Walsham, and in the villages and towns all around, you will find farmers and others willing to pay almost anything to get men and women to work for them. What I am allowed to offer is simply not attractive enough. While some of our farm servants are pleased to have a secure job, a couple have run away, despite the bonuses, extra food, clothing, and other bribes you allowed me to give them. I cannot replace them, for there are scarcely any capable servants who are willing to enter into long contracts. Instead they choose to work by the day, and then only when they feel like it."

Geoffrey was now waxing eloquent: "These lowly folk, who lack any real skills, are receiving from others outrageously high wages and extravagant free meals. I have seen them many times sitting under trees taking an early dinner and a nap, with trenchers piled high with large slices of lean meat, and pots of good ale to wash it down with. All provided by their employers."

"What about the day works owed by our lady's tenants?" asked Blakey, wearily, as if he already knew the answer.

"They find any excuse not to perform their obligations, and laugh at your threats of fines or eviction. You will find, sir, that not only Lady Rose's law but the king's law is held in contempt by laborers and peasants, and also by the lords who hire them."

It was then that Rath reported that Edmund de Welles was prominent among the multitude of employers in Walsham and the surrounding villages who were surrendering to demands from lazy and unreliable laborers, and lavishing excessive rewards on the undeserving. John Blakey was stunned into silence. He waved Rath away and swiftly dispatched a letter to Lady Rose explaining that Edmund de Welles was the chief cause of the sorry conditions on her estate in Walsham. He claimed to have proof that Sir Edmund weakly gave in to the rustics' illegal demands by offering lavish food, loans of farm equipment, and free pasturage and reduced rents, as well as excessive wages, and he advised that until Sir Edmund desisted little could be done to improve matters. As Blakey saw it, if Sir Edmund could be made to abide by the king's ordinance and not compete with Lady Rose, then, as the major employers in Walsham, the two lords would each be able to secure adequate supplies of cheap labor. In his letter Blakey reminded his lady that, under the provisions of the ordinance, those who paid excessive wages were as guilty as those who took them. A week later, Blakey received back a note of agreement from Lady Rose, to which she added the hope that if Edmund de Welles could be persuaded to join with her in enforcing the new laws, their joint attention could be focused on stopping villagers from leaving Walsham for days and even weeks on end to wander around the country looking for the highest paid work wherever they could find it.

However, John Blakey soon found that self-interest made Sir Edmund and Lady Margaret very slippery to deal with. At the meetings he attended with Edmund and his managers, everyone enthusiastically agreed that they would all be much better off if the ordinance were strictly obeyed, and no rustic offered more than the old payments of three halfpence per day and no food. However, in private Edmund continued to tell his reeve and hayward that saving money on wages was all well and good, but the highest priority had to be to find enough workers to run his estate efficiently. If that meant paying them 3d or more and feeding them, then so be it.

There was no prison in Walsham or anywhere nearby, so Lady Rose's steward decided that stocks would be built on the green in front of St. Mary's church, and that every man or woman who refused to work for the old wages would be placed in them until they relented. But, much to his humiliation, he could not find any carpenter who was willing to make the stocks for less than twice the legal daily rate of pay because they were all so busy repairing Sir Edmund's barns and fences. But even Sir Edmund balked at giving in to some of the more outrageous demands. A little old man from Essex who had lately taken up the life of an itinerant laborer caused much amusement as he passed through the village. Carrying a spade and pick on his back, he stood on the green and offered himself for hire. But only for light jobs, like digging up small trees, for which he asked 5d per day and two square meals. When he found few who were willing to hire him, he shrugged his shoulders and went on his way whistling (see figure 36).

Although he was making some progress, Blakey realized that his manorial administration required strengthening by the appointment of a new reeve as a matter of urgency to replace Walter Osbern, who had died in the plague. He appreciated that, for all his faults, Geoffrey Rath was the best he was likely to find. So he set about the distasteful task of trying to bribe him to accept the office. At first Geoffrey, who was in his fourth consecutive year of service in the office of manor hayward, was reluctant to accept the even more onerous position of reeve. Over the last few weeks, however, as some of the immediate turmoil had begun to subside, he had started to appreciate that, along with the hard work and abuse, being reeve might offer even greater opportunities for profit than he had enjoyed as hayward. So, when John Blakey pressed him again, increased the emoluments of the office, and promised him a fine outfit of clothes that had previously been worn by a footman in Lady Rose's household, he agreed to allow his name to go forward. Blakey was delighted when Rath was duly elected reeve at the court held on August 1, together with a full complement of villagers to serve in all the other offices, including John Patyl as hayward and Peter Tailor as woodward.

Having made little headway with hiring laborers, Blakey tried to improve the turnout of his lady's tenants to work their required days on her fields. Now that the immense disruption and confusion caused by the death of half the villagers had begun to die down, he was heartened by some rustics coming to their senses and accepting plots they had refused to inherit, realizing it was foolish to turn down decent cottages and farmland, and the security, sustenance, and income they provided. And while some persisted in their obstinacy, preferring the promise of quick rewards and the wayfaring life of casual laborers, it was becoming easier to find acceptable tenants from among the previously landless in Walsham and surrounding places, or even farther afield.

John Blakey's instincts told him that he could now begin to put a little more pressure on the lady's tenants to fulfill their obligations, without causing them to abandon their holdings. But he was mindful of Rath's advice on the need for caution, for nobody could be certain how to act in these days. So, although he instructed his manorial officers to threaten tenants with large fines or even eviction should they fail to perform their required labor, he often came down on the side of clemency when they failed to turn up or send an adequate substitute. It was a game of cat and mouse, bluff and compromise. By giving offenders a second chance and reducing their fines well below what had been threatened, Lady Rose's manorial officers were able to reach acceptable working relationships with the majority of occasional offenders, who usually undertook to mend their ways in the future. But persistent and impertinent rebels were another matter. The steward lost patience with John Bolle's repeated brazen refusals to serve the lady and seized all his lands until he relented.

But John Blakey's careful planning failed when it came to gathering in the harvest. Try as he might, he simply could not get anywhere near enough workers onto the fields when they were most needed. Time was always of the essence at harvest, and during the unprecedented wet autumn of 1349 it was crucial. There were precious few fine days in late August, and when the sun finally shone long enough in the second week of September to dry the grain, the tenants rushed to reap their own lands and gather in their own crops, and would not be threatened or bribed to work on the lady's farm instead. When, on the steward's orders, Geoffrey Rath and John Patyl chastised the delinquents, they were brazenly asked why they should neglect the crops in their own fields to save the lady's. The fact that the law of the manor required them to, and that they and their predecessors had always done so, since time out of mind, no longer held sway, and the best they offered were substitutes who were too old or too young to be useful, or promises to work for the lady when their own harvest had been gathered in. With time running out to complete the harvest, it was a thankless task, and so was the effort involved in making those who eventually did turn up work diligently. Rath and his foremen were forced to spend much time wandering round the fields, where they repeatedly came across groups of idlers sitting on the ground drinking, singing, and playing games of chance in hidden corners of the fields, away from prying eyes. In desperation, as the grain rotted on the ground, Geoffrey had urged Blakey to relent and hire laborers to fill the gaps caused by absent and idle tenants. But since Lady Rose was among the least generous employers in Walsham, her corn was left to wait, and was duly drenched and flattened by further heavy rainfall. Blakey finally relented and sanctioned a modest cash bonus and improved refreshments, but at the end of September they were still trying to gather in the last remnants of crops with the least able workers. The harvest had been ruined, and Geoffrey was blamed.

With most of the stalks beaten down to the ground, and with intermittent rain disrupting the reaping, binding, and stacking of sheaves, the amount of grain harvested from Lady Rose's fields was disastrously low. Instead of gathering the normal yield of around four times the wheat and barley seed that had been sown, Blakey and Rath estimated that the barn contained little more than twice the seed that had been scattered. And, as if that were not bad enough, when Geoffrey inspected the sheaves a couple of weeks later he found many of the damp husks were already showing signs of sprouting.

As John Blakey prepared to return to Lady Rose, he knew that the disastrous harvest, the low price of grain, and the high cost of labor would combine to slash the profits of her demesne farm. This was going to be the worst year he had ever experienced as steward, and he doubted whether Lady Rose had ever had a poorer year in the seventy or more she had lived. However, this was far from being the only bad news he had to report to his lady. The plans he and she had hatched to bring Walsham's tenants speedily to order were in disarray. In the hurly-burly of these days, his manorial officers were so overburdened with pressing matters that they were forced to turn a blind eye to many misdemeanors. And so manifold breaches of his lady's rights, of the ancient customs of the manor, and even of good community bylaws went unpunished. Even when the perpetrators were brought to court and fined, many neglected to pay. As a consequence, paths were obstructed and boundaries transgressed, fences and hedges went unrepaired, cattle and sheep were not properly controlled and caused extensive damage to neighboring fields. More than this, Blakey and Rath suspected that not all of the damage was careless or accidental, and that some villagers were deliberately grazing their animals where they should not.

Then, just as Blakey was preparing to ride out, he learned that a group of unfree villagers were refusing to pasture their sheep on his lady's fields. From time out of mind, Walsham's villein farmers had obediently erected hurdles and folded all their sheep on their lady's demesne fields after the harvesting had been concluded, so that her soil could be enriched with their manure before the winter plowing. But now, Rath told him, a number of prominent tenants were plotting to resist this ancient obligation by defiantly folding most of their sheep on their own lands. When Rath suggested turning a blind eye as long as these tenants folded a fair part of their flocks on the demesne, Blakey disagreed, saying that if others saw that it was possible to disregard the lady's will without punishment, they too would be tempted to send only part of their flocks to the communal folds. But Rath remained adamant, saying that it would be foolish to try and force the rustics to obey in the face of such widespread defiance, and he warned that any attempt to coerce them was likely to provoke more serious conflicts in which he and his bailiffs might be assaulted. Blakey, shaken by this claim, reluctantly told Rath to await further orders from his lady.

The orders, when they came, were for Geoffrey and the hayward to crush the peasants' resistance by seizing their sheep. Lady Rose, urged on by her son, Henry, had instructed her steward to toughen policies toward the villagers rather than seek the compromises the reeve advised. Put under increasing pressure, Geoffrey began to feel ever more uncomfortable in his position as both a member of the village community and an agent of their lady. Whatever he did, he found himself criticized either by Blakey, who constantly berated him for failing to produce satisfactory results, or by his fellow villagers, who chastised him for imposing unwelcome lordship on them, restricting their freedom, and denying them opportunities to prosper.

It did not take Geoffrey long to decide that henceforth he would make only a pretense of following every wish of his lady and every command issued by her steward. Actually he would plow his own furrow by opting for a quiet and profitable life, rather than an arduous, unpopular, and unrewarding one. He knew that Blakey, in addition to coming to hold the four courts each year, would visit Walsham only three or four times, and that on each visit he would stay only a week or so. Thus, for most of the time, Geoffrey reasoned, he would be unsupervised and left to follow his own inclinations. If he exercised cunning and took steps to cover his tracks, he could look after his own interests better than he looked after his lady's, and do so without fear of retribution.

So, after Blakey's departure, Geoffrey turned a blind eye when most of the villein tenants continued to refuse to fold all their sheep on the lady's recently harvested fields and instead held them back to fertilize their own farms with their droppings. But that autumn the lady's demesne farm suffered from far more than a lack of nutriment. When, at plowing time, the tenants once again made endless excuses for not performing their customary duties, ranging from feigned ill health to simple forgetfulness, Geoffrey and his local officers displayed a marked lack of enthusiasm in pursuing the absentees. Instead of draconian punishments, most defaulters were allowed to escape by promising to fulfill their duties conscientiously in the future, and those who committed multiple misdemeanors were often excused in return for a small bribe. Nor were Geoffrey's efforts to hire plowmen and harrowers much more effective. Since the rates of pay and perquisites he was permitted to offer were comfortably exceeded by other employers, Geoffrey ended up hiring second- and third-choice people who had been rejected by others on the grounds of age, frailty, or incompetence, and sometimes all three. Consequently the lady's plowing was both late and inadequately performed. Scarcely any acres received the benefits of double plowing, and the harrowing too was slipshod. Eventually, when severe damage had been done to the prospects of the next harvest, Blakey relented and gave the reeve permission to boost the workforce by hiring women for many jobs around the farm that had previously been done by men. But this made very little difference, for few women were willing to work for the wages Geoffrey was allowed to pay them (see figure 37).

September to December, 1349

The Black Death has often been seen as heightening the conflict between lords and the peasant and laboring masses. Some historians stress the potency of what is termed the "seigneurial reaction," when landlords, backed by the government (which was, of course, composed of landlords), strove not merely to reassert control over the lower orders but to impose new restrictions and burdens on them in order to bolster their weakening authority and reverse falling revenues. For other historians it is the success of peasants and laborers in winning substantial concessions on rents and conditions of tenure and large increases in their wages and perquisites that is paramount.

However, the problems caused to the ruling elites by plunging population were far from being solely demographic and economic. The increased availability of land and work, beyond simply putting more money in the pockets of the lowly, massively enhanced their bargaining power. In turn this new power fostered self-confidence among people who had formerly been servile, which then helped to promote a robust questioning of authority and lordship, first at local level and then more widely. Nor did potentially fatal threats to the venerable social order come from recalcitrant rustics and artisans alone. The scale and diversity of the forces set in train by the pestilence impacted almost all areas of life to a greater or lesser extent. In the eyes of contemporaries, the new world stimulated equally selfish and sinful behavior from members of the other two estates, the clergy and the lords. The rapid response of the king and his barons signaled the depth of their concern about the way things were deteriorating. On September 5, 1349, before the pestilence had finally departed all regions of the realm, the king sent a letter to his bishops expressing alarm that lessons had not been learned. The recent evil tribulations, he wrote, had been inflicted by a just God who was offended by the guilt of mankind. But rather than reforming their behavior, sinfulness and pride were constantly increasing in the people. As a result, he warned, an even greater calamity might be inflicted.

We can see clearly in William Langland's great allegorical poem, Piers Plowman, *the first version of which dates from the early 1360s, the intense hostility displayed toward those who used conditions after the plague to pursue their own interest and thereby threaten the cherished social order. Langland was a devoted priest and a charitable defender of the poor, but in the poem he repeatedly castigates those who refuse to work, demand excessive rewards, and refuse to be disciplined. In a striking passage, Piers calls on Hunger to chastise such delinquents and takes great delight in observing the salutary effects that a dose of starvation has on their willingness to labor and conform. Langland, in keeping with so many of his educated or elite contemporaries, was at pains to distinguish between the deserving poor—those who were entitled to alms because they were unable to support themselves—and the plethora of false beggars and idlers who sprang up in the aftermath of the great pestilence. The narrator of this book is from the same social strata and of the same mind.*

⊣☐⊢

As the lords prayed that the world would soon return to normal, the common folk celebrated their good fortune and followed their self-interest, insofar as they were able to determine what it was. Peasants, laborers, tenants, and artisans, especially the smallest and least worthy of people, were courted by their betters, and daily existence became for them less miserable and more bearable. Men and women who had spent most of their lives desperately seeking poorly paid work in competition with scores of their fellows, hoping without expectation one day to acquire a piece of land or a cottage, or even the ability to keep themselves and their families moderately well fed, clothed, and warm, now found themselves sought after by employers and landlords.

For the first time, lowly folk were enjoying a sense of their own worth, and it gave them satisfaction and confidence. Increasingly, the old ways of doing things, the old levels of rents and wages, and the old customs were no longer accepted without question. Instead there was a feeling that matters should be decided on their merits rather than precedent. Some even argued that rents and fines should be set at whatever anyone was willing to pay, and that if a farmer was prepared to offer 3d per day and food, and a man was prepared to sell his labor at that price, then no one should interfere in this free contract. It mattered little to such people whether or not Lady Rose or Edmund de Welles had custom supporting their demands.

Since time out of mind, the village and the manor had been run according to custom and precedent. What had always been was the prime means of deciding what should be—who should inherit, what rent and dues should be paid, how much wood could be collected from the manor's woodlands, how many animals could be grazed on its communal pastures, how long a labor service on the lady's demesne should last, and even how large the loaf given to harvest workers should be. But in the new world custom was proving irksome and restrictive. While the peasant community had always been resolute in defending custom when lords and ladies were threatening to breach it and increase their burdens, now they had every interest in breaching it themselves. People of all sorts, richer tenants as well as landless laborers, wanted the freedom to pick and choose, negotiate, and refuse if it suited them.

Nor was it only former troublemakers who evaded their time-honored obligations. Time and again folk who had previously been law-abiding or even subservient now needed much persuasion to continue to render all the payments, services, fines, and duties that they, and their fathers and grandfathers before them, had rendered all their lives. Naturally, others viewed the rising fortunes of the rustics in a different light, for the improved benefits the lowly now enjoyed had invariably been won at the expense of their betters. This made the elites both angry and fearful, and the new state of affairs was bewailed in the houses of gentlemen and in sermons from the pulpit. Much to the surprise of Master John, he was invited to Ixworth to hear the prior of the abbey preach against the evils of the present times, and though he was loath to admit it to himself, John found there was much in the sermon with which he agreed.

"When they were held low by many travails and woes," the prior began, "and forced to labor hard for scarcely enough beans and water to keep them alive, the rustics were deserving of our charity. But today their hearts are waxing stout and rebellious and they will neither work nor listen to reason. They have got the upper hand, and instead of sympathy they are deserving of harsh discipline and punishment. If they are not soon brought to heel they will cause chaos and destruction, and bring down further scourges from an angry God."

The prior, who was a learned man, despite being foolish and worldly, knew his Aelfric and his Bartholomew Anglicus well, and he went on to proclaim how those who were born to govern knew that the world was ordained by God to be divided into three permanent estates—*bellatores, oratores, laboratores*—warriors, prayers, laborers—the barons and knights who defended and ruled society, the clergy who prayed and attended to the cure of souls, and those who labored for a living. Few in his audience could doubt that it was essential to the well-being of the world that the great mass of rustics at the base of society performed the work and paid the rents and other dues that provided the sustenance and wealth needed to maintain the other two estates, the clergy and the nobility and gentry. "How could it be otherwise?" he asked without fear of dissent. "If they did not do so, knights and bishops, priors and squires, lawyers and monks would have to become plowmen and herdsmen in order to survive, and so would be forced to abandon their higher vocations. These are the commandments of God. But now, instead of being turned from their sinful ways in fear and penitence, as God wished when he unleashed the terrible pestilence that we have just suffered, the common people are setting their hearts against his commandments, and by their selfishness, arrogance, and immorality they are putting the world in grave danger of another terrible punishment delivered by his anger" (see figure 38).

The prior's audience, consisting largely of senior clerics, gentry, lawyers, burgesses, and merchants, nodded in agreement with his diagnosis of the ills of time. But the common folk saw it differently. They had no desire to rise up against their lords but simply wanted to be free to choose the most attractive among the opportunities which presented themselves. During their lives they had been taught harsh lessons that beggars could not be choosers, but in the space of a few months they had ceased to have to beg for work and subsistence. Instead, those set above them now had to beg them for their services and their compliance. Since they were no longer bullied by hardship and poverty, they would no longer allow themselves to be bullied by bailiffs and lords. As they frequently told each other, and when emboldened, the officials of their lord and lady as well, they would choose when and whether to work, and when and whether to take on the lease of a property; and they would haggle over their wages, their rents, and their services if they wanted to.

In Walsham, as elsewhere throughout the realm, the lords were uncomfortably aware that the common people were becoming less docile and more questioning of authority. In these days, when lowly rustics should have been working, Master John, as well as John Blakey and Edmund de Welles, observed that they could be found spending much of their time and money drinking in the alehouses, hanging around in groups, gossiping and plotting to thwart their betters, idling in local markets and fairs, playing unsuitable and immoral games of chance such as dice, cards, and alpenyprick, poaching rabbits, fowl, and fish, and organizing football matches, which were an excuse for riotous behavior. What is more, shame to say, it was now becoming fashionable for some villagers to pretend they were gentlemen by hunting with dogs and sometimes with horses as well.

It was because this lamentable situation prevailed throughout the realm that King Edward spent long hours during the summer in pious meditation with his spiritual advisers. The king was anxious to provide the leadership that a good monarch ought to offer in such a time of turmoil and danger, so he sought advice on what should be done, not just from his nobles but from the leading churchmen of his realm. His counselors expressed themselves both amazed and appalled that sinners who had been spared from the lashings of the pestilence had not been humbled by the terrible judgments and lessons of God. Instead of being cowed, most had emerged unchastened, ungrateful, and obstinately recalcitrant. Everywhere one looked, sinfulness and pride was constantly increasing in the people, and charity was growing unusually cold. Fearing that an even greater disaster was sure to be visited on the world by a God offended by the guilt of the people, the king decided to write to all bishops in the realm entreating them to do all they could to ensure that the flocks of every priest in every parish repented of their sins, in the hope that the penances and prayers of the faithful might pacify a furious God.

The king's letter was duly dispatched in early September, when the plague had departed into the far north of England and the borders of Scotland. A few weeks later a copy was passed to Master John by the prior of Ixworth, with the admonition that he should pay close heed to its content and act swiftly on it. As John read the letter, he was pleased that the king was greatly disturbed by the persistence, and indeed the increase, of sinfulness. John was impressed that the king showed himself to be a faithful Christian by proclaiming that "there is nothing that prayer cannot achieve when accompanied by entreaty, humility, fasting, and the other defenses of virtue." He was also a humble man, since he wrote "we have little trust in our own merits," and finally he was a wise man when he beseeched the clergy, "who have been chosen to make offerings and sacrifices for sins on behalf of mankind, to offer God devout prayers and sacrifices for our salvation and that of our people."

The king's letter was a comfort for Master John, and he was determined to act on it. As required, he would spare no effort in persuading his parishioners to follow the exhortation of the king and repent their sins and give themselves up to prayer, fasting, and the exercise of virtue, and turn away from evil. He would also promise his flock that if they were able to drive out spiritual wickedness from their hearts, God would give them peace, tranquility, and health of body and soul, and that the malignancy of the air and of the other elements would also depart and not return. But there were doubts in his heart that the clergy alone could save mankind, since all their efforts had failed to halt the advance of the pestilence. What is more, he noted ruefully, since the pestilence even more churchmen of high and low status were displaying clear signs of sinfulness themselves, by acting in just such a greedy and selfish fashion as the common people they so derided.

Master John hoped his parishioners would be impressed by the grave concerns of the king, but he decided to force the message home by delivering a sermon reminding them of the transience of life and their recent narrow escape from death. Before the great pestilence, time and again, he had seen how the sight of corpses and weeping made men and women think on their own death, and he had often marveled how death could serve as a very effective spur to put away sin. But the pestilence had been so dreadful and the numbers of corpses so huge that the survivors appeared less sensitive to the threat of death, and instead gave themselves over to pride, luxury, and lechery. He would therefore ask them from the pulpit of St. Mary's, "Where now are the evil lovers of the world, who a little time ago were with us? Where are the haughty, where the envious, the lustful, the gluttonous?" And he would tell them, when they had looked to him for an answer, "For all their love of riches, their delicacies and luxuries, they now have nothing, and the worms have their bodies."

On Sunday, at the main Mass, Master John duly read the king's letter about the obstinacy of the sinful in the face of God's wrath, and he reminded all who attended of the other message that King Edward had sent them a little while ago, against the malice of idle servants who would not work without taking outrageous wages. Such selfish and destructive behavior was certain to be severely punished by God as well as by the king. He had been asked many times by Lady Rose, and by Sir Edmund and Margery de Welles, to preach against the excesses of workmen and to urge parishioners to obey the king's ordinance, or suffer the pains of Hell for their sins. Now he needed no further prompting, for it was his own loathing of disorder and the disruption caused by people who did not know their place in God's hierarchy which drove him to berate his congregation for sloth, greed, and arrogance.

"The sins of pride and avarice can be found everywhere about, within Walsham and without. In case there are any among you who believe that God is offended only by the misbehavior of the rich and powerful, I tell you that your own misdeeds and the sinfulness which abounds among you in this very parish offends him just as deeply. The poor man can be as guilty in his heart of the vices of pride and avarice as the rich man. Every villager in Walsham, by forgetting how lowly he or she is, threatens the well-being of the whole of society and with it the divine order that God imposed on the world. You risk provoking him into sending us all another chastisement. The king and his highest counselors sought to restore order, but his ordinance has been ignored, and servants serve their masters worse from day to day. How can we doubt that God is angered by every slothful workman, who scarcely does in two days what he could do in one? They are laggards who think only of their wages, and the food and drink that their master will give them, rather than of completing the job well which they have contracted to do. As the goat does not know how to stay in one place, so many servants do not know how to stay loyal in good service, but change from master to master in order to hide their bad qualities."

Then, to drive his message even further into their hearts, he chose an example much closer to home: "Are you too obstinate to learn from the awful lessons God has so recently taught you within your own parish and within your own families? Have you so soon forgotten how God dealt with those among us who refused to perform their divinely allotted role in society, and defied their earthly lords along with their heavenly savior? I remind you, then, of the harvest before the pestilence when eleven men out of selfishness and arrogance refused to work for Lady Rose and Sir Hugh, of blessed memory, in the fields of their great farm, as custom and the manor law requires, by helping to reap their lords' corn, bind it into sheaves, and cart it into the barns. These men all swore oaths of fealty when they accepted their lands and were obliged to do their lords' bidding, yet out of pure rebelliousness, they conspired together to deprive their lord and lady of what was theirs by right. They abused the reeve and ignored his lawful summons. But they could not ignore the summons of the Lord of Heaven. His commands cannot be defied. His punishment, more awful than any torture on earth, cannot be avoided. Of those eleven rebels, only John Rath and William Warde are alive today. For our Lord struck dead with pestilence fully nine for their sinfulness. You will do well to remember their names: Walter Osbern, Robert Lene, Robert Springold, Peter Jay, William Cranmer, William Hawys, Thomas Fuller, Thomas Dormour, and Stephen Cooper. We will now remember their souls in our prayers, that they may be speedily delivered from torment.

"Nor should the sinful and the idle among you here believe that you have escaped just punishment. This time of plenty will not last forever, and Hunger will soon haste himself hitherward to chastise wasters who ruin the world. Just think on the sparseness of this year's harvest, destroyed by the rain sent by God. Just look in the barns of Lady Rose and Sir Edmund, and in the prior's tithe barn, and you will see stocks of grain as meager as any I have ever seen. When you go to market you will find that prices are already a little more than they were last year, and listen to the dealers and you will find them predicting that food prices will rise even higher. When food is dear and your wages fall back to their former levels, then you will work hard and be respectful to your betters. When hunger returns you will regret your present excesses."

Master John was deeply saddened that he had to chastise his parishioners in this manner. All his life he had felt sympathy and compassion for the heavy oppressions that the poor and lowly had to endure, and he had never previously shared the hostile sentiments of those preachers who believed that rustics had to be held low by fear and dread to make them subservient. But now he lamented how irreverently they behaved when they were not cowed by hunger. Those who had little or nothing of substance were displaying disrespect for those of a higher estate. All around he saw parishioners, who only a few months before had led industrious and dutiful lives, refusing to work unless they received excessive payments. What is more, when they deigned to take on a job, they were lazy and inefficient. However, when it came to taking pleasures, many of which were sinful, the villagers gave themselves wholeheartedly to gratification. Laborers, smallholders, and beggars complained loudly about the rich but, to Master John's mind, they were now showing that they would behave just as badly as their betters if they were advanced to riches and possessions.

Master John had always taught his flock that charitable giving is one of the finest acts of mercy. He led by example, and many times from his own meager resources he supported those who had fallen on bad times with money, food, and shelter. These unfortunate folk, he had always believed, were fully deserving of alms. But of late, he had become concerned that there were many men and women in Walsham, strangers as well as residents, who deliberately chose a life of idleness and begging rather than honest labor. When offered a job they pretended to be sick or disabled, and pleaded for alms despite being fit enough to work for a living. They preyed upon the kindness of their fellows who, anxious to perform good works, seemed willing to give their money away too freely.

He recalled that the king's ordinance was concerned not only with avaricious laborers but with ridding the realm of the sturdy beggars who had appeared since the pestilence, who lived in idleness and sin, and sometimes by theft and other crimes. So Master John read again the copy of the royal ordinance he had kept, and his eyes alighted on a passage that proclaimed imprisonment "for any person who under the color of pity or alms gave anything to anyone who was able to labor for a living, and thereby cherished them in their sloth." He was shocked, for he did not feel that this was a just penalty for Christians who acted out of kindness, even if they did so without sufficient care. So, remembering what he had been taught at school, he weighed Cato's advice against that of Gregory, and he found much to favor in Cato's view that we should take care who we give alms to, so that the genuinely needy are not deprived by undeserved gifts to those able to support themselves. Gregory's injunction to give to all who asked seemed unsuitable to the present times, for almsgivers must choose carefully between those who deserved charity and those who undermined the law of Christ and the law of the king by pretending to be what they were not. Nowadays, there was a duty to distinguish between deserving folk who were too old or too young to work, and those who did not wish to work; between those burdened with too many children, those who were genuinely sick or with twisted limbs or unseeing eyes, and those who were able but slothful.

Master John spent much time pondering the problem of whether guilt should attach to those who gave to a false beggar, and he concluded that it should not. Except, that is, when the giver acted stupidly or out of a reckless and selfish desire for indulgence. In most cases, the blame and the sin should attach to the false beggar. But try as he might, he was unable to resolve the more difficult question of whether compassionate almsgivers who were tricked by clever idlers should derive any spiritual reward for the gifts they made. It was when faced with issues like these that he longed for the intellectual support and companionship of his lifelong friend Richard, the infirmarer of Bury abbey. But Richard had perished three months earlier along with forty of his brethren, and the dormitory of the famous monastery was now barely half full, despite recently taking in numerous boys scarcely old enough to be away from their mothers.

In late September, a flurry of excitement swept through the parish over news that a band of followers of the Brotherhood of Flagellants had landed for the first time in England. Master John knew that these zealots had arisen like a flood across Europe in the chaos and hysteria caused by the pestilence, and he had often reflected in a scholarly fashion on stories of their frenzied activities. Their name, he had discovered, came from the whips, *flagella*, with which they scourged themselves. They were also known as "cross bearers" on account of the crosses they carried on their travels and the cross-like manner in which they lay prostrate on the ground with their arms outstretched. Master John had listened intently to fascinating accounts of how innumerable large bands of flagellants, including women as well as men and drawn from all ranks of society, had traversed through many countries overseas, threatening the authority of the Church and calling for the death of Jews and other unbelievers. Gripped by extreme penitential fervor and beseeching God to stay his anger, these bands processed through towns and villages along their way, chanting in unison and whipping themselves and each other until the blood ran freely down their backs and shoulders (see figure 39). It was said that many had died in a state of ecstasy from their beatings. Wherever they went hundreds flocked to join them, and thousands welcomed them into their communities, singing with them the flagellants' hymn and hoping that their abasement and suffering would ensure their town or village exemption from God's pitiless scourge:

Your hands above your head uplift
That God the plague may from us shift
And now raise up your arms withal
That God's mercy on us fall

But as far as Master John was aware, nothing so hysterical or so violent had yet occurred anywhere in England. Now, however, a group of agitated villagers stopped him by the church door soon after the feast of Michaelmas and told him that more than a hundred devout men of the Brotherhood of Flagellants had arrived in London on ships from Flanders. Excitedly they ushered the priest toward a nearby alehouse where, they assured him, he would find a carter who had seen these holy people processing in and around St. Paul's church in the city of London. As John hurried along, he tried desperately to order his thoughts. On the one hand, he knew for certain that God was favorably influenced by penitential processions. What is more, the young clerk had told the monks at Bury abbey that Pope Clement himself had joined with a group of flagellants on a number of occasions while the plague raged in Avignon in the spring of 1348. On the other hand, John had also heard that the pope had subsequently changed his mind and was now thinking of banning the movement, because he and other Church leaders were alarmed at the huge numbers that had flocked to join and the fanaticism of some adherents. Flagellants were unlicensed laypeople who were challenging the power of the Church by public preaching and praying. Some claimed that they and their brotherhood could save mankind from the death-dealing pestilence, whereas the Church had failed.

As they drew near, Master John could see a stranger regaling a large group of villagers outside Alice Pye's alehouse. When he caught sight of the priest, the carter announced that he would begin his story again. This he did, but not before stooping to pick up a fresh jug of ale which one of his audience had bought for him. "I was going about my business near the huge river in the center of the great city, picking up goods from this merchant and that, loading up my cart with the things you like to buy in these parts when I kept bumping into people who urged me to go to St. Paul's to see a band of strange pious folk, including many noblemen, who had come from the Low Countries, to take the sins of you and me on their shoulders and save us from the plague. So I hurried to that huge church and stood in the massive crowd of people gathered outside. All went silent as we heard the faint sound of beating drums and mournful chanting. As the drumming and chanting grew louder, I saw in the distance a host of brightly colored banners held aloft. And as they drew nearer I could see that those who bore them were followed by men carrying crosses, dressed in strange hoods and white cloth, and behind them the wondrous sight of a long procession of men of the brotherhood. The brethren were all dressed alike, and they marched in lines, moving in time with each other and with their chanting. As they drew close, I could see that each was barefoot and stripped to the waist, and wore a white cloth which hung down from loins to ankle. On their heads they had hats with a red cross painted on the front and back, and in their right hands they carried a whip with three thongs in it. The thongs were tied into a knot, and I saw that some of these whips had sharp needles inserted through the knots. They walked slowly, and as they did they whipped themselves with these scourges on their naked, bloody bodies. Four of the leaders chanted in their native tongue, and the rest answered as in a litany. Then, as we were crossing ourselves and praying, the procession stopped, and everyone in the procession threw themselves down on their faces on the street, making with their arms and bodies the shape of the cross. Then, still singing, beginning with the man at the end of the line, they each in turn stepped forward over the others, giving a stroke of the scourge to each man lying beneath, as they did so. And they did this until all those lying down had got up and performed the same ritual. This they repeated twice until, bloodied and weakened, they finally put on their usual clothes and retired to their lodgings."

When the carter had finished his description, a dozen or more of his audience turned to Master John and demanded, "What does this mean? Is this what God wants us to do here in Walsham to stop the plague returning?" The priest could only answer, "These people cannot know the will of God better than the clergy and the highest leaders of the Church. They do these things ill-advisedly."

1350

Women enjoyed unprecedented opportunities for employment in the times of acute labor scarcity that characterized the years after the Black Death. The king and his council recognized that female labor had a crucial role to play if the gap between supply and demand was to be closed, when they required able-bodied women as well as men to work when asked to do so. An abundance of eager employers not only meant higher wages for women, but a far greater choice of occupations than ever before, including work as assistants to skilled artisans. Records of prosecutions of offenders against the Ordinance and Statutes of Laborers show the existence of gangs of workers which included women as well as men, and also lone women "who move from place to place" demanding excessive wages for their work.

 It usually made better sense for farmers to pay high wages than to have essential jobs not done, and employers of all ranks competed fiercely with each other for the few available workers, commonly offering free food, clothes, and bonuses in cash and kind to attract and retain them. The east of England was an early target for the commissions set up to enforce the Ordinance of Laborers. In February 1350 justices of the peace were sent into the counties of Cambridgeshire and Norfolk, which bordered Suffolk to the west and the north, and into Essex, to the south, soon afterward. Suffolk was the subject of commissions issued in November 1350 and March 1351, headed by Sir John de Aspale. The preamble to the first Suffolk commission states that it was issued in consequence of complaints of the nonobservance of the ordinance that reached the king's council, and that special justices were appointed to punish all offenders. Visits by the justices caused great alarm and resentment.

In normal years pressure on farmers was always greatest at harvest time, when they had a limited period to get their crops reaped and safely stored before they deteriorated, and naturally workers were quick to seize any opportunity to maximize their earnings. Therefore, it is not surprising that in the general turbulence of 1350 conditions at harvest time were especially chaotic. Statistics from demesne farms across the country show that the 1350 harvest, with yields of wheat and barley little more than 70 percent of normal, and oats around 60 percent, was not much better than the disastrously poor harvest of the previous year. As a consequence prices began to rise in the ensuing months.

Viewed from a distance of time, the long-term changes that took place in the later Middle Ages assume a clarity and inevitability that must have appeared anything but clear or fated to those who lived through the early years after the Black Death. Here we are dealing with the first weeks and months, when the shock of the massive mortality gave rise to an abundance of confusion and doubt, and nowhere was this more in evidence than in religious and spiritual life. To the survivors of the mid-fourteenth century, the pestilence was undoubtedly the work of God. But what sort of God would have wreaked such cruel devastation, and why? The faith of many of the clergy must have been severely tested, along with that of the laity. A new and urgent hunger for moral and spiritual guidance was exhibited by the laity, which they sought not only from their priests but from a growing corpus of spiritual literature. The works of Richard Rolle, who died of plague in 1349, were especially popular. But few clergy were equipped, either theologically or temperamentally, to provide all that the laity demanded. Moreover, many pious folk were insufficiently learned and had a tendency to take teachings out of context or apply them too literally.

The pestilence multiplied the workload of parish priests by taking away, through death or promotion, most of the formerly prolific freelance and assistant clergy. Even experienced parish priests might be enticed into performing the light duties of chantry priests retained to sing Masses for the souls of the departed in private chapels, selling their services to parish guilds or acting as confessors and spiritual guides in rich households. Moreover, many of the more conscientious and rigorous clergy who continued to toil in their parishes found themselves seriously out of joint with the times and the formidable and often conflicting challenges they threw up. These could range from seemingly audacious demands of the pious to be taught ever more of the mysteries of the relationship between man and God, to the dangerous impiety of those who, by striving to take advantage of a world turned upside down, were subverting the divine order and threatening divine retribution.

꜒ꜜ

Although Lady Rose possessed other manors and properties, she relied heavily on the profits from her Walsham farm to maintain her household, and was shocked to hear of the late and shoddy plowing. When, soon after Christmas, further reports about the poor state of the manor were brought by her treasurer, who had just returned from a visit to collect some of the cash Geoffrey Rath had accumulated from the sales of farm produce, she dispatched Blakey and her son, Henry, back to Walsham in haste. Rath had little warning of their arrival and was dismayed to learn that there was scarcely anyone working on the farm when they visited it. The next day, when he and the hayward accompanied Sir Henry and Blakey on a tour, the visitors discovered that little muck had been spread on the fields, and they had been poorly plowed and sown. Many hedges and fences were broken, ditches were blocked, the roof of the barn was leaking badly, and the dairy was in disorder. The pessimism of the lady's emissaries was confirmed in the afternoon when they inspected the demesne livestock and found them in very poor condition, with many animals showing clear signs of malnutrition, disease, and neglect.

Geoffrey attempted to assure Sir Henry and Blakey that everything possible was being done to rectify the faults and headway was being made, but they curtly brushed aside his excuses. Geoffrey then started to blame the sorry state of the livestock on the shortage of staff, and the scab the sheep were suffering from on the wet weather. He bemoaned the lack of experience of those few shepherds and herdsmen he had managed to get to replace the trusty servants who had died in the pestilence, but Sir Henry was in no mood to listen. His mother was facing hardship because of reduced revenues from all her estates, and Walsham was performing particularly badly. Yet again, Lady Rose had been forced to postpone her hopes for a substantial improvement in her income until the next harvest, and although it was eight months away, from what Sir Henry had already seen this was unlikely to happen. No longer could he tolerate his mother's rights being trampled by incompetent and malicious rustics. What annoyed

him most of all was the behavior of the reeve and his cronies. Geoffrey
had dressed in his finest outfit in order to impress Sir Henry but had angered him instead.

"No wonder the manor is being so badly run," Sir Henry ranted to
John Blakey. "This mere base reeve looks more like a knight than a knave.
He is more concerned about the state of his dress than the state of the
farm! Where did he get the money to buy such luxuries? They offend
against all order and decency."

Blakey did not answer but tried to placate his lady's son by saying that
things were bound to get back to normal soon, and in the meantime they
would have to be patient.

So outraged was Sir Henry by the demeanor of Geoffrey Rath that he
began asking around Walsham what the villagers thought of their reeve
(see figure 40). He soon learned, from those who bore grudges, that
Rath had committed as many offenses against the poor rustics as he had
against Lady Rose. So Geoffrey found himself subjected to interroga-
tion. Ignoring the evidence that the reeve had taken a succession of
small bribes, for he knew these were commonplace on every manor, Sir
Henry concentrated on charges that Rath had repeatedly kept his fine
new horse in the stables of the manor house, where it had consumed
large quantities of Lady Rose's oats, and that he had routinely claimed
far too much for the wages of the laborers he hired and recorded far too
little from the receipts of grain, livestock, and other produce he had sold.
Geoffrey readily admitted stabling his horse at the manor house but
claimed he had done so rarely, and then only when the urgency of business on his lady's behalf made it necessary—to stop thefts of corn from
her barns, for example. He strenuously denied false accounting or cheat-
ing his lady of money, and asserted that the accusations were invented by
troublemakers he had refused to hire at excessive wages or to sell grain
to at low prices. He went to his cottage and came back bearing tally
sticks on which he had marked every major transaction since he had become reeve six months earlier. But Sir Henry waved them aside, saying
that they could be false as well.

It was especially worrying for Sir Henry that the reeve and hayward
appeared to be far too close to the rustics. In fact, Henry gained the distinct impression that the two of them often connived with the villagers

against his mother. As Blakey had foretold, every attempt Henry made to persuade Geoffrey to take a tough line with the tenants was met with cunning counterarguments about the advisability of trying to win them over by offering compromises, and warnings that excessive severity would force them to abandon their holdings. Finally Sir Henry could stand it no longer and instructed John Blakey to summon Geoffrey Rath and tell him that he was going to be brought before the upcoming February court and fined heavily for his manifold defaults. Much as Blakey had predicted, Geoffrey responded to this by threatening to leave his post, and he stormed out abusing both Blakey and Sir Henry.

In the following days tempers cooled and a compromise was reached: the charges against Geoffrey would be dropped if he swore to amend his behavior. Geoffrey had a keen sense of his own value to Lady Rose. He was convinced that if he left she would not be able to get anyone nearly as competent or more honest to replace him. Certainly she would not find the qualities she wished in the second choice reeve, John Nobel. Thus he decided not to reform his behavior but simply to take greater care to cover his tracks.

During the new year Agnes Chapman attended Mass meticulously and was never absent when prayers were said for the souls of those who had recently died. On these occasions, which were very frequent, her thoughts were plagued with fears for the plight of her husband, John, who had not been fully confessed when he departed the world, and for her three dead brothers, who had shared a similar fate. As John's life slipped away before her eyes, Agnes had not been able to rouse him from his ramblings and had stupidly failed to remember the correct words of the Placebo, so condemning him, she believed, to suffer torments in Purgatory that would be prolonged far beyond his just deserts. Even worse, she kept recalling the harsh words of the traveling friar who had recently visited Walsham to impart a warning that another plague would surely come soon to punish them for their continuing sinfulness. For him, the majority of the victims of the late plague were now in Hell because they had died unshriven. And he pronounced to his terrified audience: "In Hell a man shall weep more than all the water in the earth—alms, Masses, and prayers shall not avail him. Heaven is for those who serve God, and those who died in the plague did not serve God" (see figure 41). Master John had driven the friar from the parish and poured scorn on his erroneous views, but doubts remained in some minds.

As Agnes stood in the crowded church and listened to the priest bid them "pray for all the souls that abide in the mercy of God in the pains of Purgatory," she fervently beseeched St. Katherine, her favorite saint, to ensure that the prayers were heeded by God and benefited the soul of her dead husband. But doubts often crowded into her mind. She knew that souls in Purgatory could not pray for themselves and depended on the prayers of the living, but she feared that collective prayers might not achieve much. For it was commonly accepted by both the clergy and the laity, that the benefits bestowed on individual souls were diluted in proportion to the numbers of dead for whom the prayers were said. And, of course, it was John's further misfortune that the numbers of recent dead were far too many to be counted. At the same time, Agnes was comforted by the words of Master John, who frequently reminded his flock that no prayers were more powerful than those recited by the clergy and echoed by the congregation during a Mass in St. Mary's church. Nonetheless, whenever she could afford it, Agnes would purchase a candle and place it before the newly painted statue of the Virgin to the left of the altar. Agnes, too, prayed many times each day before the little shrine to St. Katherine, which she had made near the window in her cottage, and before she ate she always said the De Profundis, or as much of it as she could remember, just as she had been urged to do by an old lady who used to work as a servant at Ixworth priory, who assured her that reciting it before eating would feed her dead husband's soul and enable it to suffer the pains of Purgatory with more patience.

Only a few months ago, on the eve of the pestilence, Agnes had a husband, four brothers, and a daughter. Now she was left with only her daughter, having recently learned that her brother Henry, who had left the village more than two years before, was also dead. Agnes was forever indebted to John Wodebite for his caring guardianship of her precious daughter through the darkest days of the pestilence and, fittingly, the Wodebites had been favored by God and fate and touched but lightly by the pestilence. Among his close family John Wodebite had lost only his sister-in-law Margery. It was because of her deep gratitude that Agnes continued working for John one or two days a week, cooking and cleaning in his house and looking after his pigs and poultry, although he paid her only a halfpenny more than he had paid before the pestilence, which was much less than she could have earned elsewhere.

Like all the widows and single women in Walsham, Agnes thought about remarrying or cohabiting. Although she would have liked more assistance on her smallholding, she had not received any offers that were attractive enough for her to give up her independence. Her heart had pounded when John Wodebite's wife died suddenly from a seizure a few weeks after the pestilence had departed, but her hopes were crushed when he quickly took up with a young woman and married her just a few weeks later. Agnes remained devoted to the family, but she was not sorry when John failed to invite her to his wedding party. She was delighted soon afterward, however, to be a guest at the grand feast that celebrated the marriage of his daughter, also called Agnes, to Edmund Lene in November. John Wodebite considered it a splendid match because Edmund was one of the richest villagers in Walsham. But Agnes was a little sad, for although Edmund showered gifts on his bride, he was at least twenty years older than the young woman.

Agnes's friendship with her sister-in-law blossomed as Alice's pregnancy advanced. However, Alice, unlike Agnes, felt driven to replace her dead husband, and soon after the birth of her son she took up with John Packard, whose wife had died in the plague. Alice had been left to run a large farm, and although Agnes appreciated that it was difficult for her to cope alone, she did not like Packard and was suspicious of his motives. Packard was a substantial landholder in his own right, but he had a reputation for greed and deceit. Agnes could not help feeling that he was courting Alice and was willing to take on the burdens of raising her child in order to get his hands on her land. But perhaps it was the long-standing enmity between the Packards and the Wodebites, which had its origins in a bloody assault ten years earlier by Packard's wife on John Wodebite's mother in a row about an unpaid debt, that most swayed Agnes against him. Despite her opposition, Alice married John Packard in May 1350.

It was in late July 1350 that Agnes first became interested in joining the gang of wayfaring workers that William Warde was recruiting in the village. Because of commitments to her smallholding, her child, and John Wodebite, she had so far not been able to profit much from the high wages on offer in Walsham, and she was determined to take better advantage of the approaching harvest season. Harvests had always offered good wages and lots of ale and food for those who gathered in the crops, even when the village was heavily populated with willing hands. Now, with workers so scarce, there were prospects of extraordinarily high wages, even for menial tasks such as gathering and binding the stalks after reaping. But rumors were rife in Walsham that Lady Rose and Sir Edmund and Margery de Welles had entered into a compact with each other to hold wages down and coerce other farmers into doing the same. What is more, it was said that they were threatening to bring in the king's justices to prosecute anyone who refused to work at the wages they offered.

William Warde was well-known among the village elite as an agitator. Even before the pestilence, he was often to be found instructing workmen on their rights and how to gain the best wages and conditions, and now he had a much larger and more sympathetic audience as he encouraged villagers to join with him and leave Walsham at harvest time to find better pay in the villages around. Employers and their foremen, worried by the influence he was now exerting, tried to pour scorn on Warde's notions, pointing out that he was a person of no substance, a failure who had twice been forced to dispose of what little land he possessed in order to pay his debts. But they failed to stop him winning the confidence of many of the common people. For Warde was not just a talker, he was a doer. He was renowned for organizing the strike of harvest workers on Lady Rose's demesne farm two years before, and he had been one of the first to demand greatly increased wages in Walsham during the pestilence; when he was refused he quickly found well-rewarded work down the road in Ixworth.

Now that Lady Rose's steward, John Blakey, was trying to lower expectations by swearing to hire workers for the forthcoming harvest only at the old rates and was cajoling Sir Edmund and other large farmers to do the same, Warde found no shortage of potential recruits to his gang. People were extremely angry that they were being persecuted in their own village, and Warde offered a solution: join him and leave to seek work elsewhere. However, the reeve of Sir Edmund and Margery de Welles had already spoken in confidence with Warde and offered attractive terms for the supply of ten workers, so he intended to harvest their crops first, as long as they lived up to their promise to pay good wages. Then he planned to lead his band of workers out of Walsham into neighboring villages seeking the highest rates of pay they could get. Warde was convinced from all he had heard that they would be welcomed everywhere by farmers anxious to get their crops in at the optimum time, and willing to pay handsomely for it. Warde also knew that as gang master he could negotiate fat bonus payments for himself.

At Hilary Typtoft's urging, Agnes Chapman finally spoke to William Warde in Robert Rampoyle's alehouse. She was thrilled by his warm greeting and his cheery optimism. He told Agnes that she would be very welcome and assured her that he would have no difficulty finding her as much work as she wanted, and at 2d per day rather than the 1d per day she would be lucky to get in Walsham. Nor would it be a problem if she brought her young daughter along with her. When Agnes questioned whether farmers would hire women to do work normally done by men, Warde laughed and said that at harvest time they would take anyone who was available—even young children and the old and decrepit. "In a couple of weeks farmers everywhere will be desperate to bring the harvest in. They will have to pay us what we want or they will see their crops rot in the fields. Isn't it better to pay us a few extra shillings than lose wheat, barley, and oats worth a few pounds?" Then Warde raised his voice to address the whole tavern: "The rich here are threatening to deny us our deserts, but in all the villages around there are farmers who will welcome us as the answer to their prayers. You can rely on me to get you the very best deal for reaping each field, and not just in coin. I will see to it that you'll eat as well as you have ever done, and for free. There'll be no cold, stale vegetables or barley bread for us, nor no penny ale. But hot meals, with slices of meat hanging over the sides of the platter, wheat bread and tuppeny ale to wash it down with."

When Agnes looked incredulous, Warde shrugged his shoulders. "If they won't pay, then we'll just move on to the next farm. They'll soon learn their lesson, you believe me."

At that point two young men joined them, asking Warde how much they would be paid if they joined him. Warde said he would pay them according to the amount of work they did, which would never be less than 3d a day, with food on top. "Obviously if you reap less or bind fewer sheaves than the others, then you'll get less money. But if you do more, you'll get paid more."

The men then looked at Agnes, and Warde told them that, as women generally took longer to do the same amount of work as men, they would get paid less. But so would old men, lazy men, or young boys. That was only fair. Naturally, if Agnes took time off to look after her child, she would lose money, but if she worked extra hard afterward she could make it up.

As Agnes shook hands on the deal, Warde told her and the two men that he had work waiting for anyone who joined him on three farms within fifteen miles of Walsham. Anticipating Agnes's next question, he assured her that there was no pestilence to be found anywhere in the region.

A couple of days later, Agnes went to tell Hilary Typtoft that she would be joining her in William Warde's band of traveling harvest laborers. But, to her surprise, Hilary replied that she would not be going with them after all as she had found something better to do. Agnes's surprise turned to amazement when Hilary, who had spent all her life working as a domestic servant for little more than board and lodging, announced that she had just started working as an assistant to a local thatcher, and that she was receiving regular work at 1.5d a day and a free dinner with ale. According to Hilary, there was so much work to do and so few people to do it, that many women were being taken on by tilers, carpenters, plasterers, plumbers, and suchlike. In fact, Hilary had heard that in nearby Bradfield a woman and her daughter had taken over the running of the blacksmith's workshop after the death of her husband in the pestilence.

Later the next week, just as the harvest was ripening, at Lady Rose's suggestion John Blakey spread a rumor that the king's justices were on their way from nearby Cambridgeshire to Walsham to force the lazy to work and fine or imprison anyone who had taken excessive wages. The intention was to break the resistance of rebellious laborers, but the effect was to encourage them to flee. William Warde hastily got his gang of laborers together and they left Walsham. Soon they were earning very good money in the villages round about, and Agnes had all the work she could wish for, and more money in her purse than she had ever dreamed of.

The succession of male deaths in the wealthy Cranmer family had left Olivia and her sister Hilary, both widows in their thirties, in possession of very substantial lands, mostly around Cranmer Green and High Hall manor, for which they paid only modest rents. Naturally they faced the same problems of the scarcity and high cost of servants and day laborers as all large farmers, but they fared better than most because they were especially good and innovative managers, and had many insights into how to run their affairs to the best advantage. Olivia, in particular, enjoyed a reputation as an astute trader who could predict how prices would move, and in the 1340s she had speculated successfully in the corn market by buying cheaply and selling dear.

Immediately on gaining their inheritance, the sisters began to work together as partners and manage all their lands and assets jointly. Then they decided to specialize in animal husbandry. This was to prove a masterly policy that would bring them even greater wealth. Along with the other farmers of Walsham and Suffolk, the sisters had been depressed by the poor prospects for their neglected and rain-sodden harvest, and the cost and trouble of finding enough laborers to help them cultivate their lands. But instead of lamenting their predicament, they decided to improve it. This they did by drastically cutting back on crop cultivation and expanding their herds and flocks. As Olivia explained to Hilary, growing corn and legumes took far more labor than looking after livestock. In the course of a year every acre of arable might require ten or more likely fifteen days' work: plowing, sowing, harrowing, weeding, muck spreading, reaping, binding, and so on. Where would they find the workers they would need, and how could they afford to pay them when the price of corn was so low and the yields so pitiful? But even large herds of cattle and flocks of sheep could be managed with relatively few hands, and there was plenty of cheap pasture available in Walsham. What is more, the yields of wool, butter, cheese, milk, meat, and leather were far more reliable than those of wheat, barley, and oats, and the prices better too. As Olivia and Hilary were quick to appreciate, livestock could be bought very cheaply in the months after the pestilence, especially from the reeves of Lady Rose and Edmund and Margery de Welles. So, with money in their pockets from their father's chest, they set about buying good livestock on a grand scale for bargain prices, which they pastured on rented plots as well as their own lands (see figure 42).

The Cranmer sisters' strategy soon began to pay off. For the appetite for milk, butter, cheese, and meat rose strongly as the villagers of Walsham eagerly spent a large part of their increased income on better and more varied food. Thus Olivia and Hilary prospered and did not find it at all difficult paying the frequent fines imposed on them when their animals strayed into neighboring fields and damaged crops. They even managed to deliver promptly seven bushels of barley to the barn of Edmund and Margery de Welles, in compensation for the destruction caused when no less than sixteen of their cows and bullocks broke through the fences onto the field called Abovethewood. Though on this occasion the sisters did sack the boy who should have been looking after their herd.

In 1338 Olivia had married Robert Hawys, a union forced on her after she had been fined and shamed in both the manor court and the church court for giving birth to an illegitimate child in the previous year. The marriage had not been happy but had been mercifully short, and Olivia had no intention of marrying again. She enjoyed her independence, and the last thing she wanted was for a new husband to take control of her money and property, as the law of the manor and of England decreed. Hilary, however, thought differently, and she went with a number of suitors before settling on John Margery, a free tenant of independent means whom she married in late 1350. By this time the success of their business ventures had made the Cranmer sisters famous in the village, and it did not take long for Lady Rose's son Henry to hear of the match. Well aware that Hilary was of unfree status, and therefore by custom liable to pay a fine to the lady of the manor for marrying, he charged her the unprecedented sum of 13s 4d in the November court. Hilary made it clear to her new husband that she would continue her joint ventures in sheep farming and cattle rearing with Olivia, and John

Margery, conscious of the pleasing income they produced, was happy to go along with his wife's wishes.

Although Olivia was the main driving force behind the joint ventures, the close collaboration with her sister proved very helpful to her on occasion, not least when her mind began to turn toward making a pilgrimage to Rome. Olivia had been a founding member of the fraternity of Corpus Christi, and with her growing wealth and intensifying devotion, as well as the demise of so many of her fellows, she had risen to a position of prominence in that guild. When, after a private Mass, the priest told the assembly that Pope Clement, with remarkable foresight, had some seven years previously declared this year to be a Roman Jubilee, Olivia set her heart on making a pilgrimage to the holy city. The priest added to the excitement by predicting that many thousands of pilgrims would be traveling from all parts of Christendom to the basilica of the blessed apostles Peter and Paul and St. John in the holy city, there to give thanks to God for their deliverance from death. Her resolve was further strengthened when the priest went on to say that the pope had also announced that everyone who made the journey to Rome at any time during the whole of the year 1350 would be rewarded with a plenary indulgence, as long as they were fully confessed and truly penitent. The priest was unable to explain quite what a plenary indulgence meant, but Master John said that each pilgrim would receive the full divine remission of the penance due on all the sins they had committed in their life. The pope, Master John said, was able to do this because he held the keys to a vast treasury, in which was stored the merit accumulated by Christ, the Virgin Mary, and all the saints, martyrs, and other exceptionally good folk during their lifetime that was in excess of the quantity needed for their own salvation.

Olivia was exhilarated by the prospect of gaining her plenary indulgence. For, although God had shown favor to her by sparing her during the pestilence, she still felt a great weight of sin pressing on her for her youthful fornication. The other members of the Corpus Christi fraternity were very supportive, since they appreciated that Olivia's pilgrimage would produce great spiritual benefit for them all. A number of the richer members asked her to try and obtain an indulgence for them in their absence, and she received many donations toward the cost of the journey.

Soon Olivia obtained confirmation that the pestilence had not been seen in Rome for many months. In fact, she was reliably told that the dreadful scourge had departed from the city well before it had left Walsham, and the whole region of Italy had been entirely free of the disease for many months. As far as she could gather, the pestilence was now to be found only in the cold northerly regions of the world, whereas the route she had to follow would take her safely to the south.

But there were many other perils and obstacles to be faced on such a journey. The route the pilgrims followed across France and down into Italy had to be very carefully planned, as England and France were at war. So Master John took Olivia to the library of the abbey at Bury, where the old librarian got out the itinerary composed by the chronicler Matthew Paris in the late thirteenth century. He showed her the recommended routes that proceeded southward from either Calais or Boulogne right down to the Alps, and that the mountains were to be crossed using the Mont Cenis pass. Then Olivia had to obtain a special license permitting her to visit the lands of the king's enemies, which she did from an official of the sheriff of Cambridgeshire when she visited Cambridge. A few weeks later, by a stroke of good fortune that was surely due to divine intervention, she heard that a vessel was soon to sail from Ipswich to Calais, with a small band of pilgrims bound for Rome, so she made her way to the Suffolk port with all haste.

With good reason, Lady Rose continued to fret about the state of Walsham manor. As frequently as they could be spared, she dispatched John Blakey and her son Henry to inspect it. Although there were some encouraging signs of a slow but fitful recovery of interest in a few of the less unattractive pieces of vacant land, buoyed by an upward drift in grain prices, she received no assurance that her Walsham tenants were becoming any more inclined to obey her wishes. What is more, as Henry had warned her many times, this year's harvest was likely to be even worse than last year's.

So, when he was summoned for an audience with his mother the day before he left to conduct the midsummer court session with Blakey, Henry expected to receive lengthy instructions on good business practice and efficient farm management. To his surprise, however, his mother told him that she had another task for him to perform while he was in Walsham, which she implored him to treat as an even higher priority than restoring her revenues. She wished to endow a chantry in memory of her dead husband, in which priests would forever sing Masses for his soul and the souls of all departed members of their family. When Henry protested at the exorbitant cost of setting up such a chapel at a time when money was very short and priests very expensive, Rose agreed as a temporary measure to hire only one priest rather than two. And, after further pressure, she accepted for the time being that instead of a costly new building, the chapel could be housed in the small church close to her manor house, in a prominent niche fenced off by wooden rather than stone screen work. To humor the clearly disgruntled Henry further, she told him that the priest would also sing Masses for the soul of Henry's father, Sir Edmund de Pakenham, who had died when he was but an infant in 1331. Henry was scarcely mollified by these concessions, as he could see his inheritance draining away. But his mother would budge no further, adding that the priest they chose would soon have to sing for her soul as well, as she was bound to die before long. And, she insisted, if they were going to have to make do with only one priest, that priest had to be Master John, one of the most holy clerics she had ever encountered, whose prayers would carry far more weight with God than those of greedy and ill-educated young upstarts or tired and lazy old priests in retreat from their parishes.

Lady Rose was delighted when Henry enthusiastically agreed that Master John should be their chantry priest. But he had had reasons other than piety for favoring Walsham's vicar. He knew that Master John could be hired very cheaply, since he was an otherworldly man who had little interest in money. Hiring this ascetic and making a small chapel in the local church were excellent ways of keeping the costs of this extravagant venture down.

Unfortunately for Lady Rose and her son, Master John would not consider for a moment giving up his cure of souls to sing masses for sweet silver. So, after a series of fruitless attempts to persuade him, Henry hired Master John's new assistant as chantry priest instead. This assistant was a promising but very young cleric, who had arrived in Walsham a few weeks before, fresh from Norwich, having been ordained by the bishop at the unprecedented age of twenty-two years. When he first reported he handed a letter to Master John from the bishop, in which it was explained that, because of the great scarcity of priests and the urgency of filling the multitude of vacant posts at all levels in the church, occasioned by the recent disastrous pestilence, the minimum age of ordination had been reduced below twenty-five years for the most promising young deacons. But the bishop had done this only on the understanding that such young men would be entrusted into the care of experienced clergy, and he finished the letter by saying that he deemed Master John worthy to supervise his further training.

Before the pestilence Master John would have railed against such a lowering of standards, which would inevitably follow from the ordination of the young and immature. But now he recognized that vacancies had to be filled for the sake of his parishioners, and that it was better to appoint good young men than to ordain older men who were illiterate or ignorant, or recently widowed and lacking a sense of vocation. However, no sooner had Master John reconciled himself to accepting the new young priest, than he heard that the bishop of Norwich was contemplating seeking papal dispensation for ordaining clerks as young as twenty years, since so many of his parishes were without priests. Master John let his opposition be known, but his protests were to no avail, and in October 1350, with the permission of the pope, the bishop ordained no less than sixty clerks who had barely reached this tender age. However, Master John was delighted to learn that the bishop was founding a school for the education and training of young boys for the priesthood, and also a college in Cambridge to secure a supply of educated priests for his diocese. It was also encouraging that in the same city the Guild of St. Mary and the Guild of Corpus Christi were contemplating joining together to found another new college, and endow it with sufficient property and possessions to fulfill in perpetuity the dual purposes of singing Masses for the souls of its benefactors and educating young men for a career in the Church.

The desertion of his recent recruit to Lady Rose's family chantry chapel hit Master John exceptionally hard, and his morale plunged further when another chaplain, John Kebbil, sublet the lands in Walsham that he had inherited from his father and accepted a benefice in a nearby parish. But the causes of John's depression extended far beyond his acute need for assistance in carrying out all the essential tasks in the parish. The state of the world, and his inability to correct the behavior of his flock or fathom the purpose behind God's actions, had cast him into deep despair. Though he knew of a couple of priests in parishes near Cambridge who spoke warmly of the stream of instruction they received from the bishop of Ely, John was a fiercely independent man by nature, and he had little time for the spiritual guidance offered to him by officials of the bishop of Norwich, and he resisted the intermittent interference of the prior of Ixworth and the handful of monks who remained alive in his small monastery.

Much as he strove to restore order to the religious life of the parish and get things great and small back to where they had been, Master John found himself constantly buffeted by new concerns and new fashions. New fashions could take many forms, in worship as well as in clothing and morals, and one of the latest modes was for the celebration of a Mass created by the pope while the pestilence raged in Avignon, which had come to be called Missa pro Mortalitate Evitanda. Through its appeals for mercy to "pie Jesu" and the Mother of Mercy, it was believed that this Mass had helped to bring the pestilence to an end in that city. Now an influential group of pious but simple parishioners began demanding that it be regularly celebrated in St. Mary's. As word spread that the Mass gave 260 days of indulgence to all who heard it while truly contrite and confessed, and a guarantee that those who heard it on five consecutive days, while kneeling with a burning candle in their hands, would not suffer a sudden death, the pressure on Master John to agree became intense. But he resisted the calls. Not only was he was deeply skeptical of claims that this Mass would grant such rich privileges, he had difficulty tracking down a reliable copy of the liturgy.

While Master John hesitated, however, the eager young priest retained by the fraternity of Corpus Christi celebrated a corrupt version for his employers almost as often as they desired. This inexperienced hireling, as Master John termed him, repeatedly assured his eager audience that the indulgence and freedom from sudden death they craved "is certain and was proved in Avignon and neighboring regions," before he launched into his recitation of the office: "Remember, O Lord, your covenant, and say to the scourging angel, 'Now hold your hand,' so that the earth is not laid waste and you do not lose every living soul."

Another discomfort for Master John was that he was called regularly to High Hall manor house to attend to the spiritual needs of Margery de Welles. Since the pestilence Margery had spent much of her time reading pious works, and of late she had become anxious to discuss many things contained in a book she had acquired from the estate of a dead relative, written by a hermit called Richard Rolle. It was called *The Form of Living*, and it was in English, for Margery knew no Latin. She found the author's "song of love" most affecting, and devoutly following Richard Rolle's advice to keep it in remembrance, she had taken to reciting it at mealtimes, as well as on many other occasions during each day:

> *Loved be thou, king,*
> *and thanked be thou, king,*
> *and blessed be thou, king,*
> *Jhesu, all my joying,*
> *Of all thy gifts good,*
> *that for me spilt thy blood,*
> *and died on the rood,*
> *thou give me grace to sing,*
> *the song of thy loving.*

Memorizing and reciting prayers was the easy part for Margery, but when reading other passages in the book she became overly excited and deeply troubled. As Master John patiently explained, Rolle was a renowned hermit who had devoted his whole life to meditation and trying to attain perfection in a contemplative life, far removed from the everyday world. His book was not a manual to be followed to the letter by someone like Margery, who had a busy household to run. It should be read for insights into an ideal life, which was for someone like her to admire rather than to attain. Master John encouraged Margery to concentrate on the closing pages of the book, which contained excellent guidance for those who led an active life, by keeping the commandments and loving one's neighbor as oneself. After a long series of visits to her chamber and many hours of teaching, Master John felt satisfied that he had at last settled Margery's troubled mind.

Yet within a few days he received an urgent summons from High Hall and arrived to find Margery in a euphoric state. She beckoned him into her chamber, where she sat by the window and pointed excitedly with her finger to a passage in Rolle's book. There he read the dedication: "Loo, Margaret, I have briefly said the form of living, and how you may come to perfection." Despite his best efforts, including discovering that the Margaret to whom Rolle had dedicated the book was a nun and a recluse, not a rich widow, Margery saw the similarity between their names as a sign, and for many months afterward she strove for spiritual perfection in everything she did and said, and on a number of occasions she was transported into a state of religious ecstasy. This frustrated and even angered Master John, who blamed such books for confusing the minds of simple folk who should rely only on what they were taught by their priests. In his efforts to cool her ardor, Master John had the support of Margery's brother Edmund, who was driven to frequent outbursts of profanity by her mystical affectations.

Master John's dealings with a number of ardently pious individuals and groups within his parish were becoming a daily burden to him rather than a source of delight and fulfillment. He was continually pestered by parishioners who demanded more and more explanation of the will of God, and more and more explication of the word of God, all of which was far beyond what was proper for them to be told, and sometimes far beyond John's wit to tell. Such folk would not be satisfied unless they were offered frequent sermons and innumerable Masses, including those containing the latest version of any rites they had happened to hear about. They were no longer content to follow the methods of teaching that he had used all his life, such as looking in awe at rituals and learning to recite by heart. Now they had seemingly inexhaustible appetites for explanation and participation. Stimulated by loose sermons given by friars and traveling preachers in the open air, by discussions in parlors with their fellows and unsupervised reading in their homes, they strove in a clumsy fashion to interpret God's will and the Church's laws and procedures, which they should have left entirely to clerks learned in these matters.

Master John was also troubled by the growing numbers of folk who believed in omens and magic, and had come to pay greater heed to the evil casting of lots, the superstitions practiced by old women, and the auguries and chattering of birds, than they did to following the right and true faith in which he steadfastly tried to instruct them. But when he chastised them, they replied saying why should they abandon trust in the ancient knowledge and magical powers of old women and men at his bidding, when the Church with all its pomp and authority had failed to avert God's anger and left them defenseless to face the pestilence.

Everywhere about him John saw sinners in their daily lives refusing to abide by the old ways, since they found the new so alluring. Daily he witnessed acts of selfishness and sinfulness in a world of greed and deceit, and he knew such behavior was bound to bring down the wrath of God again. It was against the commandments of God, as well as those of the king, for lowly laborers of little skill with nothing but their own hands to feed them, and clergy without vocation or learning, to demand wages far in excess of the value of the work they did, but everywhere employers clamored for their services and gave them what they desired. This led to the lowly being puffed up with pride and the ignorant misleading their charges. Master John preached and counseled against greed, but he was powerless to persuade laborers to work in his own fields or clergy to labor in his own parish for the old moderate rates of pay. Nowadays contracts and oaths were held lightly and broken on a whim. Since time out of mind, all tenants in Walsham had paid homage and sworn oaths of fealty to their lord or lady, to be faithful to them and render the services due from the tenements they held. Many had sworn thus just a few months ago when they entered into their inheritances on the death of their kin in the pestilence. Yet now these upstarts were breaking their solemn oaths and withholding, withdrawing, diminishing, and knowingly concealing services and rights due to their lords, and in so doing committing perjury and theft.

Many of the rustics, poor villeins as well as rich freemen, gathered together and made conventicles and illicit pacts, bringing false accusations against each other and against the officials of their lords. Disrespect was spreading like a poison through the village. Not only had tenants refused to serve their lady at harvest, there had been a spate of thefts of Lady Rose's corn. These thefts had not been carried out by poor hungry folk, desperate for food for themselves and their children, for there were few of those in

Walsham now. They had been perpetrated by those who were greedy rather than needy, by people who stole rather than labored. Only a few of the thieves had been identified and fined in the manor court, as John the dairyman and John Ryvel had been. But Master John took care to name and publicly rebuke the miscreants from the pulpit of St. Mary's.

Master John was tired and growing old. He had not recovered from his extreme physical and mental exertions during the months of the pestilence, and found it an increasing struggle to maintain either his authority over his flock or his unquestioning faith in his God. In early March he was briefly elated when King Edward issued a decree pronouncing that the pestilence was nowhere to be found in England. A few days later, while reciting prayers of thanksgiving in St. Mary's, Master John took care to calm the elation of the villagers gathered there by warning them of the king's earlier message that their sinfulness and pride was likely soon to bring down on their heads another and probably even more terrible retribution. Nor did he waver from continuing to impart this message, although few cared to listen and even fewer to heed the old man.

Throughout the spring and summer of 1350 Master John often felt unwell, and on some days he found it difficult to rise from his bed, although he rarely failed to do so by six. Whereas he used to find visiting sick or distant parishioners a welcome chore, he now tired when walking farther than a few steps. What was worse, he had become prone to wonder whether many of these visits were worthwhile. While performing Mass in late September, on the Sunday before the feast of St. Michael the Archangel, Master John collapsed, breathless, with pains in his chest while raising the Host and died just a few minutes later (see figure 43). Mercifully, he was rewarded for his holy life with a good death. He lived long enough to be ably confessed by the two priests who rushed to his side, and he passed away surrounded by members of his devoted flock in the house of the Lord, while clutching the Lord's body and having drunk his blood. Master John's soul was protected and speeded to salvation by their prayers, on this day and for many years thereafter (see figure 44).

⇥ EPILOGUE ⇤

After the immediate turmoil of the Black Death had subsided, the ensuing years saw relatively few further dramatic changes. In fact, many social and economic forces were working to return the world to normal. So alarmed were bishops by the multitude of vacant positions in the Church that they introduced a range of initiatives to increase the supply of priests, including substantially lowering the age at which young men were permitted to enter holy orders and drastically shortening the time permitted to progress from acolyte to priest. As a result of these measures and the expansion of schools and colleges, ordinations of new priests soared in the early 1350s and remained very high thereafter. Because there was no shortage of people seeking social advancement and the Church remained an attractive career, it proved far easier to fill vacancies in the clergy than in the ranks of laborers and small peasants massed at the base of the social and economic hierarchy. Consequently laborers retained much of the improved bargaining power that the pestilence had bestowed on them. Although wages fell back from the peaks they touched in the chaotic year of the great pestilence, they stayed high as labor remained very scarce.

Landlords and large farmers experienced some respite when grain prices rose sharply as the ruinous harvest of 1350 was followed by an even worse one in 1351, and then stayed high for the rest of the 1350s despite improving yields. High food prices increased the attraction of farming and strengthened the value of land, and so a progressive refilling of vacant holdings and recovery in rents took place, and lords were encouraged to continue cultivating their demesne farms. But, as the Walsham and High Hall records show, the severe difficulties in running their manors that lords continued to experience were not simply due to the shortage and high cost of laborers. Finding and keeping competent and honest reeves had become a major problem, as Edmund and Margery de Welles found when John Packard refused to accept election as reeve in the High Hall court of September 29, 1350, although John Wodebite did agree to serve as their hayward.

Geoffrey Rath was not chosen to continue as reeve of Walsham manor in the autumn of 1350, but we do not know whether this was the choice of Geoffrey, Lady Rose, or the community of tenants. What is clear, however, is that the election of John Spileman in his stead created even greater problems for Lady Rose and her son, Henry. In November 1350, after a few months in office, Spileman was judged responsible for losing a great part of the lady's crops in the recent harvest and fined the huge sum of 40s. He seems not to have lasted as reeve for much longer, for we soon learn that Geoffrey Rath returned to replace him. Some of the reasons for dissatisfaction with Spileman are spelled out in the January 1351 court, when he faced a long list of charges including failing to "raise the common [sheep] fold" on the lady's recently harvested fields, misusing the lady's cart and the time of her carpenter, neglecting the lady's woodland, and stealing various small items. But Rath too was soon in trouble and also accused of failing to raise the sheepfold as well as keeping his horse at the lady's expense. Symptomatic of the fraught relations between the lady and her local peasant officers were the fines levied on John Spileman for insulting Henry, the lady's son, and on Geoffrey Rath for insulting John Blakey. Things did not improve, and later the same year Geoffrey Rath was again fined heavily for failing to rectify various faults on the manor, and so were the two manorial shepherds for neglecting their duties and allowing a great part of the lady's lambs to die. Unsurprisingly, Rath was not reappointed at the end of the year.

From the records of Walsham and High Hall, which by now have become patchy, it can be seen that disputes between the lords of the two manors and their tenants continued to flare up throughout the 1350s. In autumn 1353 an unprecedentedly large, concerted action arose soon after the death of Lady Rose, when fourteen tenants refused to perform labor services at the harvest, thirty-four tenants refused to perform the winter *works required soon after, and ten women refused to winnow corn for the wages they were offered. Other signs of discord include the unlicensed departure of villeins to settle in other villages or towns and refusal to return, failure to swear fealty, and continuing disputes and negotiations over conditions of tenure, work, wages, and so on. These small-scale disputes and hard bargaining were repeated between villagers and their landlords and employers in thousands of manors across England, as the survivors of the great pestilence struggled to gain some control over the dramatically changed circumstances in which they found themselves. Cumulatively they were symptoms of the genesis of a universal transformation in the most important relationship in the Middle Ages, that between lords and their tenants, between land and labor. The famous Peasants Revolt of 1381 was a milestone in this struggle, for even if it was not primarily the rising against serfdom and landlords that it was once thought to be, it was certainly a formidable demonstration of the newfound confidence and independence of the lower orders.*

Such an ordered account of change can, of course, only be constructed by historians using the benefit of hindsight. But even historians find it difficult to unravel what happened in the confusion and instability that followed immediately after the Black Death, and for the survivors living through these turbulent years the task of discerning the new realities from the merely transitory, and enduring changes from short-term oscillations, must have been all but impossible. Lords and social elites longed for the world to be returned to normal, but the chances of this happening faded fast as the next decade opened with the awful news that pestilence was once again stalking the world. A second virulent epidemic erupted in England in the spring of 1361, this time choosing its victims disproportionately from the young, and it was followed by further major national outbreaks in 1369 and 1375.

The Black Death unleashed forces of immense power, and many of these forces were rendered irresistible by the long succession of deadly pestilences that punctuated the later fourteenth and fifteenth centuries and drove population down. The enhanced power that peasants and laborers derived from their scarcity was to prove a potent driving force behind revolutionary changes in economic and social institutions, including the decline of serfdom and feudalism, and a golden age for peasants and laborers. But it should always be remembered that the rising living standards and improved status that the ordinary folk came to enjoy were bought at the huge cost of high and unpredictable mortality.

Dance of Death from Ingmar Bergman's *The Seventh Seal*

ILLUSTRATION CREDITS

1. *A reconstruction of a peasant cottage.* Weald and Downland Open Air Museum, West Sussex, England.
2. *A poor parson from the Ellesmere Chaucer.* Huntington Library Art Collections and Botanical Gardens, San Marino, California.
3. *Celebrating mass: raising the Host.* Cambridge University Library, Ee.4.24, f.25r.
4. *Derision.* British Library, Royal 6E VII, f.500.
5. *A deathbed scene.* British Library, Royal 6E VI, f.302.
6. *Bust of the Virgin.* Metropolitan Museum of Art, New York, Cloisters Collection.
7. *Painting of the Day of Doom.* St. Thomas Church, Salisbury, courtesy of the Ecclesiological Society.
8. *The Battle of Crécy.* Bibliotheque national de France, MS FR2643, f.165v.
9. *Gathering in the sheaves.* Bodleian Library, Selden Supra 38, f.21v.
10. *A nativity scene.* Corpus Christi College, Cambridge, Parker MS 53, f.8r.
11. *Pope leading a penitential procession in time of plague.* Les tres riches heueres du Duc de Berry, Musee Conde, Chantilly, MS 65, courtesy of Art Resource, New York.
12. *In fear of the plague.* Stained glass window, north aisle, Trinity Chapel, Canterbury Cathederal.
13. *The Thornham Parva Retable.* Thornham Parva church, Suffolk.
14. *Miracle of the Virgin's Milk.* British Library, Egerton 2781, f.24v.
15. *Figure of God.* Church of St. Mary and St. Clement, Clavering, Essex.
16. *Pelican in her piety.* Church of St Martin, Tuddenham St Martin, Suffolk, courtesy of Simon Knott.
17. *Scene from the Book of Revelation.* Corpus Christi College, Cambridge, Parker MS 20, f.16v.
18. *Torments of Hell.* Corpus Christi College, Cambridge, Parker 20 MS f.66r.

19. *A clerical procession.* Fitzwilliam Museum, Cambridge, MS 298, f.1.

20. *Pardoner from the Ellesmere Chaucer.* Huntington Library Art Collections and Botanical Gardens, San Marino, California.

21. *Preaching in a churchyard.* Fitzwilliam Museum, Cambridge, MS 22, f.55.

22. *Lay communion with houseling cloth.* British Library, Royal B VII, f.207v.

23. *Cemetery.* British Library, Royal 6E VI, f.267v.

24. *Patient with bubonic plague.* Public domain image courtesy of Oracle ThinkQuest.

25. *Death strikes.* Fitzwilliam Museum, Cambridge, Macclesfield Psalter, f.235v.

26. *Demons seizing the soul of an unconfessed man.* British Library, Royal B VII, f.214v.

27. *Burying plague victims.* Bibliotheque Royale de Belgique, MS 13076–7, courtesy of The Granger Collection, New York.

28. *Mass for plague victims.* Bodleian Library , Douce 313, f.394v.

29. *Holbein: Death drives the plow.* Hans Holbein the Younger.

30. *Corpus Christi procession.* Trinity College, Cambridge, MS B11.3, f.155r.

31. *Laborer digging.* Bodleian Library, Douce 104, f.39.

32. *Plowman.* Fitzwilliam Museum, Cambridge, Macclesfield Psalter, f.77r.

33. *A court scene.* British Library, Royal 6E VI, f.233.

34. *Drinking game.* British Library, Add. MS. 42130, f.157v.

35. *Man and woman dancing.* Bodleian Library, Auct. D. 32, f.238.

36. *Man digging up a tree.* Beinecke Rare Book and Manuscript Library, Yale University, Le livre de Lancelot du Lac, f.169.

37. *Harrowing.* British Library, Add. MS 42130, f.171r.

38. *Preaching to an elite audience.* Thomas Arundel preaching, from a medieval tapestry.

39. *Flagellents.* Bibliotheque Royale de Belgique, MS 13076–7, courtesy of The Granger Collection, New York.

40. *Reeve from the Ellesmere Chaucer.* Huntington Library Art Collections and Botanical Gardens, San Marino, California.

41. *Souls in peril and torment.* Corpus Christi College, Cambridge, Parker MS 20, f.20.

42. *Two women driving cows and a bull.* British Library, Royal B VII, f.74b.

43. *Death of a cleric.* Les tres riches heueres du Duc de Berry, Musee Conde, Chantilly, MS 65, courtesy of Art Resource, New York.

44. *Dance of Death.* The Seventh Seal, dir. Ingmar Bergman, Svensk Filmindustri, 1957.

⊰ NOTES ⊱

WALSHAM IN THE MIDDLE AGES

The key original records on which this book is based are the fourteenth-century Walsham court rolls, which have been edited and translated in two volumes by Ray Lock, *The Court Rolls of Walsham le Willows, 1303–1350* (Suffolk Records Society, vol. 41, 1998); and *The Court Rolls of Walsham le Willows, 1351–99* (Suffolk Records Society, vol. 45, 2002). R. Lock, "The Black Death in Walsham le Willows," *Proceedings of the Suffolk Institute of Archaeology* 37 (1992), also contains material of interest. Readers wishing to learn more about the history and topography of Walsham le Willows should consult S. E. West and A. McLaughlin, *Towards a Landscape History of Walsham le Willows, Suffolk* (East Anglian Archaeology, Suffolk County Council, 1998); K. M. Dodd, *The Field Book of Walsham le Willows, 1577* (Suffolk Records Society, vol. 17, 1974); and David Dymond, "The Parish of Walsham le Willows: Two Elizabethan Surveys and Their Medieval Background," *Proceedings of the Suffolk Institute of Archaeology* 33 (1974). Those wishing to learn more about the region around Walsham, as well as the Middle Ages, are fortunate that an attractive and extremely informative new history has just been published: M. Bailey, *Medieval Suffolk: An Economic and Social History, 1200–1500* (Woodbridge, 2007).

CHAPTER 1

13 *Geoffrey Chaucer's portrait of a poor parson*: Chaucer's portrait of "a poor parson" is contained in the Prologue to the *Canterbury Tales*, of which there are innumerable modern editions. Unfortunately Master John's favorite manual, William Pagula's *Oculis Sacerdotis*, which was deliberately chosen for this book as it was written before the Black Death, has not been published. However, there is a modern edition of a manual

written in the 1380s which borrows heavily from Pagula: *John Mirk's Instructions for Parish Priests,* edited by G. Kristensson (Lund, 1974). Discussions of the role of the parish priest, together with excerpts from a wide range of contemporary sources, are provided in J. Shinners and W. J. Dohar, eds., *Pastors and the Care of Souls in Medieval England* (University of Notre Dame Press, 1998); and R. N. Swanson, ed., *Catholic England: Faith, Religion, and Observance Before the Reformation* (Manchester, 1993).

14 *Robert Shepherd, a man who was more interested*: There are abundant references in the Walsham court rolls to Robert Shepherd, chaplain, which show him engaged in money lending and dealing in land between 1329 and 1348 (e.g., Lock, *Walsham Court Rolls,* I, pp. 172, 173, 195, 204, 207, 231, 238, 297, 298, 307, 312).

15 *Time and again John had disappointed*: In this he was unlike the priests "in modern times," satirized by John Mirk (quoted in Owst, *Literature and Pulpit,* pp. 276–277).

16 *If gold rust, what shall iron do?*: From Chaucer's Prologue, as is the reference to the "shiten shepherd."

17 *two of his favorite*: For the first mentions of John Beck, chaplain, and John Kebbil, chaplain, see Lock, *Walsham Court Rolls,* I, pp. 305, 324.

18 *Master John, like William Pagula, saw*: The matters contained in this and succeeding paragraphs are based on the *Oculus Sacerdotis.* For a discussion of this work and its author, see W. A. Pantin, *The English Church in the Fourteenth Century* (University of Notre Dame Press, 1962), pp. 195–202; for an extended quotation, see Shinners and Dohar, *Pastors and the Care of Souls,* pp. 138–151.

19 *He expected his flock to know*: This program of religious instruction, recommended by Pagula, was laid down by Archbishop Pecham in the Provincial Council of Lambeth in 1281, and was also used by Archbishop Thoresby of York as the basis of his catechism in 1357 (Pantin, *English Church,* pp. 193–194, 199–200).

19 *warned how easily an infant might be killed*: Following William Pagula's advice (Pantin, *English Church,* p. 199).

19 *Master John was quick to reprove*: For a recent study of the treatment of fornication and illegitimacy, see J. M. Bennett, "Writing Fornication: Medieval Leyrwite and Its Historians," *Transactions of the Royal Historical Society,* 6th ser., 13 (2003).

20 *In the face of considerable criticism*: In the Walsham court held on November 12, 1345, both the fining of Catherine Cook, "for giving birth outside wedlock," and her death were noted (Lock, *Walsham Court Rolls,* I, p. 286).

CHAPTER 2

21 *the importance of a "good death"*: Descriptions of the drama and liturgy of the deathbed, funeral service, and burial in England in the late Middle Ages are contained in E. Duffy, *The Stripping of the Altars* (New Haven, 1992), pp. 301–337; P. Binski, *Medieval Death: Ritual and Representation* (British Museum, 1996), pp. 33–50; and C. Daniell, *Death and Burial in Medieval England, 1066–1550* (London, 1997), pp. 30–64. G. R. Owst, *Literature and Pulpit in Medieval England* (Cambridge, 1933), pp. 335–347, provides many graphic quotations from contemporary sermons of the ordeal of dying, including temptation by fiends, the decay of the body, the pains of Purgatory and Hell, and suchlike.

22 *William Wodebite was close to death*: Notice of William Wodebite's death, together with details of his landholdings, heirs, death duties, and so on, were recorded in the High Hall manor court held on September 24, 1345 (Lock, *Walsham Court Rolls,* I, p. 283).

23 *Then, one by one, he put on*: F. A. Gasquet, *Parish Life in Medieval England* (London, 1907), is an informative guide to the vestments and accoutrements of parish priests, and to funeral processions.

24 *Hail! Light of the world*: Gasquet, *Parish Life,* pp. 204–205.

24 *with bowed heads, devotion of heart*: Gasquet, *Parish Life,* pp. 203–204.

24 *the image of thy savior*: Duffy, *Stripping of the Altars,* p. 314 (from Julian of Norwich, *A Book of Showings*).

25 *thou art not my God*: Duffy, *Stripping of the Altars,* p. 315 (from *Monumenta Ritualia*, III). The late medieval church was well aware of the dangers of the worship of images.

25 *the Seven Interrogations*: These passages are based on John Mirk, *Instructions for Parish Priests* (quoted in Shinners and Dohar, *Pastors and the Care of Souls,* pp. 195–196).

27 *As one of the prominent tenants*: Many references to occasional events in William Wodebite's life between 1317 and 1345 can be found in Lock, *Walsham Court Rolls;* the remarkable business venture with John Baude is briefly described on p. 92.

28 *dying, in their last sickness*: Owst, *Preaching in Medieval England* (Cambridge, 1926), p. 342 (from *The Boke of the Craft of Dying*).

28 *There are invisible demons here* and *For the Mother of Mercy*: John Mirk, *Instructions for Parish Priests* (quoted in Shinners and Dohar, *Pastors and the Care of Souls,* p. 210).

28 *took his sprinkler and scattered holy water*: This description is taken from the chronicler Thomas Walsingham's account of the death of the Black Prince in 1376.

28 *William grudgingly admitted*: References to Wodebite's dealings with Packard and Syre can be found in Lock, *Walsham Court Rolls*, I, pp. 165, 245.

29 *ego auctoritate dei patris omnipotentis*: Latin was the language used for most of the liturgy and for the highest form of prayer uttered by the priest. It was considered holier than the vernacular. It was not understood by more than a tiny proportion of the laity.

29 *seal his contrition*: Any gifts made by William Wodebite have not been recorded, but for those given by William Lene some years before, see Lock, *Walsham Court Rolls*, I, 135.

30 *Master John placed the rest*: The giving of the last sacraments, and the accidents that can occur, are described in M. Rubin, *Corpus Christi: The Eucharist in Late Medieval Culture* (Cambridge, 1991), pp. 77–82.

30 *shriven and cleansed of his sins*: This is from Mirk, *Instructions for Parish Priests* (quoted in Daniell, *Death and Burial*, p. 43).

31 *purge me with hyssop*: Psalm 51:7.

32 *sight of corpses and weeping*: In John Mirk's *Festial* (quoted in Owst, *Preaching in Medieval England*, p. 268).

32 *might have lived a hundred years*: From *Gesta Romanorum* (quoted in Owst, *Preaching in Medieval England*, p. 342).

32 *very seldom does any man*: From the fourteenth-century *Book of the Craft of Dying* (quoted in Swanson, *Faith, Religion, and Observance Before the Reformation*, p. 139).

32 *a hall whose roof*: From John de Bromyard, *Summa Predicantium* (quoted in Owst, *Preaching in Medieval England*, p. 343).

32 *a mirror for us all*: The rest of the sermon is based on John Mirk's late-fourteenth century example of a sermon for the burial of the dead (quoted in Shinners and Dohar, *Pastors and the Care of Souls*, pp. 208–211).

33 *Six wethers, four piglets*: Details of the sumptuous "common feast" held in Walsham on the day of William Lene's funeral in 1329 are given in Lock, *Walsham Court Rolls*, I, 135, together with the expenses of sending a friar from Babwell to the shrine of St. Thomas of Lancaster at Pontefract in accordance with Lene's last wishes.

CHAPTER 3

35 *There are thousands of surviving records*: Discussions of the nature of court rolls and the information they contain, as well as details of many of the surviving collections, are given in Z. Razi and R. Smith, eds., *Medieval Society and the Manor Court* (Oxford, 1996). M. Bailey, *The English Manor, c. 1200–c. 1500* (Manchester, 2002), is an excellent, accessible

guide to the medieval manor and its principal records. For descriptions and analyses of rural England in the decades before the Black Death, see E. Miller and J. Hatcher, *Medieval England: Rural Society and Economic Change, 1086–1348* (London, 1978); and M. Bailey, "Peasant Welfare in England, 1290–1348," *Economic History Review* (1998). Data on harvest yields and grain and livestock prices are abundant, since they are meticulously recorded in the comprehensive accounts of the operation of demesne farms drawn up for landlords, which survive in great numbers. See, for example, the national series compiled from such records by D. H. Farmer in *The Agrarian History of England and Wales,* vols. 2–3 (Cambridge, 1988 and 1991).

A brief, accessible account of the early stages of the Hundred Years War is given in B. Tuchman, *A Distant Mirror: The Calamitous Fourteenth Century* (1978), pp. 70–91. Most of the plethora of books on the Black Death pay some attention to the origin and spread of the devastating epidemic, and a number attempt detailed discussions. See, in particular, O. Benedictow, *The Black Death, 1346–1353: A Complete History* (2004), pp. 44–67; and M. W. Dols, *The Black Death in the Middle East* (Princeton, 1977), pp. 35–67, both of which examine the testimony of Gabriele de' Mussi.

37 *For those who might forget*: The description of the doom painting is based on the one above the chancel arch of "St. Thomas" Church, Salisbury.

38 *Acrimony between Walter Cooper:* The dispute between Walter Cooper and Thomas Bec can be followed in Lock, *Walsham Court Rolls,* I, pp. 282–286.

38 *Few quarrels, however, were as remorselessly bitter*: The tumultuous affairs of William Wodebite's children were recorded in successive High Hall court rolls: Lock, *Walsham Court Rolls,* I, pp. 283–284, 290–291, 295–297, 299–300, 307–308.

42 *a glorious victory in the war*: This description of the battle of Crécy is based on the account written by the famous contemporary court chronicler, Jean Froissart.

43 *her private confessor*: Later fourteenth-century writings abound in criticisms of the friars, who operated largely outside of the jurisdiction of the English Church hierarchy and posed a threat to the local regular clergy by diverting revenues from parish priests and competing with their authority in spiritual matters. Many of the failings of the Franciscan friar in Walsham are taken from the portrait of the friar in Chaucer's Prologue to the *Canterbury Tales.*

44 *Lady Margery, who was particularly fond*: Chess was a popular game in the Middle Ages, and a moralized game of chess was often used to drive

home lessons from the pulpit. This sermon is based on that quoted by C. Smyth, *The Art of Preaching: A Practical Survey of Preaching in the Church of England, 747–1939* (SPCK, 1940), pp. 89–90 n. 2.

44 *Devils and demons are with us*: Demons are commonly featured in fourteenth-century sermons, especially Tutivillus (Owst, *Literature and Pulpit*, pp. 512–514).

46 *The harvest of autumn*: The fourteenth century was a period of climatic deterioration, including markedly increased rainfall and lower temperatures (M. Bailey, "Per Impetum Maris: Natural Disaster and Economic Decline in Eastern England, 1275–1350," in B. M. S. Campbell, ed., *Before the Black Death: Studies in the "Crisis" of the Early Fourteenth Century* (Manchester, 1991). The famines and agrarian crises of 1315–1322 were among the worst that Europe ever experienced: I. Kershaw, "The Great Famine and Agrarian Crisis in England, 1315–22," *Past and Present* 59 (1973).

48 *from the lands of the Great Khan*: Based on a highly imaginative account written by an anonymous Flemish cleric who relied on a letter sent from the papal court at Avignon, in southern France by Louis Heyligen (quoted in P. Ziegler, *The Black Death* [New York, 1971], p. 14).

50 *a London merchant visiting Bury*: Largely based on Gabriele de' Mussi of Piacenza, who relied on travelers' tales for his account of the early spread of the pestilence (quoted in R. Horrox, *The Black Death* [Manchester, 1994], pp. 16–18).

50 *the doings of Idonea Isabel*: Examples of Idonea Isabel's rebelliousness can be found in Lock, *Walsham Court Rolls*, I, pp. 238, 284, 295.

CHAPTER 4

53 *The spread of the pestilence*: The precise dating of the spread of the pestilence across the known world is a difficult task, owing to inconsistencies and inaccuracies in both contemporary sources and the works of modern historians. The most recent and most comprehensive chronology is provided in Benedictow, *The Black Death*. Gui de Chauliac's description and analysis of the pestilence in Avignon is contained in his *Chirurgia*, and a translation of a key passage is given in S. K. Cohn Jr., *The Black Death Transformed: Disease and Culture in Early Renaissance Europe* (2002), p. 87. For histories of the town and abbey of Bury St. Edmunds, see M. D. Lobel, *The Borough of Bury St Edmunds: A Study in the Government and Development of a Medieval Town* (Oxford, 1935); and A. Goodwin, *The Abbey of St Edmundsbury* (Oxford, 1931). A recent account of aspects of monastic life, including diet, health, and the

infirmary, is given in B. Harvey, *Living and Dying in England: The Monastic Experience* (Oxford, 1993). Monastic chroniclers are discussed in A. Gransden, *Historical Writing in England: c. 1307 to the Early Sixteenth Century* (Cornell, 1983).

54 *model of the stable at Bethlehem*: For the widespread use of such models in the Middle Ages, see B. Hamilton, *Religion in the Medieval West* (1986), p. 74.

58 *there had once been twenty thousand people*: Gilles li Muisis, abbot of St. Giles in Tournai, southern France (quoted in Horrox, *Black Death*, p. 47).

58 *Just four days ago a young clerk*: The testimony of the young clerk fleeing the papal court at Avignon is based on a letter written during the plague by a young musician in the papal court, Louis Heyligen, a close friend of Petrarch, that was sent to his friends in Bruges and ended up being copied into an anonymous Flemish chronicle. Lengthy excerpts are quoted in G. Deaux, *The Black Death 1347* (New York, 1969), pp. 100–103; and Horrox, *Black Death*, pp. 41–45.

58 *from the city of Avignon*: It should be noted that the clerk had fled from Avignon during the early, pneumonic phase of the pestilence.

60 *on the persons of the Genoese*: It was widely accepted at the time that the plague had been brought to Europe on the ships of Genoese fleeing from Caffa, a trading port on the Black Sea that was besieged by the Tartars.

61 *A sick man had to be cured*: The Fourth Lateran Council of 1215 admonished the sick to first seek cures for the ills of their souls. With spiritual health restored, medications and physical remedies would provide greater benefit.

CHAPTER 5

63 *Pilgrimages were incessant*: J. Sumption, *Pilgrimage: An Image of Medieval Religion* (London, 1975), provides an accessible introduction to pilgrimages and shrines; for Walsingham, see J. C. Dickinson, *The Shrine of Our Lady of Walsingham* (Cambridge, 1956). This chronology of the spread of the pestilence has been based on many sources, medieval and modern. For the death of Princess Joan in Bordeaux, see N. F. Cantor, *In the Wake of the Plague: The Black Death and the World It Made* (New York, 2002), pp. 42–52.

65 *wrestling matches in the churchyard of St. Mary's*: On the use of Suffolk churchyards for various sports and entertainments, see D. Dymond, "God's Disputed Acre," *Journal of Ecclesiastical History* 50 (1999).

66 *pray before the magnificent altarpiece*: The painted and gilded altarpiece, now known as the Thornham Parva Retable, has been recently restored.

69 *At this Margery Wodebite*: Some of the characteristics attributed to Margery Wodebite have been borrowed from Margery Kempe, a famous and highly eccentric mystic who lived in King's Lynn at the turn of the fourteenth and fifteenth centuries. For a sympathetic portrait, see "The Making of Margery Kempe: Individual and Community," in D. Aers, ed., *Community, Gender, and Individual Identity* (Routledge, 1988).

70 *had a special talent for finding lost keys*: For the belief that saints could help find lost keys, see Owst, *Literature and Pulpit*, pp. 147–148.

70 *bearing trays of badges*: Large quantities of pilgrims' badges and souvenirs from the fourteenth century survive, many of which are equally as shoddy as today's tourist wares. A well-illustrated standard book is B. Spencer, *Pilgrim Souvenirs and Secular Badges* (London, 1998).

71 *When, after a very long wait*: Descriptions of the Lady Chapel and its contents are contained in S. Morrison, *Women Pilgrims in Late Medieval England: Private Piety As Public Performance* (London, 2000); and Dickinson, *Shrine of Our Lady.*

73 *plague has never been heard of*: This and the other opinions of the pestilence voiced by the pilgrims have all been taken from contemporary sources. See, for example, those cited in Cohn, *Black Death*, pp. 224–226.

74 *It was delivered with calm*: Sir Robert Godlington's account of the plague in Avignon is based on the letter written by Louis Heyligen while he was in the papal curia in 1347–1348 (quoted at length in G. Deaux, *The Black Death 1347* [New York], pp. 100–103; Horrox, *Black Death*, pp. 41–45).

76 *Ipswich sea captain*: The seaman's report of the stories circulating in Bruges are based on the letter Heyligen sent to his friends in Bruges (quoted in Ziegler, *Black Death*, p. 67; Horrox, *Black Death*, pp. 41–45).

78 *dog left pissing against the wall*: This picturesque phrase is attributed to Cola di Rienzo, a colorful Roman who was exiled in Abruzzi at the time of the pestilence.

78 *scarcely one in seven survived*: Gabriele de' Mussi, in Horrox, *Black Death*, pp. 20–21.

79 *shrift and housel*: The last sacraments of confession and Communion, to which "annealing," the anointing of the body with oil, was usually added.

CHAPTER 6

81 *Many bishops wrote letters*: A selection of these letters is provided in Horrox, *Black Death*, pp. 111–118. The quotations from Boccaccio, Giles li Muisis, and the Neuberg chronicler are in Horrox, *Black Death*, pp. 26, 49, 70. For the dating of the earliest plague outbreaks in England and a

discussion of the probable length of time between first contamination by microorganisms and their carriers and the recognition of the presence of plague in human communities, see Benedictow, *Black Death*, pp. 57–60, 126–133.

83 *Almighty God uses thunder*: The letter read by Master John combines passages from letters written by the archbishop of York on July 28 and the bishop of Bath and Wells on August 17. There is no such surviving letter written by the bishop of Norwich.

84 *O Lord God*: Psalm 94; "For the Lord is a great God," a version of Psalm 95.

84 *the ruin that was justifiably prophesied*: Drawn from the letter of bishop of Bath and Wells, August 17, 1349.

84 *Who can tell if God will turn*: Jonas 3:9–10.

85 *Remember not our former iniquities*: Psalm 78:8.

86 *All things are subdued to God's will*: The sentiments expressed by Master John have been taken from a number of the episcopal letters written at this time, and directly reflect prevailing attitudes among church leaders.

86 *conjunction of ill-fated stars and planets*: Astrology was commonly used to explain events in the late Middle Ages. These statements are taken from the report of the Paris Medical Faculty into the causes of the pestilence, completed in October 1348 (in Horrox, *Black Death*, pp. 158–163).

87 *death of the two-headed child monster*: This story is from the chronicle of Meaux Abbey, Yorkshire, written by Thomas Burton (in Horrox, *Black Death*, pp. 69–70).

87 *It is said in Avignon*: King Andrew of Hungary was murdered in September 1345, and his widow Jeanne I was suspected of complicity. She fled to Avignon, where Pope Clement VI acquitted her of the charges and gave her permission to marry again (letter of Louis Heyligen from Avignon, printed in Horrox, *Black Death*, p. 40).

88 *pestilence that threatens us*: A number of chroniclers criticized the behavior of gentlewomen at tournaments held in the years before the Black Death, which included dressing like men and fornication or adultery with knights and champions. This speech is drawn from Henry Knighton (Horrox, *Black Death*, p. 130).

88 *extravagant and unseemly dress*: Fashions in clothes began to change with unusual speed in the mid-fourteenth century and attracted great criticism. The tailor's speech is based on an anonymous Westminster chronicler's entry for 1344 (Horrox, *Black Death*, p. 131).

89 *Jesus has now become English!*: This intriguingly jingoistic assertion comes from Henry Knighton's chronicle, which tells us that verses were found written up in various places in France claiming it mattered little that the

pope was French because "Jesu devenu Engleys" (Pantin, *English Church*, p. 82).

89   *the set of glass windows*: Stained glass windows, like statues and paintings, were an important part of the instruction of the laity in medieval churches.

90   *Acting together in a community*: Religious guilds established by parishioners flourished in the later Middle Ages and were especially numerous in East Anglia (V. Bainbridge, *Guilds in the Medieval Countryside: Social and Religious Change in Cambridgeshire* (Boydell, 1996). Walsham had a Guildhall Street, but it is not known when its guild was founded.

91   *Corpus Christi was a new and exhilarating feast*: For a detailed study of the cult of Corpus Christi and its rise in the fourteenth century, see Rubin, *Corpus Christi*. For the guild of Corpus Christi in Cambridge, see also C. P. Hall, "The Guild of Corpus Christi and the Foundation of Corpus Christi College," in P. Zutshi, ed., *Medieval Cambridge: Essays on the Pre-Reformation University* (Woodbridge, 1993), pp. 65–91.

91   *made of a pelican in its piety*: The pelican was a common symbol of Corpus Christi.

91   *Pious Pelican, Lord Jesus*: A prayer dating from the thirteenth century (in Rubin, *Corpus Christi*, p. 311).

92   *among the seven acts of mercy*: The other acts were to feed the hungry, give drink to the thirsty, clothe the naked, and comfort those in prison.

93   *As I live, saith the Lord God*: Ezekiel 33:11.

94   *even the houses and clothes*: From an account of the plague in Padua (Horrox, *Black Death*, p. 34). People trusted the evidence of their own eyes and experience, even if it conflicted with the medical analysis of doctors and academics. They were right to do so, for we now know that the houses and clothes of plague victims would have been likely to harbor infected rats and fleas.

95   *yields of corn turned out*: For all main crops the harvest of 1348 was a substantial improvement on those of the preceding two years, and significantly above the long-term average. Consequently grain prices fell very sharply indeed, sometimes by almost a half (D. L. Farmer, "Crop Yields, Prices, and Wages in Medieval England," *Studies in Medieval and Renaissance History* (1983), p. 125; *Agrarian History*, II, p. 791).

96   *now lying in narrow pits in the earth*: Taken from a mid-fourteenth-century sermon by the Dominican friar, John Bromyard (Owst, *Literature and Pulpit*, p. 293).

96   *I looked, and beheld a pale horse*: Revelation 6:8. The preacher's other declamations are from Revelation 6–12.

97   *for God has said*: From Gabriel de' Mussi (Horrox, *Black Death*, p. 15).

98   *For those that shall be damned*: These visions of Hell come from a number of contemporary sermons, many are quoted at length in Owst, *Preaching in Medieval England*, pp. 336–337.

98   *when the head quaketh*: From *Fasciculus Morum*, a fourteenth-century preacher's handbook (quoted in Daniell, *Death and Burial*, p. 41).

99   *in Hell a man shall weep*: Quoted in W. J. Dohar, *Black Death and Pastoral Leadership*, p. 62.

CHAPTER 7

101   *Knowledge of the plague in London*: The scarcity of information on the Black Death in London is extremely frustrating, and most general books and articles tend to recycle the same scant evidence. For new work, however, see B. Megson, "Mortality Among London Citizens in the Black Death," *Medieval Prosopography*, 19 (1998); and R. Britnell, "The Black Death in English Towns," *Urban History* 21 (1994). An accessible and informative, if rather dated, account of magic in the Middle Ages is given in K. Thomas, *Religion and the Decline of Magic* (London, 1971), pp. 27–56. The letter of the bishop of Bath and Wells is in Horrox, *Black Death*, pp. 271–273.

103   *William Sr. purchased*: Details of these arrangements were recorded in the Walsham manor court of October 24, 1348 (Lock, *Walsham Court Rolls*, I, pp. 312–313, 315).

104   *Terrible is God toward the sons*: The bishop of London's letter is in Horrox, *Black Death*, pp. 113–114.

106   *assemble in our churchyard*: From a letter sent by the bishop of Winchester on October 24, 1348, to all the major officeholders and vicars in his diocese. For the text, see Horrox, *Black Death*, pp. 115–117, where the penitential psalms are given as Psalms 6, 31, 37, 50, 101, 129, 142, and the psalms of degrees as 119–133.

107   *During the proceedings*: The proceedings of this court are printed in Lock, *Walsham Court Rolls*, I, pp. 312–316.

108   *twenty-three of the twenty-six monks*: Shrewsbury, *Bubonic Plague*, p. 60.

109   *These cities, castles, towns, and villages*: Taken from the bishop of Winchester's letter of October 24, 1348 (Horrox, *Black Death*, p. 116).

110   *laid them side by side*: A similar account is given by the Sienese chronicler who wrote, "And I, Agnolo di Tura, called the Fat, buried my five children, with my own hands." W. M. Bowsky, ed., *The Black Death: A Turning Point in History?* (1971), pp. 13–14.

111   *Parliament in Westminster in late January*: The pestilence, which was said to have subsided in late December, clearly flared up again in January (Shrewsbury, *Bubonic Plague*, p. 84).

112 *beseech all the saints in heaven*: From an account of the conduct of processions, possibly the work of John Mirk (Owst, *Preaching in Medieval
England,* p. 202).

112 *The flock was repeatedly warned*: These sentiments and the story of the devout woman who withheld a small sin at confession are taken from *Fasciculus Morum: A Fourteenth-Century Preacher's Handbook,* edited by S.
Wenzel (University of Pennsylvania Press, 1989), p. 497.

114 *hungered no less fervently*: The phrase is from the Sarum Manual (*Manuale
ad Usum Percelebris Ecclesie Sarisburiensis,* edited by A. Jefferies Collins
[Henry Bradshaw Society, 1960], p. 4). The bread was given in lieu of the
Host and regarded as a medicine for the sick and a preservation against
the plague (Thomas, *Religion and the Decline of Magic,* pp. 31–33).

114 *the well of Our Lady*: See C. Paine, "The Chapel and Well of Our Lady of
Woolpit," *Proceedings of the Suffolk Institute of Archaeology and History* 38
(1993).

115 *at least be able to see*: This phrase comes from Robert Rypon, subprior of
Durham in the late fourteenth century (Owst, *Literature and Pulpit,* p. 140).

115 *When you kneel before the images*: From an anonymous treatise on the
Decalogue (Owst, *Literature and Pulpit,* pp. 140–143).

116 *confession might be made*: This dispensation and the reasons for it are
spelled out in a mandate issued by the bishop of Bath and Wells on January 10, 1349 (Shinners and Dohar, *Pastors and the Care of Souls,* pp.
284–285).

117 *contrition could not slay mortal sin*: This passage on the unique power of
confessing to a priest is drawn from William Langland's later fourteenth-
century poem *Piers the Plowman* (Penguin ed.), p. 169.

117 *They presented themselves*: Exceptionally high numbers of clerks had been
ordained to first tonsure and holy orders in the nearby diocese of Ely in
1346 and 1347. J. Aberth, "The Black Death in the Diocese of Ely: The
Evidence of the Bishop's Register," *Journal of Medieval History* 21
(1995), p. 283.

CHAPTER 8

119 *The monks charged with*: For the office of infirmarer and the operation of
the infirmary at Westminster Abbey, see B. Harvey, *Living and Dying in
England, 1100–1540: The Monastic Experience* (Oxford, 1993), pp.
81–111. For an accessible introduction to medieval medicine, see C.
Rawcliffe, *Medicine and Society in Later Medieval England* (1995).

123 *authority of the great Greek master*: The works of the ancient Greek writers Hippocrates and Galen formed the basis of medical education in the

Middle Ages. Their writings were first rediscovered in the Middle East and reached the West through Latin and Hebrew translations of Arabic texts. For Galen's theories, see R. E. Seigel, *Galen's System of Physiology and Medicine* (Basel, 1968).

123 *Galen might well have lived*: There is no evidence in Galen's time or before of a disease anything like the Black Death.

124 *Galen taught us that the body*: For a brief discussion of Galen's three emunctoria and the symptoms of plague, see Cohn, *Black Death Transformed*, pp. 68–71.

124 *Unnatural lumps are to be divided*: Excerpts from *The Art of Medicine* are contained in *Galen: Selected Works*, edited and translated by P. N. Singer (Oxford, 1977). The quotations are from page 369.

126 *flee the plague quickly*: This is the most certain and common advice given by doctors and the writers of plague tracts (Cohn, *Black Death Transformed*, p. 118).

126 *Rufus of Ephesus*: The preventatives and cures of Rufus of Ephesus were prescribed during the Black Death over thirteen hundred years after he had first proposed them (Deaux, *Black Death*, pp. 60–61).

126 *advised Master John to buy as much oil*: The price of wax used to make church candles rose sharply in 1349, but there is insufficient information on the price of oil (Thorold Rogers, *History of Agriculture and Prices*, vol. 1, pp. 445–450).

127 *witnesses to the liturgy*: Duffy, *Stripping of the Altars*, pp. 91–130, provides much information on the Mass in late medieval England. See also M. Rubin, *Corpus Christi*.

128 *These plain-minded folk complained*: Such sentiments were expressed by some pious lay folk who shunned what they saw as excessive displays and ceremonies, long before Wyclif and the Lollards (e.g., Owst, *Preaching in Medieval England*, p. 133).

129 *Pardoners, unlicensed as well as licensed*: See the portrait of the pardoner given in Chaucer's Prologue to *The Canterbury Tales*. J. J. Jusserand, *English Wayfaring Life in the Middle Ages* (Methuen, 1961), contains much of interest on pardoners, as well as wandering preachers, friars, herbalists, and charlatans.

130 *Before him went the pestilence*: Habakkuk 3:5; *there shall be famines*: Matthew 24:7–8.

131 *a cloud of infection*: For a lively survey of contemporary medical advice on the avoidance of infection, see J. Kelly, *The Great Mortality: An Intimate History of the Black Death* (London, 2005), pp. 170–175.

132 *ordering incense to be burned*: Horrox, *The Black Death*, pp. 101–106, provides a brief, accessible introduction to the role of astrology and humoral

theory in medieval medicine. For more advanced information, see E. J. Kealey, *Medieval Medicine: A Social History of Anglo-Norman Medicine* (Baltimore, 1981); and N. G. Siraisi, *Medieval and Early Renaissance Medicine* (Chicago, 1990).

CHAPTER 9

135 *The early onset of plague*: Details of the outbreak of plague in Suffolk may be found in the excellent chronology provided in Bailey, *History of Medieval Suffolk*, pp. 176–184. Benedictow, *Black Death*, pp. 123–145, provides the most recent examination of the evidence for the spread of the Black Death through the British Isles. The crucial Walsham court rolls, with their notices of the deaths of tenants, are printed in Lock, *Walsham Court Rolls*, I, pp. 317–327. The ceremonies of Lent and Easter, as well as the other festivals of the late medieval liturgical year, are described in Duffy, *Stripping of the Altars*, pp. 11–52.

139 *News of the imminence of the pestilence*: Land markets in many manors were exceptionally active in early 1349, as people tried to get their affairs in order before the pestilence arrived (Bailey, *Medieval Suffolk*, p. 179).

141 *Wyverstone, Wetherden, Elmswell*: Based on the information that new priests had been instituted in these parishes between mid and late May (*The Register of William Bateman, Bishop of Norwich, 1344–55*, vol. 2, edited by P. E. Pobst [Canterbury and York Society, 1996], pp. 88–93).

142 *railed against the brewers*: Such complaints about retailers and traders, especially of food and drink, were common currency in the moral literature of the later fourteenth century.

142 *the time of Lent is entered*: From a contemporary Lenten sermon (Owst, *Preaching in Medieval England*, p. 147).

143 *As Holy Week approached*: The ceremonies of Holy Week are described in Duffy, *Stripping of the Altars*, pp. 22–29.

144 *Behold, then, that good Lord*: from a contemporary sermon quoted in Owst, *Literature and Pulpit*, p. 508.

145 *Master John came down from his pulpit*: The liturgy of the Easter sepulcher is described in Duffy, *Stripping of the Altars*, pp. 29–37.

147 *careful to wrap their fingers*: Duffy, *Stripping of the Altars*, p. 110.

CHAPTER 10

149 *accounts of the sickness and deaths*: The contention that rages about the nature of the Black Death is exemplified in the two most recent schol-

arly books on the epidemic: Cohn, *The Black Death Transformed;* and Benedictow, *The Black Death, 1346–1353.* Both contain lengthy descriptions and analysis of contemporary evidence of the pestilence and modern medical knowledge of plague. However, they differ radically in their interpretations, with Cohn insisting that the Black Death was "any disease other than the rat-based bubonic plague," and Benedictow insisting that it was nothing other than rat-based bubonic plague, allowing scant significance to pneumonic and septicemic plague. The accounts given here are based on a host of primary and secondary sources which, like de' Mussi, provide invaluable clues if not always consistency (Gabriele de' Mussi, *Historia de Morbo,* translated in Horrox, *Black Death,* pp. 24–25).

151 *It was the second marriage*: Evidence for the statements in this paragraph can be found in numerous entries in the Walsham and High Hall court rolls. For example, the marriage of Agnes Helpe and John Chapman is recorded in the High Hall court roll of April 16, 1345 (Lock, *Walsham Court Rolls,* I, p. 281) and the name and age of their daughter, Agnes, is recorded in the court roll of May 25, 1349 (Lock, *Walsham Court Rolls,* I, p. 319).

157 *Death gives no certain respite*: Quoted by Duffy, *Stripping of the Altars,* 310.

157 *Without confession the just man*: From *Fasciculus Morum,* edited by Wenzel, p. 35.

157 *a crowd of grinning demons*: From a mid-fourteenth century sermon of John Bromyard (Owst, *Preaching in Medieval England,* p. 343).

158 *recited the* Placebo *as best she could*: The Placebo was a prayer from the Office of the Dead, the liturgy of funeral Masses, named after its first word.

158 *both the Goche brothers are dead*: The High Hall court recorded that John Goche and his wife died and left two sons, Walter, age ten, and John, age two; and that Peter Goche and his wife died and left a son John, age four (Lock, *Walsham Court Rolls,* I, p. 325). Daughters would not have been mentioned in the court roll because they had no right of inheritance if there were surviving sons.

CHAPTER 11

163 *Precise death rates*: Numerous examples of death rates from manors in many parts of England are given in Benedictow, *Black Death, 1346–1353,* pp. 342–379; and J. Hatcher, *Plague, Population, and the English Economy, 1349–1530* (1977), pp. 21–25. See also R. Lock, "Black Death in

Walsham," for estimates of the death rate and pattern of mortality in Walsham. This sermon is by Thomas Brinton, a monk at Norwich before becoming bishop of Rochester, who lived through the Black Death. It is quoted in Owst, *Preaching in Medieval England,* pp. 206–207, which also contains many other examples, as does Owst, *Literature and Pulpit.* For selections from many of the chronicles of the period, see Horrox, *Black Death.*

165 *far more would die in a month*: An average of six tenant deaths occurred each year from 1327 to 1348, compared with 109 in 1349 (Lock, "Black Death in Walsham," p. 322).

166 *So great was the ceaseless press*: This description follows, *inter alia,* passages written by Boccaccio and Heyligen (Horrox, *Black Death,* pp. 32–33, 44).

167 *a portion, perhaps one in five*: Spontaneous recovery from untreated bubonic plague can exceed 20 percent.

168 *The passage of death*: From the *Book of Dying,* quoted in Swanson, *Catholic England,* p. 126.

169 *Dread of catching the pestilence*: Similar sentiments are a commonplace of contemporary descriptions of communities during the pestilence.

171 *Why is God scourging us*: Questions like these were commonly posed during and after the pestilence, as can be seen from the many attempts of preachers to answer them in a rhetorical fashion in their sermons. See also William Langland's lament that "Since the plague, friars and other impostors have thought up theological questions just to please the proud" (*Piers Plowman,* Attwater ed., p. 78).

172 *So he repeatedly scoured his memory*: The bishop of Winchester struggled with a similar problem when he wrote in October 1348, "It is not within the power of man to understand the divine plan. But it is to be feared that the most likely explanation is that human sensuality—that fire that blazed up as a result of Adam's sin and which from adolescence onwards is an incitement to wrongdoing—has now plumbed greater depths of evil, producing a multitude of sins which have provoked the divine anger, by a just judgment, to this revenge" (Horrox, *Black Death,* p. 118).

172 *God drowned the whole world*: Genesis 6:5.

173 *Sometimes, in a hostile or angry manner*: This paragraph and quotations are based loosely on Thomas Brinton's sermon on pestilence, taking the text "Be Watchful" (Horrox, *Black Death*, pp. 144–148).

173 *Prayers have no power this pestilence*: from Langland's late-fourteenth-century poem *Piers Plowman,* (Attwater ed., p. 78).

174 *supervised the adding of quicklime*: This was the practice followed for the bodies of plague victims in Christchurch priory, Canterbury.

176 *henceforth be called the bede roll*: Drawn from the experiences of the Corpus Christi guild of Cambridge (Hall, "The Guild of Corpus Christi and the Foundation of Corpus Christi College," p. 69).

176 *Yet piety and steadfastness*: The next three paragraphs draw on a range of contemporary descriptions of behavior in communities during the pestilence, especially in Florence, as described by Boccaccio. G. H. McWilliam, ed., *Decameron* (Penguin Classics, 1972).

178 *Particularly disgraceful were the piles*: Again, drawn from Boccaccio.

178 *sheep, cows, oxen, and horses strayed unchecked*: As Henry Knighton stresses in his account of the effects of the Black Death (Dobson, *Peasants' Revolt*, pp. 59–63).

CHAPTER 12

179 *The lords of the little manor*: High Hall manor has excellent court rolls, but unfortunately few other manor records have survived, and there is even less for Walsham manor until the fifteenth century. A comparison between High Hall account rolls in the 1370s and Walsham's in the 1400s suggests that Walsham may have been worth five times as much each year as High Hall. All the High Hall and Walsham records are deposited in the Suffolk Record Office at Bury St. Edmunds. Given the intrinsic interest of the subject, there are remarkably few studies of rural communities during and immediately after the Black Death to complement E. Levett's pioneering "The Black Death on the Estates of the See of Winchester," in P. Vinogradoff, ed., *Oxford Studies in Social and Legal History*, vol. 5 (Oxford, 1915). But see P. D. A. Harvey, *A Medieval Oxfordshire Village: Cuxham, 1240–1400* (Oxford, 1965); and B. Harvey, "The Abbot of Westminster's Demesnes and the Black Death of 1348–1349," in M. Meek, ed., *The Modern Traveller to Our Past* (2006). Invaluable evidence of Suffolk in the Black Death is contained in Bailey, *Medieval Suffolk*, pp. 176–184. Studies taking a somewhat longer perspective include R. H. Britnell, "Feudal Reaction After the Black Death in the Palatinate of Durham," *Past and Present* 128 (1990); and J. Hatcher, "England in the Aftermath of the Black Death," *Past and Present* 144 (1994).

182 *Edmund made up his mind*: The court was held on May 25 (Lock, *Walsham Court Rolls*, I, pp. 318–319).

185 *Robert Sare, who had theatrically*: These deaths were reported at the next court, held on July 23, 1349, along with those of a further three tenants (Lock, *Walsham Court Rolls*, I, pp. 325–326).

187 *the pestilence was no longer raging*: The disappearance of plague is usually even more difficult to date than its appearance, but the registers of the dioceses of Salisbury and Bath and Wells display a striking decline in deaths in the opening months of 1349 (Shrewsbury, *Bubonic Plague* [Cambridge, 1970], pp. 59, 64).

188 *Those participating in the procession*: For Corpus Christi day processions and jostling for precedence, see Rubin, *Corpus Christi*, pp. 243–271.

190 *there were more than 250 acres*: Based on the acreage under crops in the early fifteenth century (Suffolk Record Office, Bury St. Edmunds, HA504/3/5).

192 *Blakey remonstrated with Rath*: The local peasant reeves usually had the responsibility for hiring laborers to work on their lords' farms, but the wages they paid them were subject to the approval of their superiors. In many surviving manorial accounts claims made by reeves for wages have been crossed out by the auditors for being excessive. For evidence of how wages and additional bonuses were handled by reeves and estate accountants, see Hatcher, "The Aftermath of the Black Death," pp. 20–25.

192 *demanding yet another shilling to be paid*: Evidence of sharply increased demands in late 1349 is abundant (e.g., Harvey, "Westminster's Demesnes and the Black Death," pp. 293–295; and Harvey, *Cuxham*, pp. 168–171).

193 *I don't give a pea*: William Langland's rebellious hired worker put Piers and his plow at the price of a pea in *Piers Plowman* (Attwater ed., p. 55).

193 *Most of those who have turned up*: Contemporary writings are full of complaints about the high cost and low productivity of workers (Hatcher, "The Aftermath of the Black Death," pp. 13–19). John Gower, writing in the 1370s, stated, "One peasant insists on more than two demanded in days gone by . . . Yet [then] one performed more service than three do now." William Langland portrays hired laborers sitting down, drinking ale, and singing when they should be working *(Piers Plowman*, Attwater ed., p. 54).

195 *I have tried, but I have only*: Henry Knighton wrote in his *Chronicon* of these times: "A horse that was formerly worth 40s could be had for half a mark [6s 8d], a fat ox for 4s, a cow for 12d" (Dobson, *Peasants' Revolt*, p. 60). Knighton seems to have exaggerated somewhat, but the broad truth of his testimony is borne out by statistics gathered from contemporary manorial accounts.

196 *with generous slices of meat*: The diet demanded by servants and laborers improved markedly in the weeks after the Black Death, and generous allowances of food became a major part of their additional remuneration. Langland writes angrily of common workers refusing to be fed on cheap

ale, bean bread, vegetables, and bacon, and demanding instead fresh meat and fried fish served warm or hot, with fine wheat bread and copious quantities of good ale (*Piers Plowman*, Attwater ed., p. 58).

196 *a brightly colored doublet and gown*: Clothing called livery was frequently supplied to servants engaged on long contracts, and this too became part of the remuneration that was bargained over. Contemporary literature and sermons contain many amusing descriptions of lowly servants and laborers dressed in what the authors saw as ridiculously inappropriate clothing. There was concern also that the social order was being disrupted, and in 1363 Parliament passed a statute against the "outrageous and excessive apparel of diverse people against their estate and degree."

198 *Blakey had brought with him a rental*: No rental of Walsham manor has survived, but there are two rentals for High Hall manor dating from the 1330s.

200 *the legitimate means to compel heirs*: Under common and manorial law the lord of the manor had the right to compel the unfree to take up vacant lands, although this had scarcely ever needed to be exercised in the preceding era of population pressure (Hatcher, "English Serfdom and Villeinage," *Past and Present* 90, 1981).

CHAPTER 13

201 *Such momentous mortality*: Lock, "Black Death in Walsham," pp. 329–336, provides a valuable listing of the Walsham tenants who died in 1349, their holdings, the heriots paid, and their heirs, if any. An informative analysis of the transmission of landholdings to heirs and successors in 1349–1350 on Coltishall manor, Norfolk, is contained in B. M. S. Campbell, "Population Pressure, Inheritance, and the Land Market in a Fourteenth-Century Peasant Community," in R. M. Smith, ed., *Land, Kinship, and Life-Cycle* (Cambridge, 1984), p. 98.

201 *One such record is the roll*: This momentous court roll is translated and printed in Lock, *Walsham Court Rolls*, I, pp. 319–325.

209 *Suitable guardians had to be found*: For social security offered to the weaker and disadvantaged members of fourteenth-century rural communities, see E. Clark, "Some Aspects of Social Security in Medieval England," *Journal of Family History* (1982).

211 *John Kebbil, avorite protégé*: The court roll entry records that the heir to Richard Kebbil's landholding "is John his son, chaplain, who has entry" (Lock, *Walsham Court Rolls*, I, p. 324).

213 *two women had produced bastards*: The imposition of a double fine, presumably for twins, might be unique in English records.

216   *remaining male member of the Cranmer family*: There is no trace of a male
      Cranmer in the Walsham and High Hall court rolls from 1350 to 1399
      (Lock, *Court Rolls of Walsham*, II).

CHAPTER 14

217   *The alarm that elites felt*: The Ordinance of Laborers, passed by an
      emergency meeting of the king's council on June 11, 1349, is translated
      in A. E. Bland, P. A. Brown, and R. H. Tawney, eds., *English Economic
      History: Select Documents*, pp. 164–167. The ordinance sought to re-
      strict the prices charged by craftsmen such as shoemakers and tailors,
      as well as the wages of agricultural laborers. The classic study of the
      legislation is B. H. Putnam, *The Enforcement of the Statutes of Laborers
      During the First Decade After the Black Death, 1349–1359* (New York,
      1908). The price of wheat between the harvests of 1348 and 1349 was
      a third lower than it had been in the previous year, and the prices of
      rye, barley, oats, and peas were 45–53 percent lower (*Agrarian History*,
      III, p. 791).

219   *When stock was taken of the victims*: On High Hall manor, 75 percent of
      all tenant deaths occurred by May 25, and on Walsham more than 95
      percent of all deaths occurred by June 15. The next Walsham court, held
      on August 1, 1349, noted that only five tenants had "died since the last
      court," and no deaths were recorded in the subsequent courts held at
      Walsham on November 18 and High Hall on November 30.

220   *The great monastery had lost*: R. S. Gottfried, *Bury St. Edmunds and the
      Urban Crisis, 1290–1539* (Princeton, 1982), pp. 51–52. For Norwich, see
      Harper-Bill, "The English Church," p. 97.

222   *But they were no longer*: The abundant "complaint literature" of the
      post–Black Death era is full of lamentations about the idleness and inso-
      lence of the laboring and peasant masses. For a brief review see Hatcher,
      "England in the Aftermath of the Black Death," pp. 13–19, and for a
      more comprehensive study, see J. Coleman, *English Literature in History,
      1350–1400: Medieval Readers and Writers* (Hutchinson, 1981).

223   *a pair of quite ordinary shoes*: From Henry Knighton, *Chronicon* (Dobson,
      Peasants' Revolt, p. 62). Once again Knighton's near contemporary state-
      ments are borne out by the price statistics collected by historians
      (Thorold Rogers, *History of Agriculture and Prices*, I, p. 591).

225   *people were rushing into matrimony*: An upsurge in marriage was a com-
      mon response to the Black Death, and Walsham and High Hall manors
      were no exception. Court rolls are imperfect records of the numbers of
      marriages, even involving unfree tenants, but it is significant that in the

records of the courts held in Walsham in the whole of 1347 just six marriages were noted, while in the records of the court held on November 18, 1349, eight marriages are mentioned. For peasant marriage in medieval England, see P. R. Schofield, *Peasant and Community in Medieval England, 1200–1500* (Palgrave Macmillan, 2003), pp. 90–127.

226 *Robert Terwald, had just been appointed rector*: Terwald's appointment on August 13, 1349, is recorded in the Norwich diocesan register (*The Register of William Bateman, Bishop of Norwich, 1344–55*, II, ed. P. E. Pobst (Canterbury and York Society, 2000), p. 134).

227 *inexperienced and incompetent chaplains*: Knighton writes, "A chaplain was scarcely to be had for £10 or 10 marks [whereas] before the pestilence a chaplain could be had for 4,5 or even 2 marks with his board" (Dobson, *Peasants' Revolt*, pp. 61–62). A mark was 13s 4d.

229 *lords being fined if they paid*: The ordinance prescribed that "if the lords of towns or manors shall presume in any wise to contravene our present ordinance . . . then prosecution shall be made against them," and that "no man, under the penalty of imprisonment, shall presume under color of pity or alms to give anything to such as shall be able profitably to labor."

231 *if the rustics should get the upper hand*: The voice of elite conservatism which resonates through the years after the Black Death is eloquently expressed in John Gower's poem, probably written in the late 1370s (Dobson, *Peasants' Revolt*, p. 97):

> *But it is certainly a great error*
> *to see the higher estate*
> *in danger from the villein class.*
> *It seems to me that lethargy*
> *has put the lords to sleep*
> *so that they do not guard against*
> *the folly of the common people.*

CHAPTER 15

233 *a long-term and dramatic shift*: The forces that drove the economic and social changes of the later Middle Ages are analyzed in J. Hatcher and M. Bailey, *Modelling the Middle Ages: The History and Theory of England's Economic Development* (Oxford, 2001), pp. 106–120. For surveys of the impact of the Black Death, see J. Bolton, "The World Turned Upside Down: Plague as an Agent of Economic and Social Change," in M. Ormrod and P. Lindley, eds., *The Black Death in England* (Stamford, 1996); and C. Platt, *King Death: The Black Death and Its Aftermath in*

Late-Medieval England (London, 1996). For continuing population de-cline and stagnation until the early sixteenth century, see J. Hatcher, *Plague, Population, and the English Economy, 1348–1530* (1977).

The longest and most continuous series of harvest yields, calculated from records of the forty demesne farms of the bishop of Winchester, are provided in J. Z. Titow, *Winchester Yields: A Study in Medieval Agricul-tural Productivity* (Cambridge, 1972). They show that the yields of the harvest of 1349 were lower than any since the famine harvest of 1316, which in turn was worse than any since 1211. No data survive for peas-ant harvest yields.

Accounts survive for High Hall for 1327 and 1377. They show that in normal years the de Welles could expect to receive no more than £10–15 from rents, court fines, and the sales of produce from their demesne farm. From this sum various costs had to be deducted, most notably the wages of farm servants and farm laborers and repairs to equipment and farm buildings, leaving them around £5–7 clear in cash. In addition to this cash sum, the demesne farm would have provided food and other com-modities for their household. It is likely that High Hall was the de Welles' only manor.

235 *higher receipts from the sale of corn*: There is considerable evidence that landlords, assisted by their officials, commonly applied economically ra-tional policies to the exploitation of their agricultural assets. D. Stone, *Decision-making in Medieval Agriculture* (Oxford, 2005).

237 *The court, which was held on Thursday, July 23*: The proceedings of the July 23 court are printed in Lock, *Walsham Court Rolls*, I, 325–326.

239 *let vacant holdings on very short leases*: On the basic reasoning that a little rent is better than no rent, this was a very common expedient (J. Z. Titow, "Lost Rents, Vacant Holdings, and the Contraction of Peasant Cultivation After the Black Death," *Agricultural History Review* 42 (1994).

239 *On their extensive lands*: Olivia and Hilary were ordered to pay seven bushels of barley at High Hall court on November 30 for the damage done in the lords' barley field by sixteen cows and bullocks owned by them (Lock, *Walsham Court Rolls*, I, p. 330).

239 *Alice Pye was no less entrepreneurial*: Alice was fined on November 18, 1349, for having thirty sheep in her fold on the common (Lock, *Walsham Court Rolls*, I, p. 328).

241 *the scarcity of farm servants*: This was also the experience on at least three of the Worcestershire manors of Westminster abbey (Harvey, "Abbot of Westminster's Demesnes," p. 294).

242 *the king's law is held in contempt*: Although few employers were fined under the labor legislation, there are constant complaints that they took in runaways and competed with each other by offering excessive wages (Hatcher, "Aftermath of the Black Death," pp. 19–20).

244 *he could not find any carpenter*: This anecdote is based on the carpenter who made the stocks at Knightsbridge, who refused to swear obedience to the Statute of Laborers and was paid an illegally high wage of 5.5d per day (Hatcher, "Aftermath of the Black Death," p. 24).

244 *he asked 5d per day*: This was the evidence given against an itinerant laborer called John Bishop when he was prosecuted by the justices of laborers in Warwickshire (Hatcher, "Aftermath of the Black Death," p. 25).

244 *Rath was duly elected reeve*: Lock, *Walsham Court Rolls,* I, p. 327.

245 *the steward lost patience*: Lock, *Walsham Court Rolls,* I, p. 327. In the same court, August 1, 1349, Thomas Hereward and William Jay were forgiven for "withdrawing from the lady's service without leave."

246 *Rath and his foremen*: Taken from a scene drawn by William Langland (*Piers Plowman,* Attwater ed., p. 54).

246 *but at the end of September*: There is evidence that harvests were much delayed; that at Bourton-on-the-Hill, for example, did not end until October 25 (Harvey, "Abbot of Westminster's Demesnes," p. 294). The national series shows that on average the harvest of 1349 produced for landlords yields of wheat of only 2.34 times seed and of barley of 2.81 times.

CHAPTER 16

249 *new power fostered self-confidence*: For a restatement of the venerable argument that the Black Death created tensions in the countryside that led to the Peasants Revolt, see C. Dyer, "The Social and Economic Background to the Rural Revolt of 1381," in R. H. Hilton and T. H. Aston, eds., *The English Rising of 1381* (Cambridge, 1984). The king's letter is printed in Horrox, *Black Death,* pp. 117–118.

In Book VI of *Piers Plowman* (Attwater ed., pp. 51–59) Langland first describes an idyllic scene in which everyone, including a knight and "lovely ladies," work happily at the tasks for which they are best suited. But because they are well fed, the peasants and laborers soon become lazy and truculent, refusing to work and insulting their superiors. It was only when Piers called down Hunger to chastise "these wasters who ruin the world," that the slothful began to labor (Hatcher, "The Aftermath of the Black Death," pp. 14–15).

251 *every interest in breaching it themselves*: Custom was extremely important
in regulating the relations of landlords and tenants prior up to the fourteenth century, but after the Black Death customs which had protected
the peasantry in a time of land scarcity had the potential to become ex-
ploitative in a time of land abundance (Hatcher, "English Serfdom and
Villeinage," pp. 36–39).

252 *When they were held low*: The prior's sermon is drawn from a wide range
of late-fourteenth-century sermons and homilies, as well as the opinions
of Batholomew Anglicus, who wrote presciently in the thirteenth century of the common folk: "When they be not held low with dread, their
hearts swell, and wax stout and proud against the commandments of
their sovereigns" (Miller and Hatcher, *Rural Society and Economic Change*,
pp. xiii–xiv).

253 *drinking in the alehouses, hanging around*: As John Gower put it, "They
desire the leisures of great men, but they have nothing to feed themselves
with, nor will they be servants" (quoted in Hatcher, "Aftermath of the
Black Death," p. 17).

254 *The king's letter was duly dispatched*: Printed in Horrox, *Black Death*, pp.
117–118.

255 *the evil lovers of the world*: From a later fourteenth-century sermon by
John Bromyard (quoted in Owst, *Literature and Pulpit*, pp. 293–294).

255 *servants serve their masters worse*: Henry Knighton, quoted in Dobson,
Peasants' Revolt, p. 69.

256 *eleven men out of selfishness and arrogance*: The names of the rebels are
listed in the court roll of October 24, 1348, and those who died are in the
court roll of June 15, 1349 (Lock, *Walsham Court Rolls*, I, pp. 315,
319–325).

257 *Master John was deeply saddened*: Master John's sentiments are those expressed by a host of contemporary clergy and moralists . For a concise review with many quotations, see Owst, *Literature and Pulpit*, pp. 361–370.

258 *remembering what he had been taught*: Based on Langland, *Piers Plowman*
(Attwater ed., pp. 61–62).

258 *almsgivers must choose carefully*: Close attention was paid after the Black
Death to the need to distinguish between the deserving and the undeserving poor (G. Shepherd, "Poverty in Piers Plowman," in T. H. Aston
et al., ed., *Social Relations and Ideas: Essays in Honour of R. H. Hilton*
(Cambridge, 1983).

258 *the Brotherhood of Flagellants had landed for the first time in England*:
Ziegler, *Black Death*, pp. 84–97, and Kelly, *The Great Mortality*, pp.
262–268 give introductory surveys of the movement. The description of

the flagellants in London used here is based on an account given by Robert of Avesbury (Horrox, *Black Death,* pp. 153–154).

261 *They do these things ill-advisedly*: The phrase is used by Thomas Walsingham, a monk of St. Albans who commented briefly on the visit of the flagellants to England in his great chronicle, *Historia Anglicana* (Horrox, *Black Death,* p. 154).

CHAPTER 17

263 *Women enjoyed unprecedented opportunities*: For the effect of the Black Death on the prospects of working women, see M. Mate, *Women in Medieval English Society* (Cambridge, 1999); S. Bardsley, "Women's Work Reconsidered: Gender and Wage Differentiation in Late Medieval England," *Past and Present* 165 (1999); and the debate between J. Hatcher and S. Bardsley in *Past and Present* 173 (2001). D. Aers, "Justice and Wage-Labor After the Black Death: Some Perplexities for William Langland," in *The Work of Work: Servitude, Slavery, and Labor in Medieval England,* edited by A. J. Frantzen and D. Moffat (Glasgow, 1994), provides many examples of independent and mobile female laborers appearing before the justices. Legal proceedings in Suffolk in 1361–1362 report that "Robert le Goos, laborer, goes to other workers, warns and advises them that none of them should accept less than 3d per day and food" (D. Aers, *Community, Gender, and Individual Identity: English Writing, 1360–1430* [London, 1988], pp. 28–29). B. Putnam, *The Enforcement of the Statute of Laborers During the First Decade After the Black Death* (Columbia, 1908) remains the standard work on the early years of labor legislation (the references to early commissions are on pp. 12–13 and 32*–35*).

267 *brought before the upcoming February court*: Rath was not brought before the February 1350 court, but in the court held in January 1351 he was fined heavily for a list of offenses for negligence and fraud, some of them dating back more than a year, including 3s 4d for insulting John Blakey (Lock, *Walsham Court Rolls,* II, pp. 27–31). Unfortunately, not all Walsham court records survive for 1350.

267 *the correct words of the Placebo*: The colloquial term for the Office of the Dead.

267 *In Hell a man shall weep*: A short discussion of these matters is contained in Dohar, *Black Death and Pastoral Leadership,* pp. 61–62.

268 *pray for all the souls*: A common bidding by the fifteenth century (Duffy, *Stripping of the Altars,* p. 346).

268 *the benefits bestowed on individual souls*: Or, as the Council of Lambeth in 1281 put it, "Let no man think that one mass said with pure intention for a thousand men might be considered equal to a thousand masses [for one man] also said with pure intent" (Daniell, *Death and Burial*, p. 16).

269 *celebrated the marriage of his daughter*: For the marriages of John Wodebite and his daughter, see Lock, *Walsham Court Rolls*, I, pp. 326, 331, 332.

269 *enmity between the Packards and the Wodebites*: Some details of a bloody assault ten years earlier by Packard's wife on John Wodebite's mother are given in Lock, *Walsham Court Rolls*, I, p. 245. Packard was involved in a dispute with his stepson, John Helpe, when he came of age to assume possession of his father's tenement in 1366 (Lock, *Walsham Court Rolls*, II, pp. 86–87).

269 *gang of wayfaring workers*: The activities of "enticers" or "procurers" of labor are described in S. A. C. Penn and C. Dyer, "Wages and Earnings in Late Medieval England: Evidence from the Enforcement of the Labour Laws," *Economic History Review*, 2nd ser., 43 (1990). For women in gangs of migrant laborers, see Bardsley, "Women's Work Reconsidered."

270 *William Warde was well-known*: Warde was one of the eleven tenants who refused to work for Lady Rose at the harvest of 1348 (Lock, *Walsham Court Rolls*, I, p. 315).

270 *a failure who had twice been forced*: Lock, *Walsham Court Rolls*, I, pp. 302, 311.

271 *There will be no . . . penny ale*: Taken from Langland's description of the sort of free food and drink demanded by lowly wage laborers (*Piers Plowman*, Attwater ed., p. 58).

272 *Hilary, who had spent all her life*: Far more women than before found employment as assistants to craftsmen, and the wages of these assistants rose faster than those of the craftsmen (Hatcher, "Debate, Women's Work Reconsidered").

273 *Olivia, in particular, enjoyed a reputation*: In the court of February 27, 1347, John Bonde was ordered to deliver to Olivia a quarter of wheat, which he probably owed her for a loan of money (Lock, *Walsham Court Rolls*, I, p. 299).

274 *In 1338 Olivia had married Robert Hawys*: Records of the matters referred to in this paragraph are contained on the court rolls (Lock, *Walsham Court Rolls*, I, pp. 216, 222, 334; II, 37).

275 *declared this year to be a Roman Jubilee*: The Jubilee year, the plenary indulgence, and the pilgrimage to Rome were major events (J. Sumption, *Pilgrimage: An Image of Medieval Religion*, London, 1975, pp. 231–242).

275 *remission of the penance*: There was popular confusion over whether the guilt would also be remitted.

276 *the old librarian got out the itinerary*: This and other routes are described in D. J. Birch, *Pilgrimage to Rome in the Middle Ages* (Woodbridge, 1998), pp. 43–58.

277 *she wished to endow a chantry*: A short introduction to chantries is provided in Harper-Bill, "Church and Religion after the Black Death," pp. 111–113.

277 *giving up his cure of souls*: There was much contemporary criticism of priests who abandoned their parishes for the easy life of a chantry priest.

277 *a promising but very young cleric*: There was a huge jump in the number of ordinations in most dioceses in the aftermath of the plague, which inevitably resulted in a drop in the age of the ordinands. Unfortunately no records of ordinations have survived for Norwich diocese.

278 *better to appoint good young men*: Based on Henry Knighton's criticisms of the sort of men "who flocked to take orders" after the pestilence (quoted in Dobson, *Peasants' Revolt,* p. 62).

278 *he heard that the bishop of Norwich*: Harper-Bill, "Church and Religion After the Black Death," p. 87.

278 *bishop was founding a school*: Trinity Hall was founded by the bishop in 1350; the story of the founding of Corpus Christi College in 1352 is told in Hall, "The Guild of Corpus Christi and the Foundation of Corpus Christi College."

279 *he knew of a couple of priests*: For recent studies of pastoral support and education provided in the wake of the Black Death in the dioceses of York and Hereford, see J. Hughes, *Pastors and Visionaries: Religion and Secular Life in Late Medieval Yorkshire* (Boydell, 1988), pp. 127–173, and W. J. Dohar, *The Black Death and Pastoral Leadership* (Philadelphia, 1995).

279 *inability to correct the behavior*: Harper-Bill, "Church and Religion After the Black Death," provides an introduction to some of the issues facing the clergy and the Church in the aftermath of the Black Death. For a case study of the diocese of York, see Hughes, *Pastors and Visionaries.*

279 *the celebration of a Mass created by the pope*: The new Mass is described in Duffy, *Stripping of the Altars,* p. 293, and the liturgy translated in Horrox, *Black Death,* pp. 122–124.

280 *It was called* The Form of Living: For Richard Rolle and his famous text, see M. Glasscoe, *English Medieval Mystics: Games of Faith* (London, 1993), pp. 58–115; and also Hughes, *Pastors and Visionaries.*

281 *Master John was also troubled*: The phrases come from the *Memoriale Presbiterorum,* a treatise written in 1344 (quoted in Pantin, *Church in the Fourteenth Century,* p. 209).

282 *oaths of fealty to their lord*: The swearing of fealty was adhered to with exceptional vigor on the manors of Walsham and High Hall. For its

operation there, see M. A. Williams, "The Nature of Fealty and the Tenants of the Manors of Walsham and High Hall, Suffolk, in the Fourteenth Century" (M.Phil. thesis, University of Cambridge, 2003).

282   *a spate of thefts*: An unusually large number of petty thefts is recorded in the court of November 18, 1349 (Lock, *Walsham Court Rolls*, I, pp. 327–330).